BATMAN

ARKHAM™ ORIGINS

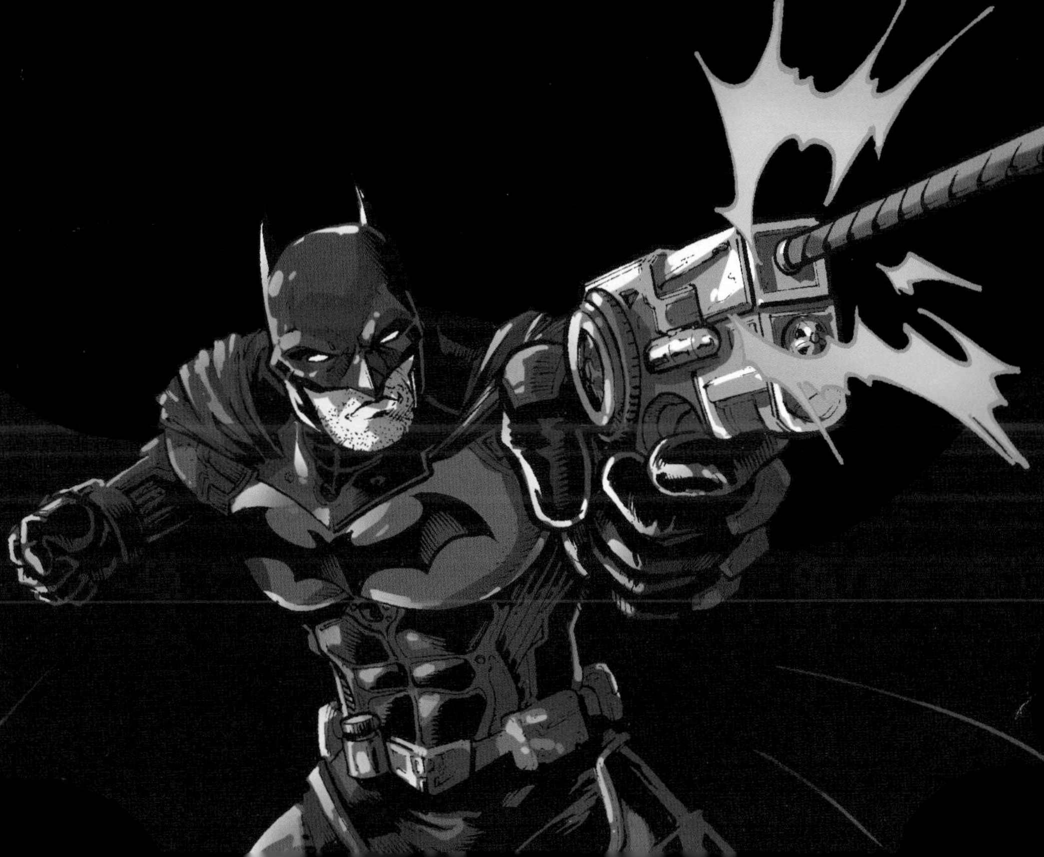

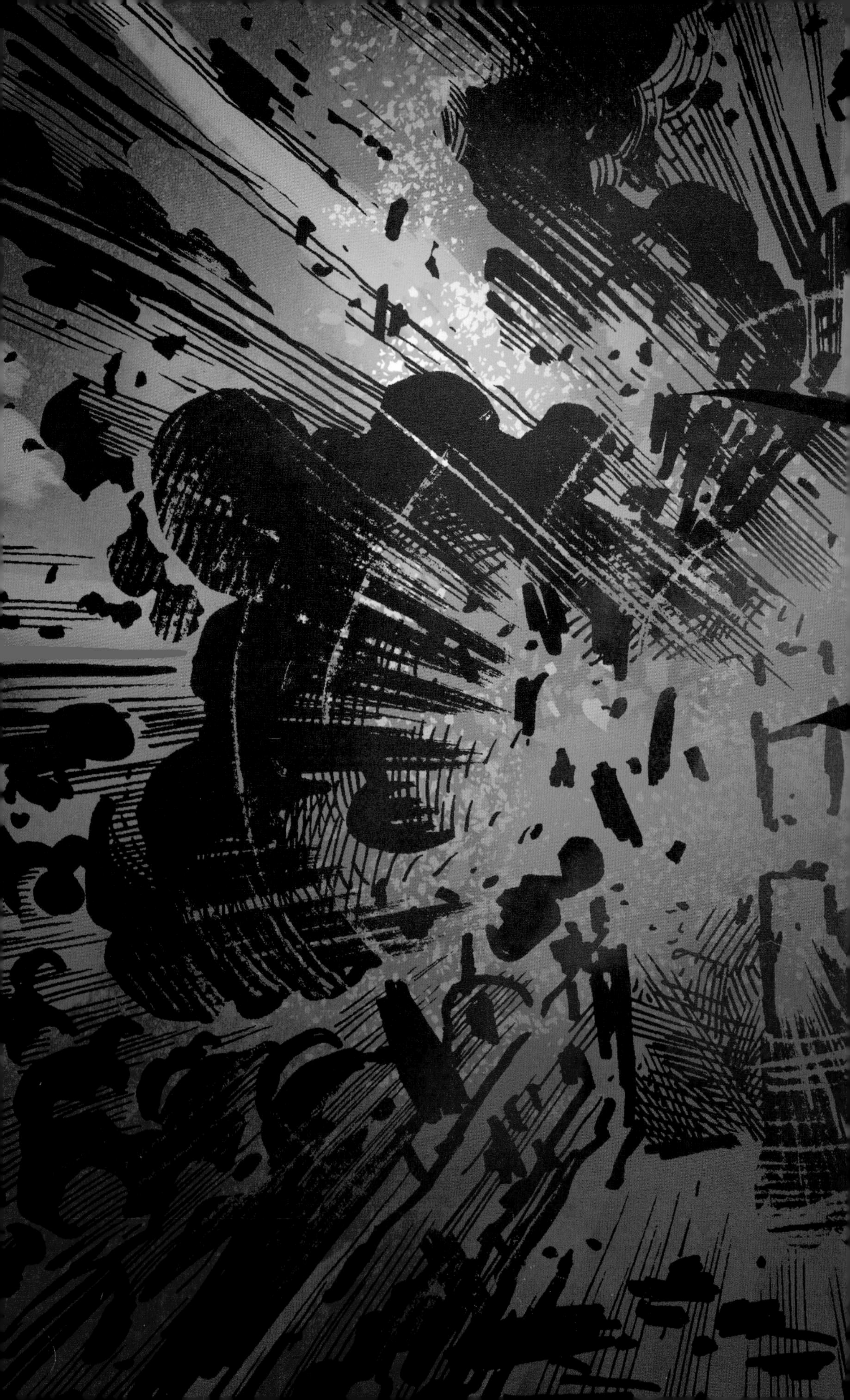

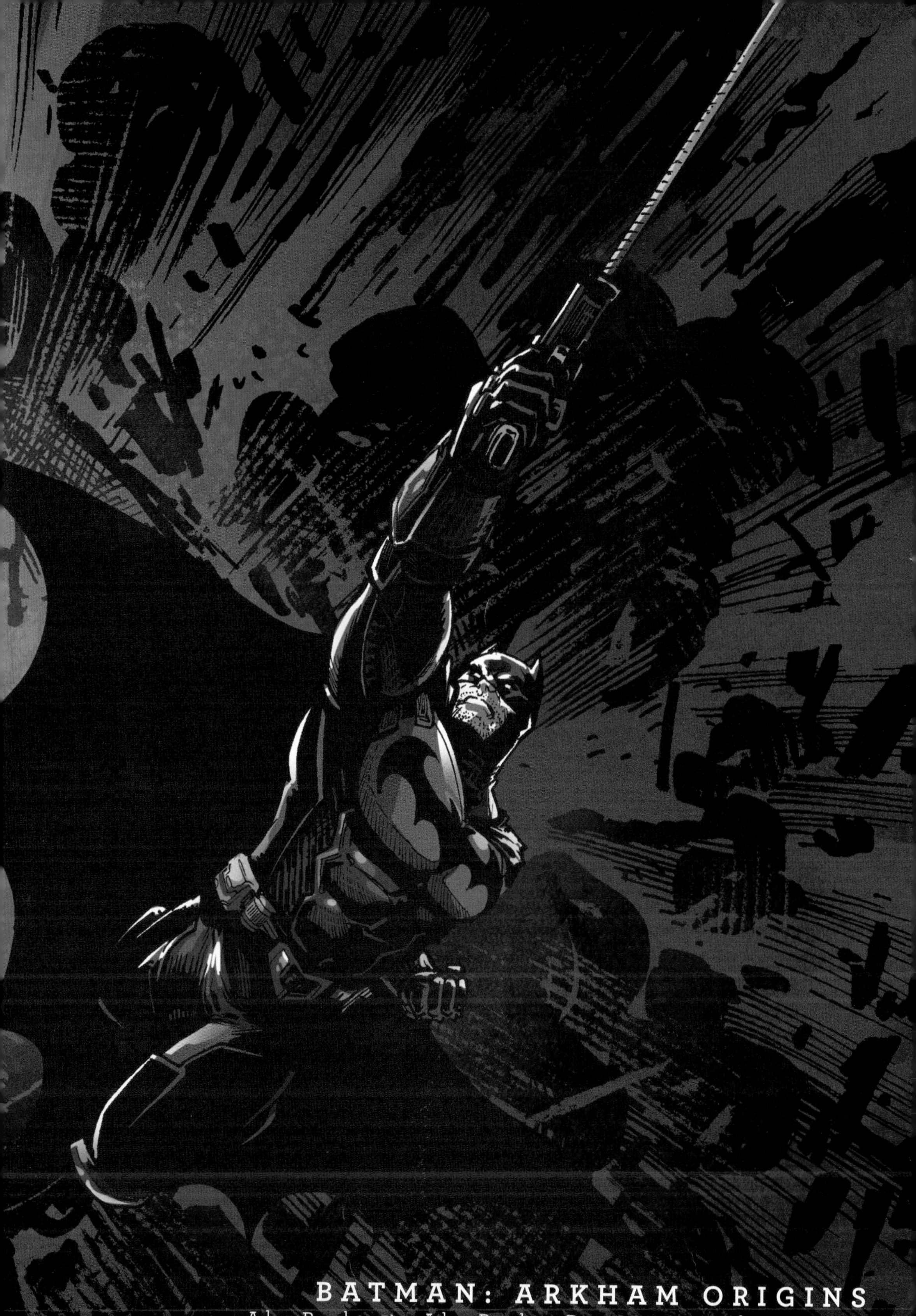

BATMAN: ARKHAM ORIGINS

Adam Beechen Plot Adam Beechen Doug Wagner Frank Hannah Script
Christian Duce Layouts Christian Duce Richard Ortiz Federico Dallocchio Vicente Cifuentes
Omar Francia Victor Drujiniu Thomas Derenick Finished Art
Santi Casas & David Lopez of Ikari Studio Colors
Travis Lanham Lettering Bryan Hitch with David Baron Collection Cover Artists
Batman created by Bob Kane

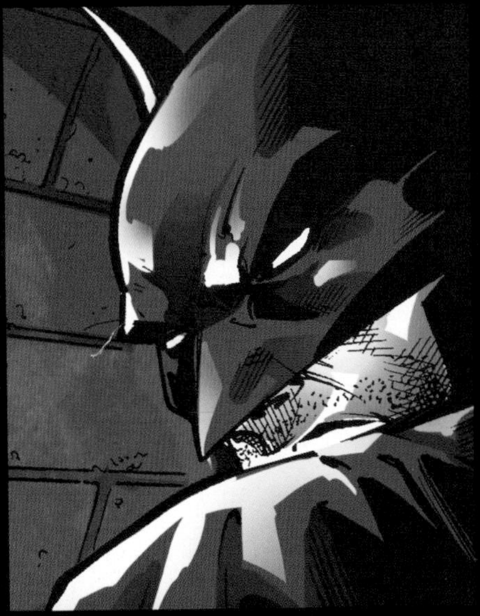

Jim Chadwick Editor – Original Series
Alex Antone Associate Editor – Original Series
Aniz Ansari Assistant Editor – Original Series
Peter Hamboussi Editor
Robbin Brosterman Design Director – Books
Louis Prandi Publication Design

Hank Kanalz Senior VP – Vertigo & Integrated Publishing

Diane Nelson President
Dan DiDio and Jim Lee Co-Publishers
Geoff Johns Chief Creative Officer
Amit Desai Senior VP – Marketing & Franchise Management
Amy Genkins Senior VP – Business & Legal Affairs
Nairi Gardiner Senior VP – Finance
Jeff Boison VP – Publishing Planning
Mark Chiarello VP – Art Direction & Design
John Cunningham VP – Marketing
Terri Cunningham VP – Editorial Administration
Larry Ganem VP – Talent Relations & Services
Alison Gill Senior VP – Manufacturing & Operations
Jay Kogan VP – Business & Legal Affairs, Publishing
Jack Mahan VP – Business Affairs, Talent
Nick Napolitano VP – Manufacturing Administration
Sue Pohja VP – Book Sales
Fred Ruiz VP – Manufacturing Operations
Courtney Simmons Senior VP – Publicity
Bob Wayne Senior VP – Sales

BATMAN: ARKHAM ORIGINS

DC Comics, 1700 Broadway, New York, NY 10019
A Warner Bros. Entertainment Company.
Printed by RR Donnelley, Salem, VA, USA.
11/21/14. First Printing.
ISBN 978-1-4012-4886-4

Library of Congress Cataloging-in-Publication Data

Beechen, Adam.
Batman : Arkham origins / Adam Beechen, Doug Wagner.
pages cm
ISBN 978-1-4012-4886-4 (hardback)
1. Graphic novels. I. Wagner, Doug, 1967- II. Title.
PN6728.B36B56 2014
741.5'973—dc23
2014011700

SUSTAINABLE FORESTRY INITIATIVE
Certified Chain of Custody
20% Certified Forest Content,
80% Certified Sourcing
www.sfiprogram.org
SFI-01042
APPLIES TO TEXT STOCK ONLY

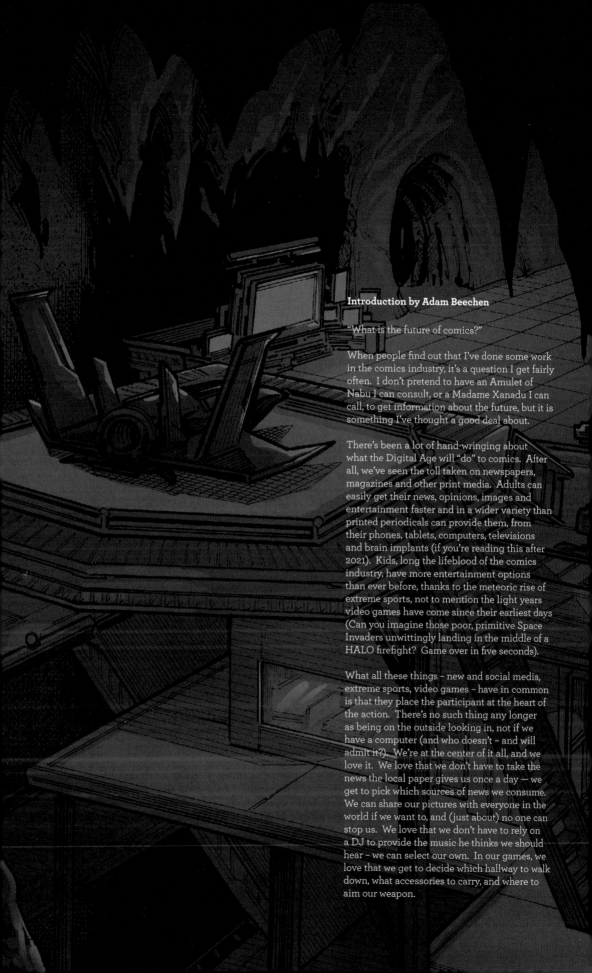

Introduction by Adam Beechen

"What is the future of comics?"

When people find out that I've done some work in the comics industry, it's a question I get fairly often. I don't pretend to have an Amulet of Nabu I can consult, or a Madame Xanadu I can call, to get information about the future, but it is something I've thought a good deal about.

There's been a lot of hand-wringing about what the Digital Age will "do" to comics. After all, we've seen the toll taken on newspapers, magazines and other print media. Adults can easily get their news, opinions, images and entertainment faster and in a wider variety than printed periodicals can provide them, from their phones, tablets, computers, televisions and brain implants (if you're reading this after 2021). Kids, long the lifeblood of the comics industry, have more entertainment options than ever before, thanks to the meteoric rise of extreme sports, not to mention the light years video games have come since their earliest days (Can you imagine those poor, primitive Space Invaders unwittingly landing in the middle of a HALO firefight? Game over in five seconds).

What all these things – new and social media, extreme sports, video games – have in common is that they place the participant at the heart of the action. There's no such thing any longer as being on the outside looking in, not if we have a computer (and who doesn't – and will admit it?). We're at the center of it all, and we love it. We love that we don't have to take the news the local paper gives us once a day — we get to pick which sources of news we consume. We can share our pictures with everyone in the world if we want to, and (just about) no one can stop us. We love that we don't have to rely on a DJ to provide the music he thinks we should hear - we can select our own. In our games, we love that we get to decide which hallway to walk down, what accessories to carry, and where to aim our weapon.

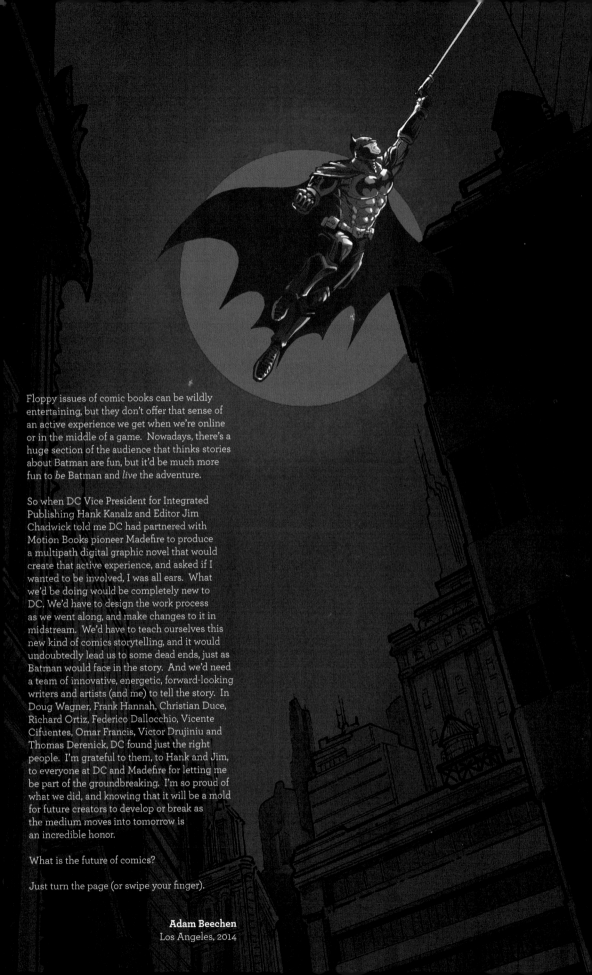

Floppy issues of comic books can be wildly
entertaining, but they don't offer that sense of
an active experience we get when we're online
or in the middle of a game. Nowadays, there's a
huge section of the audience that thinks stories
about Batman are fun, but it'd be much more
fun to *be* Batman and *live* the adventure.

So when DC Vice President for Integrated
Publishing Hank Kanalz and Editor Jim
Chadwick told me DC had partnered with
Motion Books pioneer Madefire to produce
a multipath digital graphic novel that would
create that active experience, and asked if I
wanted to be involved, I was all ears. What
we'd be doing would be completely new to
DC. We'd have to design the work process
as we went along, and make changes to it in
midstream. We'd have to teach ourselves this
new kind of comics storytelling, and it would
undoubtedly lead us to some dead ends, just as
Batman would face in the story. And we'd need
a team of innovative, energetic, forward-looking
writers and artists (and me) to tell the story. In
Doug Wagner, Frank Hannah, Christian Duce,
Richard Ortiz, Federico Dallocchio, Vicente
Cifuentes, Omar Francis, Victor Drujiniu and
Thomas Derenick, DC found just the right
people. I'm grateful to them, to Hank and Jim,
to everyone at DC and Madefire for letting me
be part of the groundbreaking. I'm so proud of
what we did, and knowing that it will be a mold
for future creators to develop or break as
the medium moves into tomorrow is
an incredible honor.

What is the future of comics?

Just turn the page (or swipe your finger).

Adam Beechen
Los Angeles, 2014

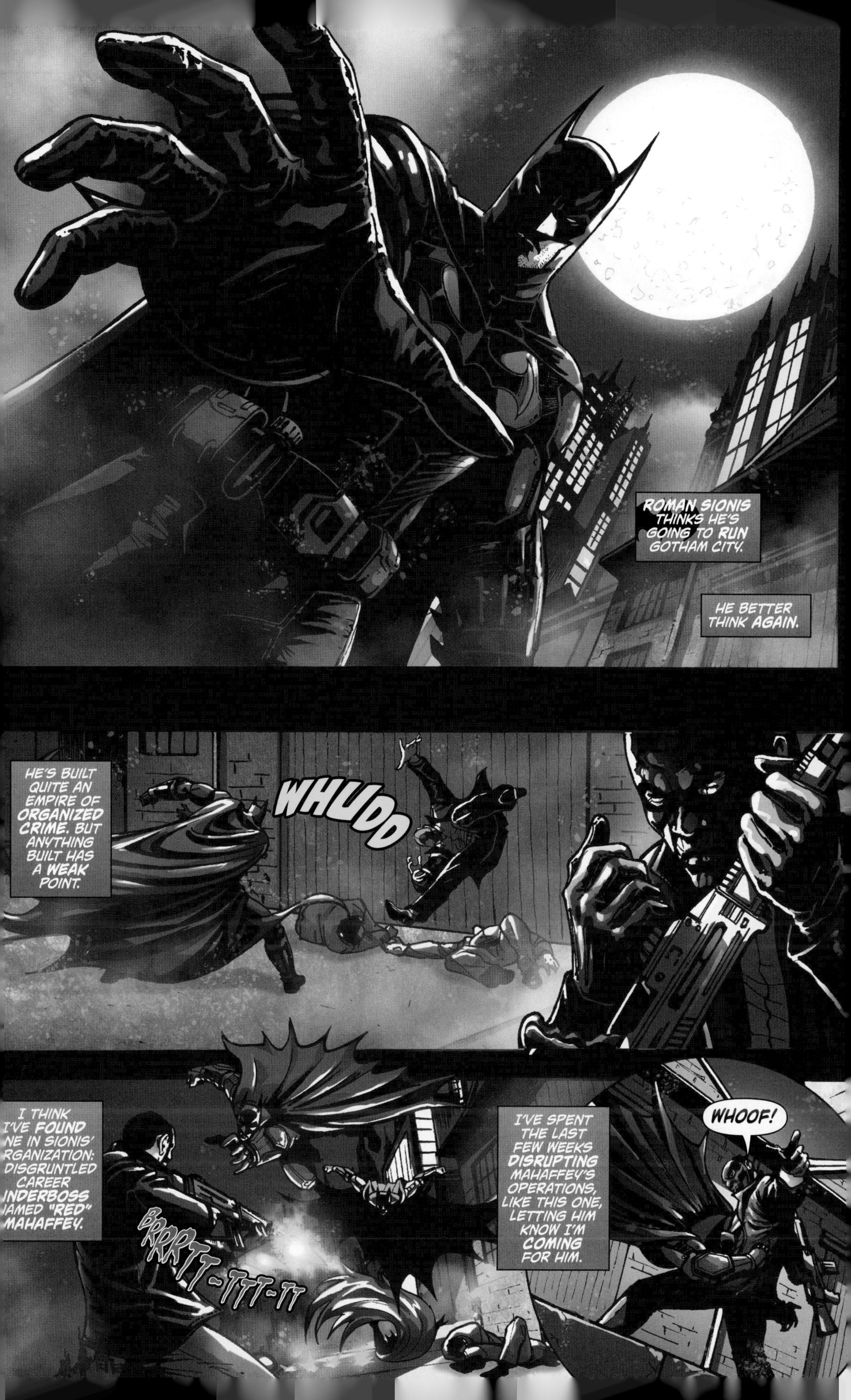

ROMAN SIONIS THINKS HE'S GOING TO RUN GOTHAM CITY.
HE BETTER THINK AGAIN.
HE'S BUILT QUITE AN EMPIRE OF ORGANIZED CRIME. BUT ANYTHING BUILT HAS A WEAK POINT.
WHUDD
I THINK I'VE FOUND NE IN SIONIS' RGANIZATION: DISGRUNTLED CAREER NDERBOSS AMED "RED" MAHAFFEY.
BRRRTT-TTT-TT
I'VE SPENT THE LAST FEW WEEKS DISRUPTING MAHAFFEY'S OPERATIONS, LIKE THIS ONE, LETTING HIM KNOW I'M COMING FOR HIM.
WHOOF!

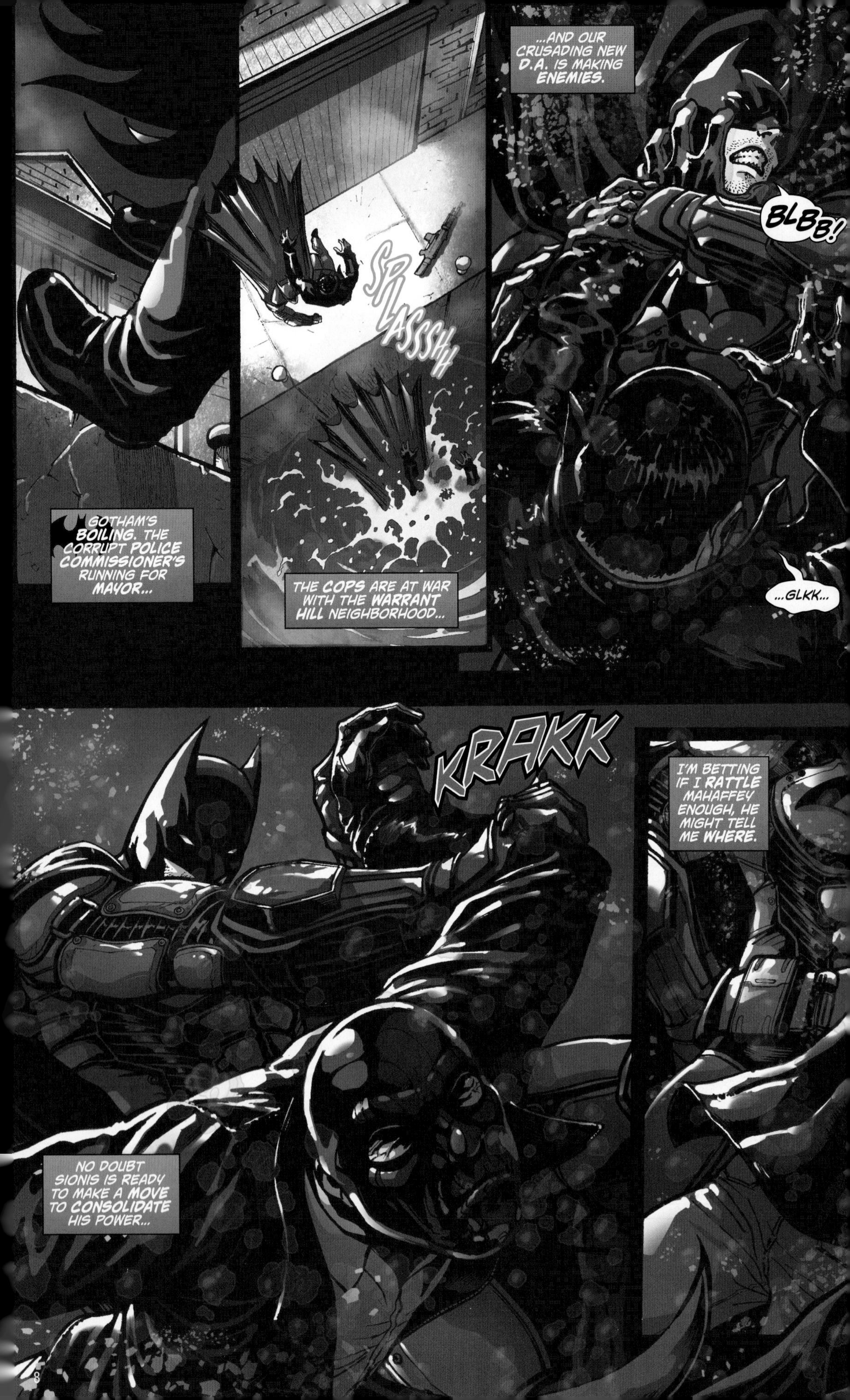
GOTHAM'S BOILING. THE CORRUPT POLICE COMMISSIONER'S RUNNING FOR MAYOR...
SPLASSSHH
THE COPS ARE AT WAR WITH THE WARRANT HILL NEIGHBORHOOD...
...AND OUR CRUSADING NEW D.A. IS MAKING ENEMIES.
BLBB!
...GLKK...
KRAKK
NO DOUBT SIONIS IS READY TO MAKE A MOVE TO CONSOLIDATE HIS POWER...
I'M BETTING IF I RATTLE MAHAFFEY ENOUGH, HE MIGHT TELL ME WHERE.

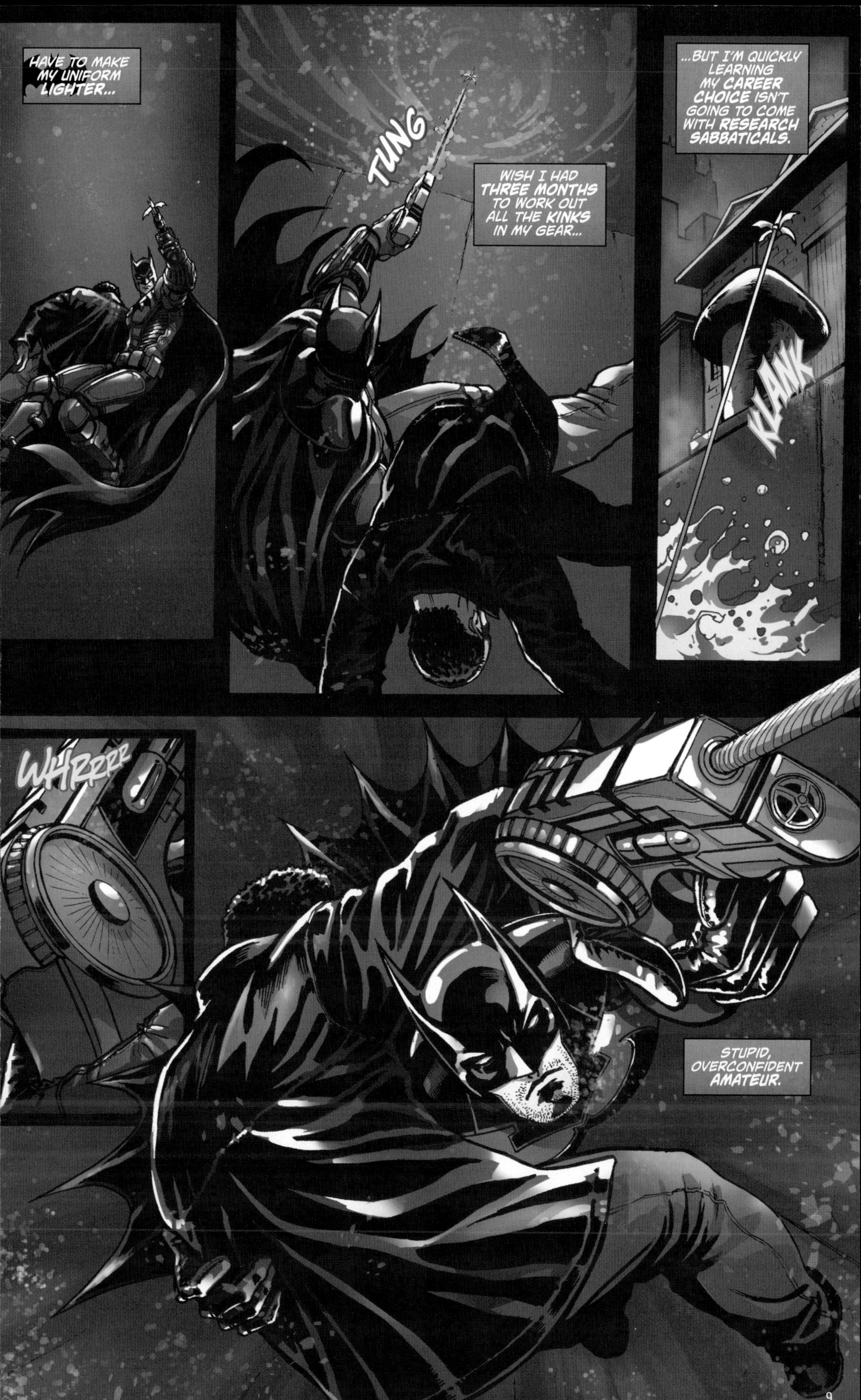

HAVE TO MAKE MY UNIFORM LIGHTER...
TUNG
WISH I HAD THREE MONTHS TO WORK OUT ALL THE KINKS IN MY GEAR...
...BUT I'M QUICKLY LEARNING MY CAREER CHOICE ISN'T GOING TO COME WITH RESEARCH SABBATICALS.
KLANK
WHRRRR
STUPID, OVERCONFIDENT AMATEUR.

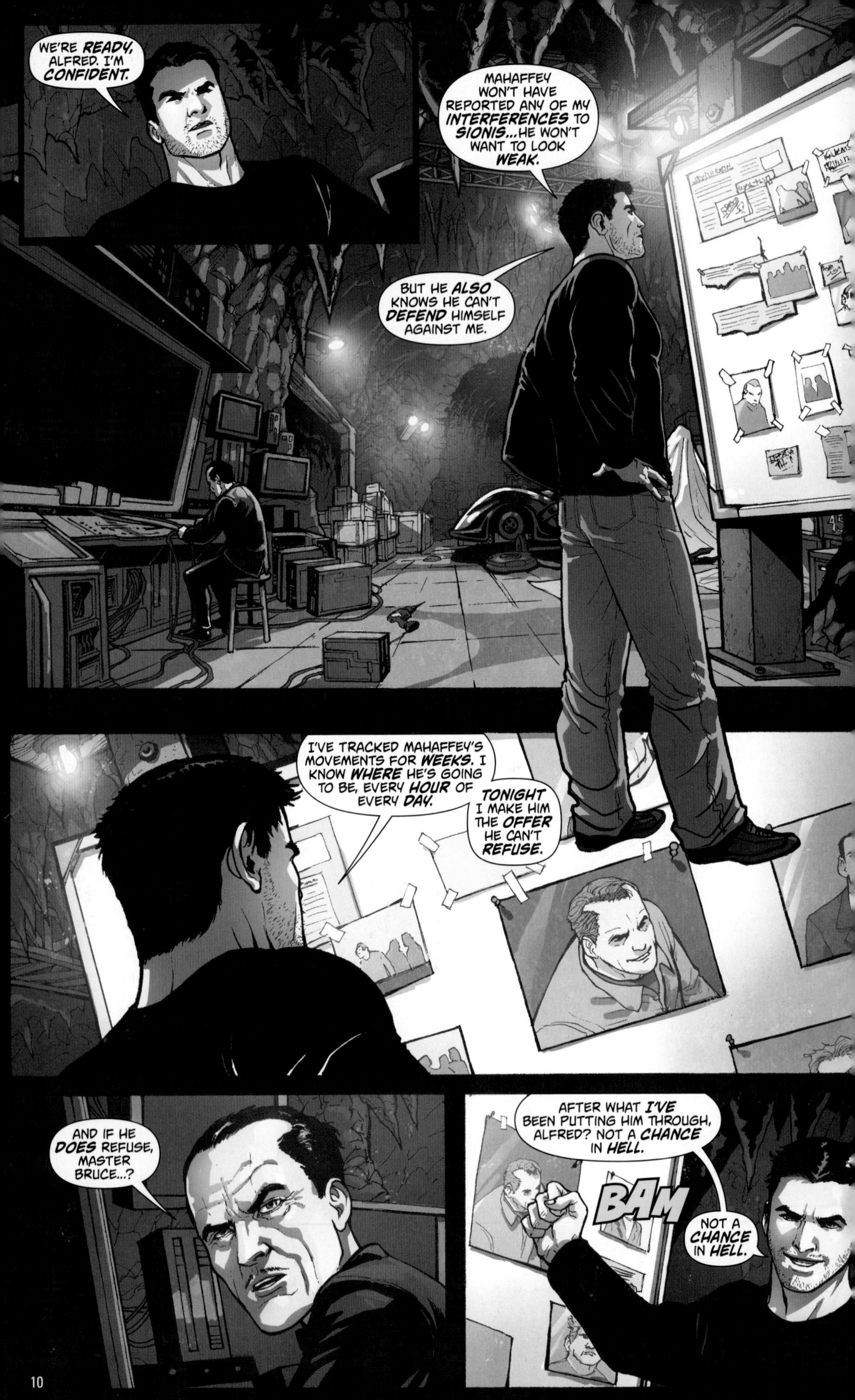

WE'RE READY, ALFRED. I'M CONFIDENT.
MAHAFFEY WON'T HAVE REPORTED ANY OF MY INTERFERENCES TO SIONIS...HE WON'T WANT TO LOOK WEAK.
BUT HE ALSO KNOWS HE CAN'T DEFEND HIMSELF AGAINST ME.
I'VE TRACKED MAHAFFEY'S MOVEMENTS FOR WEEKS. I KNOW WHERE HE'S GOING TO BE, EVERY HOUR OF EVERY DAY.
TONIGHT I MAKE HIM THE OFFER HE CAN'T REFUSE.
AND IF HE DOES REFUSE, MASTER BRUCE...?
AFTER WHAT I'VE BEEN PUTTING HIM THROUGH, ALFRED? NOT A CHANCE IN HELL.
BAM
NOT A CHANCE IN HELL.

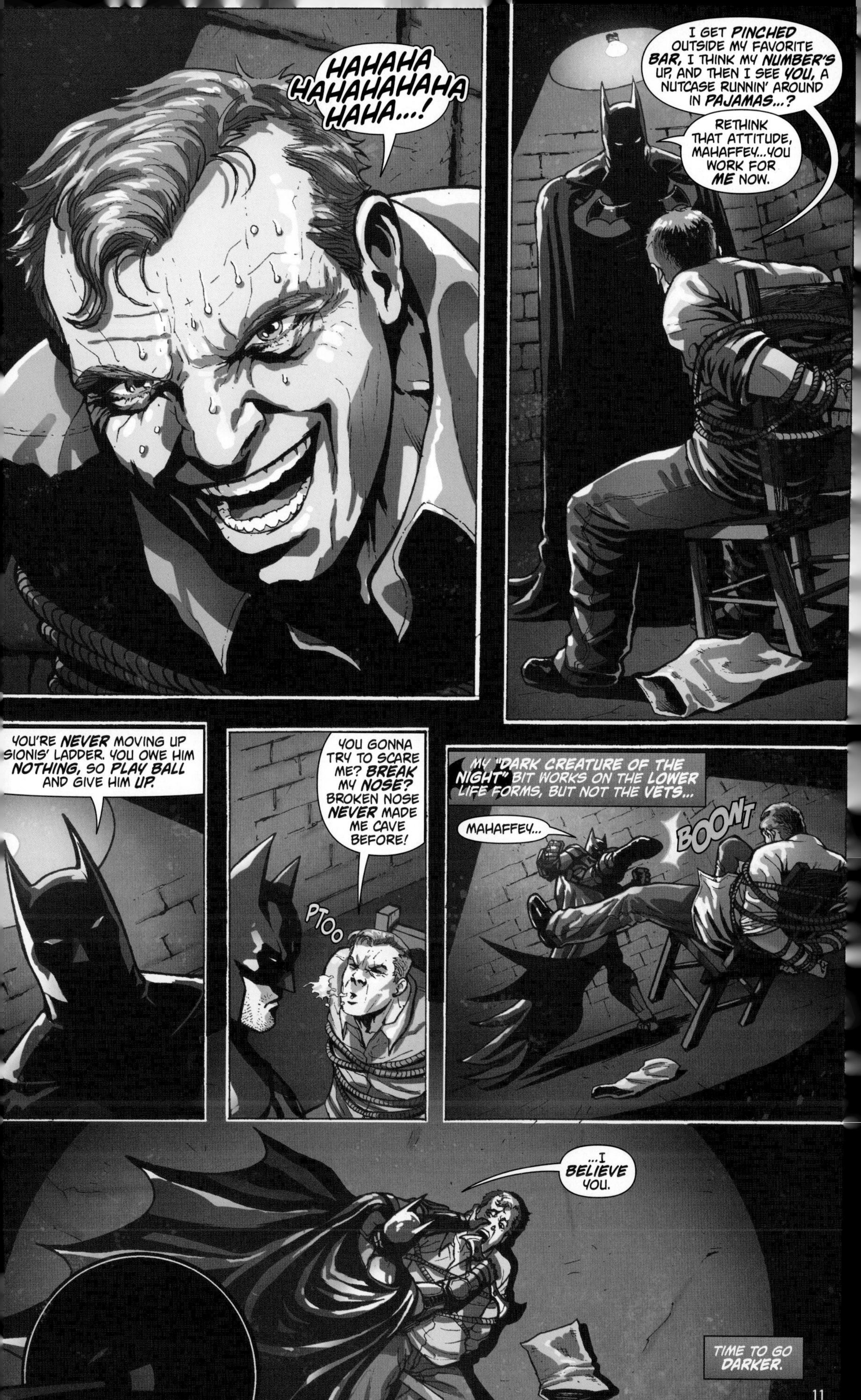
HAHAHA HAHAHAHAHA HAHA...!
I GET PINCHED OUTSIDE MY FAVORITE BAR, I THINK MY NUMBER'S UP, AND THEN I SEE YOU, A NUTCASE RUNNIN' AROUND IN PAJAMAS...?
RETHINK THAT ATTITUDE, MAHAFFEY...YOU WORK FOR ME NOW.
YOU'RE NEVER MOVING UP SIONIS' LADDER. YOU OWE HIM NOTHING, SO PLAY BALL AND GIVE HIM UP.
YOU GONNA TRY TO SCARE ME? BREAK MY NOSE? BROKEN NOSE NEVER MADE ME CAVE BEFORE!
PTOO
MY "DARK CREATURE OF THE NIGHT" BIT WORKS ON THE LOWER LIFE FORMS, BUT NOT THE VETS...
MAHAFFEY...
BOONT
...I BELIEVE YOU.
TIME TO GO DARKER.

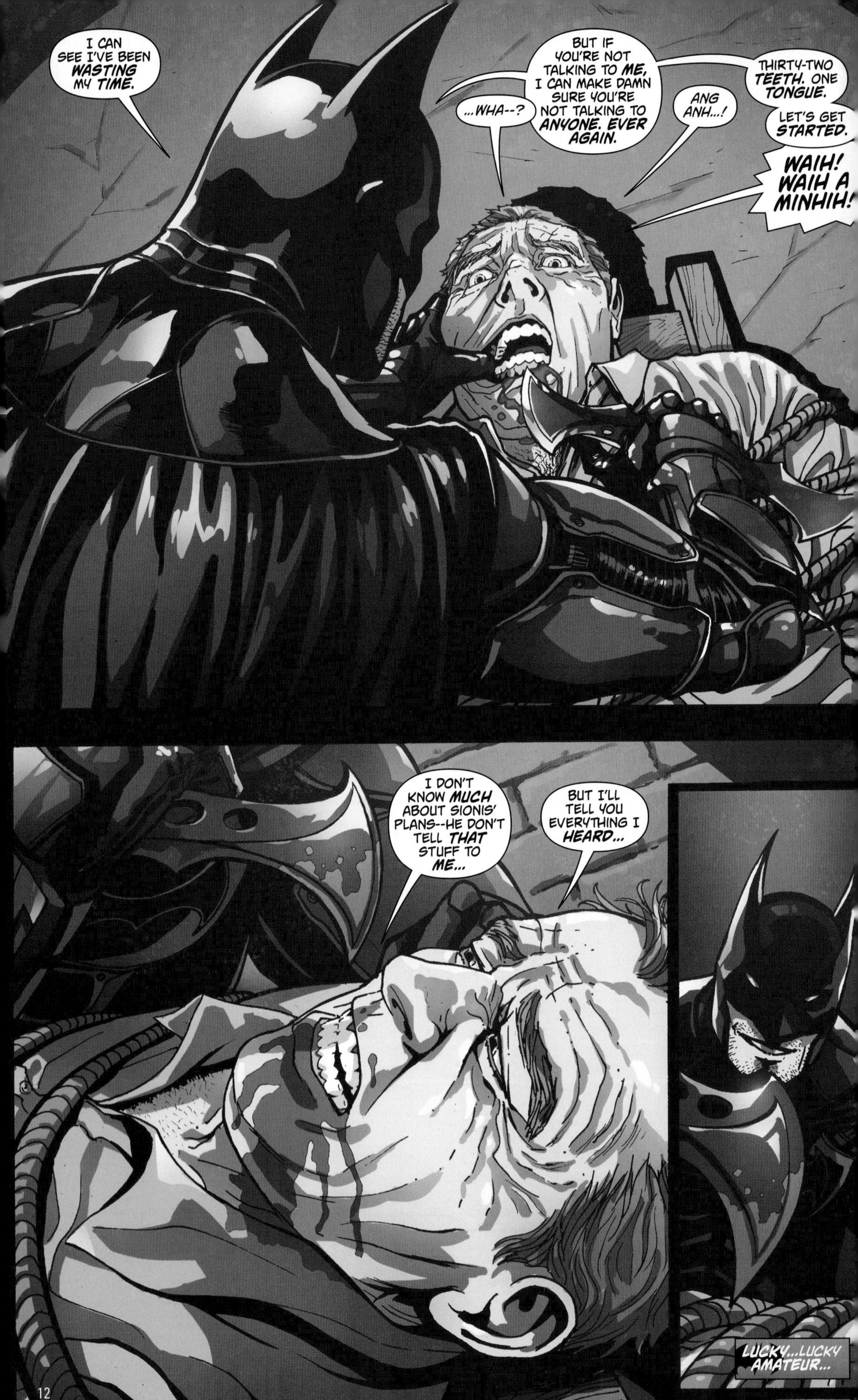

I CAN SEE I'VE BEEN WASTING MY TIME.
...WHA--?
BUT IF YOU'RE NOT TALKING TO ME, I CAN MAKE DAMN SURE YOU'RE NOT TALKING TO ANYONE. EVER AGAIN.
ANG ANH...!
THIRTY-TWO TEETH. ONE TONGUE.
LET'S GET STARTED.
WAIH! WAIH A MINHIH!
I DON'T KNOW MUCH ABOUT SIONIS' PLANS--HE DON'T TELL THAT STUFF TO ME...
BUT I'LL TELL YOU EVERYTHING I HEARD...
LUCKY...LUCKY AMATEUR...

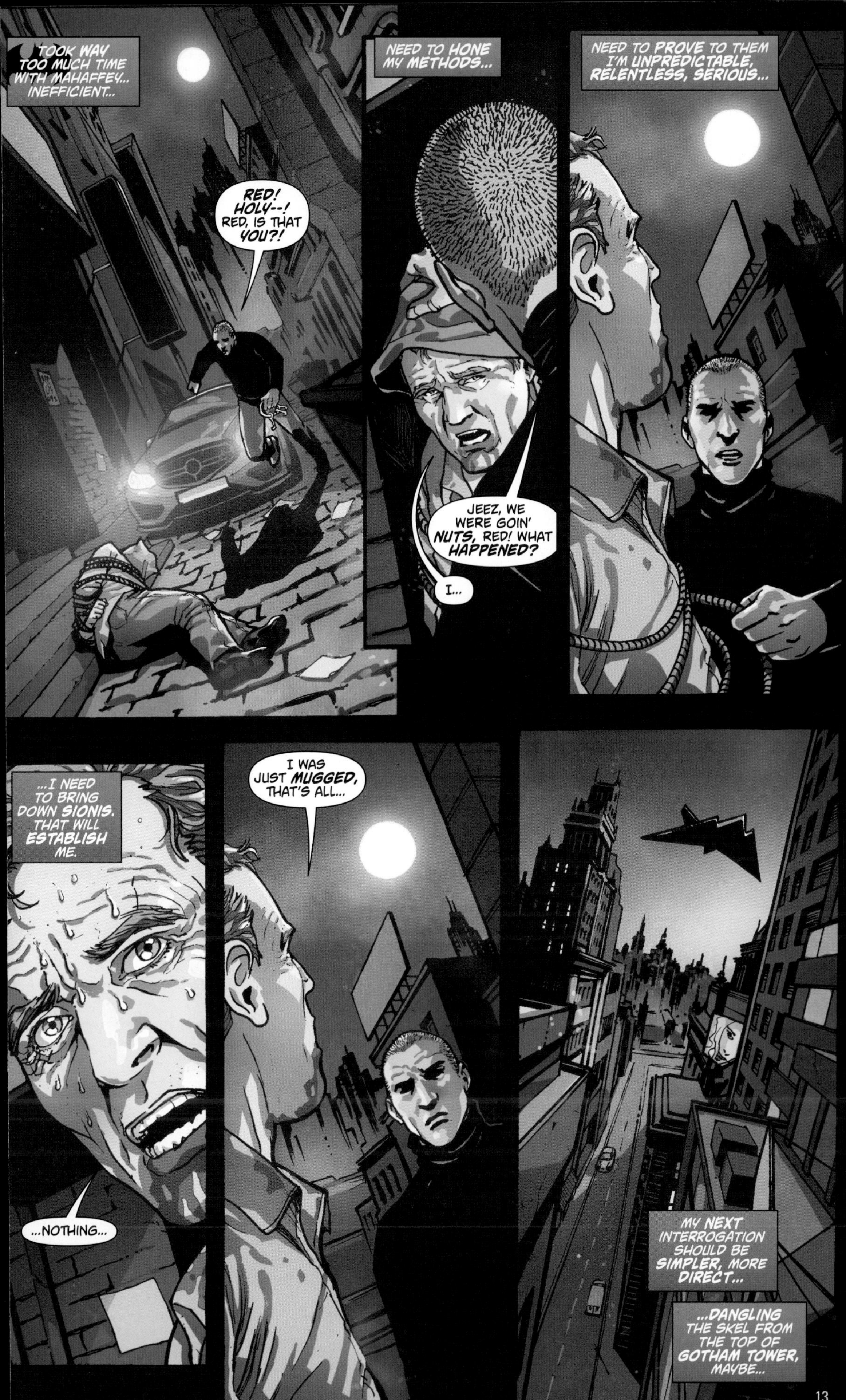
TOOK WAY TOO MUCH TIME WITH MAHAFFEY... INEFFICIENT...
RED! HOLY--! RED, IS THAT YOU?!
NEED TO HONE MY METHODS...
JEEZ, WE WERE GOIN' NUTS, RED! WHAT HAPPENED?
I...
NEED TO PROVE TO THEM I'M UNPREDICTABLE, RELENTLESS, SERIOUS...
...I NEED TO BRING DOWN SIONIS. THAT WILL ESTABLISH ME.
...NOTHING...
I WAS JUST MUGGED, THAT'S ALL...
MY NEXT INTERROGATION SHOULD BE SIMPLER, MORE DIRECT...
...DANGLING THE SKEL FROM THE TOP OF GOTHAM TOWER, MAYBE...

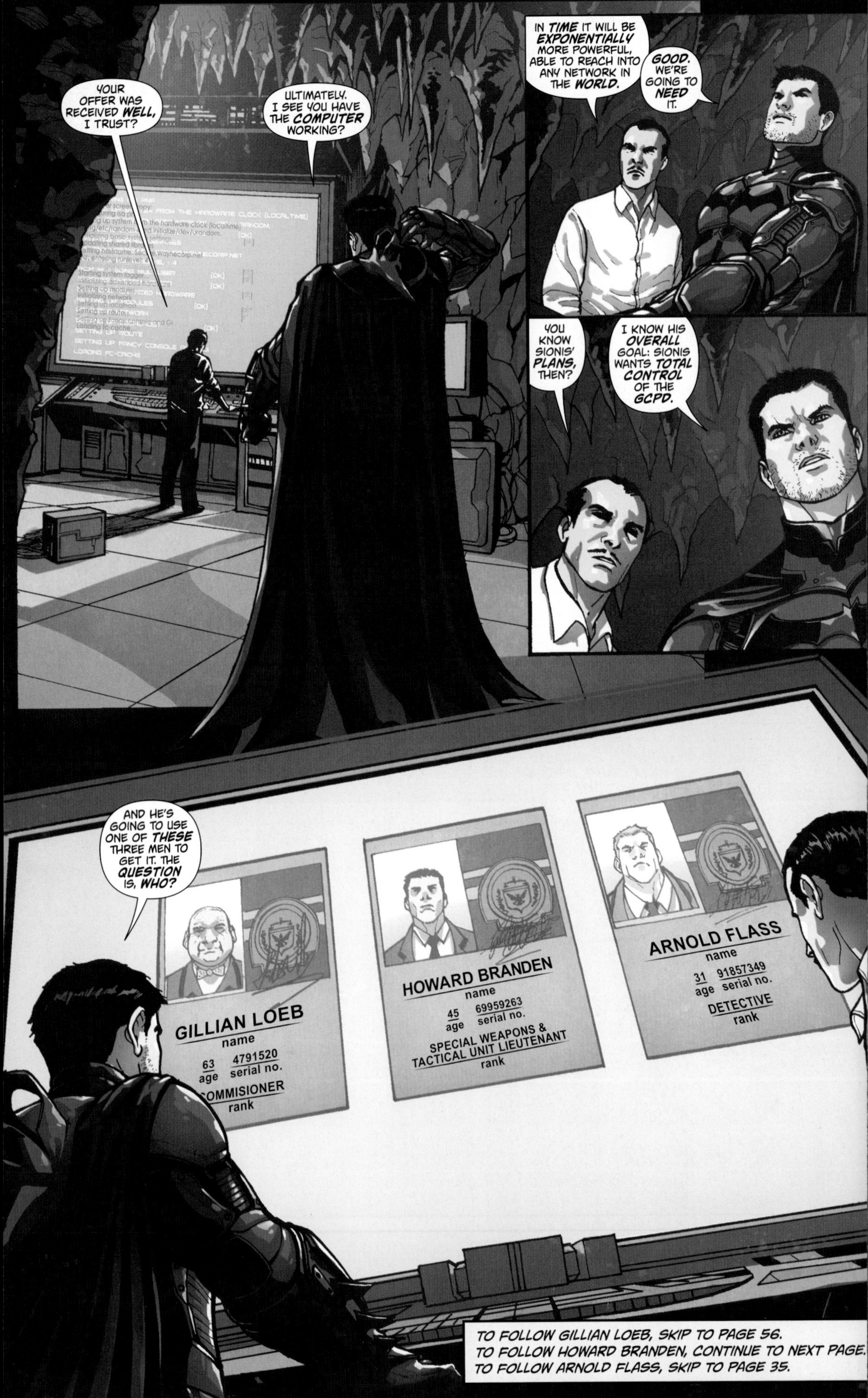
YOUR OFFER WAS RECEIVED WELL, I TRUST?
ULTIMATELY. I SEE YOU HAVE THE COMPUTER WORKING?
IN TIME IT WILL BE EXPONENTIALLY MORE POWERFUL, ABLE TO REACH INTO ANY NETWORK IN THE WORLD.
GOOD. WE'RE GOING TO NEED IT.
YOU KNOW SIONIS' PLANS, THEN?
I KNOW HIS OVERALL GOAL: SIONIS WANTS TOTAL CONTROL OF THE GCPD.
AND HE'S GOING TO USE ONE OF THESE THREE MEN TO GET IT. THE QUESTION IS, WHO?
GILLIAN LOEB
name
63 age
4791520 serial no.
COMMISIONER
rank
HOWARD BRANDEN
name
45 age
69959263 serial no.
SPECIAL WEAPONS & TACTICAL UNIT LIEUTENANT
rank
ARNOLD FLASS
name
31 age
91857349 serial no.
DETECTIVE
rank

TO FOLLOW GILLIAN LOEB, SKIP TO PAGE 56.
TO FOLLOW HOWARD BRANDEN, CONTINUE TO NEXT PAGE.
TO FOLLOW ARNOLD FLASS, SKIP TO PAGE 35.

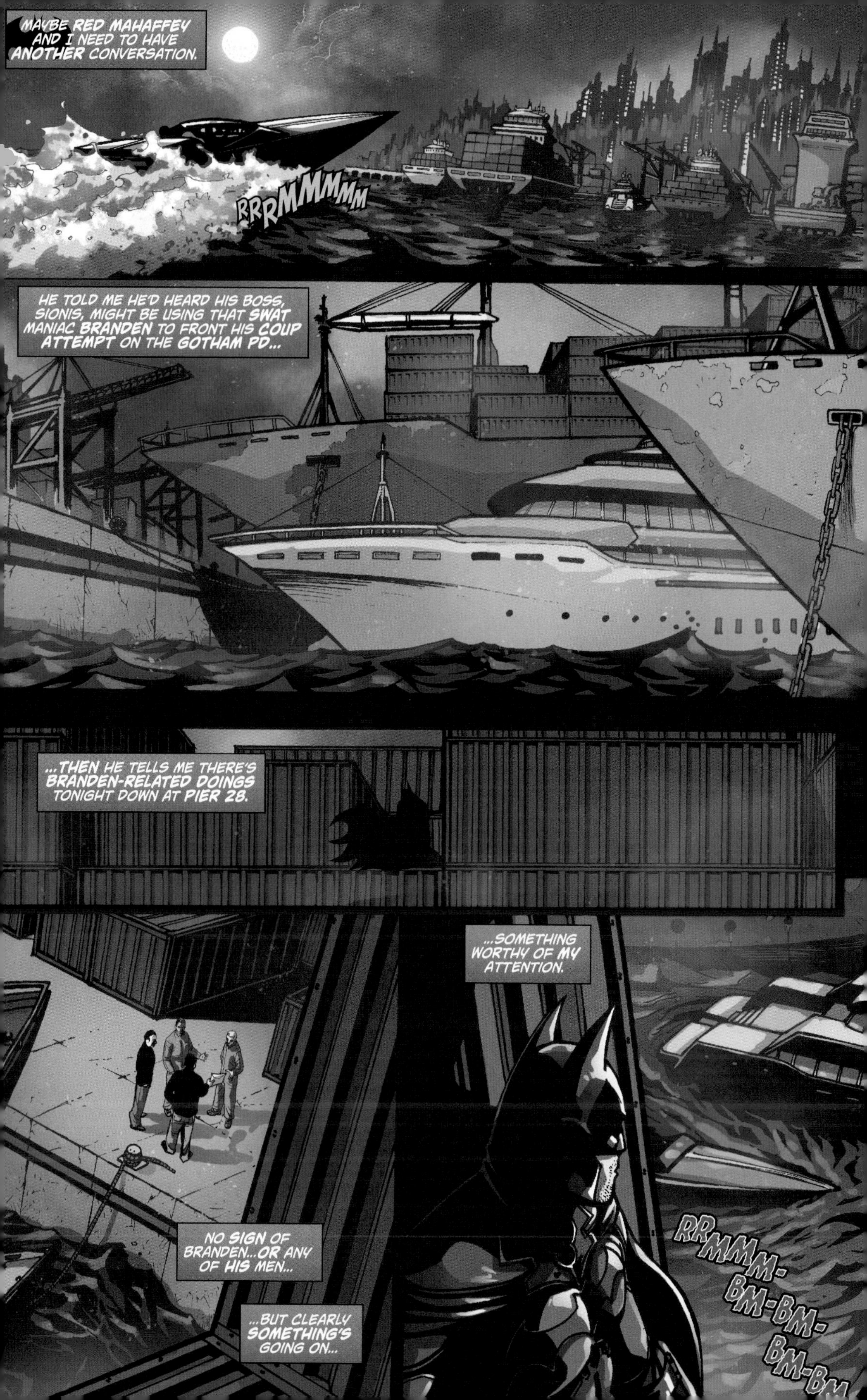
MAYBE RED MAHAFFEY AND I NEED TO HAVE ANOTHER CONVERSATION.
RRRMMMMMM
HE TOLD ME HE'D HEARD HIS BOSS, SIONIS, MIGHT BE USING THAT SWAT MANIAC BRANDEN TO FRONT HIS COUP ATTEMPT ON THE GOTHAM PD...
...THEN HE TELLS ME THERE'S BRANDEN-RELATED DOINGS TONIGHT DOWN AT PIER 28.
...SOMETHING WORTHY OF MY ATTENTION.
NO SIGN OF BRANDEN...OR ANY OF HIS MEN...
...BUT CLEARLY SOMETHING'S GOING ON...
RRMMMM-BM-BM-BM-BM

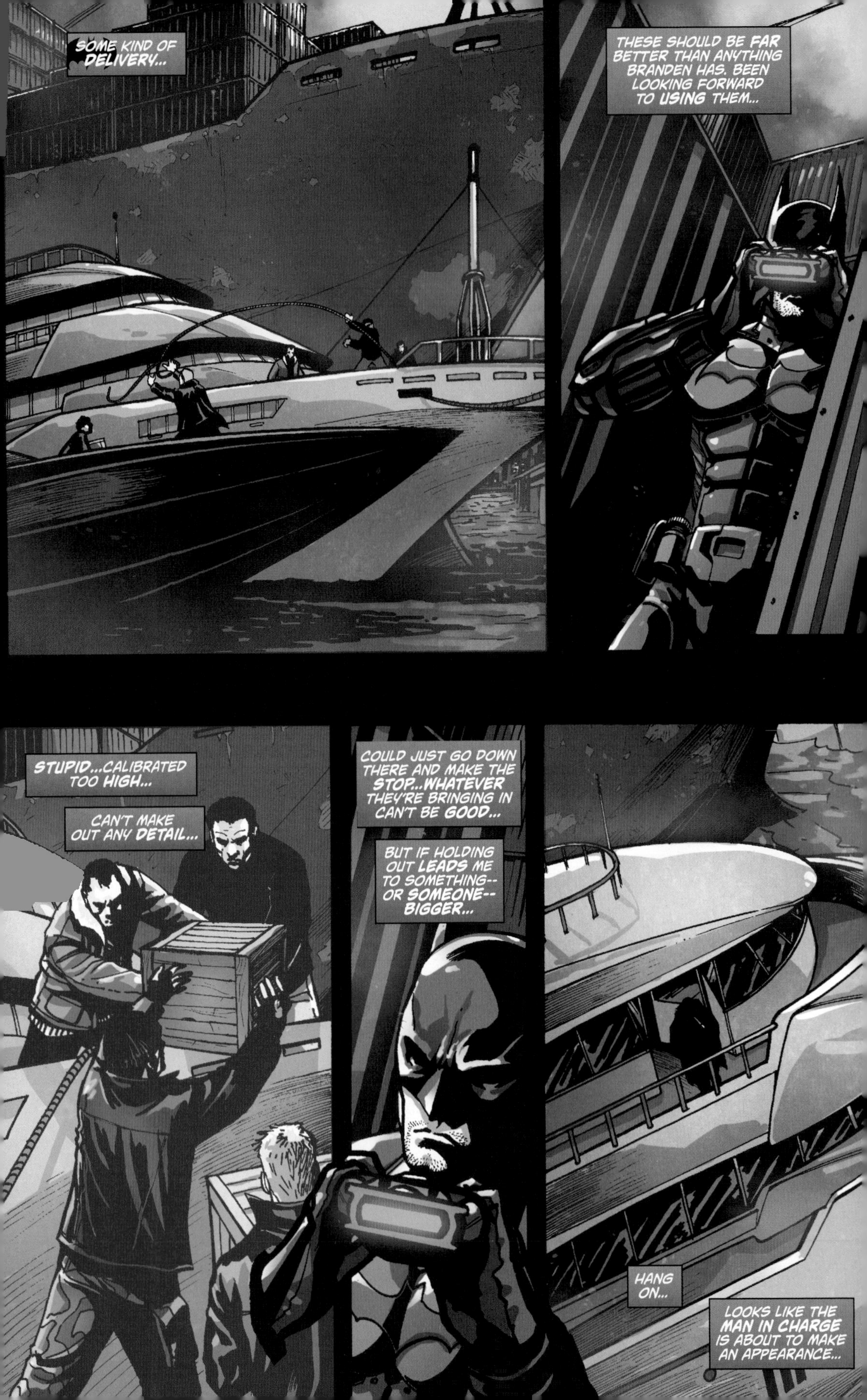
SOME KIND OF DELIVERY...
THESE SHOULD BE FAR BETTER THAN ANYTHING BRANDEN HAS. BEEN LOOKING FORWARD TO USING THEM...
STUPID...CALIBRATED TOO HIGH...
CAN'T MAKE OUT ANY DETAIL...
COULD JUST GO DOWN THERE AND MAKE THE STOP...WHATEVER THEY'RE BRINGING IN CAN'T BE GOOD...
BUT IF HOLDING OUT LEADS ME TO SOMETHING-- OR SOMEONE-- BIGGER...
HANG ON...
LOOKS LIKE THE MAN IN CHARGE IS ABOUT TO MAKE AN APPEARANCE...

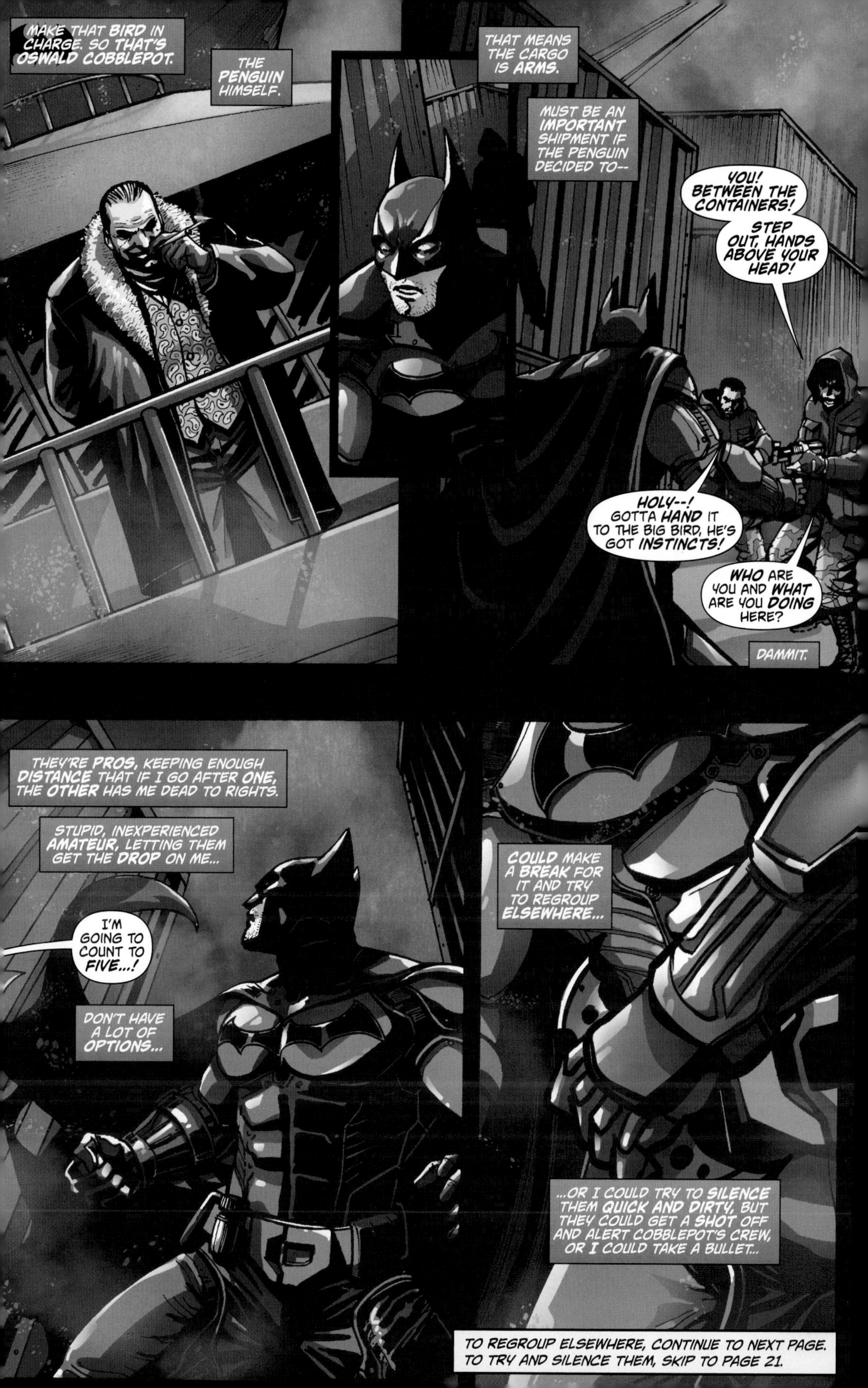
MAKE THAT BIRD IN CHARGE. SO THAT'S OSWALD COBBLEPOT.
THE PENGUIN HIMSELF.
THAT MEANS THE CARGO IS ARMS.
MUST BE AN IMPORTANT SHIPMENT IF THE PENGUIN DECIDED TO--
YOU! BETWEEN THE CONTAINERS!
STEP OUT, HANDS ABOVE YOUR HEAD!
HOLY--! GOTTA HAND IT TO THE BIG BIRD, HE'S GOT INSTINCTS!
WHO ARE YOU AND WHAT ARE YOU DOING HERE?
DAMMIT.
THEY'RE PROS, KEEPING ENOUGH DISTANCE THAT IF I GO AFTER ONE, THE OTHER HAS ME DEAD TO RIGHTS.
STUPID, INEXPERIENCED AMATEUR, LETTING THEM GET THE DROP ON ME...
I'M GOING TO COUNT TO FIVE...!
DON'T HAVE A LOT OF OPTIONS...
COULD MAKE A BREAK FOR IT AND TRY TO REGROUP ELSEWHERE...
...OR I COULD TRY TO SILENCE THEM QUICK AND DIRTY, BUT THEY COULD GET A SHOT OFF AND ALERT COBBLEPOT'S CREW, OR I COULD TAKE A BULLET...
TO REGROUP ELSEWHERE, CONTINUE TO NEXT PAGE.
TO TRY AND SILENCE THEM, SKIP TO PAGE 21.

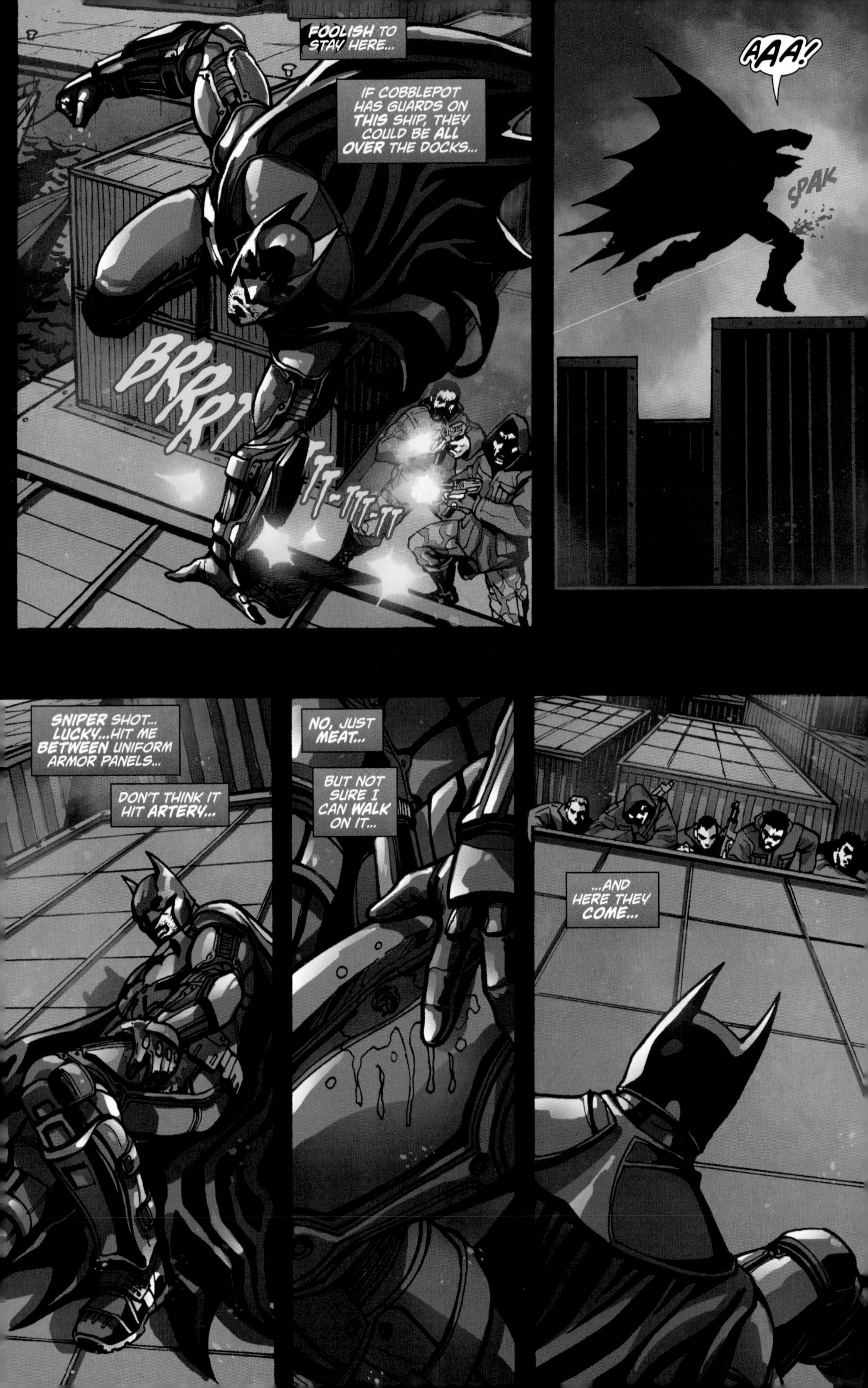
FOOLISH TO STAY HERE...
IF COBBLEPOT HAS GUARDS ON THIS SHIP, THEY COULD BE ALL OVER THE DOCKS...
BRRRT-TTT-TTT-TT
AAA!
SPAK
SNIPER SHOT... LUCKY...HIT ME BETWEEN UNIFORM ARMOR PANELS...
DON'T THINK IT HIT ARTERY...
NO, JUST MEAT...
BUT NOT SURE I CAN WALK ON IT...
...AND HERE THEY COME...

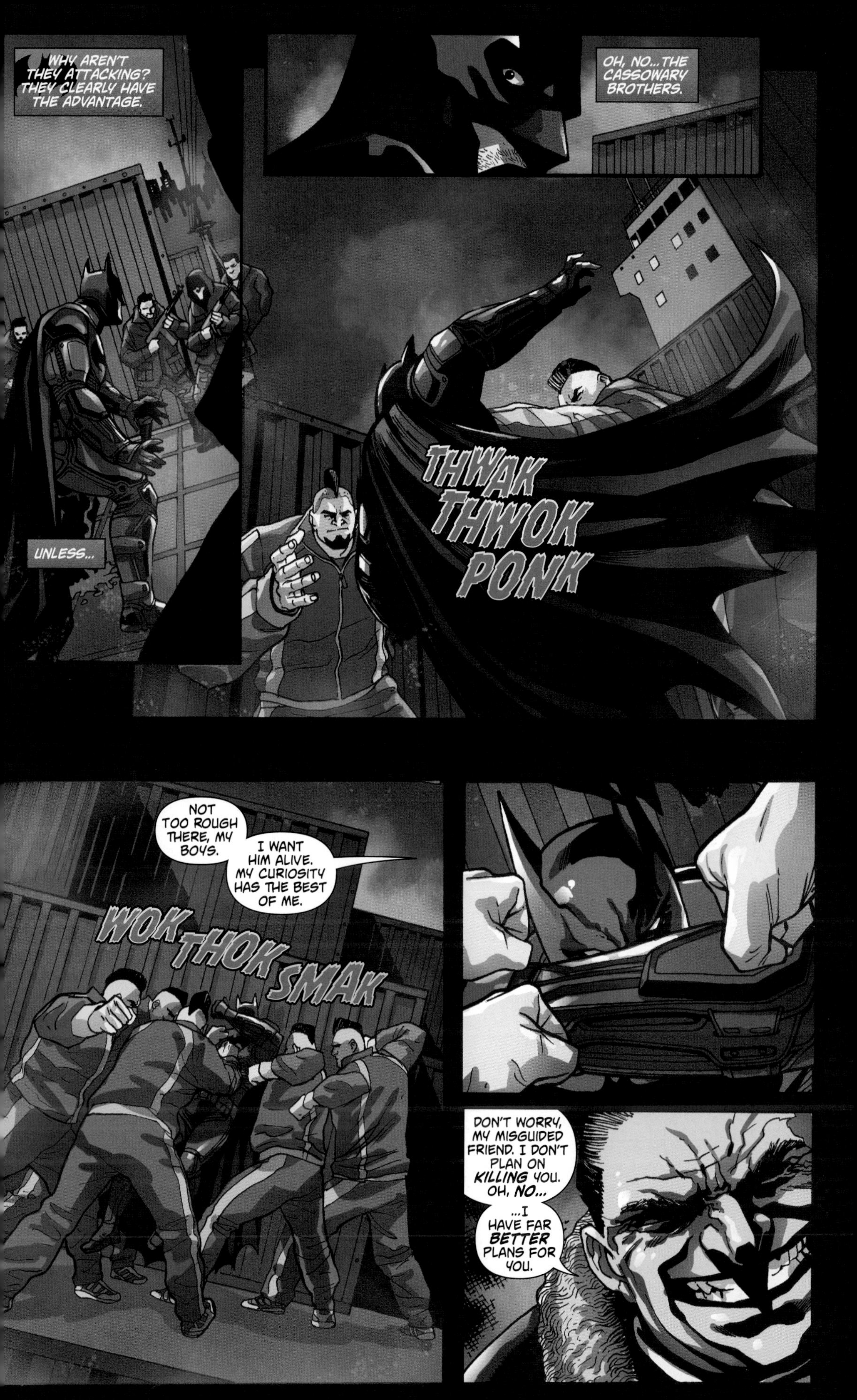

WHY AREN'T THEY ATTACKING? THEY CLEARLY HAVE THE ADVANTAGE.
UNLESS...
OH, NO...THE CASSOWARY BROTHERS.
THWAK THWOK PONK
NOT TOO ROUGH THERE, MY BOYS.
I WANT HIM ALIVE. MY CURIOSITY HAS THE BEST OF ME.
WOK THOK SMAK
DON'T WORRY, MY MISGUIDED FRIEND. I DON'T PLAN ON KILLING YOU. OH, NO...
...I HAVE FAR BETTER PLANS FOR YOU.

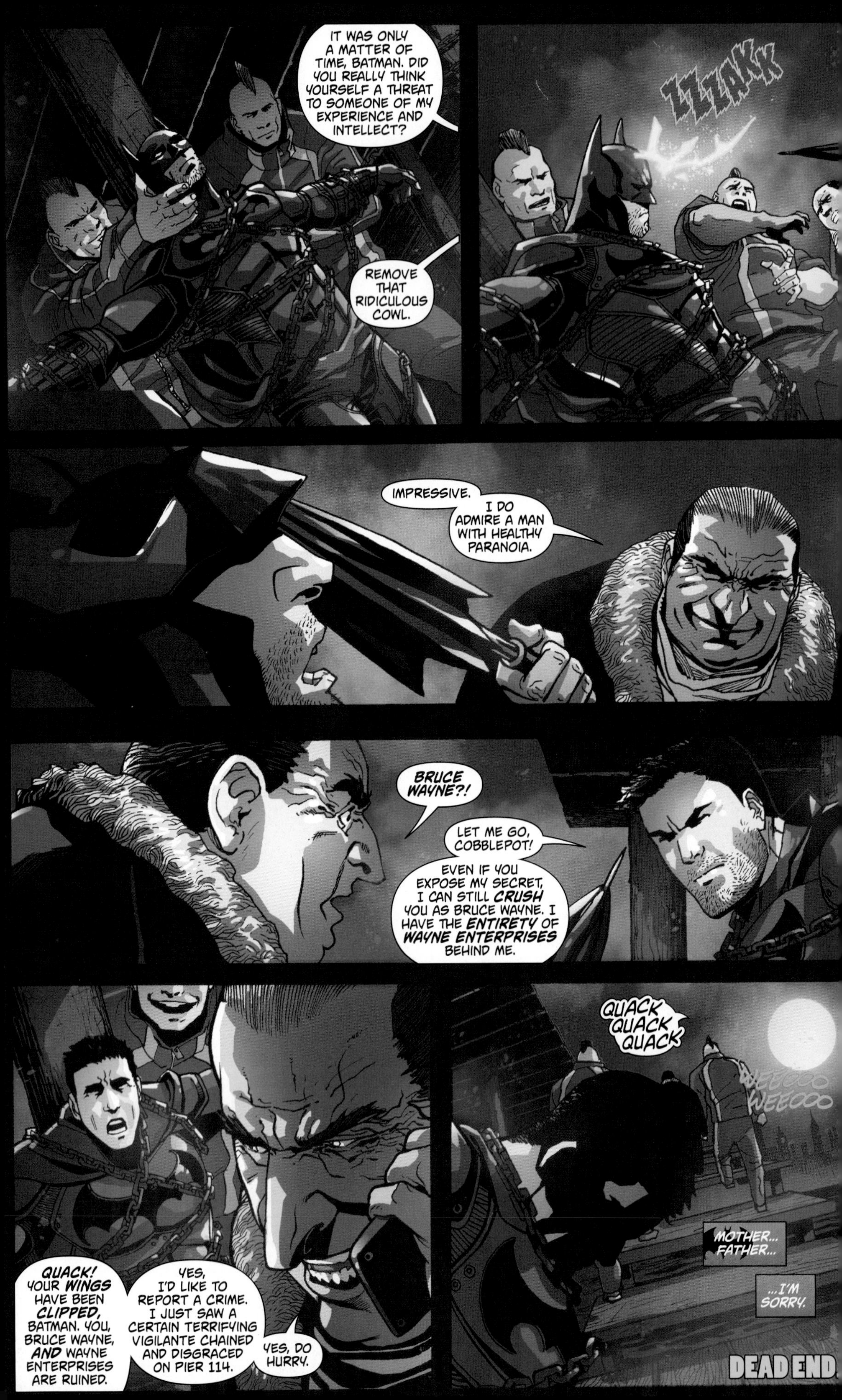
IT WAS ONLY A MATTER OF TIME, BATMAN. DID YOU REALLY THINK YOURSELF A THREAT TO SOMEONE OF MY EXPERIENCE AND INTELLECT?
REMOVE THAT RIDICULOUS COWL.
ZZZZAKK
IMPRESSIVE.
I DO ADMIRE A MAN WITH HEALTHY PARANOIA.
BRUCE WAYNE?!
LET ME GO, COBBLEPOT!
EVEN IF YOU EXPOSE MY SECRET, I CAN STILL CRUSH YOU AS BRUCE WAYNE. I HAVE THE ENTIRETY OF WAYNE ENTERPRISES BEHIND ME.
QUACK! YOUR WINGS HAVE BEEN CLIPPED, BATMAN. YOU, BRUCE WAYNE, AND WAYNE ENTERPRISES ARE RUINED.
YES, I'D LIKE TO REPORT A CRIME. I JUST SAW A CERTAIN TERRIFYING VIGILANTE CHAINED AND DISGRACED ON PIER 114.
YES, DO HURRY.
QUACK QUACK QUACK
WEEOOO WEEOOO
MOTHER... FATHER...
...I'M SORRY.
DEAD END.

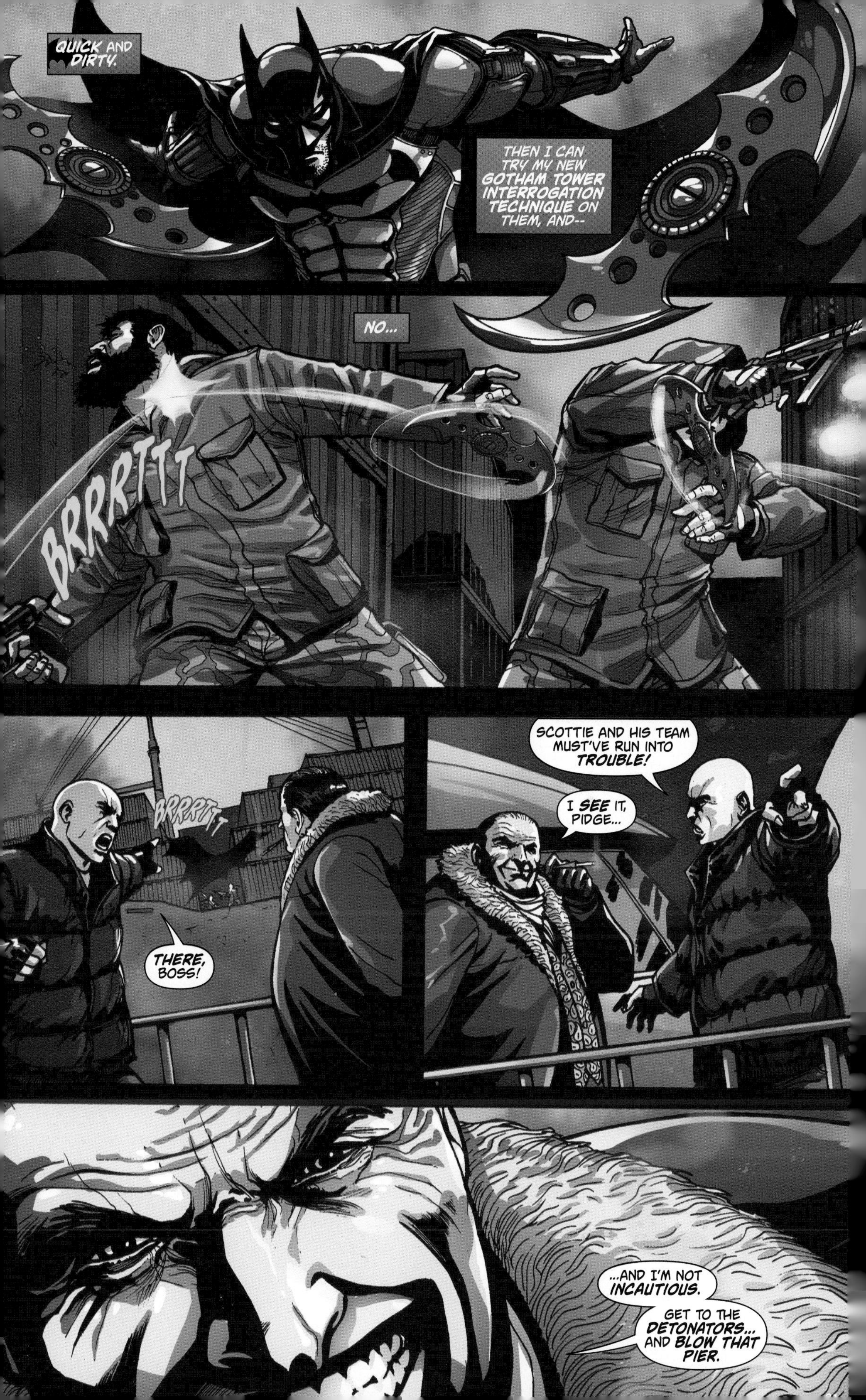
QUICK AND DIRTY.
THEN I CAN TRY MY NEW GOTHAM TOWER INTERROGATION TECHNIQUE ON THEM, AND--
NO...
BRRRTTT
BRRRTTT
THERE, BOSS!
SCOTTIE AND HIS TEAM MUST'VE RUN INTO TROUBLE!
I SEE IT, PIDGE...
...AND I'M NOT INCAUTIOUS.
GET TO THE DETONATORS... AND BLOW THAT PIER.

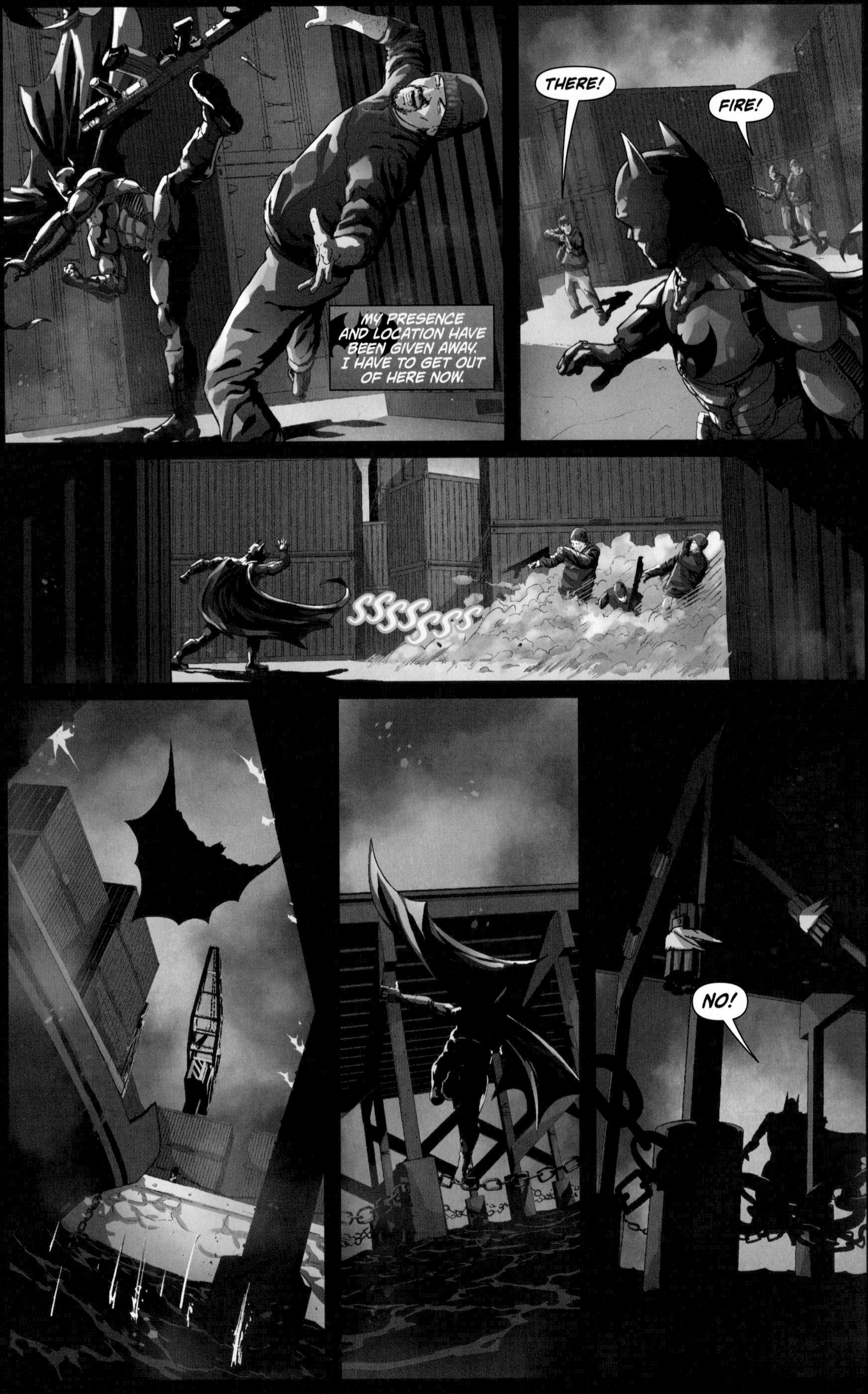
MY PRESENCE AND LOCATION HAVE BEEN GIVEN AWAY. I HAVE TO GET OUT OF HERE NOW.
THERE!
FIRE!
SSSSSSS
NO!

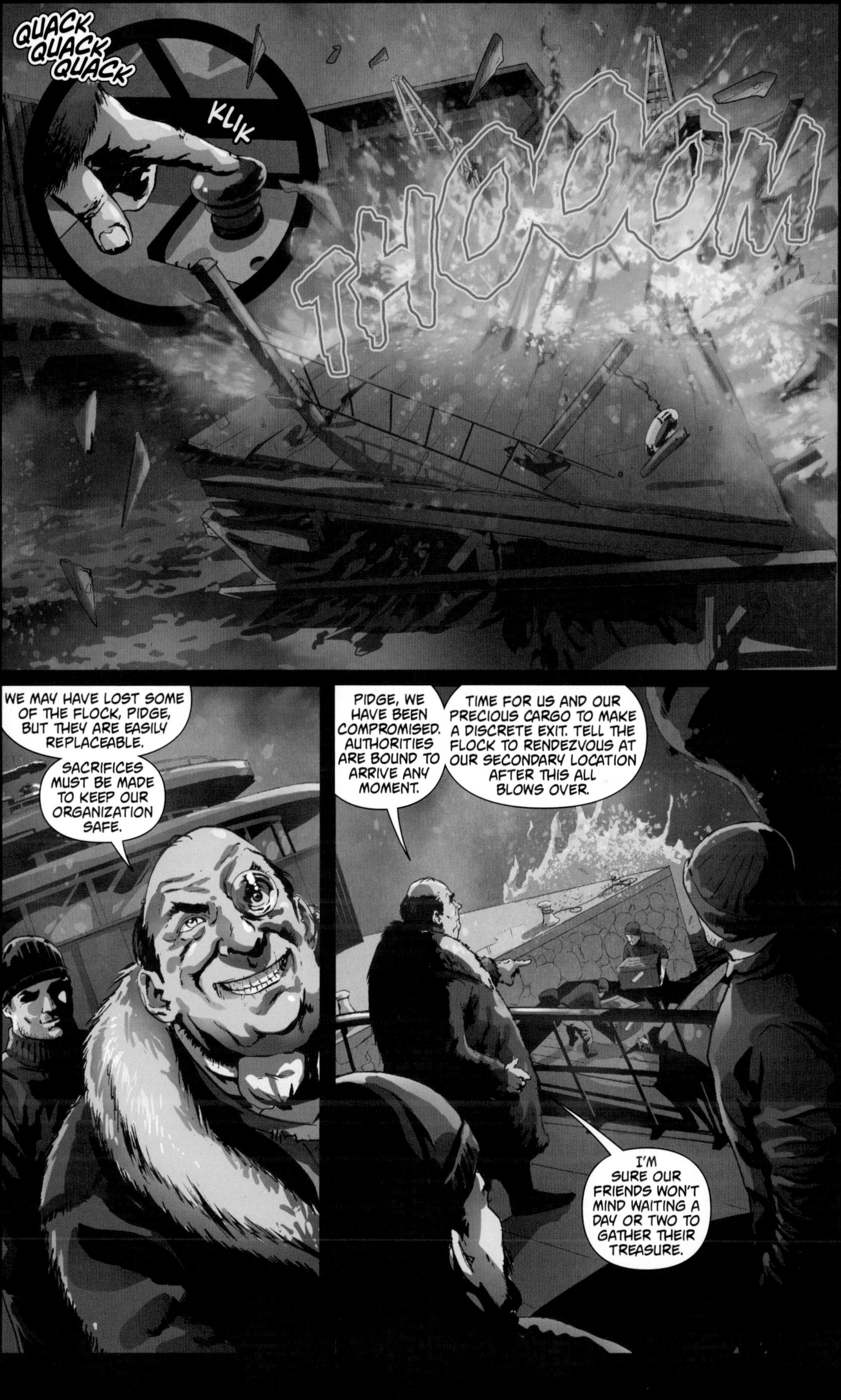
QUACK QUACK QUACK
KLIK
THOOOOM
WE MAY HAVE LOST SOME OF THE FLOCK, PIDGE, BUT THEY ARE EASILY REPLACEABLE.
SACRIFICES MUST BE MADE TO KEEP OUR ORGANIZATION SAFE.
PIDGE, WE HAVE BEEN COMPROMISED. AUTHORITIES ARE BOUND TO ARRIVE ANY MOMENT.
TIME FOR US AND OUR PRECIOUS CARGO TO MAKE A DISCRETE EXIT. TELL THE FLOCK TO RENDEZVOUS AT OUR SECONDARY LOCATION AFTER THIS ALL BLOWS OVER.
I'M SURE OUR FRIENDS WON'T MIND WAITING A DAY OR TWO TO GATHER THEIR TREASURE.

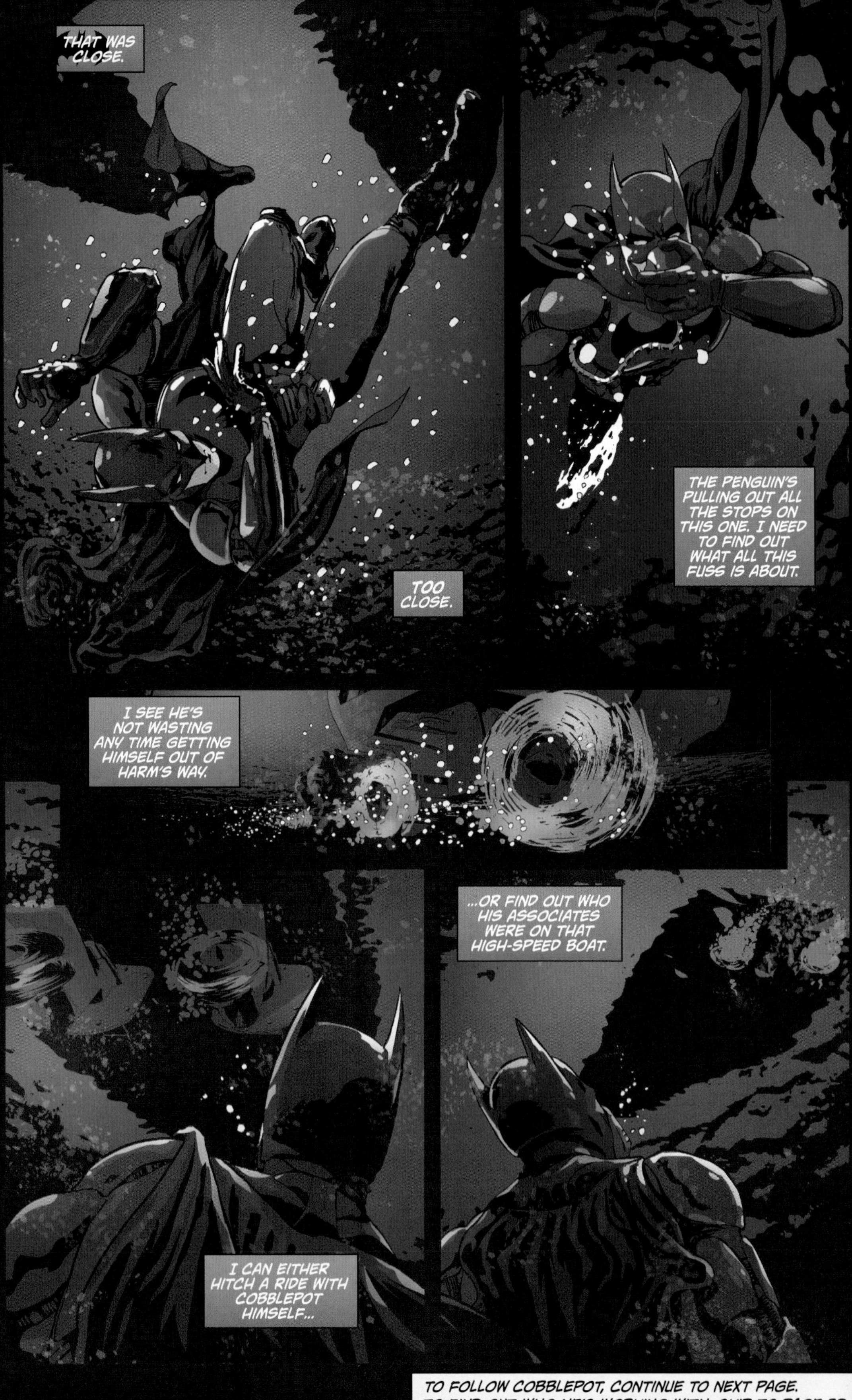
THAT WAS CLOSE.
TOO CLOSE.
THE PENGUIN'S PULLING OUT ALL THE STOPS ON THIS ONE. I NEED TO FIND OUT WHAT ALL THIS FUSS IS ABOUT.
I SEE HE'S NOT WASTING ANY TIME GETTING HIMSELF OUT OF HARM'S WAY.
I CAN EITHER HITCH A RIDE WITH COBBLEPOT HIMSELF...
...OR FIND OUT WHO HIS ASSOCIATES WERE ON THAT HIGH-SPEED BOAT.

TO FOLLOW COBBLEPOT, CONTINUE TO NEXT PAGE.
TO FIND OUT WHO HE'S WORKING WITH, SKIP TO PAGE 32.

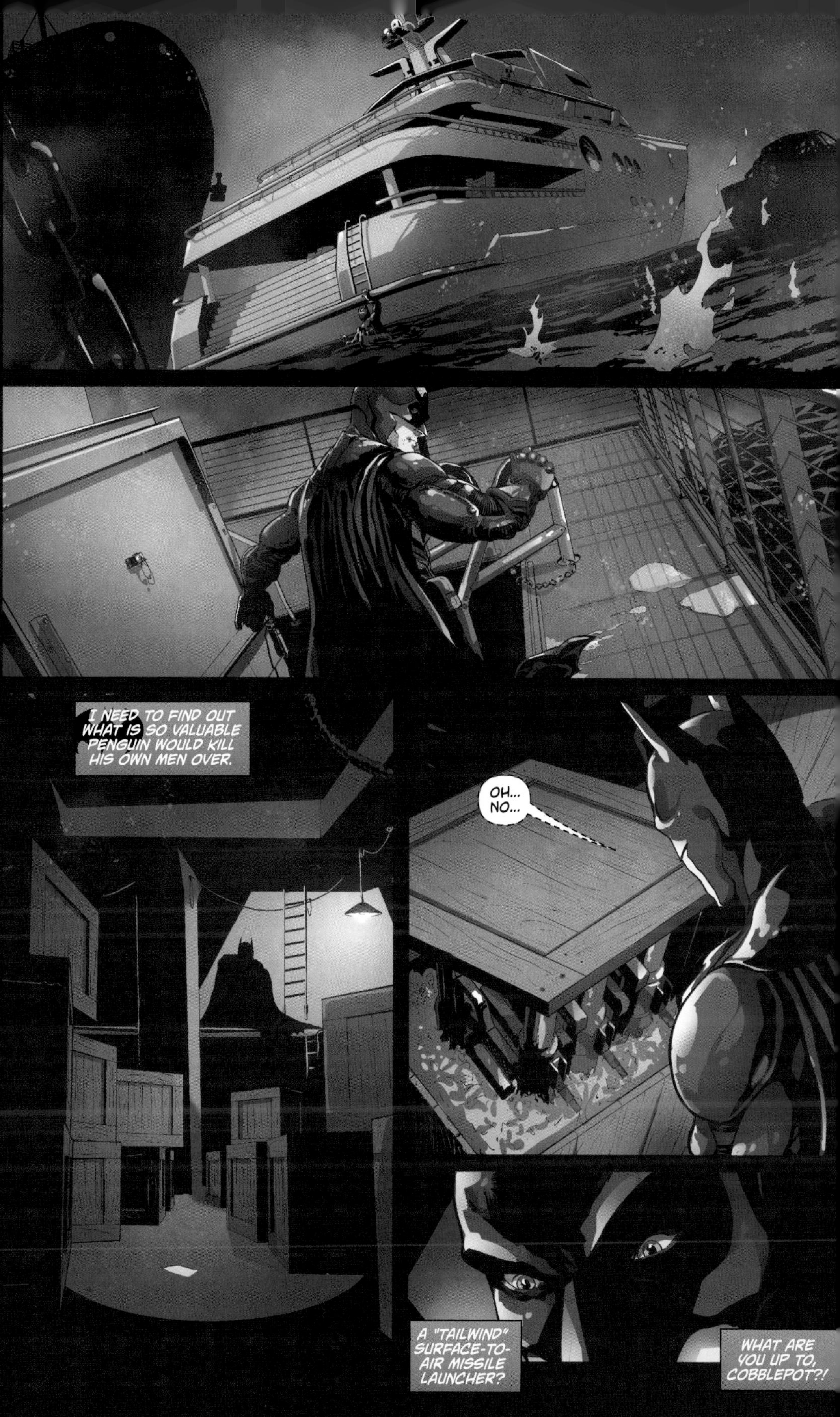
I NEED TO FIND OUT WHAT IS SO VALUABLE PENGUIN WOULD KILL HIS OWN MEN OVER.
OH... NO...
A "TAILWIND" SURFACE-TO-AIR MISSILE LAUNCHER?
WHAT ARE YOU UP TO, COBBLEPOT?!

THIS IS IMPRESSIVE. EVEN FOR A PLUCKY THIEF LIKE THE PENGUIN. IF BRANDEN IS PLANNING A COUP, THIS WOULD CERTAINLY HELP.

I DON'T WANT ANY MORE SQUAWKING FROM YOU LOT. YOU HEAR ME?!

DAMN. TIME TO MAKE MYSELF SCARCE.

I WASN'T SQUAWKING, BOSS.

FUNNY. IT SEEMS YOU'RE SQUAWKING, EVEN NOW.

THIS IS TURNING OUT TO BE A NICE LITTLE CAPER. I DIDN'T REALIZE WEAPONS COULD BE THIS SHINY. QUACK QUACK...

BOSS, LOOK! FOOTPRINTS.

GUARD THE DOOR. SEARCH THE ENTIRE HOLD. SHOOT ANYONE THAT DOESN'T BELONG. AND I MEAN ANYONE!

ONE WAY IN. ONE WAY OUT. THAT NARROWS MY OPTIONS.

KEEP WALKING, SKEL...

OF COURSE, THERE'S ALWAYS THE NUCLEAR OPTION.

WHY NOT?

FWING

NOT VERY ELEGANT. BUT IT WILL DO.

26

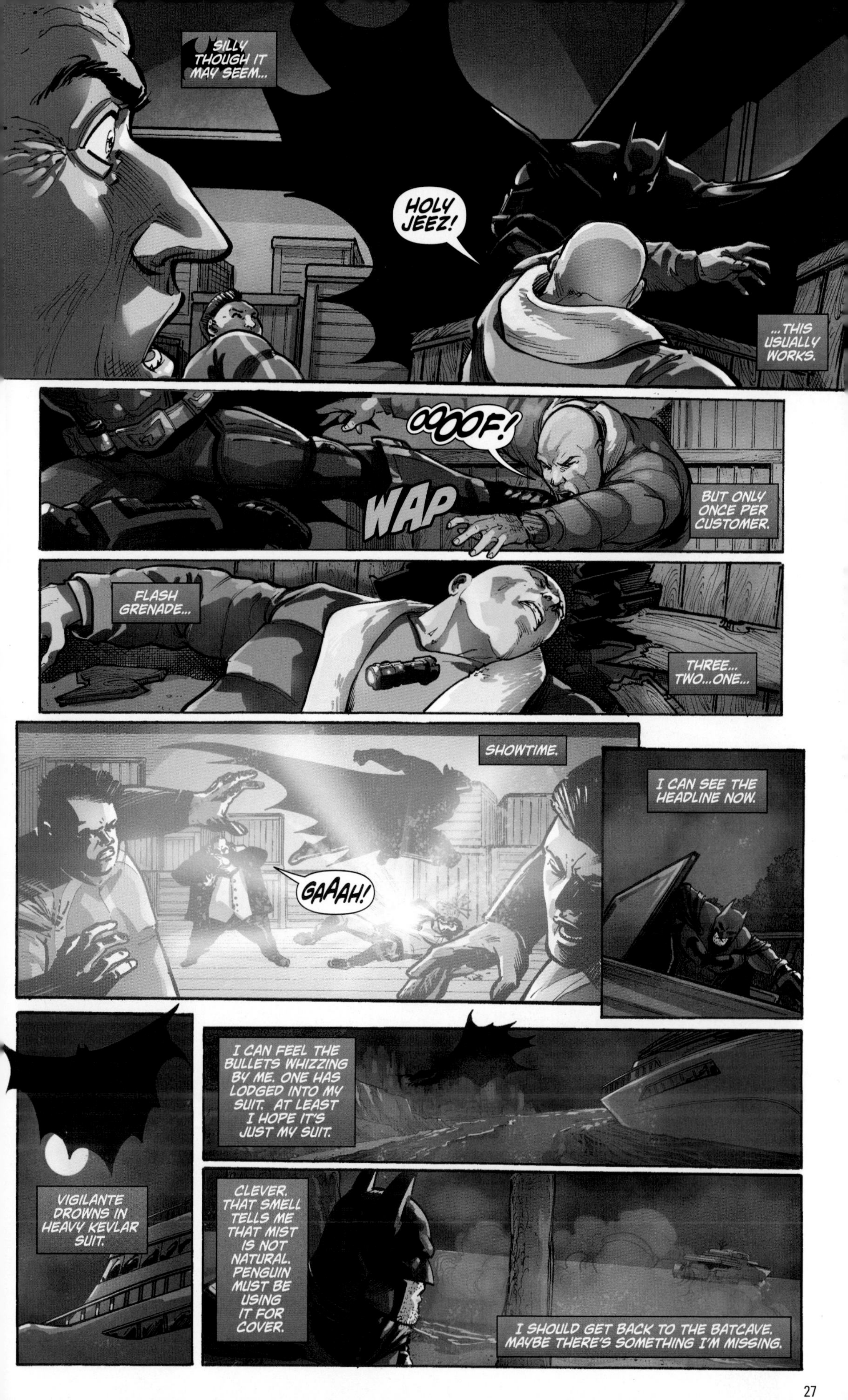
SILLY THOUGH IT MAY SEEM...
HOLY JEEZ!
...THIS USUALLY WORKS.
OOOOF!
WAP
BUT ONLY ONCE PER CUSTOMER.
FLASH GRENADE...
THREE... TWO...ONE...
SHOWTIME.
GAAAH!
I CAN SEE THE HEADLINE NOW.
VIGILANTE DROWNS IN HEAVY KEVLAR SUIT.
I CAN FEEL THE BULLETS WHIZZING BY ME. ONE HAS LODGED INTO MY SUIT. AT LEAST I HOPE IT'S JUST MY SUIT.
CLEVER. THAT SMELL TELLS ME THAT MIST IS NOT NATURAL. PENGUIN MUST BE USING IT FOR COVER.
I SHOULD GET BACK TO THE BATCAVE. MAYBE THERE'S SOMETHING I'M MISSING.

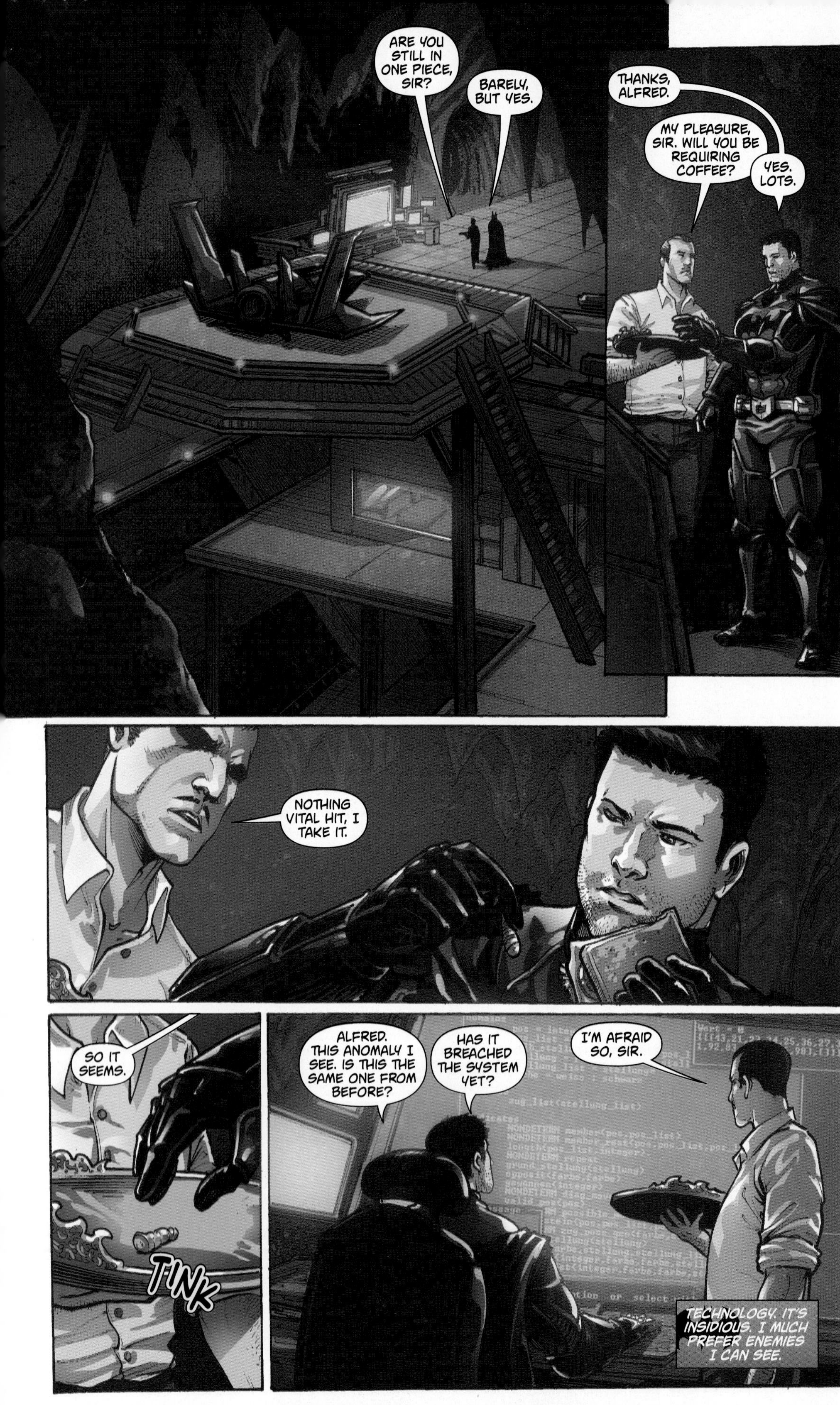

ARE YOU STILL IN ONE PIECE, SIR?
BARELY, BUT YES.
THANKS, ALFRED.
MY PLEASURE, SIR. WILL YOU BE REQUIRING COFFEE?
YES. LOTS.
NOTHING VITAL HIT, I TAKE IT.
SO IT SEEMS.
TINK
ALFRED. THIS ANOMALY I SEE. IS THIS THE SAME ONE FROM BEFORE?
HAS IT BREACHED THE SYSTEM YET?
I'M AFRAID SO, SIR.
TECHNOLOGY. IT'S INSIDIOUS. I MUCH PREFER ENEMIES I CAN SEE.

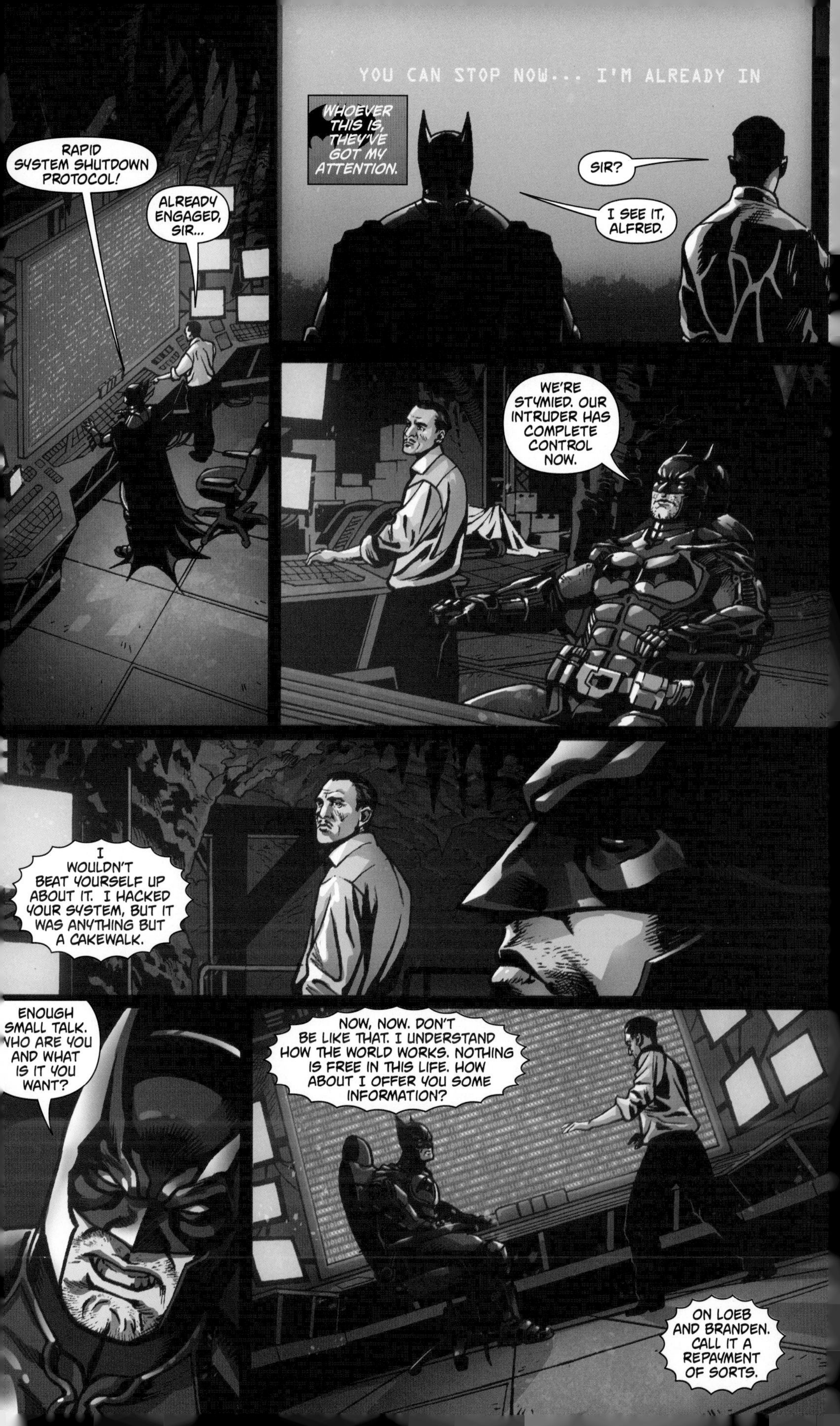
RAPID SYSTEM SHUTDOWN PROTOCOL!
ALREADY ENGAGED, SIR...
YOU CAN STOP NOW... I'M ALREADY IN
WHOEVER THIS IS, THEY'VE GOT MY ATTENTION.
SIR?
I SEE IT, ALFRED.
WE'RE STYMIED. OUR INTRUDER HAS COMPLETE CONTROL NOW.
I WOULDN'T BEAT YOURSELF UP ABOUT IT. I HACKED YOUR SYSTEM, BUT IT WAS ANYTHING BUT A CAKEWALK.
ENOUGH SMALL TALK. WHO ARE YOU AND WHAT IS IT YOU WANT?
NOW, NOW. DON'T BE LIKE THAT. I UNDERSTAND HOW THE WORLD WORKS. NOTHING IS FREE IN THIS LIFE. HOW ABOUT I OFFER YOU SOME INFORMATION?
ON LOEB AND BRANDEN. CALL IT A REPAYMENT OF SORTS.

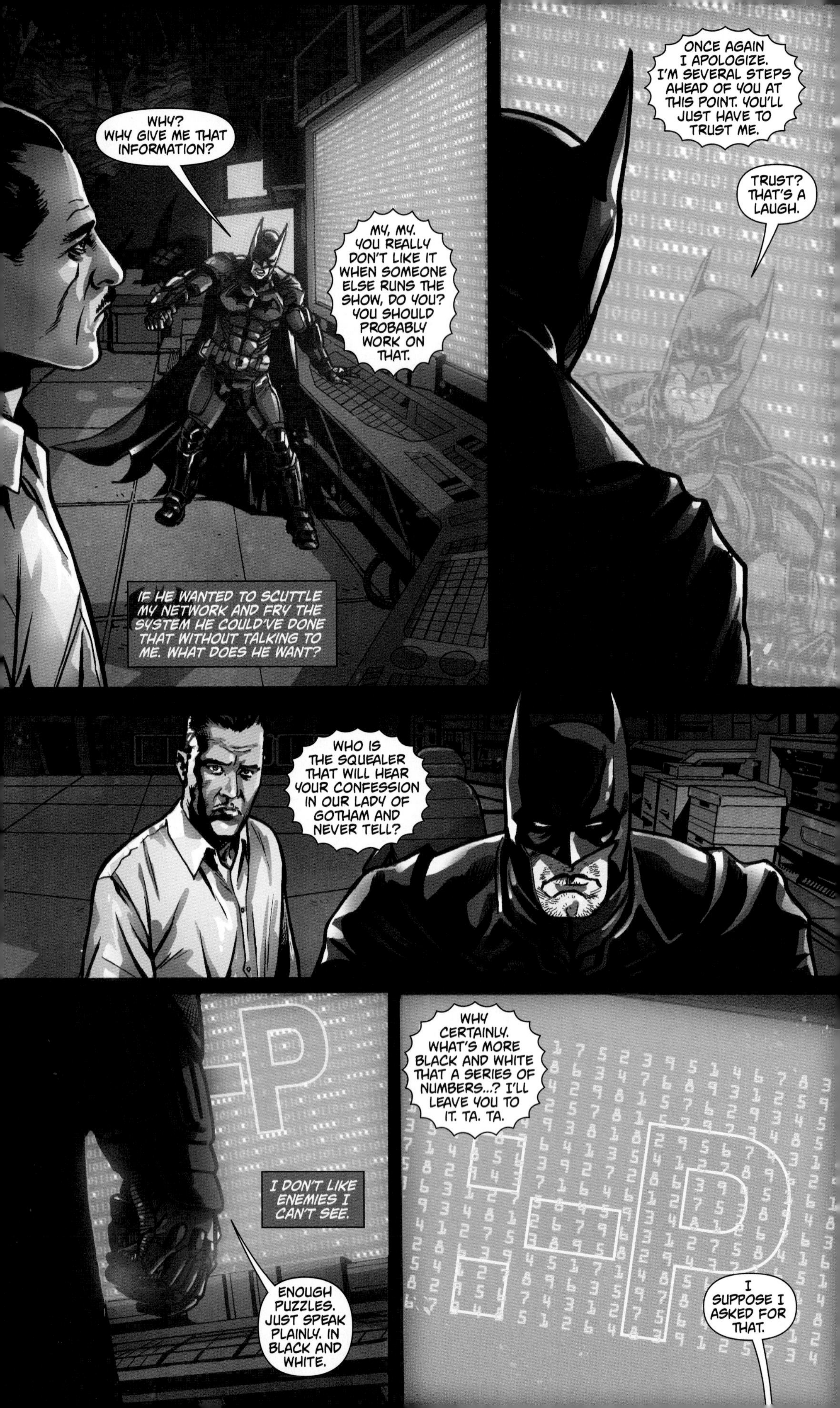
WHY? WHY GIVE ME THAT INFORMATION?
MY, MY. YOU REALLY DON'T LIKE IT WHEN SOMEONE ELSE RUNS THE SHOW, DO YOU? YOU SHOULD PROBABLY WORK ON THAT.
IF HE WANTED TO SCUTTLE MY NETWORK AND FRY THE SYSTEM HE COULD'VE DONE THAT WITHOUT TALKING TO ME. WHAT DOES HE WANT?
ONCE AGAIN I APOLOGIZE. I'M SEVERAL STEPS AHEAD OF YOU AT THIS POINT. YOU'LL JUST HAVE TO TRUST ME.
TRUST? THAT'S A LAUGH.
WHO IS THE SQUEALER THAT WILL HEAR YOUR CONFESSION IN OUR LADY OF GOTHAM AND NEVER TELL?
I DON'T LIKE ENEMIES I CAN'T SEE.
ENOUGH PUZZLES. JUST SPEAK PLAINLY. IN BLACK AND WHITE.
WHY CERTAINLY. WHAT'S MORE BLACK AND WHITE THAT A SERIES OF NUMBERS...? I'LL LEAVE YOU TO IT. TA. TA.
:-P
I SUPPOSE I ASKED FOR THAT.

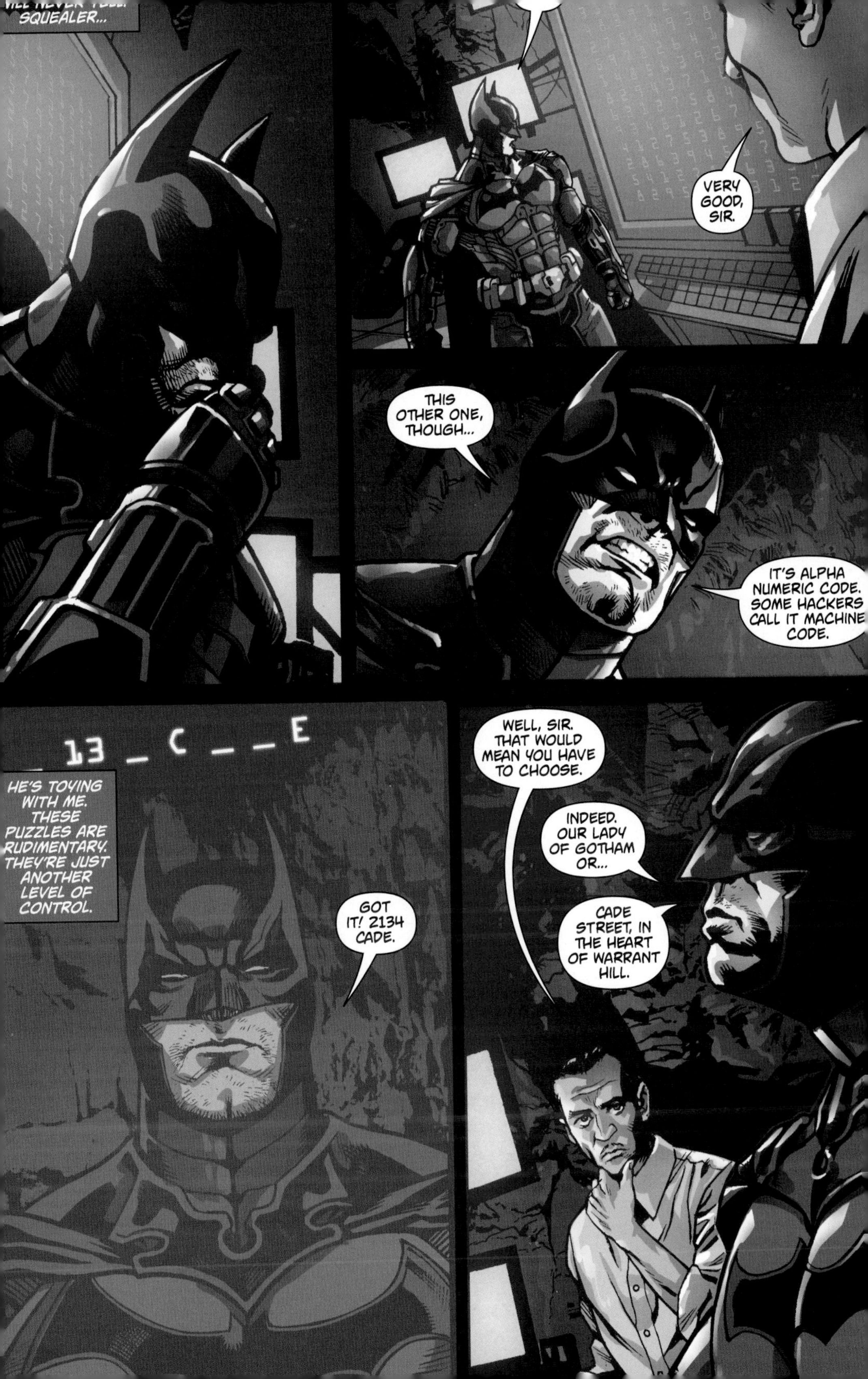
SQUEALER...
VERY GOOD, SIR.
THIS OTHER ONE, THOUGH...
IT'S ALPHA NUMERIC CODE. SOME HACKERS CALL IT MACHINE CODE.
13 _ C _ _ E
HE'S TOYING WITH ME. THESE PUZZLES ARE RUDIMENTARY. THEY'RE JUST ANOTHER LEVEL OF CONTROL.
GOT IT! 2134 CADE.
WELL, SIR. THAT WOULD MEAN YOU HAVE TO CHOOSE.
INDEED. OUR LADY OF GOTHAM OR...
CADE STREET, IN THE HEART OF WARRANT HILL.

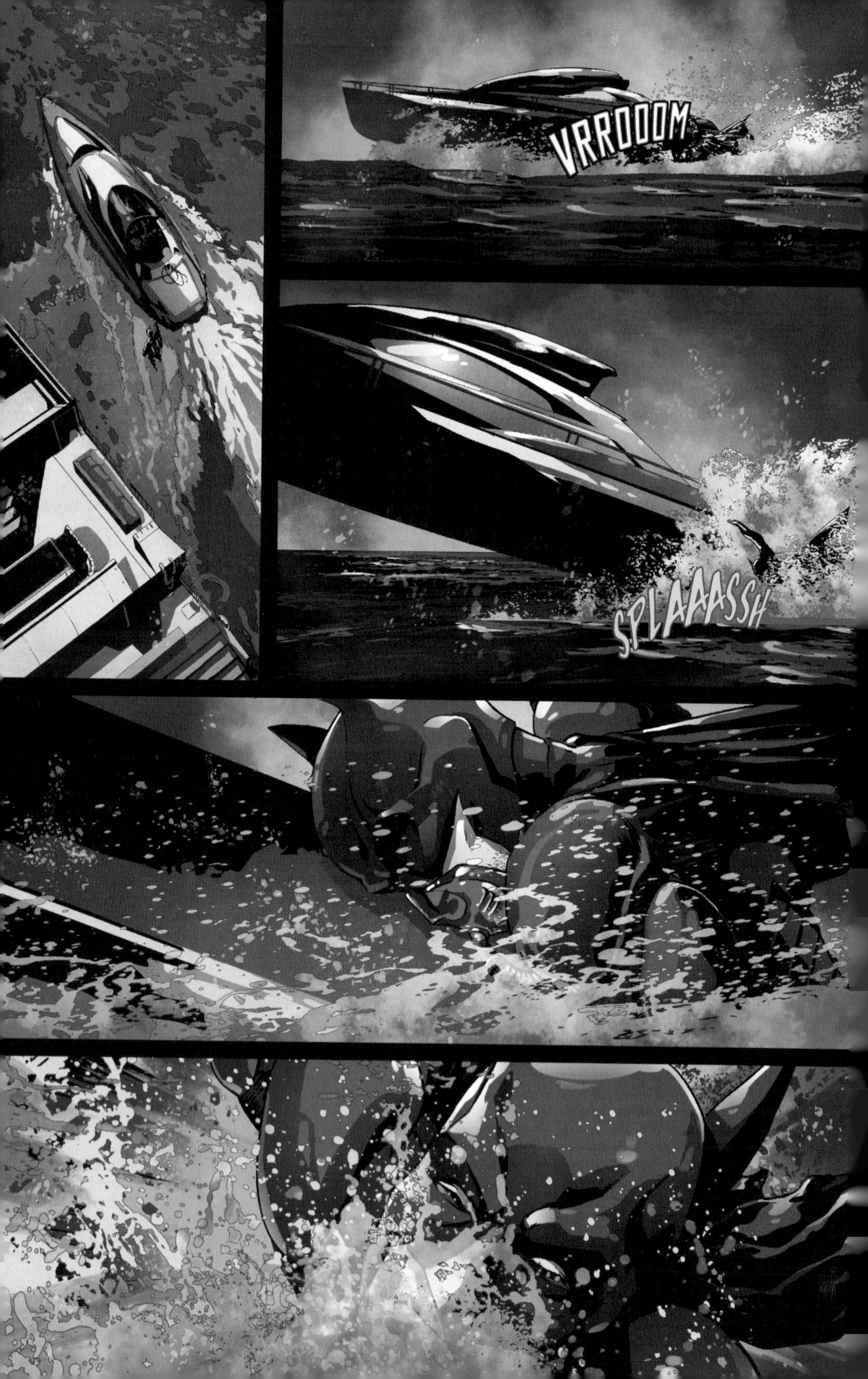
VRROOOM
SPLAAASSH

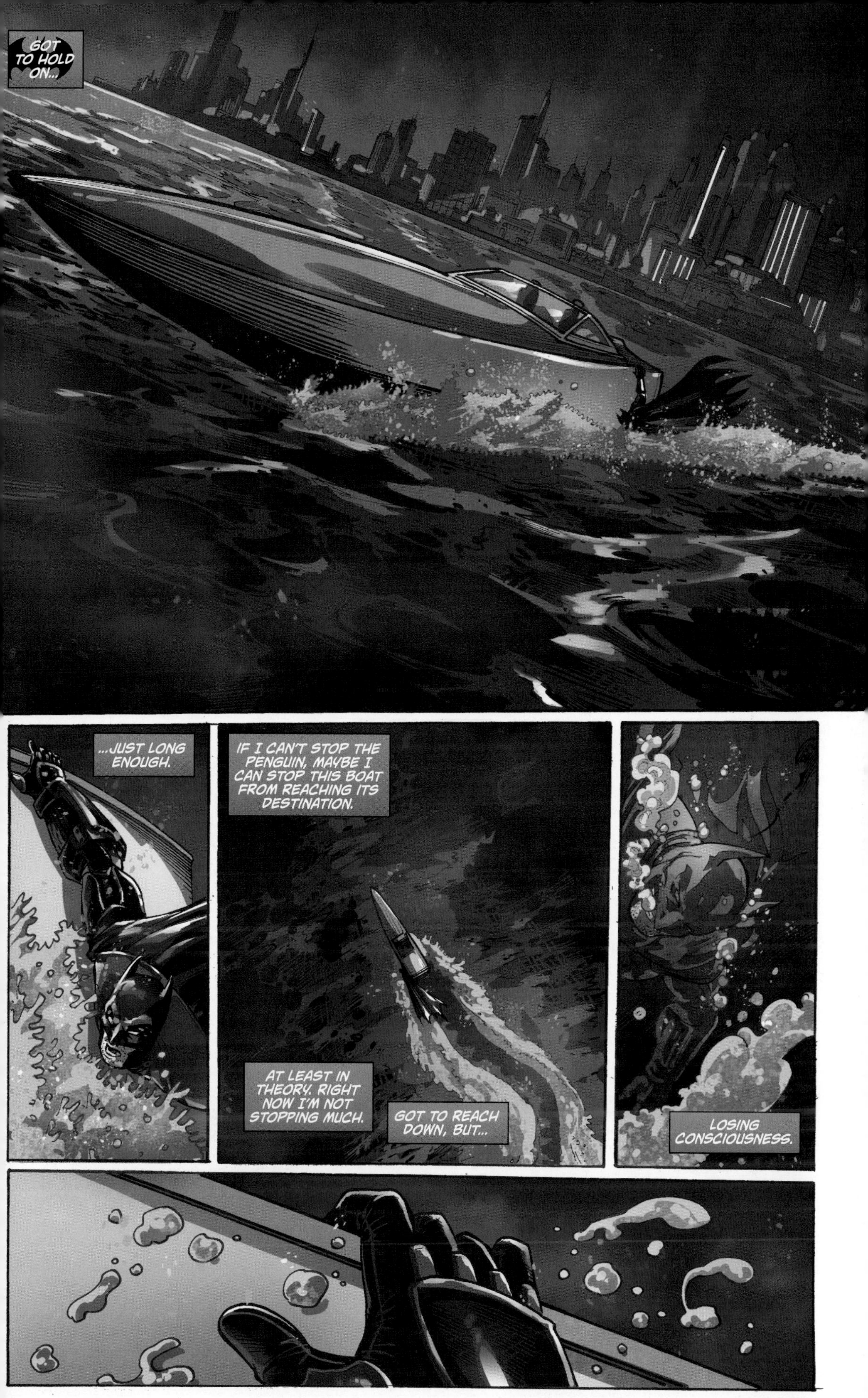
GOT TO HOLD ON...
...JUST LONG ENOUGH.
IF I CAN'T STOP THE PENGUIN, MAYBE I CAN STOP THIS BOAT FROM REACHING ITS DESTINATION.
AT LEAST IN THEORY. RIGHT NOW I'M NOT STOPPING MUCH.
GOT TO REACH DOWN, BUT...
LOSING CONSCIOUSNESS.

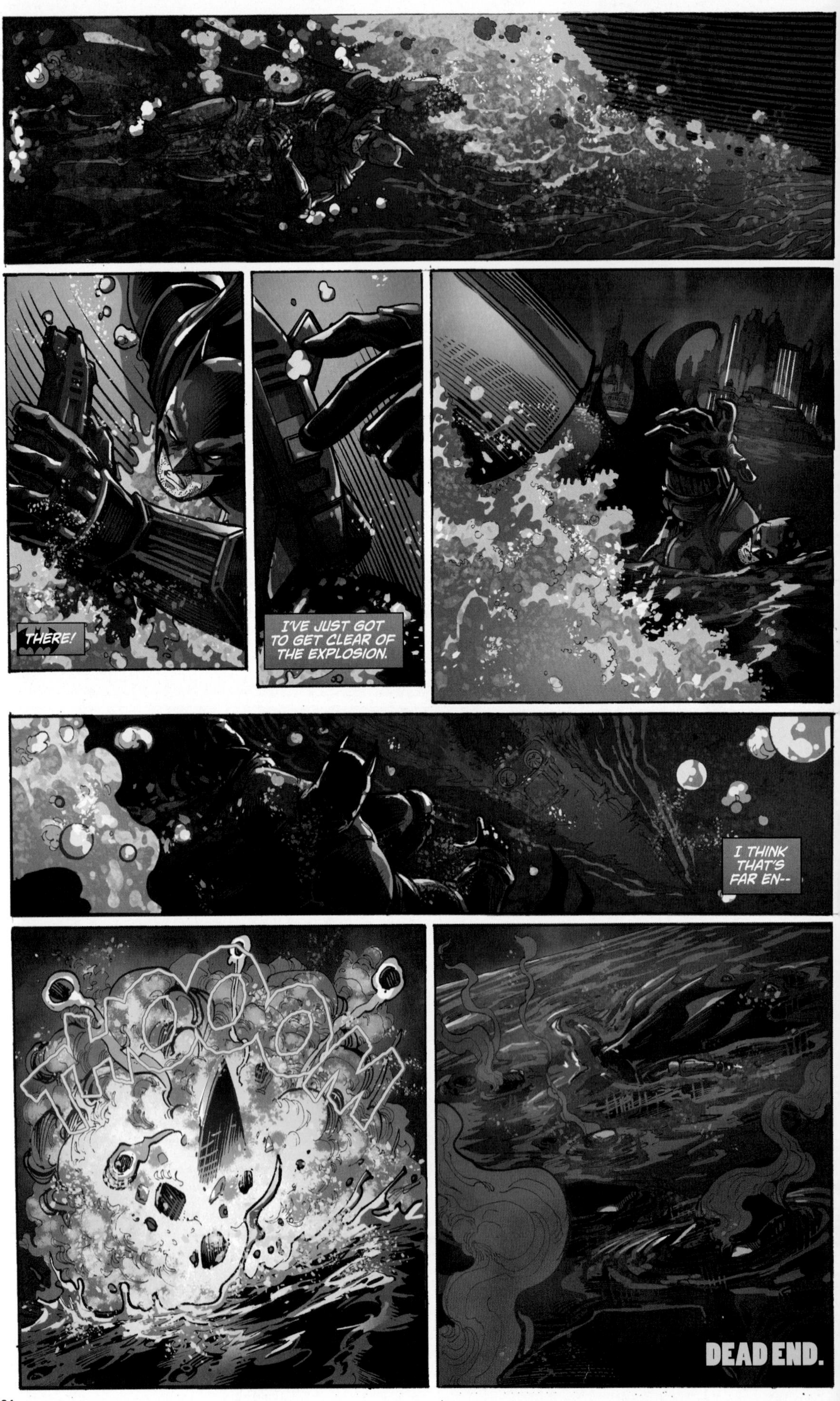
THERE!
I'VE JUST GOT TO GET CLEAR OF THE EXPLOSION.
I THINK THAT'S FAR EN--
THOOOOM
DEAD END.

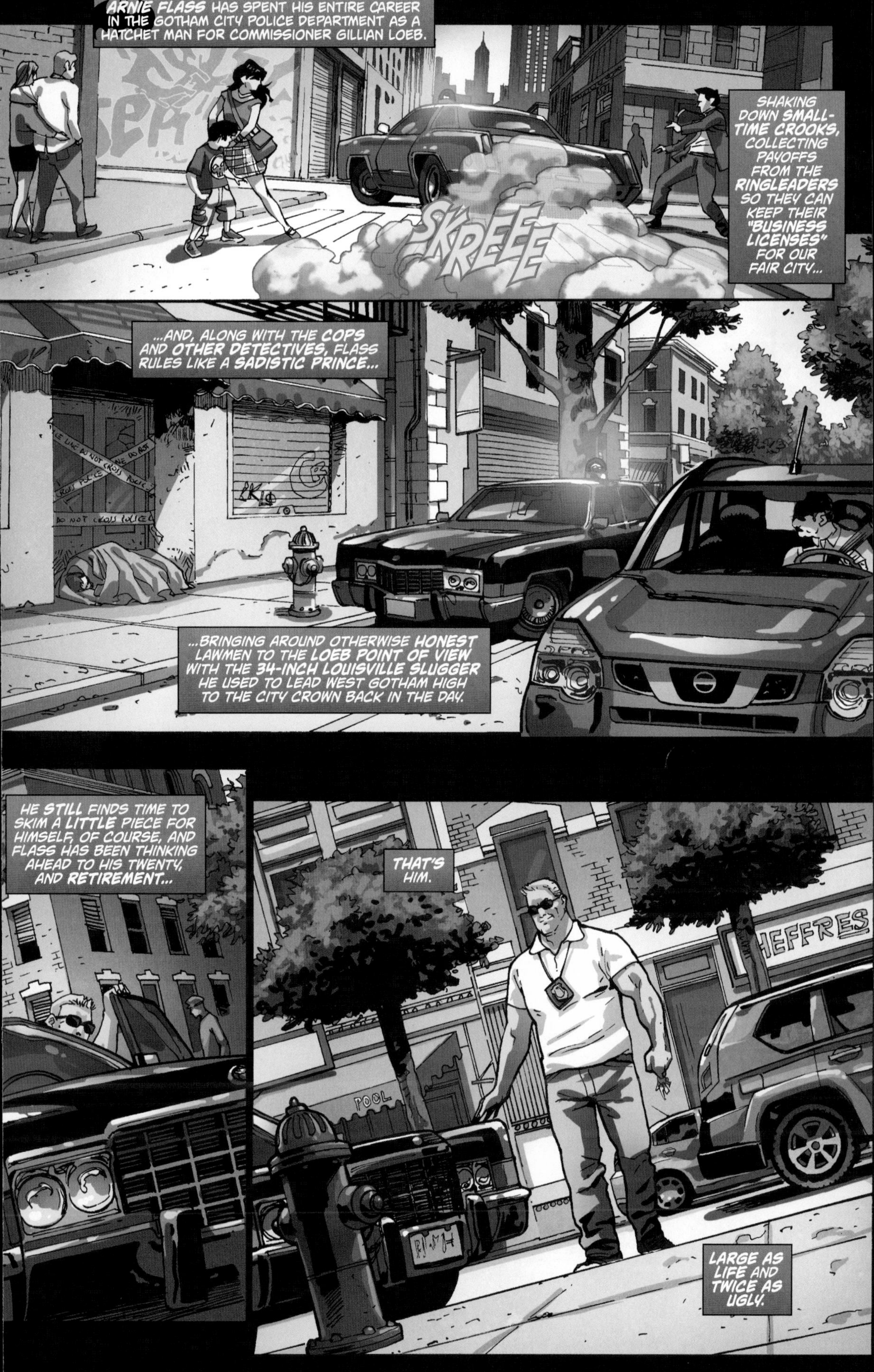
ARNIE FLASS HAS SPENT HIS ENTIRE CAREER IN THE GOTHAM CITY POLICE DEPARTMENT AS A HATCHET MAN FOR COMMISSIONER GILLIAN LOEB.
SKREEE
SHAKING DOWN SMALL-TIME CROOKS, COLLECTING PAYOFFS FROM THE RINGLEADERS SO THEY CAN KEEP THEIR "BUSINESS LICENSES" FOR OUR FAIR CITY...
...AND, ALONG WITH THE COPS AND OTHER DETECTIVES, FLASS RULES LIKE A SADISTIC PRINCE...
...BRINGING AROUND OTHERWISE HONEST LAWMEN TO THE LOEB POINT OF VIEW WITH THE 34-INCH LOUISVILLE SLUGGER HE USED TO LEAD WEST GOTHAM HIGH TO THE CITY CROWN BACK IN THE DAY.
HE STILL FINDS TIME TO SKIM A LITTLE PIECE FOR HIMSELF, OF COURSE, AND FLASS HAS BEEN THINKING AHEAD TO HIS TWENTY, AND RETIREMENT...
THAT'S HIM.
POOL
LARGE AS LIFE AND TWICE AS UGLY.

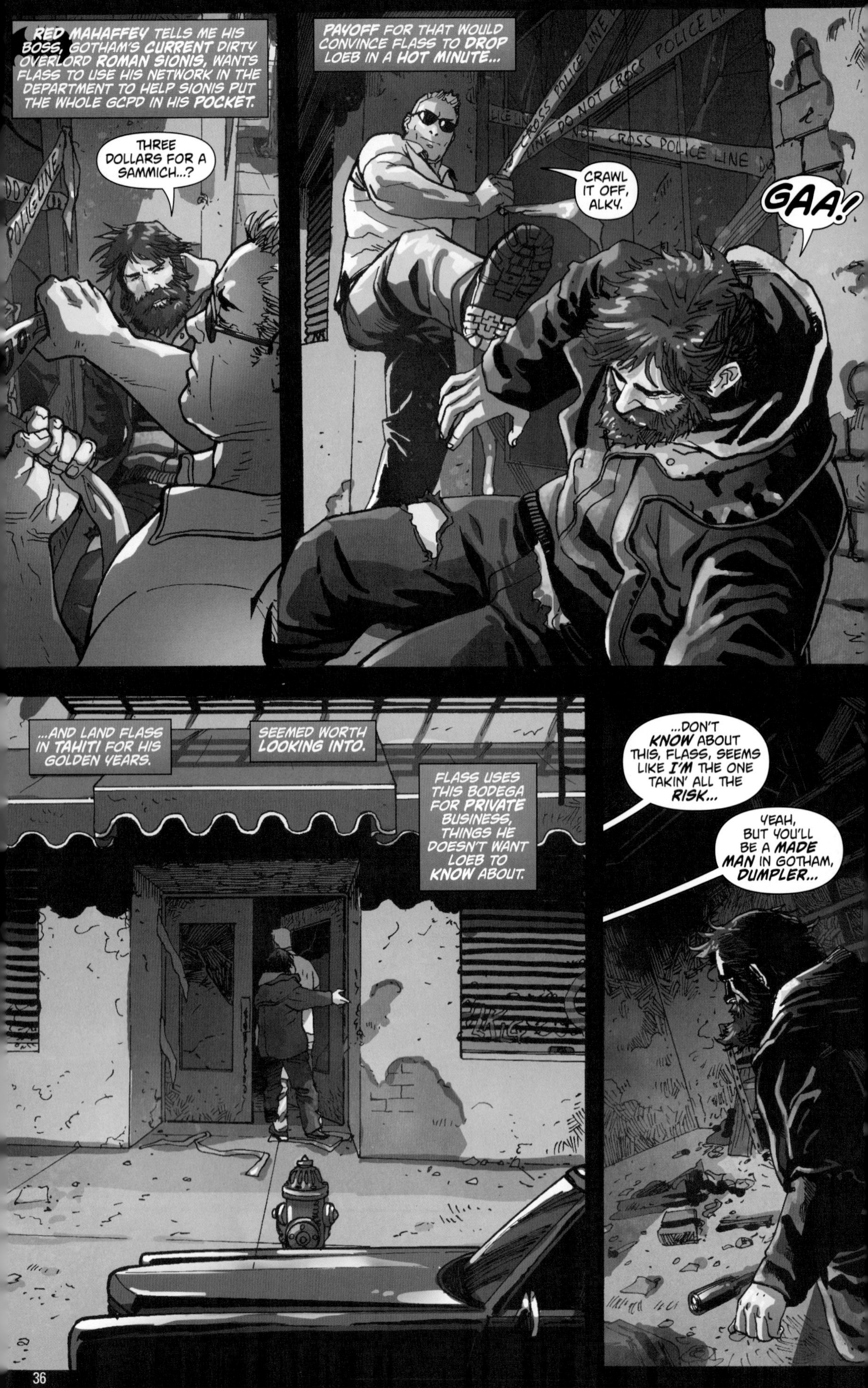
RED MAHAFFEY TELLS ME HIS BOSS, GOTHAM'S CURRENT DIRTY OVERLORD ROMAN SIONIS, WANTS FLASS TO USE HIS NETWORK IN THE DEPARTMENT TO HELP SIONIS PUT THE WHOLE GCPD IN HIS POCKET.
THREE DOLLARS FOR A SAMMICH...?
PAYOFF FOR THAT WOULD CONVINCE FLASS TO DROP LOEB IN A HOT MINUTE...
CRAWL IT OFF, ALKY.
GAA!
...AND LAND FLASS IN TAHITI FOR HIS GOLDEN YEARS.
SEEMED WORTH LOOKING INTO.
FLASS USES THIS BODEGA FOR PRIVATE BUSINESS, THINGS HE DOESN'T WANT LOEB TO KNOW ABOUT.
...DON'T KNOW ABOUT THIS, FLASS, SEEMS LIKE I'M THE ONE TAKIN' ALL THE RISK...
YEAH, BUT YOU'LL BE A MADE MAN IN GOTHAM, DUMPLER...

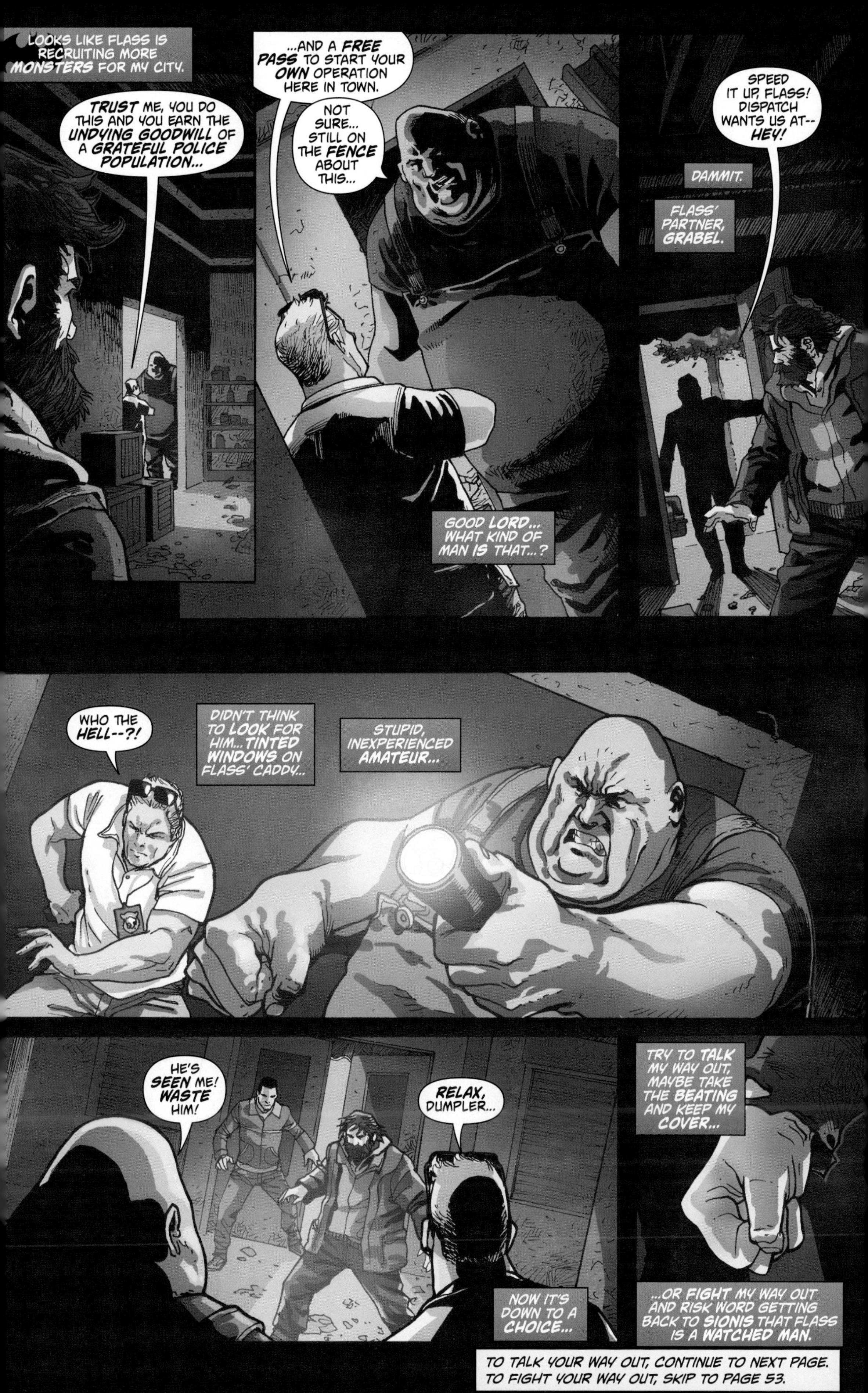
LOOKS LIKE FLASS IS RECRUITING MORE MONSTERS FOR MY CITY.
TRUST ME, YOU DO THIS AND YOU EARN THE UNDYING GOODWILL OF A GRATEFUL POLICE POPULATION...
...AND A FREE PASS TO START YOUR OWN OPERATION HERE IN TOWN.
NOT SURE... STILL ON THE FENCE ABOUT THIS...
GOOD LORD... WHAT KIND OF MAN IS THAT...?
SPEED IT UP, FLASS! DISPATCH WANTS US AT-- HEY!
DAMMIT.
FLASS' PARTNER, GRABEL.
WHO THE HELL--?!
DIDN'T THINK TO LOOK FOR HIM... TINTED WINDOWS ON FLASS' CADDY...
STUPID, INEXPERIENCED AMATEUR...
HE'S SEEN ME! WASTE HIM!
RELAX, DUMPLER...
TRY TO TALK MY WAY OUT, MAYBE TAKE THE BEATING AND KEEP MY COVER...
NOW IT'S DOWN TO A CHOICE...
...OR FIGHT MY WAY OUT AND RISK WORD GETTING BACK TO SIONIS THAT FLASS IS A WATCHED MAN.
TO TALK YOUR WAY OUT, CONTINUE TO NEXT PAGE.
TO FIGHT YOUR WAY OUT, SKIP TO PAGE 53.

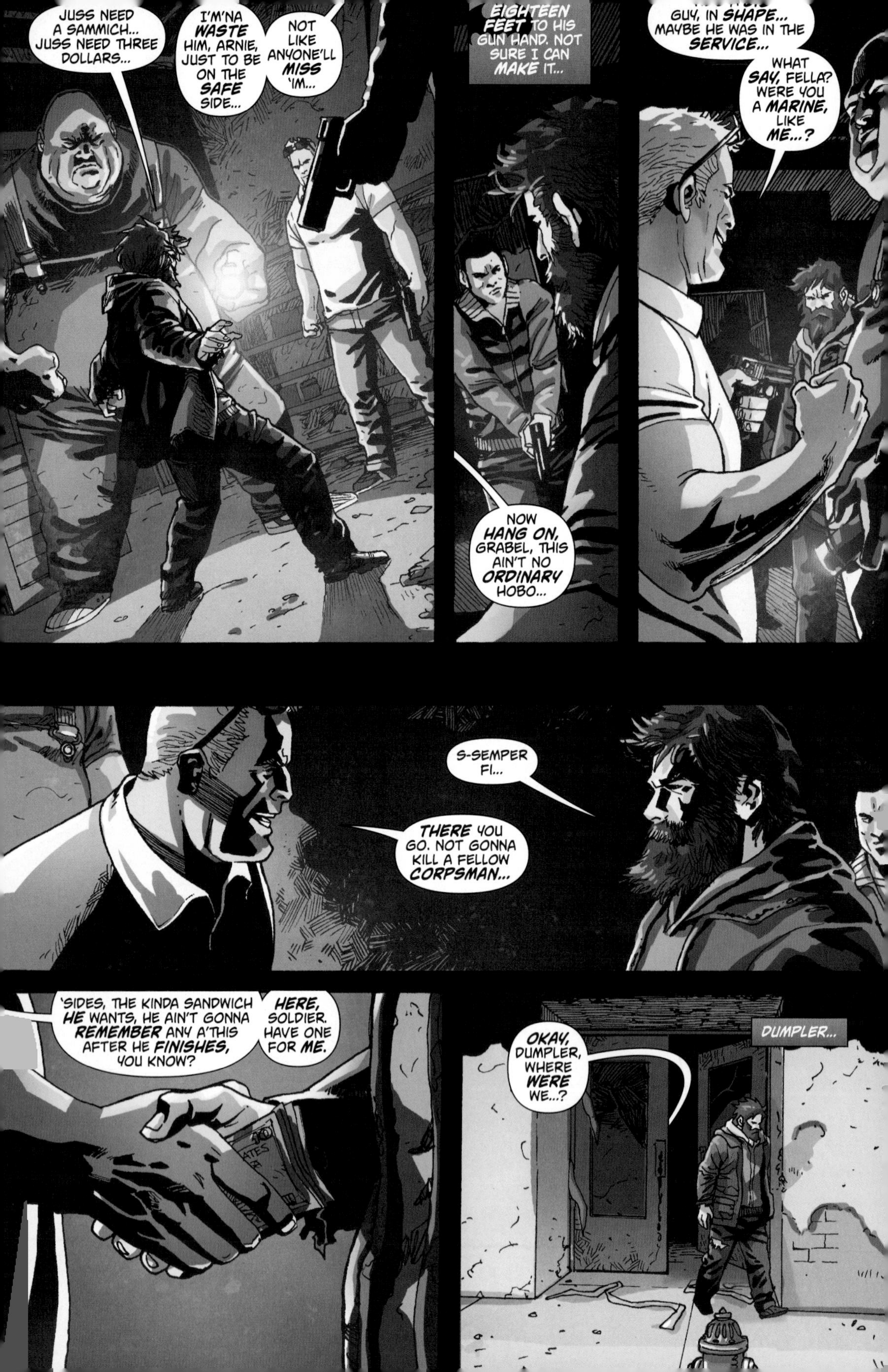

JUSS NEED A SAMMICH... JUSS NEED THREE DOLLARS...
I'M'NA WASTE HIM, ARNIE, JUST TO BE ON THE SAFE SIDE...
NOT LIKE ANYONE'LL MISS 'IM...
EIGHTEEN FEET TO HIS GUN HAND. NOT SURE I CAN MAKE IT...
NOW HANG ON, GRABEL, THIS AIN'T NO ORDINARY HOBO...
GUY, IN SHAPE... MAYBE HE WAS IN THE SERVICE...
WHAT SAY, FELLA? WERE YOU A MARINE, LIKE ME...?
S-SEMPER FI...
THERE YOU GO. NOT GONNA KILL A FELLOW CORPSMAN...
'SIDES, THE KINDA SANDWICH HE WANTS, HE AIN'T GONNA REMEMBER ANY A'THIS AFTER HE FINISHES, YOU KNOW?
HERE, SOLDIER. HAVE ONE FOR ME.
DUMPLER...
OKAY, DUMPLER, WHERE WERE WE...?

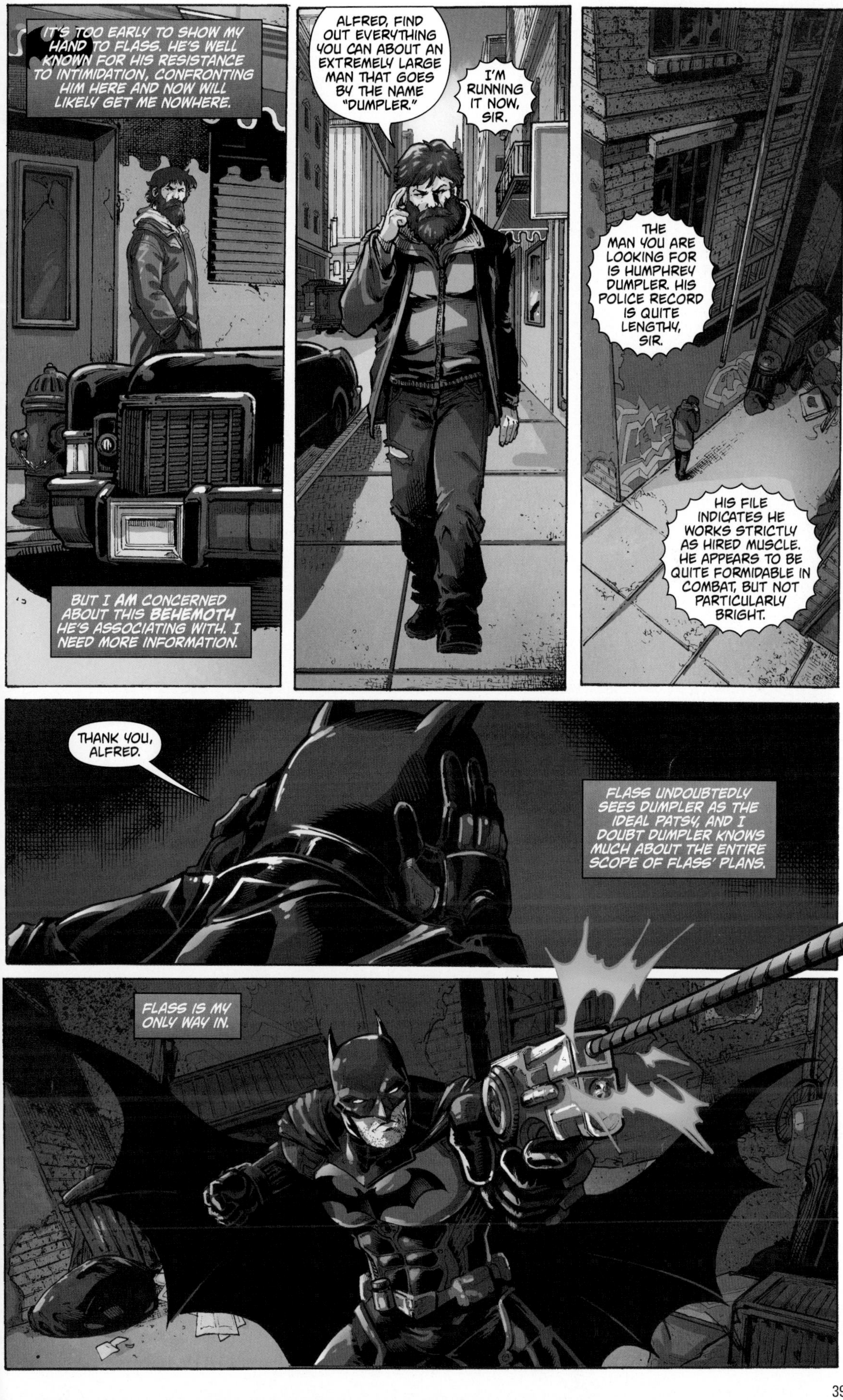
IT'S TOO EARLY TO SHOW MY HAND TO FLASS. HE'S WELL KNOWN FOR HIS RESISTANCE TO INTIMIDATION, CONFRONTING HIM HERE AND NOW WILL LIKELY GET ME NOWHERE.
BUT I AM CONCERNED ABOUT THIS BEHEMOTH HE'S ASSOCIATING WITH. I NEED MORE INFORMATION.
ALFRED, FIND OUT EVERYTHING YOU CAN ABOUT AN EXTREMELY LARGE MAN THAT GOES BY THE NAME "DUMPLER."
I'M RUNNING IT NOW, SIR.
THE MAN YOU ARE LOOKING FOR IS HUMPHREY DUMPLER. HIS POLICE RECORD IS QUITE LENGTHY, SIR.
HIS FILE INDICATES HE WORKS STRICTLY AS HIRED MUSCLE. HE APPEARS TO BE QUITE FORMIDABLE IN COMBAT, BUT NOT PARTICULARLY BRIGHT.
THANK YOU, ALFRED.
FLASS UNDOUBTEDLY SEES DUMPLER AS THE IDEAL PATSY, AND I DOUBT DUMPLER KNOWS MUCH ABOUT THE ENTIRE SCOPE OF FLASS' PLANS.
FLASS IS MY ONLY WAY IN.

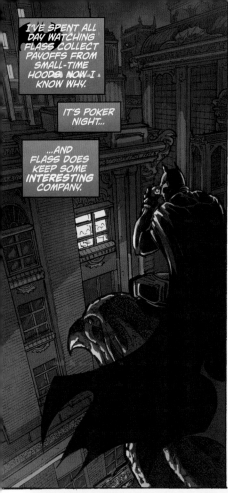

I'VE SPENT ALL DAY WATCHING FLASS COLLECT PAYOFFS FROM SMALL-TIME HOODS. NOW I KNOW WHY.

IT'S POKER NIGHT...

...AND FLASS DOES KEEP SOME INTERESTING COMPANY.

I RECOGNIZE THEM ALL. D.A.'S OFFICE, INTERNAL AFFAIRS, ORGANIZED CRIME DIVISION...

...ALL CORRUPT.

SEEMS I'M NOT THE ONLY ONE WATCHING FLASS TONIGHT.

SCAN ALL RADIO FREQUENCIES EMANATING WITHIN A 200-YARD RADIUS.

EVERYONE KEEP IN MIND THAT TWO OF THESE MEN ARE GCPD DETECTIVES AND MOST LIKELY ARMED. STAY OUT OF A FIRE FIGHT AT ALL COSTS. I NEED THEM ALL IN ONE PIECE.

THAT VOICE SOUNDS FAMILIAR, BUT I CAN'T QUITE PLACE IT.

ON MY MARK.

MOVE!
MOVE!
MOVE!

IF FLASS IS EXPOSED NOW, I COULD BE BACK AT SQUARE ONE WITH NO LEADS AND NO IDEA AS TO FLASS' PLANS FOR DUMPLER.

OR IF FLASS IS FORCED OUT OF THE PICTURE, IT COULD FLUSH A LARGER PLAYER OUT INTO THE OPEN.

DO I STOP THE INCURSION?

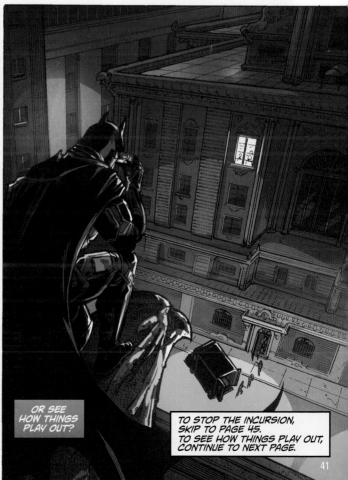

OR SEE HOW THINGS PLAY OUT?

TO STOP THE INCURSION, SKIP TO PAGE 45.
TO SEE HOW THINGS PLAY OUT, CONTINUE TO NEXT PAGE.

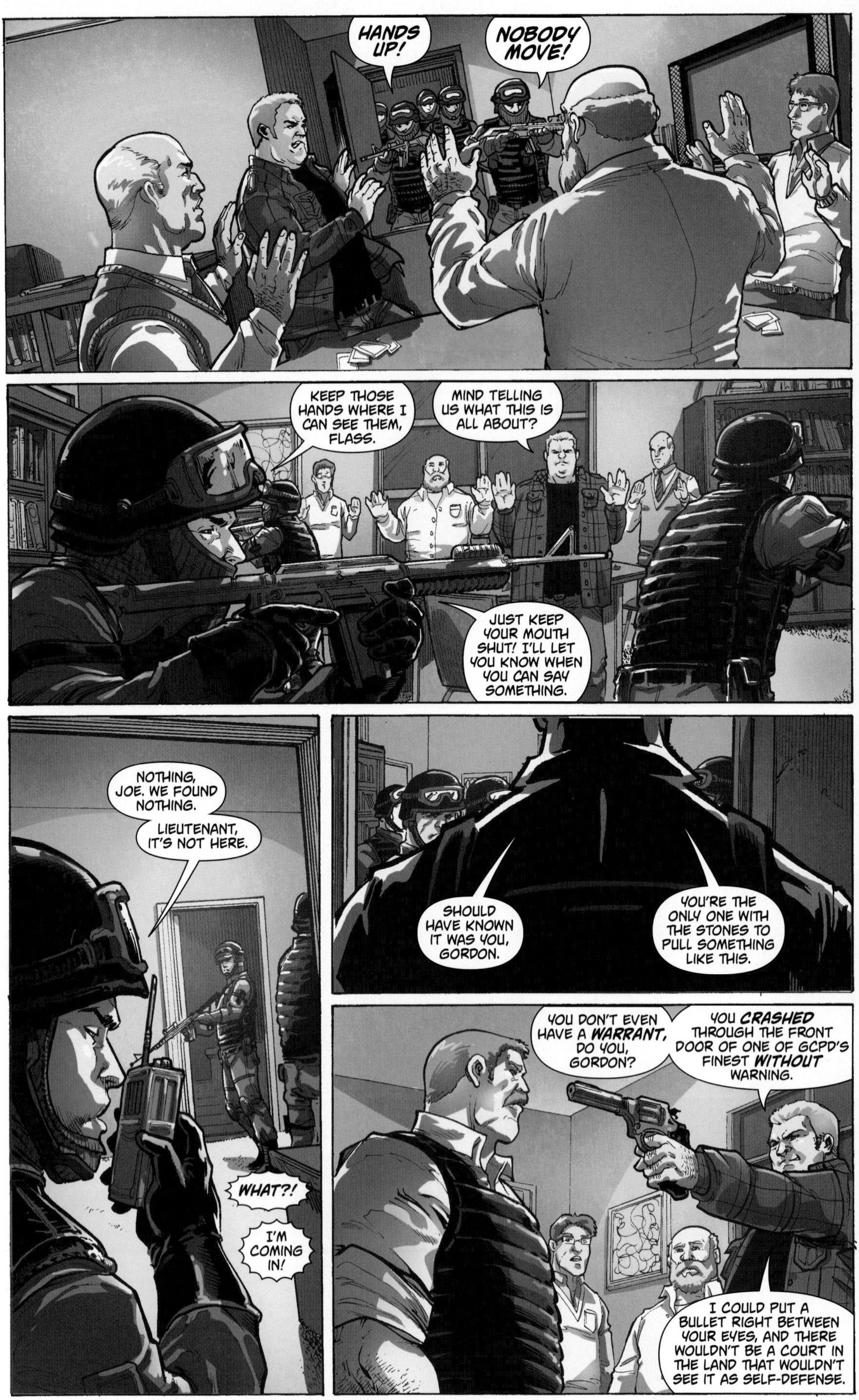
HANDS UP!
NOBODY MOVE!
KEEP THOSE HANDS WHERE I CAN SEE THEM, FLASS.
MIND TELLING US WHAT THIS IS ALL ABOUT?
JUST KEEP YOUR MOUTH SHUT! I'LL LET YOU KNOW WHEN YOU CAN SAY SOMETHING.
NOTHING, JOE. WE FOUND NOTHING.
LIEUTENANT, IT'S NOT HERE.
WHAT?!
I'M COMING IN!
SHOULD HAVE KNOWN IT WAS YOU, GORDON.
YOU'RE THE ONLY ONE WITH THE STONES TO PULL SOMETHING LIKE THIS.
YOU DON'T EVEN HAVE A WARRANT, DO YOU, GORDON?
YOU CRASHED THROUGH THE FRONT DOOR OF ONE OF GCPD'S FINEST WITHOUT WARNING.
I COULD PUT A BULLET RIGHT BETWEEN YOUR EYES, AND THERE WOULDN'T BE A COURT IN THE LAND THAT WOULDN'T SEE IT AS SELF-DEFENSE.

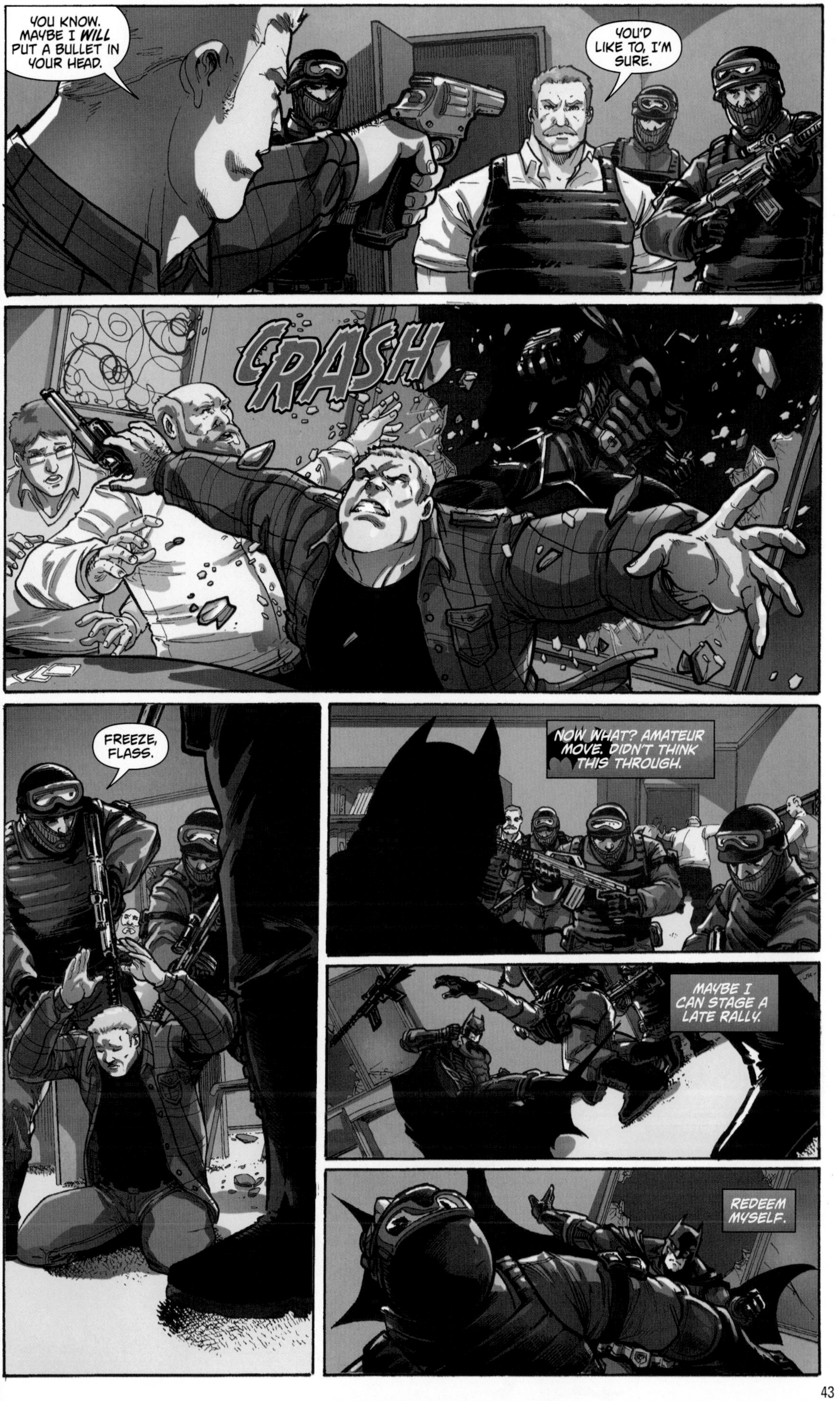
YOU KNOW. MAYBE I **WILL** PUT A BULLET IN YOUR HEAD.
YOU'D LIKE TO, I'M SURE.
CRASH
FREEZE, FLASS.
NOW WHAT? AMATEUR MOVE. DIDN'T THINK THIS THROUGH.
MAYBE I CAN STAGE A LATE RALLY.
REDEEM MYSELF.

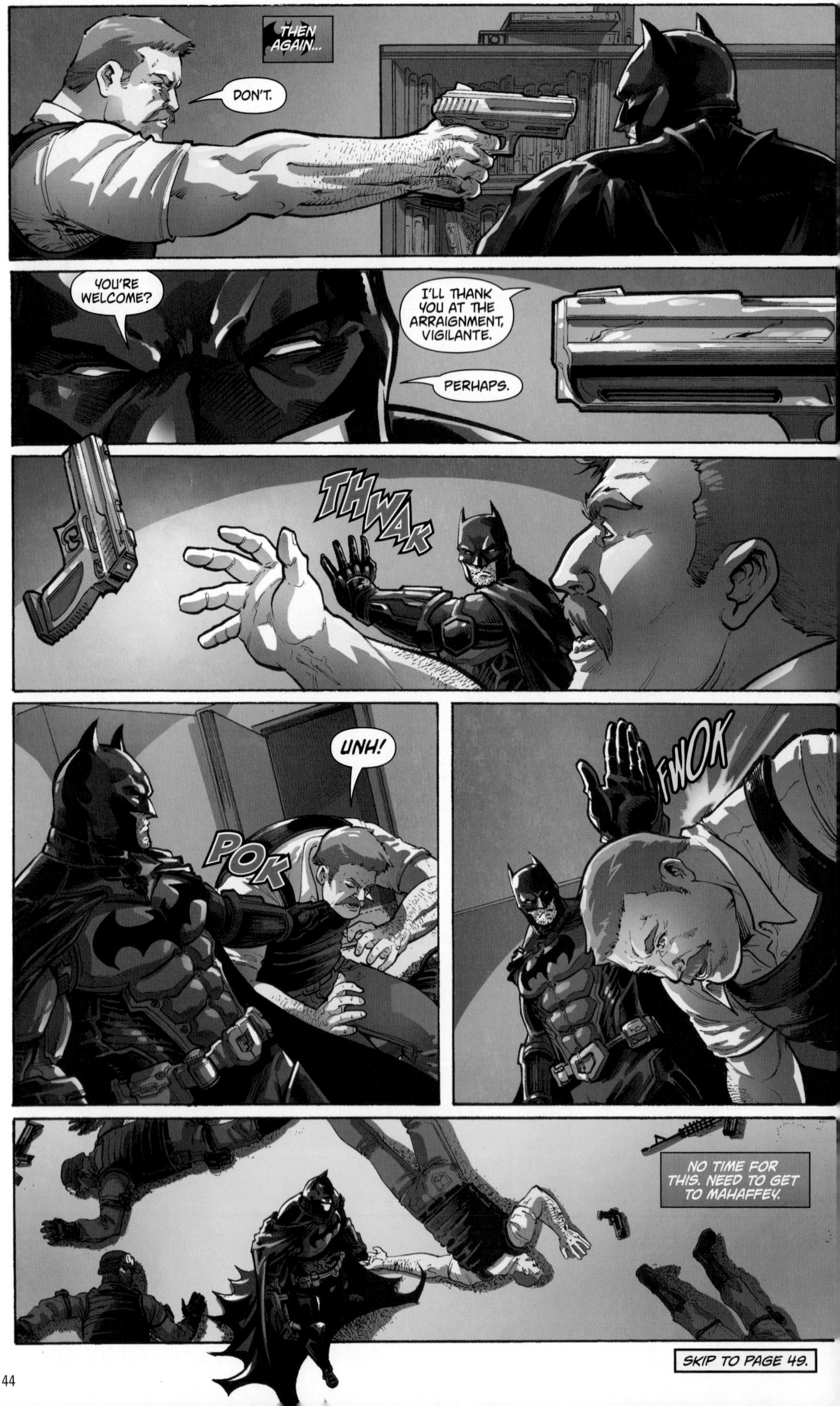
THEN AGAIN...
DON'T.
YOU'RE WELCOME?
I'LL THANK YOU AT THE ARRAIGNMENT, VIGILANTE.
PERHAPS.
THWAK
UNH!
POK
FWOK
NO TIME FOR THIS. NEED TO GET TO MAHAFFEY.

SKIP TO PAGE 49.

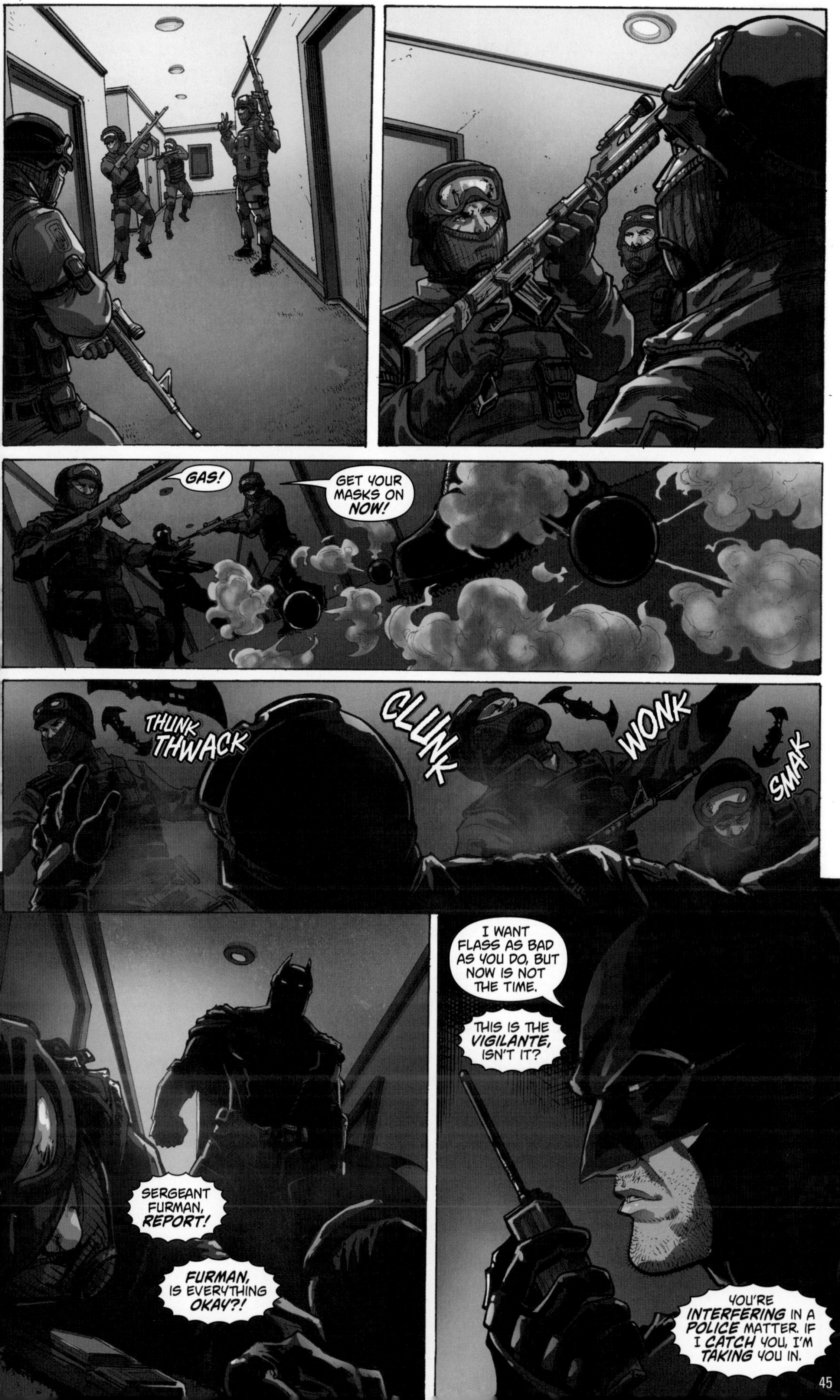
GAS!
GET YOUR MASKS ON NOW!
THUNK
THWACK
CLUNK
WONK
SMAK
SERGEANT FURMAN, REPORT!
FURMAN, IS EVERYTHING OKAY?!
I WANT FLASS AS BAD AS YOU DO, BUT NOW IS NOT THE TIME.
THIS IS THE VIGILANTE, ISN'T IT?
YOU'RE INTERFERING IN A POLICE MATTER. IF I CATCH YOU, I'M TAKING YOU IN.

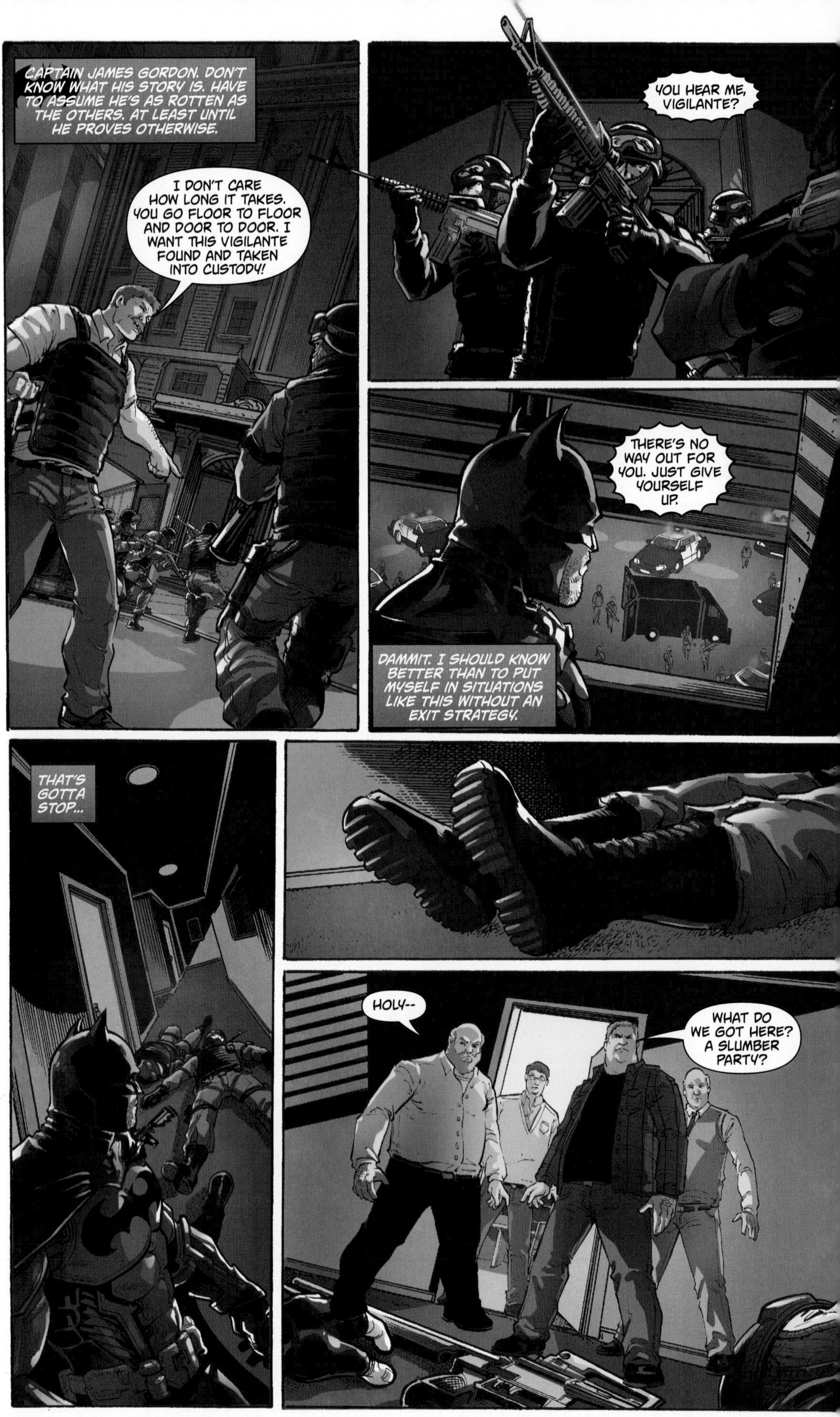

CAPTAIN JAMES GORDON. DON'T KNOW WHAT HIS STORY IS. HAVE TO ASSUME HE'S AS ROTTEN AS THE OTHERS. AT LEAST UNTIL HE PROVES OTHERWISE.
I DON'T CARE HOW LONG IT TAKES. YOU GO FLOOR TO FLOOR AND DOOR TO DOOR. I WANT THIS VIGILANTE FOUND AND TAKEN INTO CUSTODY!
YOU HEAR ME, VIGILANTE?
THERE'S NO WAY OUT FOR YOU. JUST GIVE YOURSELF UP.
DAMMIT. I SHOULD KNOW BETTER THAN TO PUT MYSELF IN SITUATIONS LIKE THIS WITHOUT AN EXIT STRATEGY.
THAT'S GOTTA STOP...
HOLY--
WHAT DO WE GOT HERE? A SLUMBER PARTY?

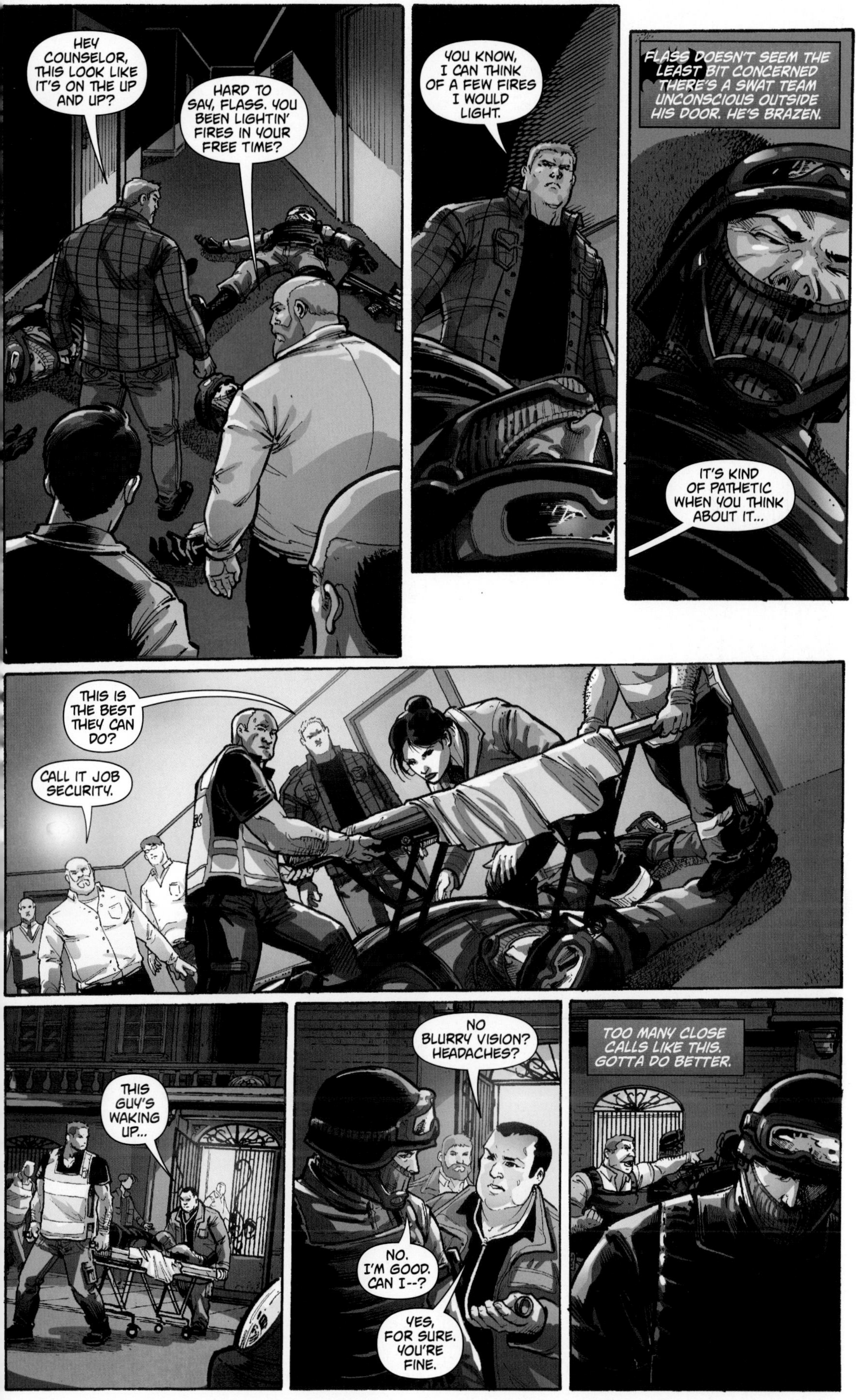
HEY COUNSELOR, THIS LOOK LIKE IT'S ON THE UP AND UP?
HARD TO SAY, FLASS. YOU BEEN LIGHTIN' FIRES IN YOUR FREE TIME?
YOU KNOW, I CAN THINK OF A FEW FIRES I WOULD LIGHT.
FLASS DOESN'T SEEM THE LEAST BIT CONCERNED THERE'S A SWAT TEAM UNCONSCIOUS OUTSIDE HIS DOOR. HE'S BRAZEN.
IT'S KIND OF PATHETIC WHEN YOU THINK ABOUT IT...
THIS IS THE BEST THEY CAN DO?
CALL IT JOB SECURITY.
THIS GUY'S WAKING UP...
NO BLURRY VISION? HEADACHES?
NO. I'M GOOD. CAN I--?
YES, FOR SURE. YOU'RE FINE.
TOO MANY CLOSE CALLS LIKE THIS. GOTTA DO BETTER.

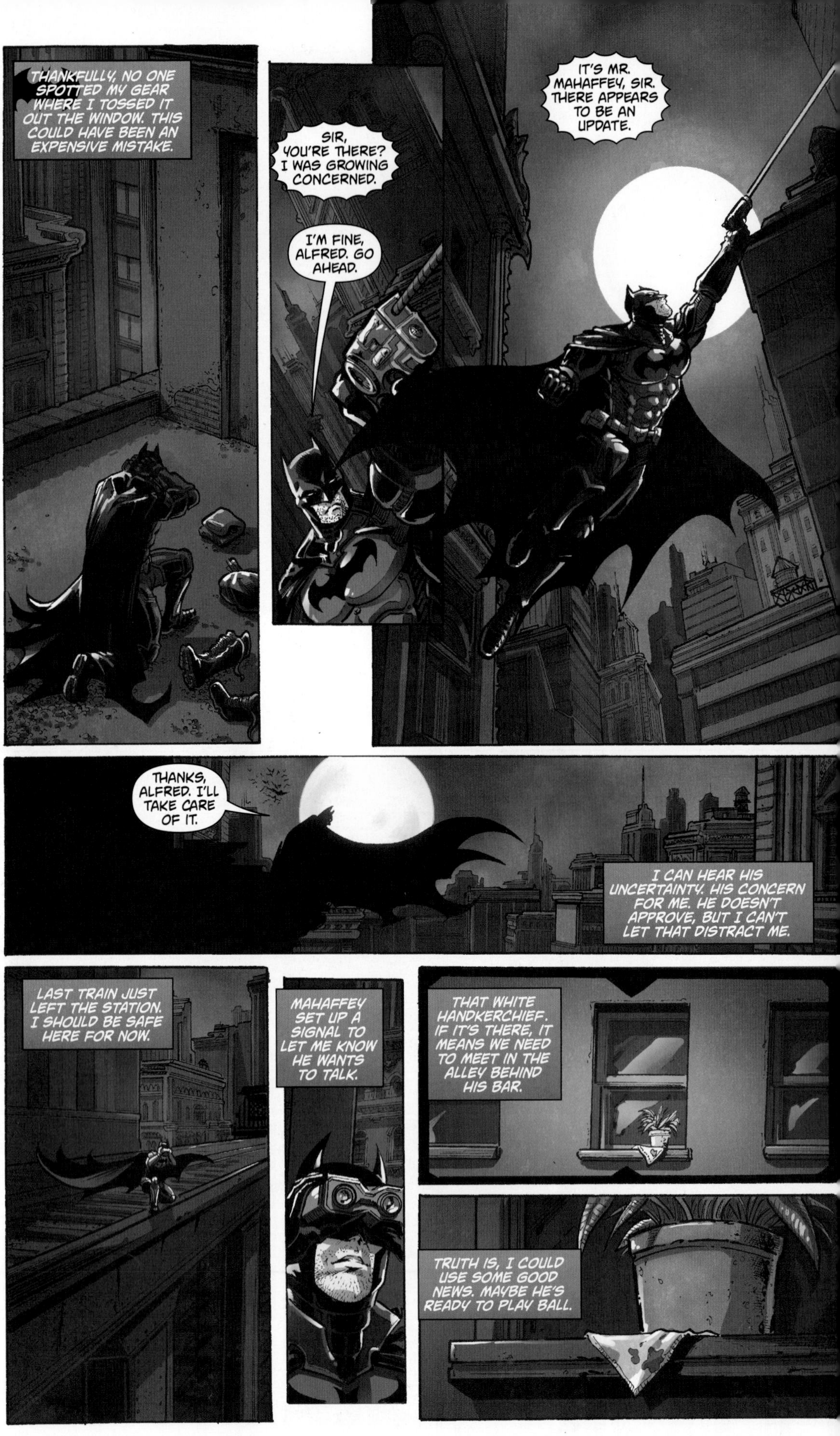
THANKFULLY, NO ONE SPOTTED MY GEAR WHERE I TOSSED IT OUT THE WINDOW. THIS COULD HAVE BEEN AN EXPENSIVE MISTAKE.
SIR, YOU'RE THERE? I WAS GROWING CONCERNED.
I'M FINE, ALFRED. GO AHEAD.
IT'S MR. MAHAFFEY, SIR. THERE APPEARS TO BE AN UPDATE.
THANKS, ALFRED. I'LL TAKE CARE OF IT.
I CAN HEAR HIS UNCERTAINTY. HIS CONCERN FOR ME. HE DOESN'T APPROVE, BUT I CAN'T LET THAT DISTRACT ME.
LAST TRAIN JUST LEFT THE STATION. I SHOULD BE SAFE HERE FOR NOW.
MAHAFFEY SET UP A SIGNAL TO LET ME KNOW HE WANTS TO TALK.
THAT WHITE HANDKERCHIEF. IF IT'S THERE, IT MEANS WE NEED TO MEET IN THE ALLEY BEHIND HIS BAR.
TRUTH IS, I COULD USE SOME GOOD NEWS. MAYBE HE'S READY TO PLAY BALL.

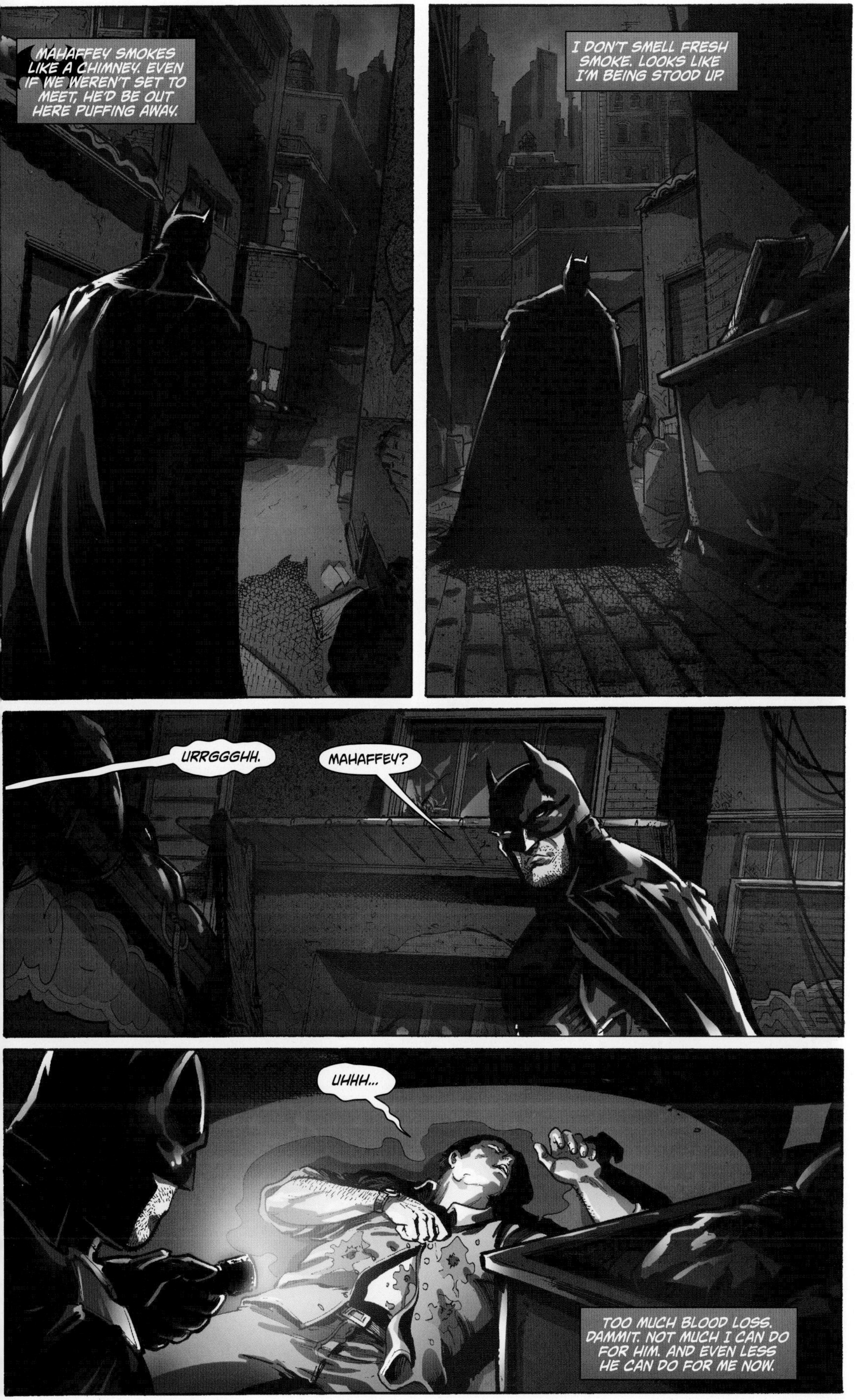
MAHAFFEY SMOKES LIKE A CHIMNEY. EVEN IF WE WEREN'T SET TO MEET, HE'D BE OUT HERE PUFFING AWAY.
I DON'T SMELL FRESH SMOKE. LOOKS LIKE I'M BEING STOOD UP.
URRGGGHH.
MAHAFFEY?
UHHH...
TOO MUCH BLOOD LOSS. DAMMIT. NOT MUCH I CAN DO FOR HIM. AND EVEN LESS HE CAN DO FOR ME NOW.

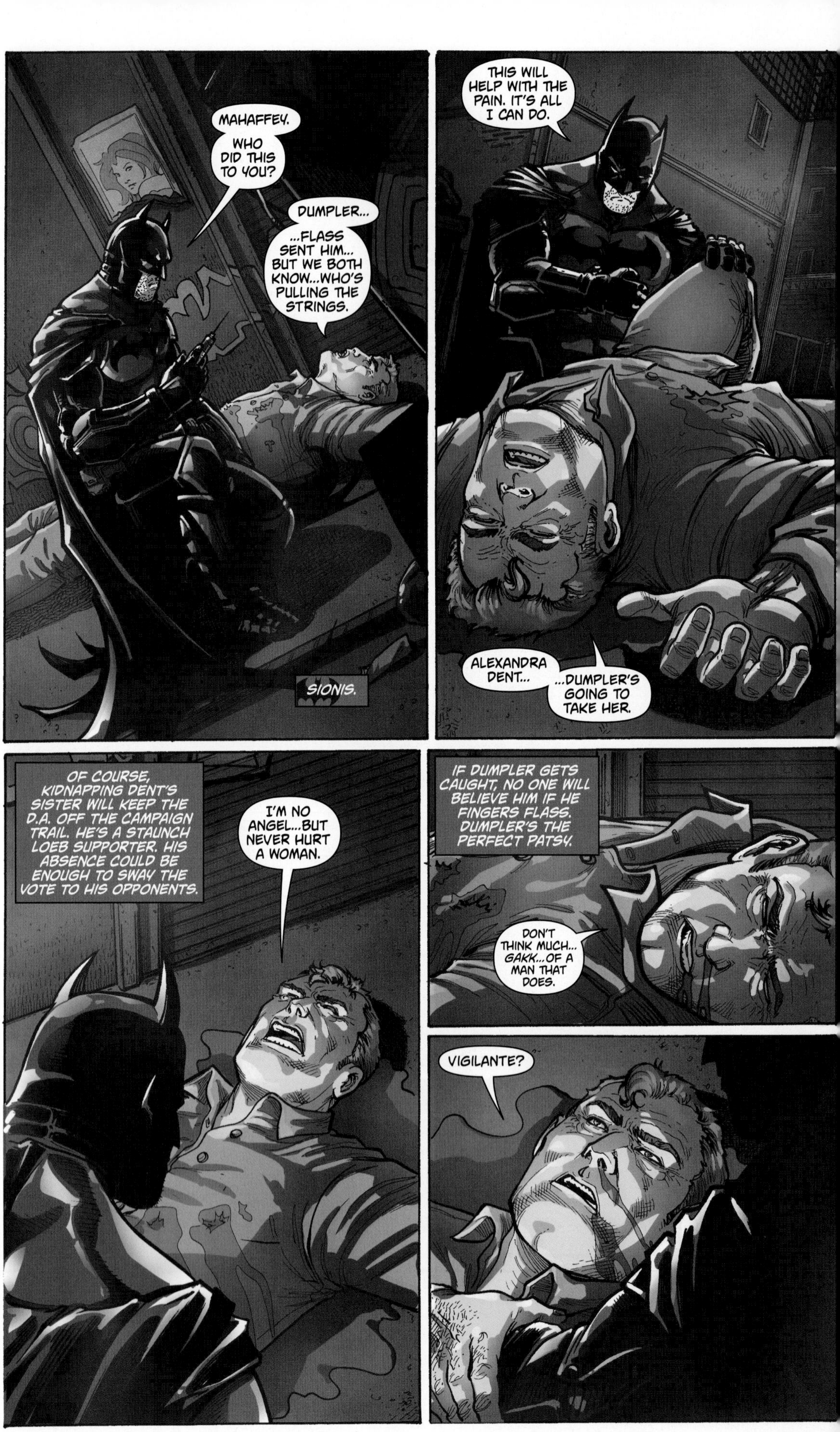
MAHAFFEY.
WHO DID THIS TO YOU?
DUMPLER...
...FLASS SENT HIM... BUT WE BOTH KNOW...WHO'S PULLING THE STRINGS.
SIONIS.
THIS WILL HELP WITH THE PAIN. IT'S ALL I CAN DO.
ALEXANDRA DENT...
...DUMPLER'S GOING TO TAKE HER.
OF COURSE, KIDNAPPING DENT'S SISTER WILL KEEP THE D.A. OFF THE CAMPAIGN TRAIL. HE'S A STAUNCH LOEB SUPPORTER. HIS ABSENCE COULD BE ENOUGH TO SWAY THE VOTE TO HIS OPPONENTS.
I'M NO ANGEL...BUT NEVER HURT A WOMAN.
IF DUMPLER GETS CAUGHT, NO ONE WILL BELIEVE HIM IF HE FINGERS FLASS. DUMPLER'S THE PERFECT PATSY.
DON'T THINK MUCH... GAKK...OF A MAN THAT DOES.
VIGILANTE?

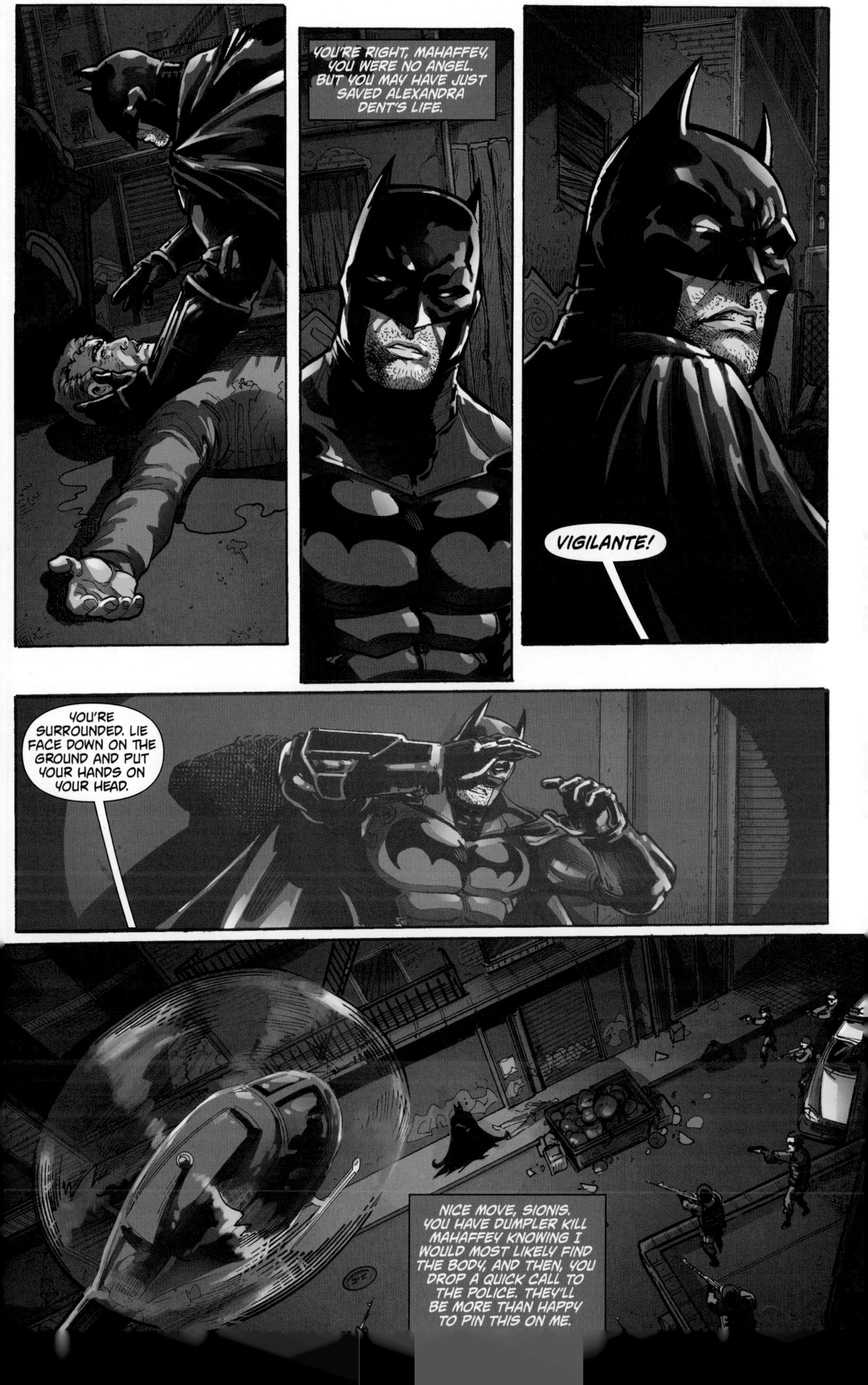
YOU'RE RIGHT, MAHAFFEY, YOU WERE NO ANGEL. BUT YOU MAY HAVE JUST SAVED ALEXANDRA DENT'S LIFE.
VIGILANTE!
YOU'RE SURROUNDED. LIE FACE DOWN ON THE GROUND AND PUT YOUR HANDS ON YOUR HEAD.
NICE MOVE, SIONIS. YOU HAVE DUMPLER KILL MAHAFFEY KNOWING I WOULD MOST LIKELY FIND THE BODY, AND THEN, YOU DROP A QUICK CALL TO THE POLICE. THEY'LL BE MORE THAN HAPPY TO PIN THIS ON ME.

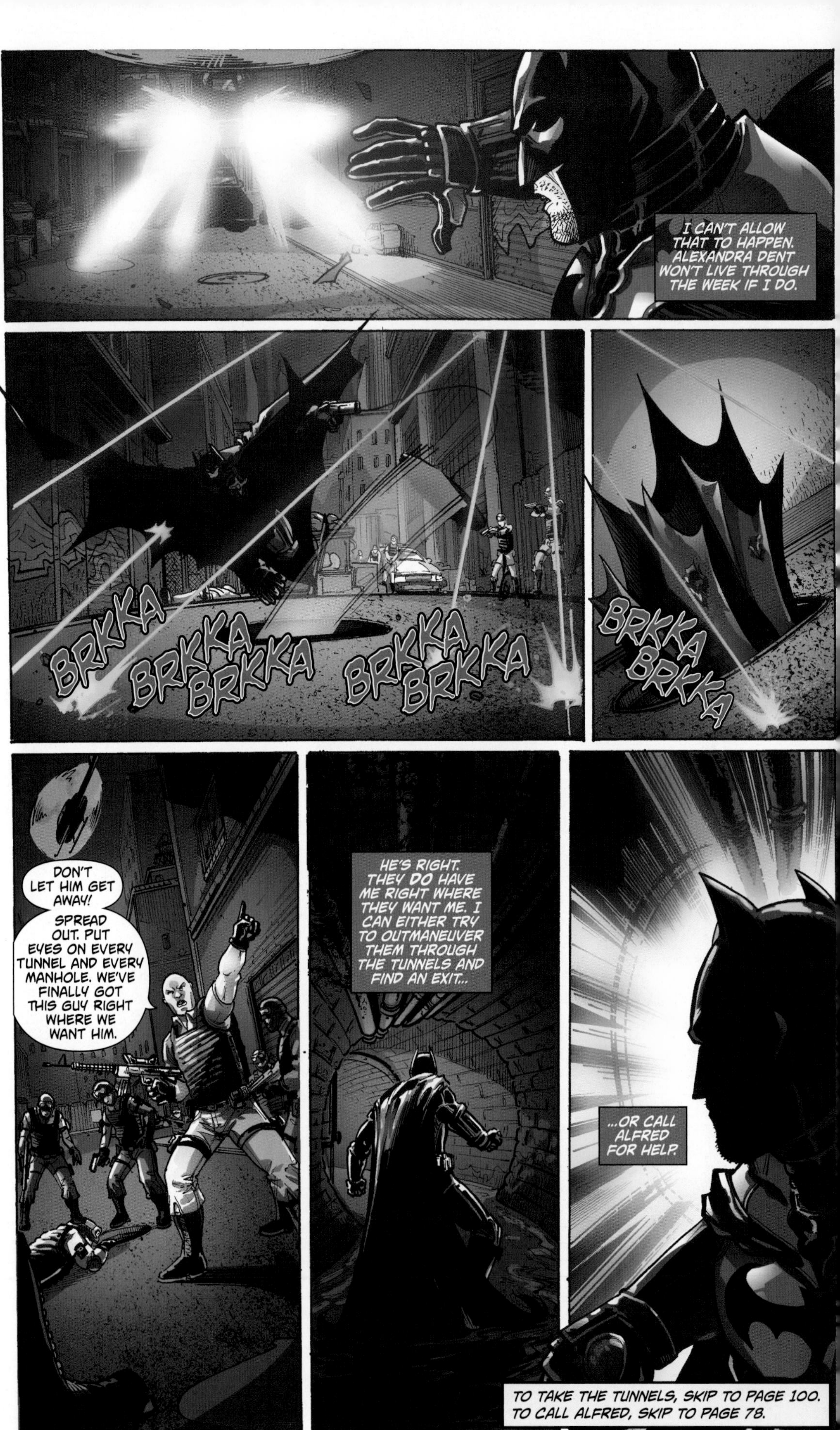
I CAN'T ALLOW THAT TO HAPPEN. ALEXANDRA DENT WON'T LIVE THROUGH THE WEEK IF I DO.
BRKKA BRKKA BRKKA BRKKA BRKKA
BRKKA BRKKA
DON'T LET HIM GET AWAY!
SPREAD OUT. PUT EYES ON EVERY TUNNEL AND EVERY MANHOLE. WE'VE FINALLY GOT THIS GUY RIGHT WHERE WE WANT HIM.
HE'S RIGHT. THEY DO HAVE ME RIGHT WHERE THEY WANT ME. I CAN EITHER TRY TO OUTMANEUVER THEM THROUGH THE TUNNELS AND FIND AN EXIT...
...OR CALL ALFRED FOR HELP.
TO TAKE THE TUNNELS, SKIP TO PAGE 100.
TO CALL ALFRED, SKIP TO PAGE 78.

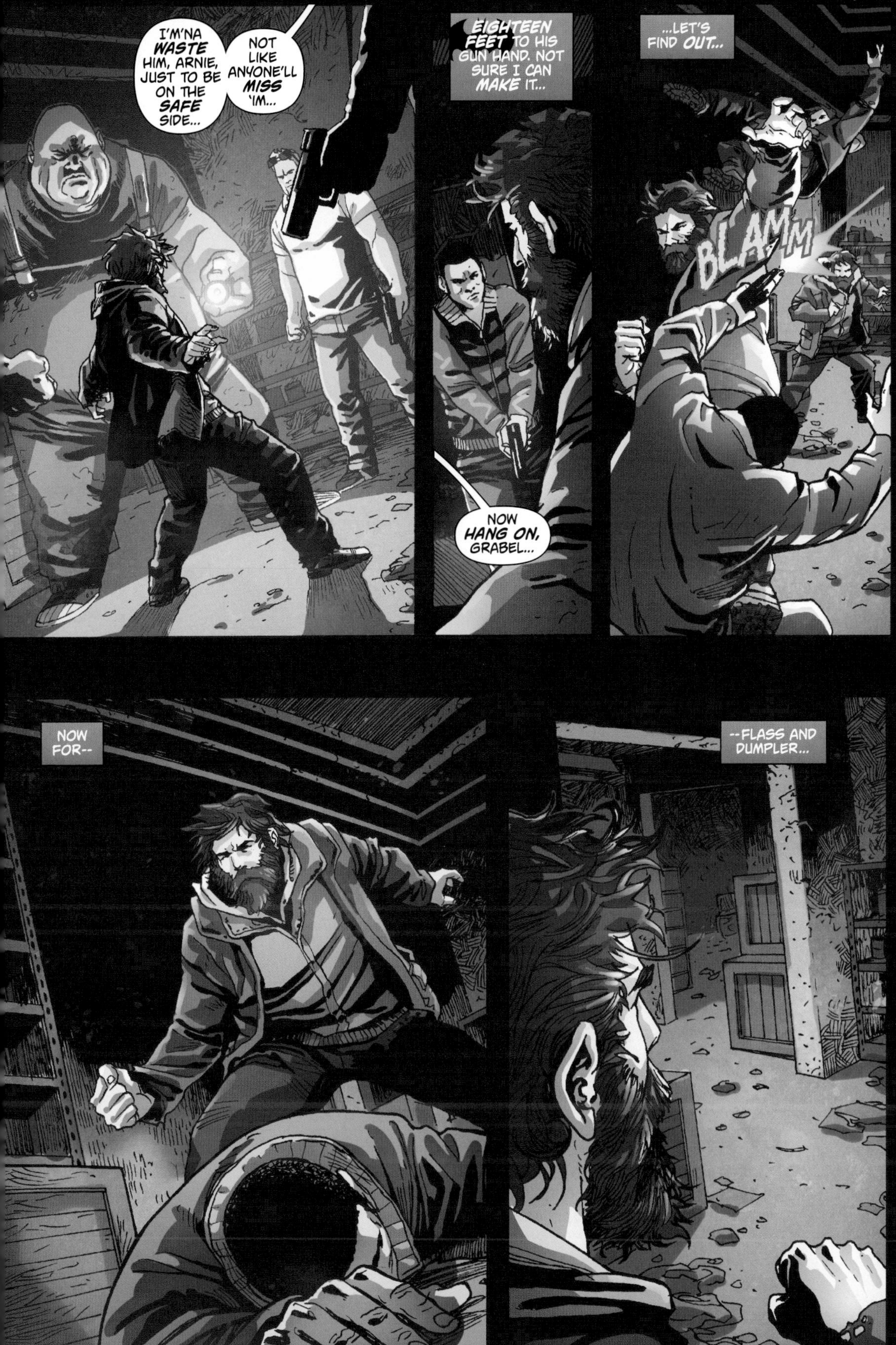
I'M'NA WASTE HIM, ARNIE, JUST TO BE ON THE SAFE SIDE...
NOT LIKE ANYONE'LL MISS 'IM...
EIGHTEEN FEET TO HIS GUN HAND. NOT SURE I CAN MAKE IT...
NOW HANG ON, GRABEL...
...LET'S FIND OUT...
BLAMM
NOW FOR--
--FLASS AND DUMPLER...

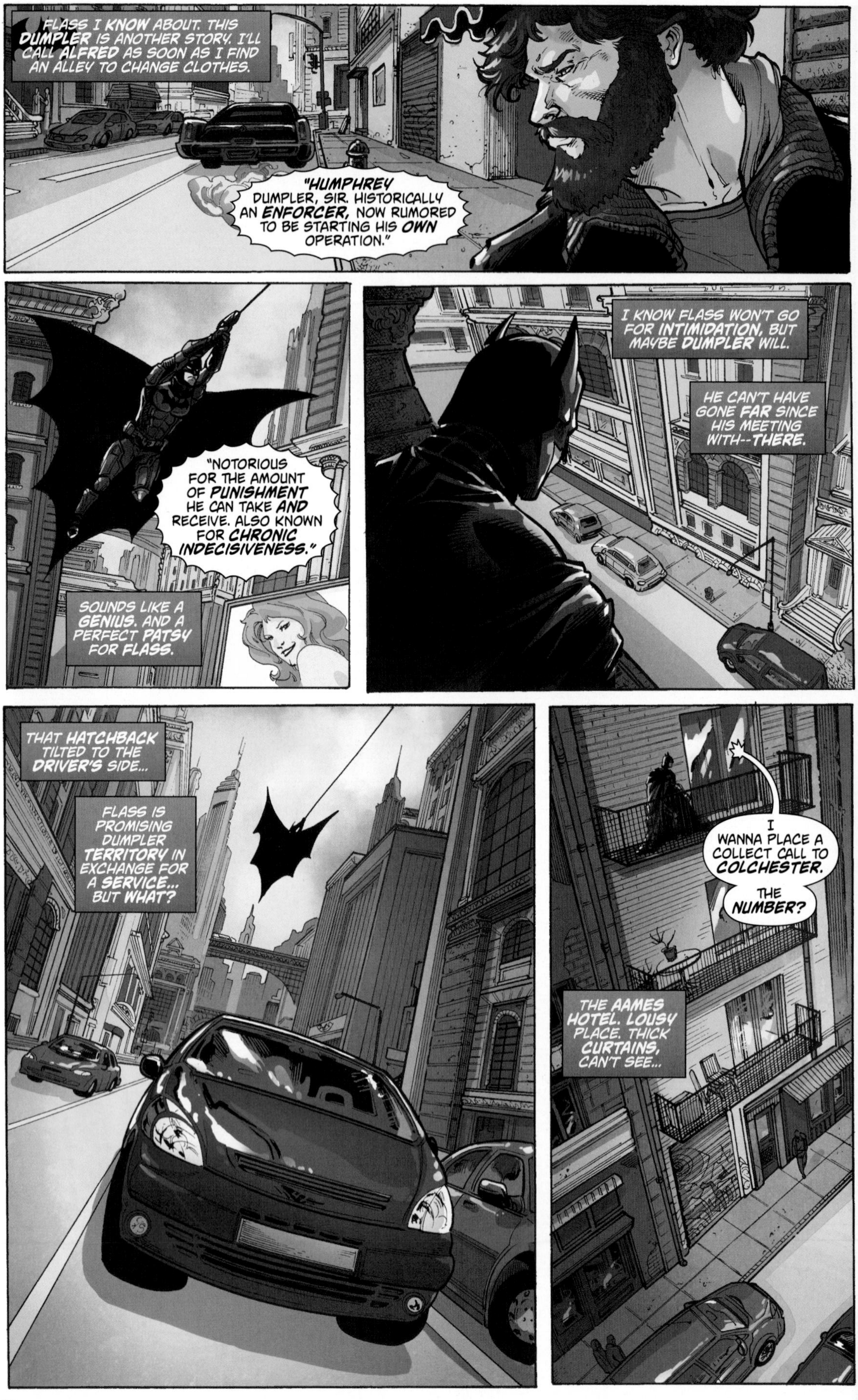
FLASS I KNOW ABOUT. THIS DUMPLER IS ANOTHER STORY. I'LL CALL ALFRED AS SOON AS I FIND AN ALLEY TO CHANGE CLOTHES.
"HUMPHREY DUMPLER, SIR. HISTORICALLY AN ENFORCER, NOW RUMORED TO BE STARTING HIS OWN OPERATION."
"NOTORIOUS FOR THE AMOUNT OF PUNISHMENT HE CAN TAKE AND RECEIVE. ALSO KNOWN FOR CHRONIC INDECISIVENESS."
SOUNDS LIKE A GENIUS. AND A PERFECT PATSY FOR FLASS.
I KNOW FLASS WON'T GO FOR INTIMIDATION, BUT MAYBE DUMPLER WILL.
HE CAN'T HAVE GONE FAR SINCE HIS MEETING WITH--THERE.
THAT HATCHBACK TILTED TO THE DRIVER'S SIDE...
FLASS IS PROMISING DUMPLER TERRITORY IN EXCHANGE FOR A SERVICE... BUT WHAT?
I WANNA PLACE A COLLECT CALL TO COLCHESTER.
THE NUMBER?
THE AAMES HOTEL. LOUSY PLACE. THICK CURTAINS, CAN'T SEE...

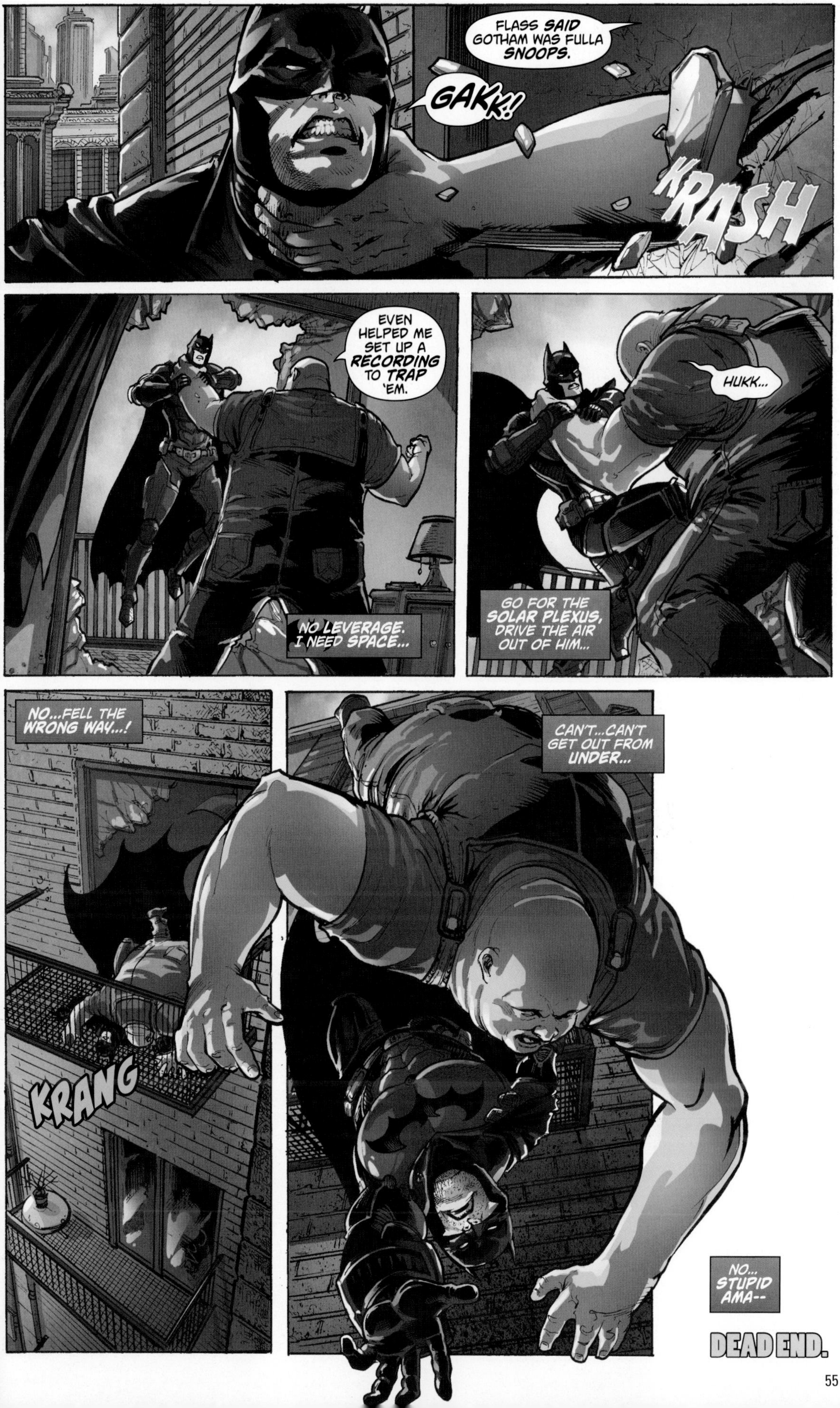
FLASS SAID GOTHAM WAS FULLA SNOOPS.
GAKK!
KRASH
EVEN HELPED ME SET UP A RECORDING TO TRAP 'EM.
NO LEVERAGE. I NEED SPACE...
HUKK...
GO FOR THE SOLAR PLEXUS, DRIVE THE AIR OUT OF HIM...
NO...FELL THE WRONG WAY...!
KRANG
CAN'T...CAN'T GET OUT FROM UNDER...
NO... STUPID AMA--
DEAD END.

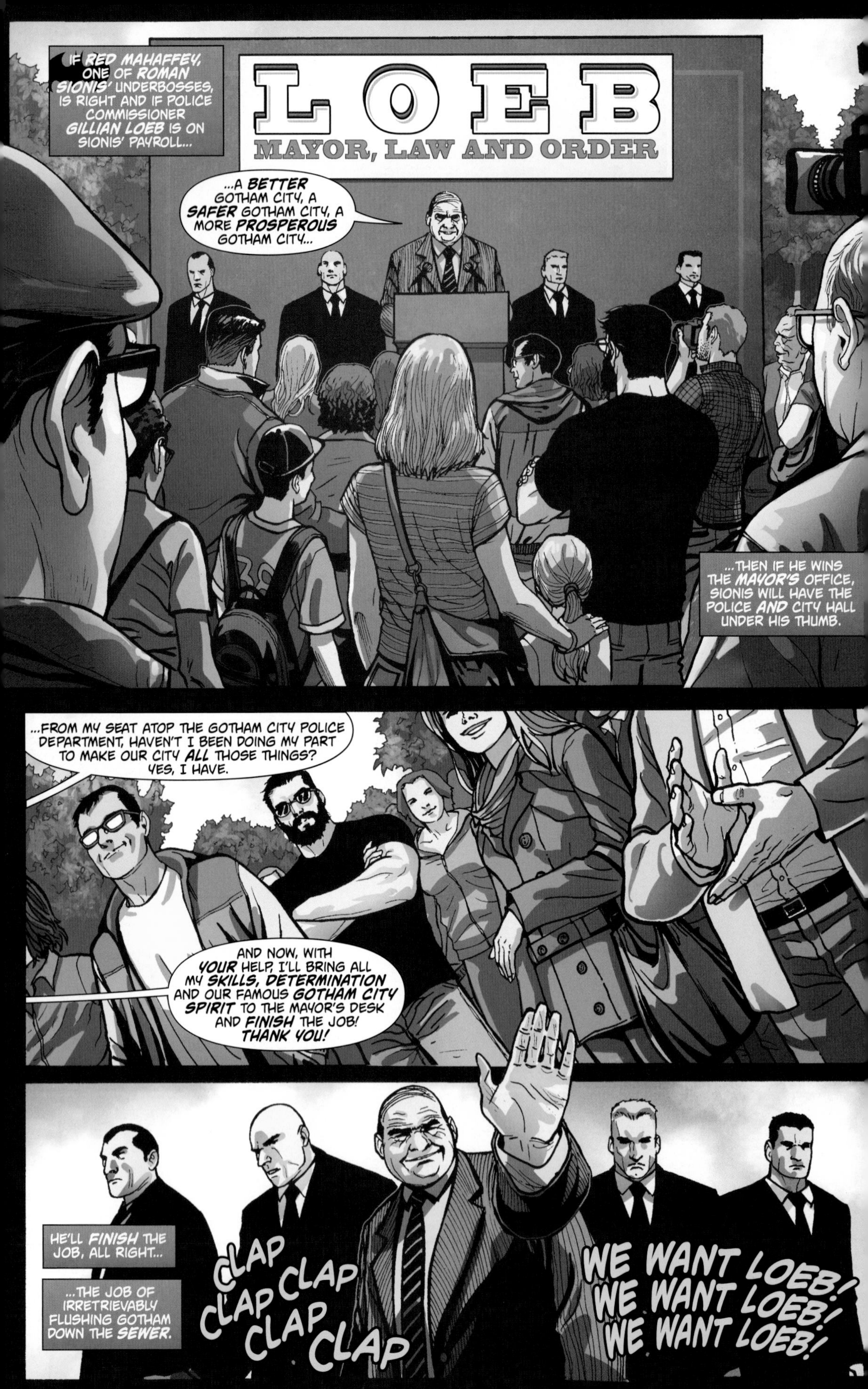
IF RED MAHAFFEY, ONE OF ROMAN SIONIS' UNDERBOSSES, IS RIGHT AND IF POLICE COMMISSIONER GILLIAN LOEB IS ON SIONIS' PAYROLL...
LOEB
MAYOR, LAW AND ORDER
...A BETTER GOTHAM CITY, A SAFER GOTHAM CITY, A MORE PROSPEROUS GOTHAM CITY...
...THEN IF HE WINS THE MAYOR'S OFFICE, SIONIS WILL HAVE THE POLICE AND CITY HALL UNDER HIS THUMB.
...FROM MY SEAT ATOP THE GOTHAM CITY POLICE DEPARTMENT, HAVEN'T I BEEN DOING MY PART TO MAKE OUR CITY ALL THOSE THINGS? YES, I HAVE.
AND NOW, WITH YOUR HELP, I'LL BRING ALL MY SKILLS, DETERMINATION AND OUR FAMOUS GOTHAM CITY SPIRIT TO THE MAYOR'S DESK AND FINISH THE JOB! THANK YOU!
HE'LL FINISH THE JOB, ALL RIGHT...
...THE JOB OF IRRETRIEVABLY FLUSHING GOTHAM DOWN THE SEWER.
CLAP CLAP CLAP CLAP CLAP
WE WANT LOEB! WE WANT LOEB! WE WANT LOEB!

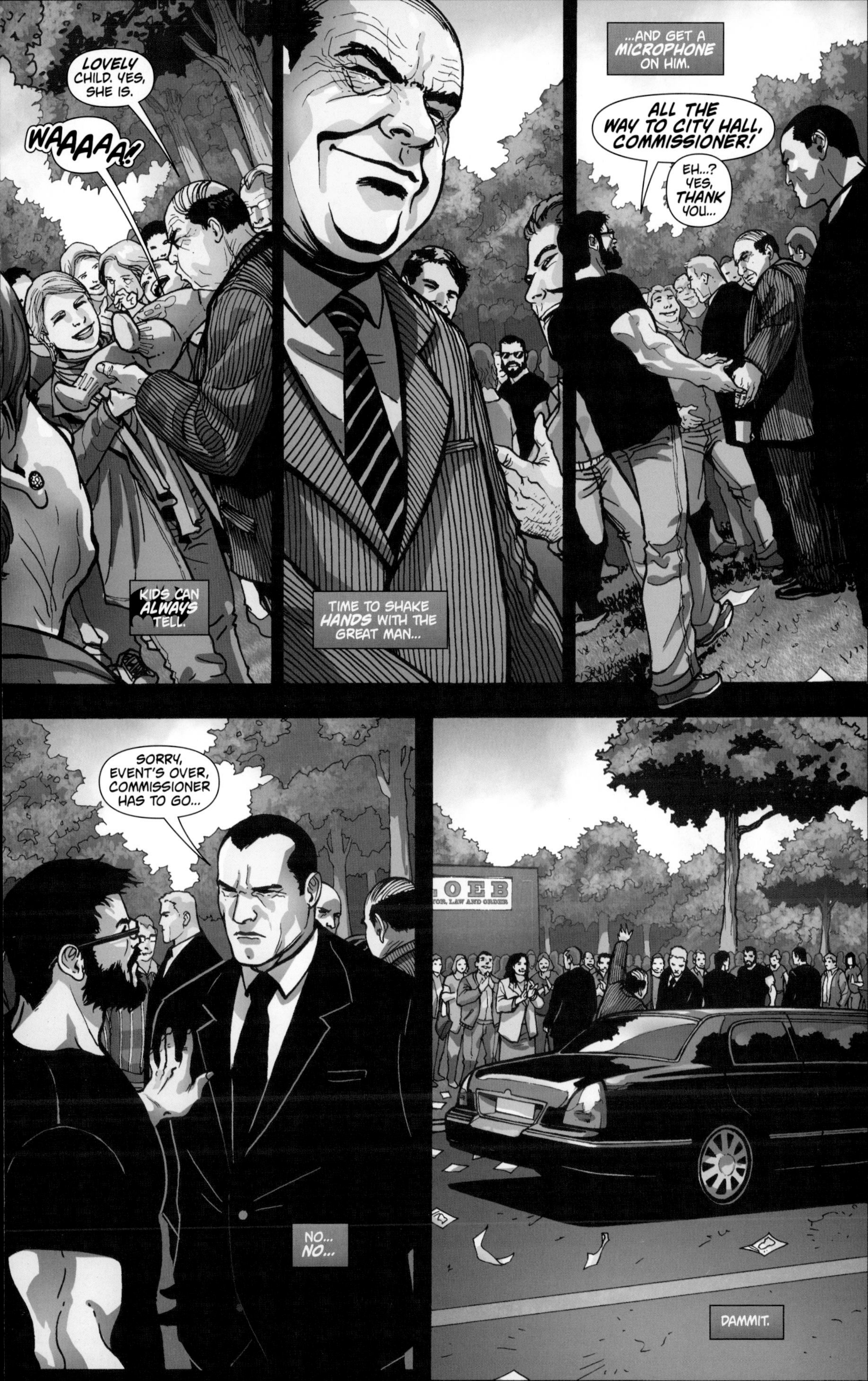
LOVELY CHILD. YES, SHE IS.
WAAAAA!
KIDS CAN ALWAYS TELL.
TIME TO SHAKE HANDS WITH THE GREAT MAN...
...AND GET A MICROPHONE ON HIM.
ALL THE WAY TO CITY HALL, COMMISSIONER!
EH...? YES, THANK YOU...
SORRY, EVENT'S OVER, COMMISSIONER HAS TO GO...
NO... NO...
LOEB
DAMMIT.

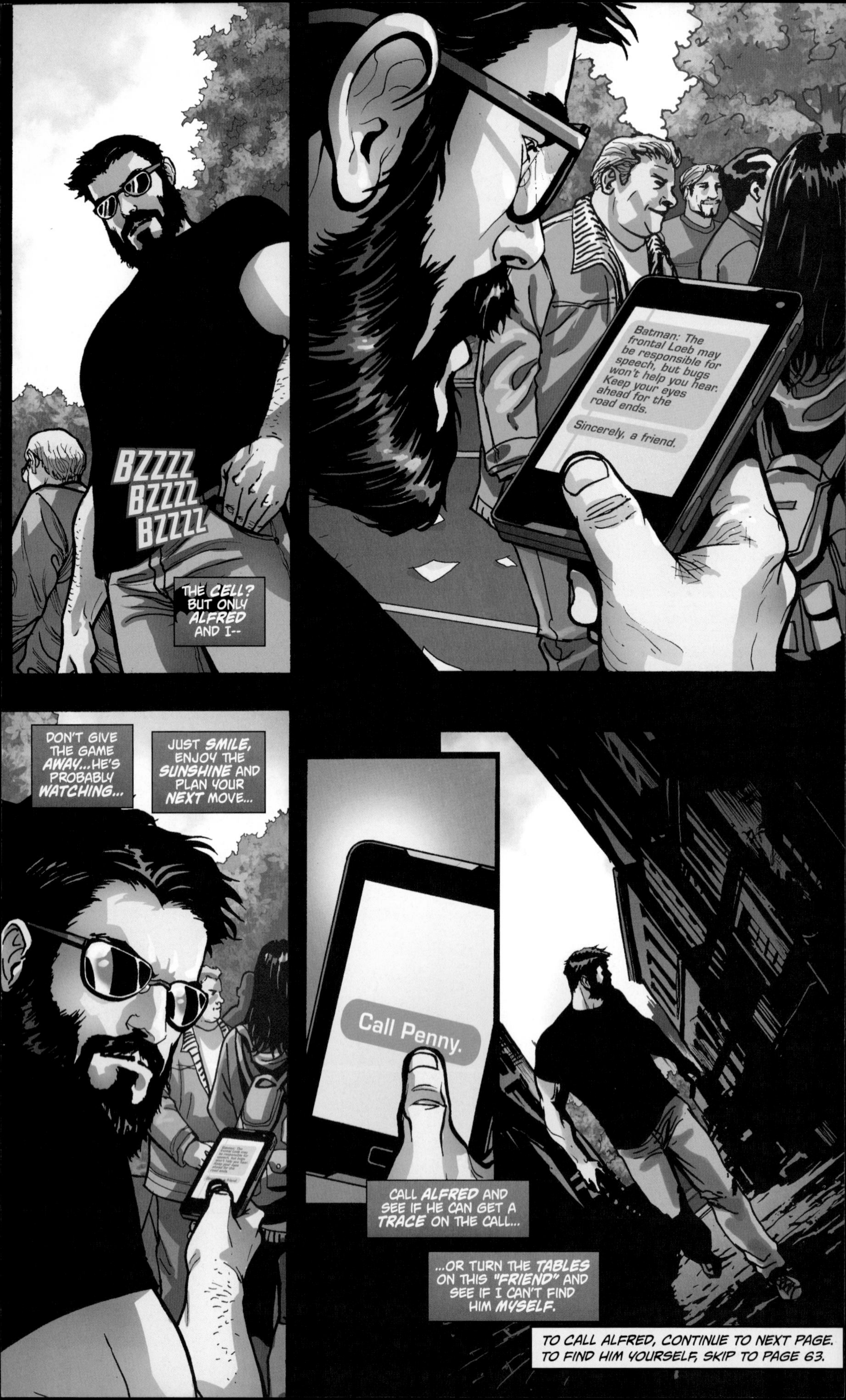
BZZZZ BZZZZ BZZZZ
THE CELL? BUT ONLY ALFRED AND I--
Batman: The frontal Loeb may be responsible for speech, but bugs won't help you hear. Keep your eyes ahead for the road ends.
Sincerely, a friend.
DON'T GIVE THE GAME AWAY...HE'S PROBABLY WATCHING...
JUST SMILE, ENJOY THE SUNSHINE AND PLAN YOUR NEXT MOVE...
Call Penny.
CALL ALFRED AND SEE IF HE CAN GET A TRACE ON THE CALL...
...OR TURN THE TABLES ON THIS "FRIEND" AND SEE IF I CAN'T FIND HIM MYSELF.
TO CALL ALFRED, CONTINUE TO NEXT PAGE.
TO FIND HIM YOURSELF, SKIP TO PAGE 63.

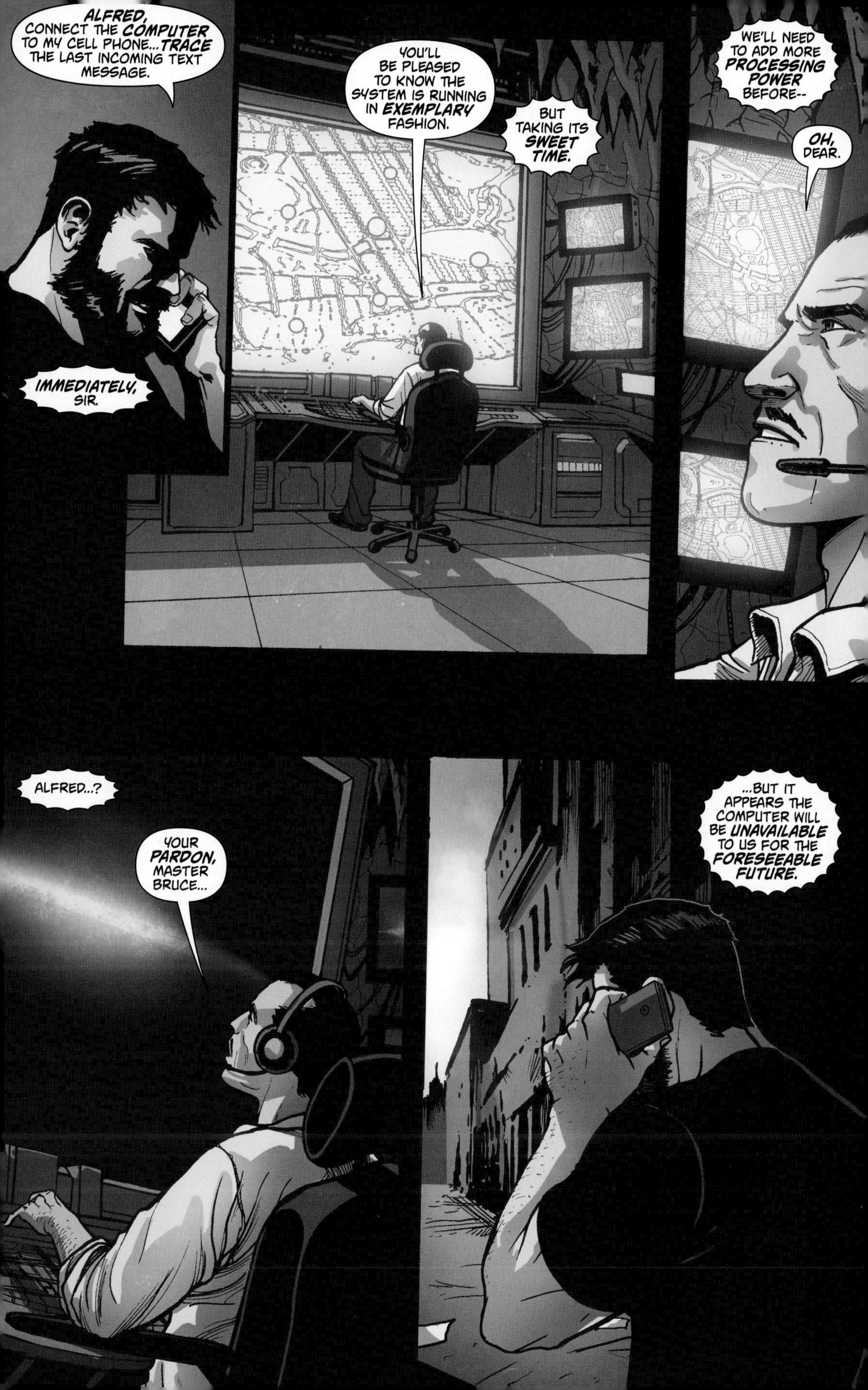
ALFRED, CONNECT THE COMPUTER TO MY CELL PHONE...TRACE THE LAST INCOMING TEXT MESSAGE.
IMMEDIATELY, SIR.
YOU'LL BE PLEASED TO KNOW THE SYSTEM IS RUNNING IN EXEMPLARY FASHION.
BUT TAKING ITS SWEET TIME.
WE'LL NEED TO ADD MORE PROCESSING POWER BEFORE--
OH, DEAR.
ALFRED...?
YOUR PARDON, MASTER BRUCE...
...BUT IT APPEARS THE COMPUTER WILL BE UNAVAILABLE TO US FOR THE FORESEEABLE FUTURE.

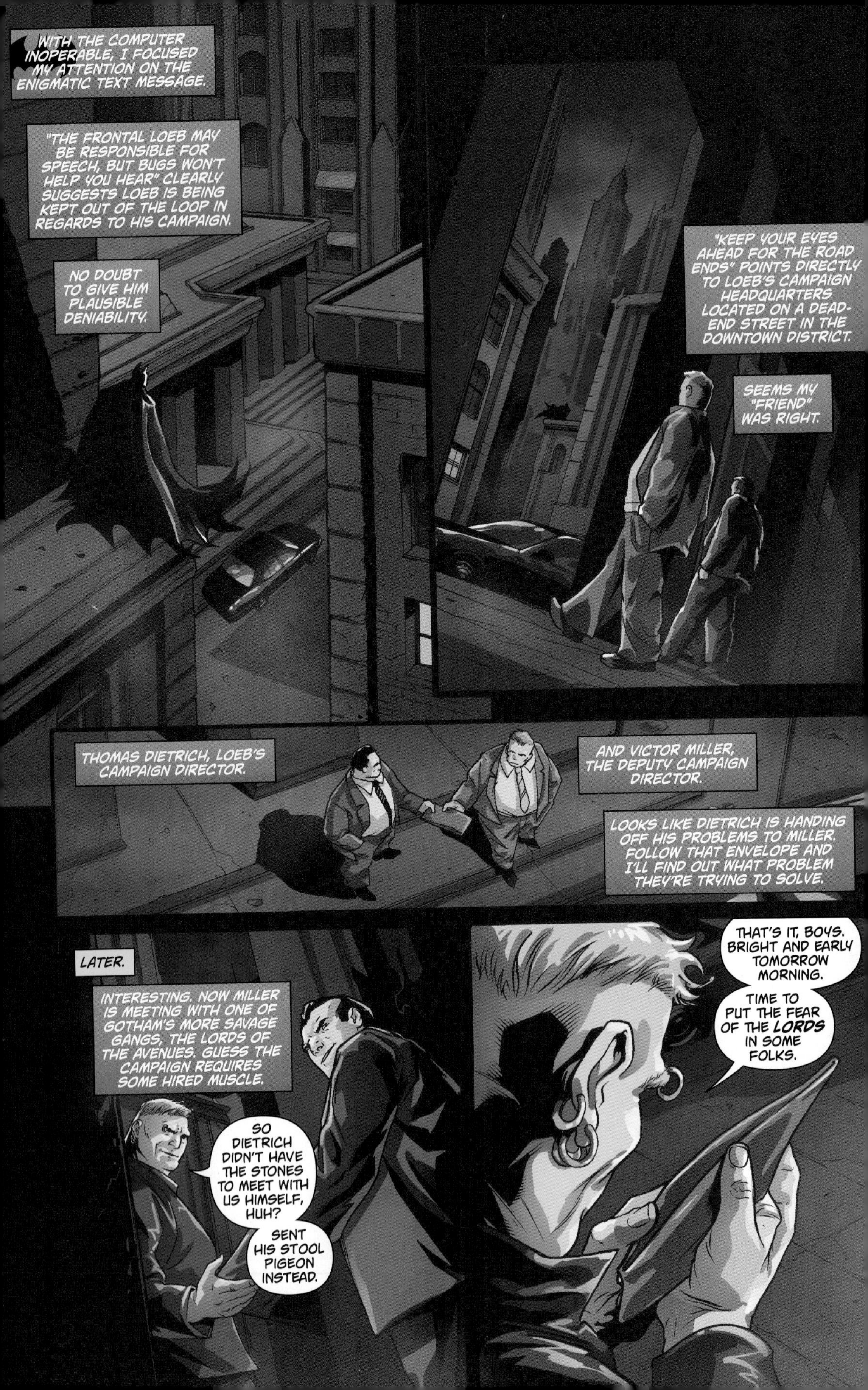
WITH THE COMPUTER INOPERABLE, I FOCUSED MY ATTENTION ON THE ENIGMATIC TEXT MESSAGE.
"THE FRONTAL LOEB MAY BE RESPONSIBLE FOR SPEECH, BUT BUGS WON'T HELP YOU HEAR" CLEARLY SUGGESTS LOEB IS BEING KEPT OUT OF THE LOOP IN REGARDS TO HIS CAMPAIGN.
NO DOUBT TO GIVE HIM PLAUSIBLE DENIABILITY.
"KEEP YOUR EYES AHEAD FOR THE ROAD ENDS" POINTS DIRECTLY TO LOEB'S CAMPAIGN HEADQUARTERS LOCATED ON A DEAD-END STREET IN THE DOWNTOWN DISTRICT.
SEEMS MY "FRIEND" WAS RIGHT.
THOMAS DIETRICH, LOEB'S CAMPAIGN DIRECTOR.
AND VICTOR MILLER, THE DEPUTY CAMPAIGN DIRECTOR.
LOOKS LIKE DIETRICH IS HANDING OFF HIS PROBLEMS TO MILLER. FOLLOW THAT ENVELOPE AND I'LL FIND OUT WHAT PROBLEM THEY'RE TRYING TO SOLVE.
LATER.
INTERESTING. NOW MILLER IS MEETING WITH ONE OF GOTHAM'S MORE SAVAGE GANGS, THE LORDS OF THE AVENUES. GUESS THE CAMPAIGN REQUIRES SOME HIRED MUSCLE.
SO DIETRICH DIDN'T HAVE THE STONES TO MEET WITH US HIMSELF, HUH?
SENT HIS STOOL PIGEON INSTEAD.
THAT'S IT, BOYS. BRIGHT AND EARLY TOMORROW MORNING.
TIME TO PUT THE FEAR OF THE LORDS IN SOME FOLKS.

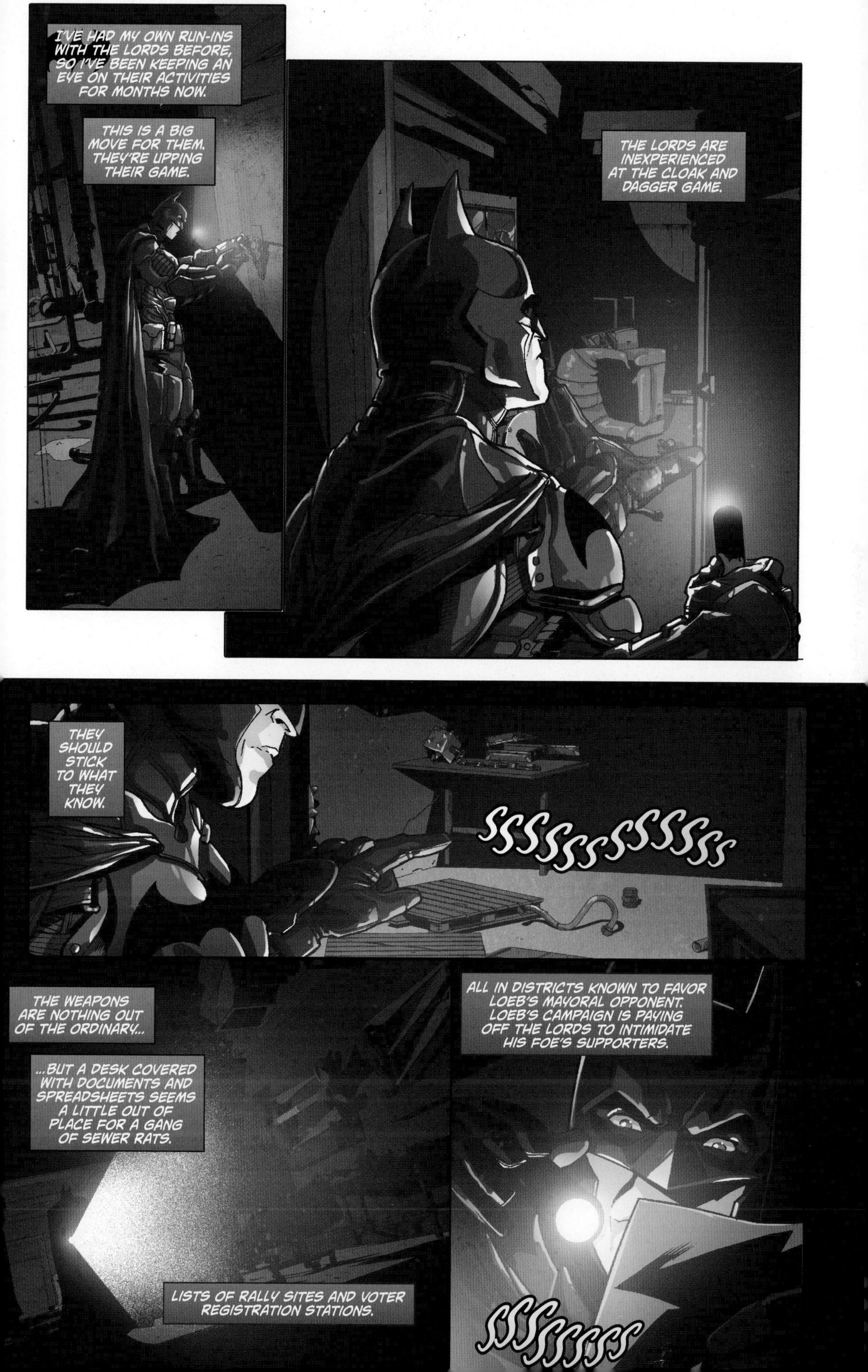
I'VE HAD MY OWN RUN-INS WITH THE LORDS BEFORE, SO I'VE BEEN KEEPING AN EYE ON THEIR ACTIVITIES FOR MONTHS NOW.
THIS IS A BIG MOVE FOR THEM. THEY'RE UPPING THEIR GAME.
THE LORDS ARE INEXPERIENCED AT THE CLOAK AND DAGGER GAME.
THEY SHOULD STICK TO WHAT THEY KNOW.
SSSSSSSSSSSSSS
THE WEAPONS ARE NOTHING OUT OF THE ORDINARY...
...BUT A DESK COVERED WITH DOCUMENTS AND SPREADSHEETS SEEMS A LITTLE OUT OF PLACE FOR A GANG OF SEWER RATS.
LISTS OF RALLY SITES AND VOTER REGISTRATION STATIONS.
ALL IN DISTRICTS KNOWN TO FAVOR LOEB'S MAYORAL OPPONENT. LOEB'S CAMPAIGN IS PAYING OFF THE LORDS TO INTIMIDATE HIS FOE'S SUPPORTERS.
SSSSSSSSS

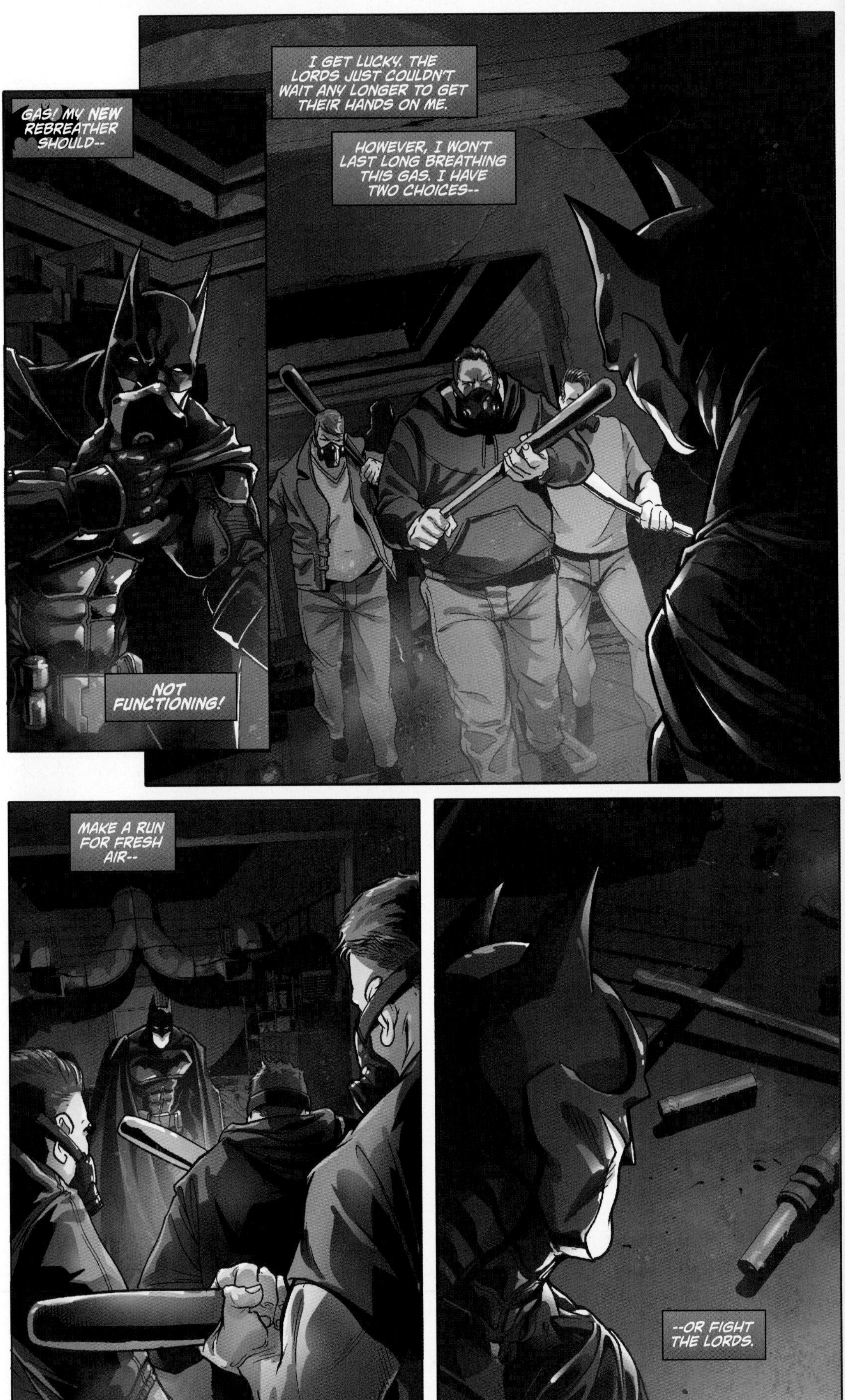
GAS! MY NEW REBREATHER SHOULD--
NOT FUNCTIONING!
I GET LUCKY. THE LORDS JUST COULDN'T WAIT ANY LONGER TO GET THEIR HANDS ON ME.
HOWEVER, I WON'T LAST LONG BREATHING THIS GAS. I HAVE TWO CHOICES--
MAKE A RUN FOR FRESH AIR--
--OR FIGHT THE LORDS.
TO RUN FOR FRESH AIR, SKIP TO PAGE 66.
TO FIGHT THE LORDS, SKIP TO PAGE 69.

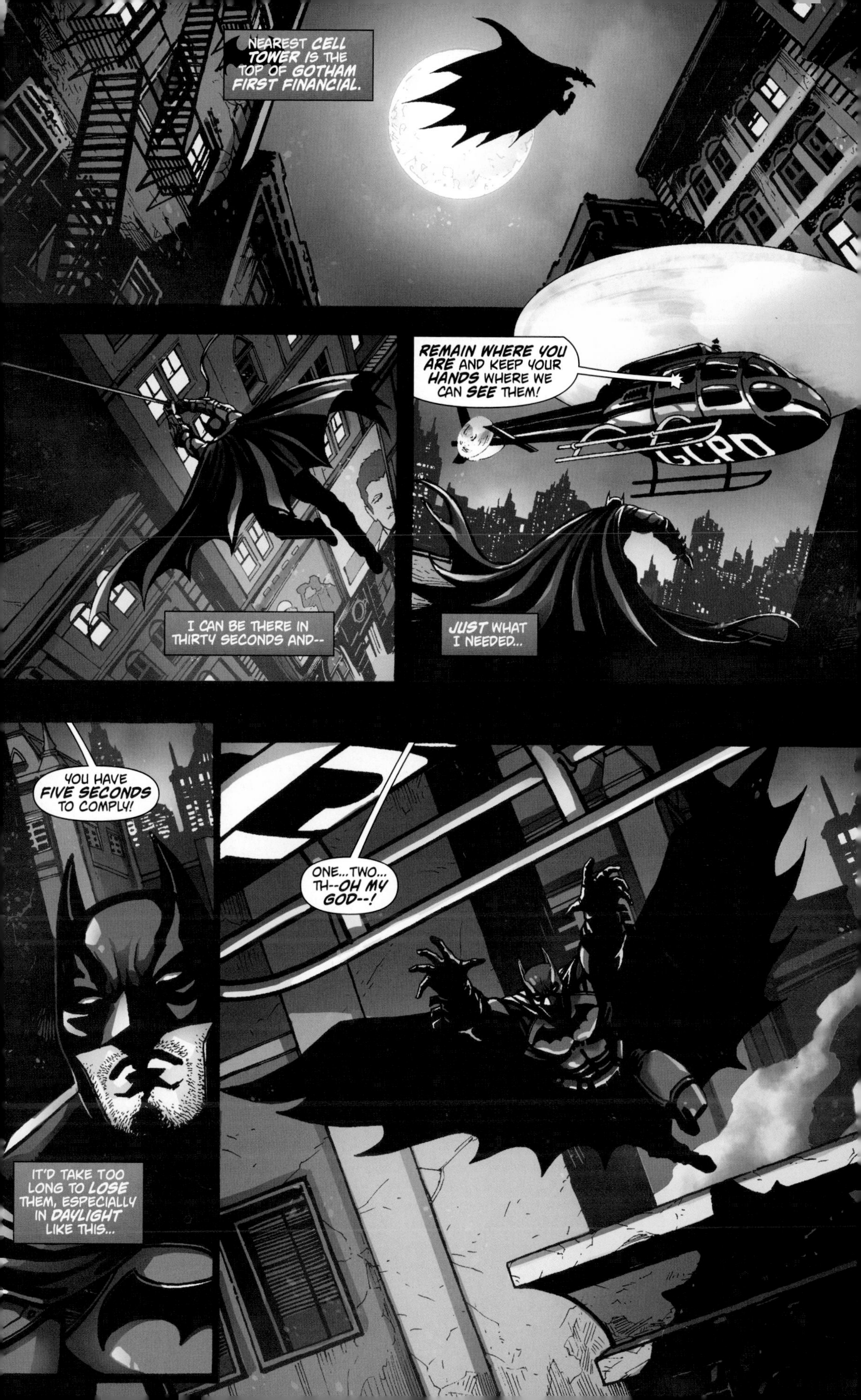
NEAREST CELL TOWER IS THE TOP OF GOTHAM FIRST FINANCIAL.
I CAN BE THERE IN THIRTY SECONDS AND--
REMAIN WHERE YOU ARE AND KEEP YOUR HANDS WHERE WE CAN SEE THEM!
GCPD
JUST WHAT I NEEDED...
YOU HAVE FIVE SECONDS TO COMPLY!
IT'D TAKE TOO LONG TO LOSE THEM, ESPECIALLY IN DAYLIGHT LIKE THIS...
ONE...TWO... TH--OH MY GOD--!

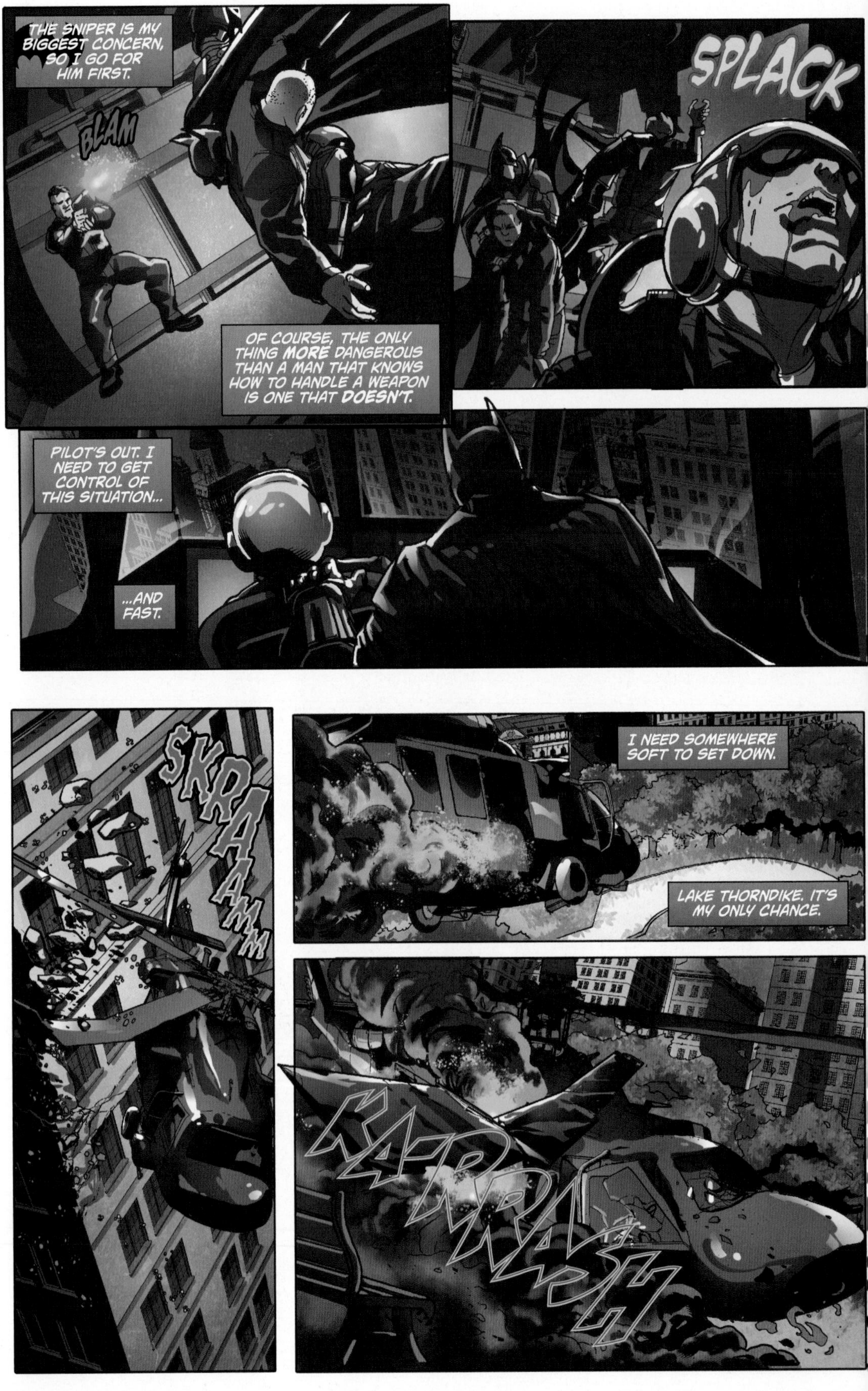
THE SNIPER IS MY BIGGEST CONCERN, SO I GO FOR HIM FIRST.
BLAM
OF COURSE, THE ONLY THING MORE DANGEROUS THAN A MAN THAT KNOWS HOW TO HANDLE A WEAPON IS ONE THAT DOESN'T.
SPLACK
PILOT'S OUT. I NEED TO GET CONTROL OF THIS SITUATION...
...AND FAST.
SKRAAAMM
I NEED SOMEWHERE SOFT TO SET DOWN.
LAKE THORNDIKE. IT'S MY ONLY CHANCE.

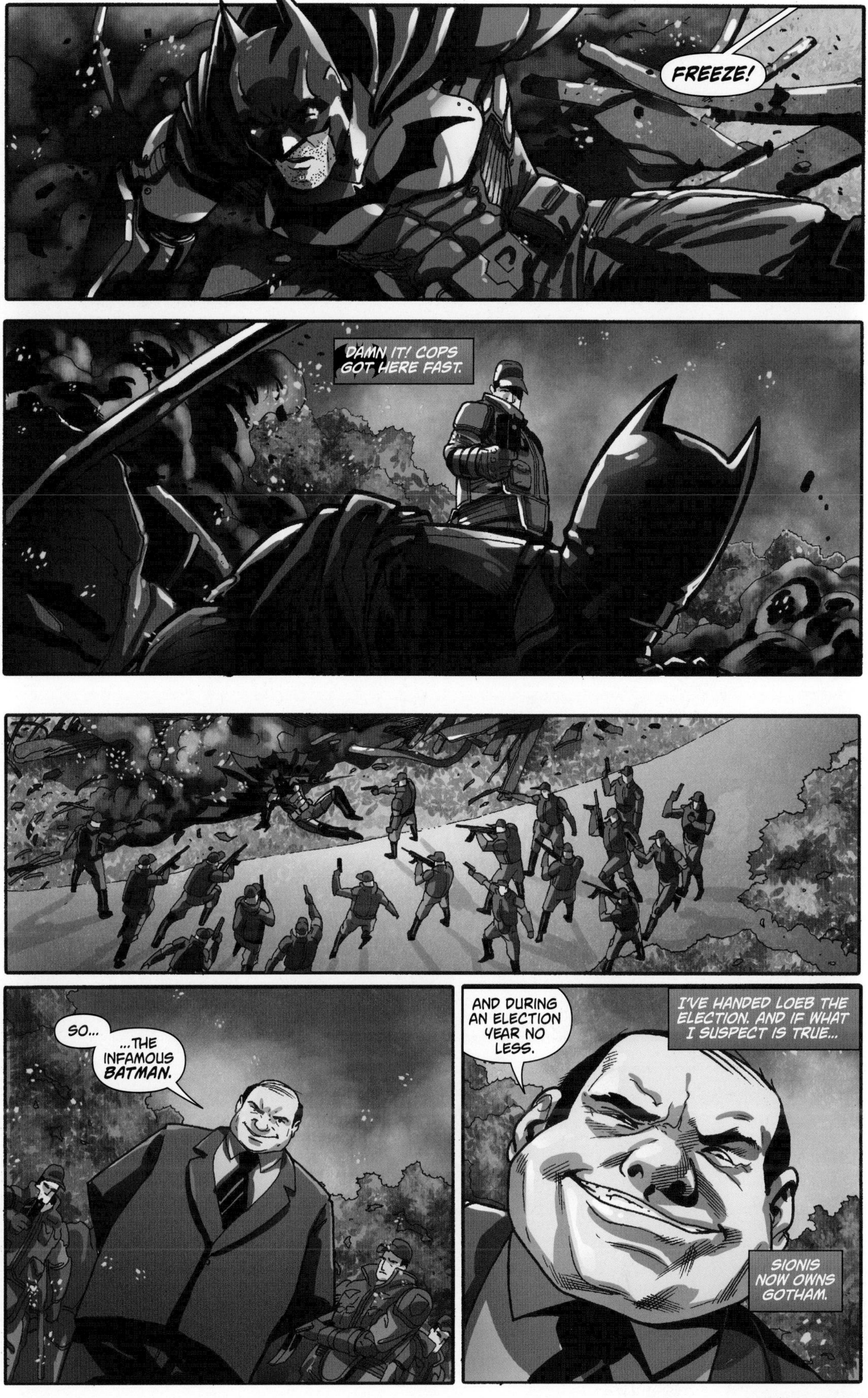
FREEZE!
DAMN IT! COPS GOT HERE FAST.
SO...
...THE INFAMOUS BATMAN.
AND DURING AN ELECTION YEAR NO LESS.
I'VE HANDED LOEB THE ELECTION. AND IF WHAT I SUSPECT IS TRUE...
SIONIS NOW OWNS GOTHAM.

DEAD END.

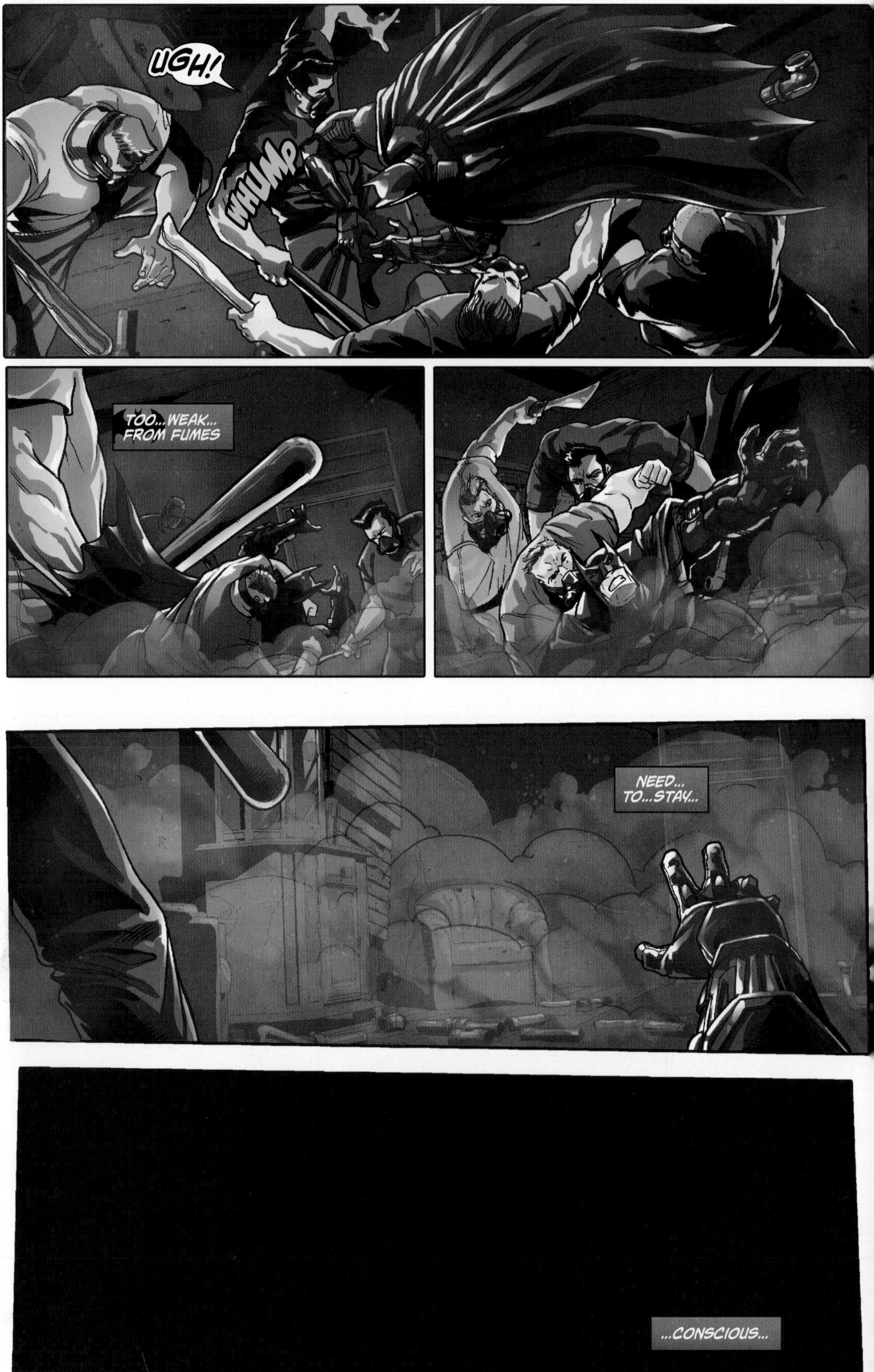
UGH!
WHUMP
TOO...WEAK...
FROM FUMES
NEED...
TO...STAY...
...CONSCIOUS...

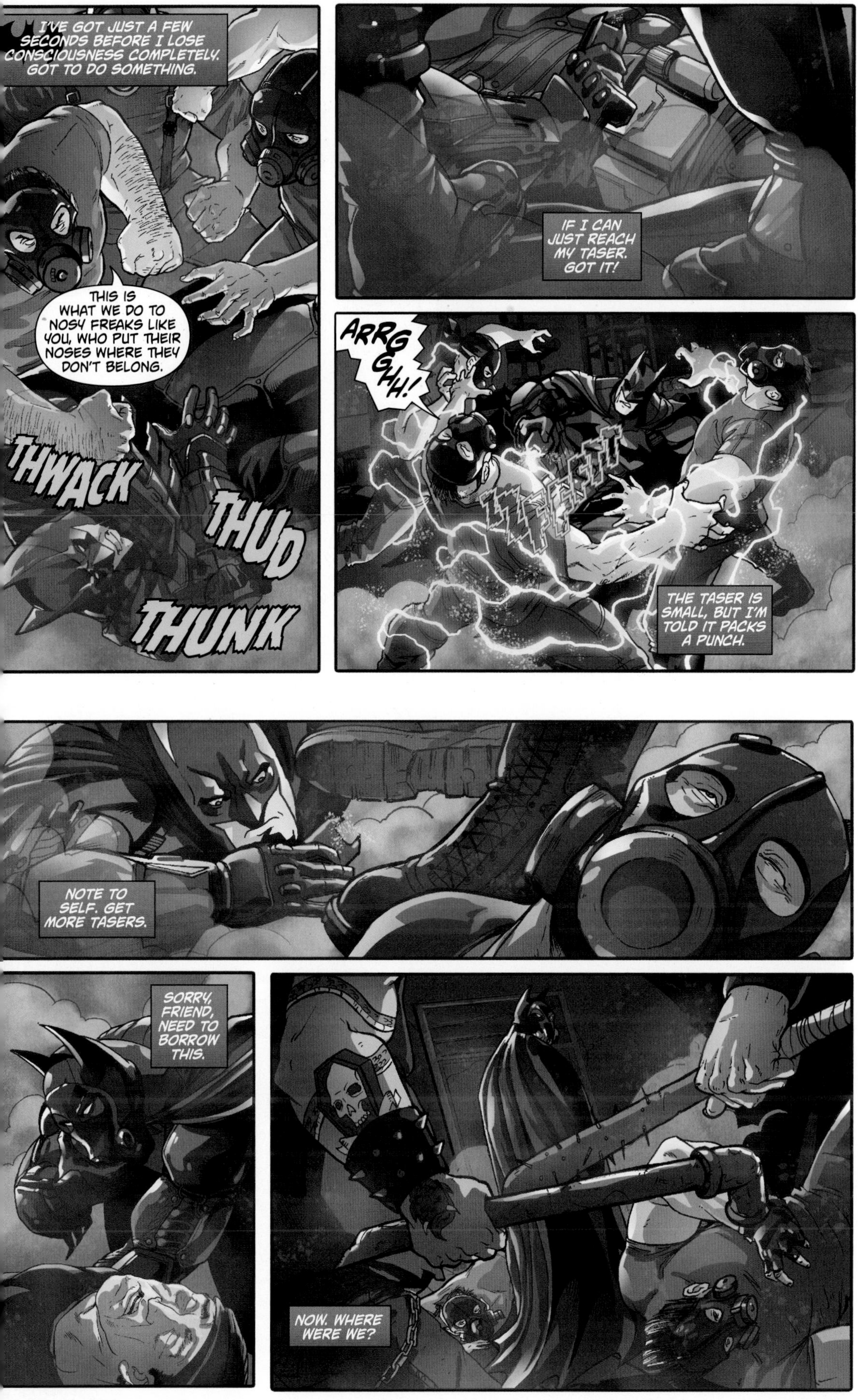
I'VE GOT JUST A FEW SECONDS BEFORE I LOSE CONSCIOUSNESS COMPLETELY. GOT TO DO SOMETHING.
THIS IS WHAT WE DO TO NOSY FREAKS LIKE YOU, WHO PUT THEIR NOSES WHERE THEY DON'T BELONG.
THWACK
THUD
THUNK
IF I CAN JUST REACH MY TASER. GOT IT!
ARRGGHH!
THE TASER IS SMALL, BUT I'M TOLD IT PACKS A PUNCH.
NOTE TO SELF. GET MORE TASERS.
SORRY, FRIEND, NEED TO BORROW THIS.
NOW. WHERE WERE WE?

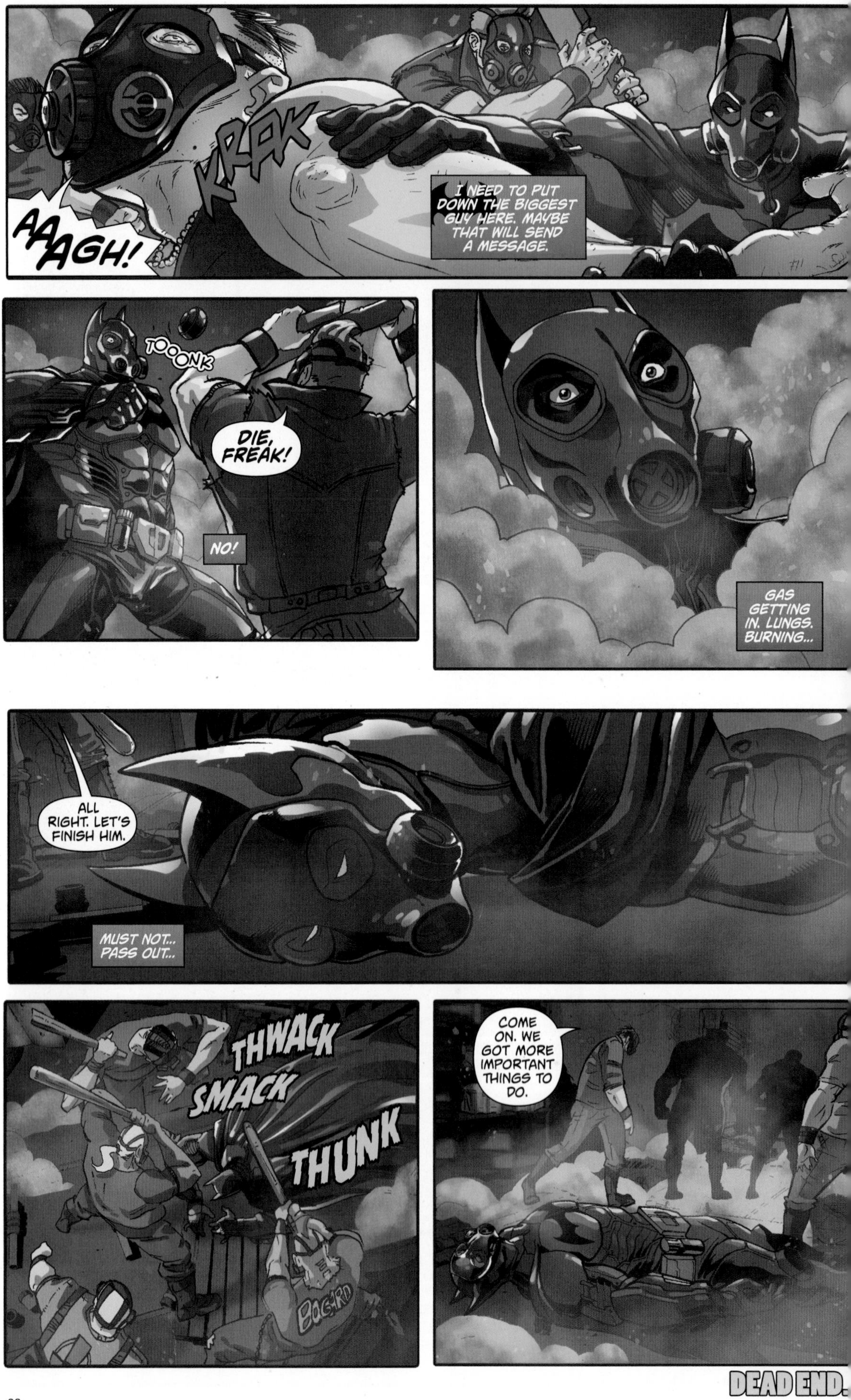
KRAK
AAAGH!
I NEED TO PUT DOWN THE BIGGEST GUY HERE. MAYBE THAT WILL SEND A MESSAGE.
TOOONK
DIE, FREAK!
NO!
GAS GETTING IN. LUNGS. BURNING...
ALL RIGHT. LET'S FINISH HIM.
MUST NOT... PASS OUT...
THWACK
SMACK
THUNK
COME ON. WE GOT MORE IMPORTANT THINGS TO DO.
DEAD END.

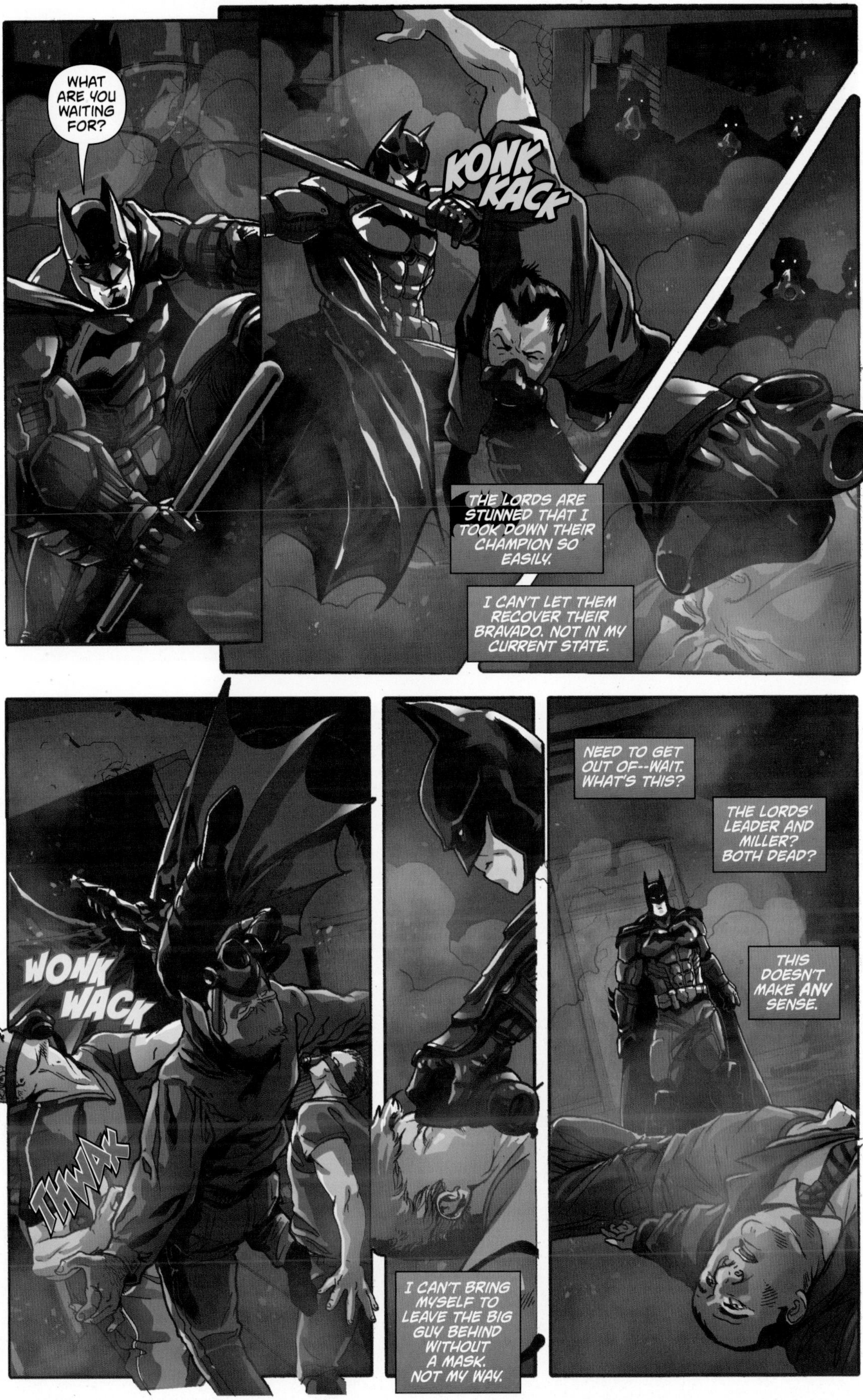
WHAT ARE YOU WAITING FOR?
KONK
KACK
THE LORDS ARE STUNNED THAT I TOOK DOWN THEIR CHAMPION SO EASILY.
I CAN'T LET THEM RECOVER THEIR BRAVADO. NOT IN MY CURRENT STATE.
WONK
WACK
THWAK
I CAN'T BRING MYSELF TO LEAVE THE BIG GUY BEHIND WITHOUT A MASK. NOT MY WAY.
NEED TO GET OUT OF--WAIT. WHAT'S THIS?
THE LORDS' LEADER AND MILLER? BOTH DEAD?
THIS DOESN'T MAKE ANY SENSE.

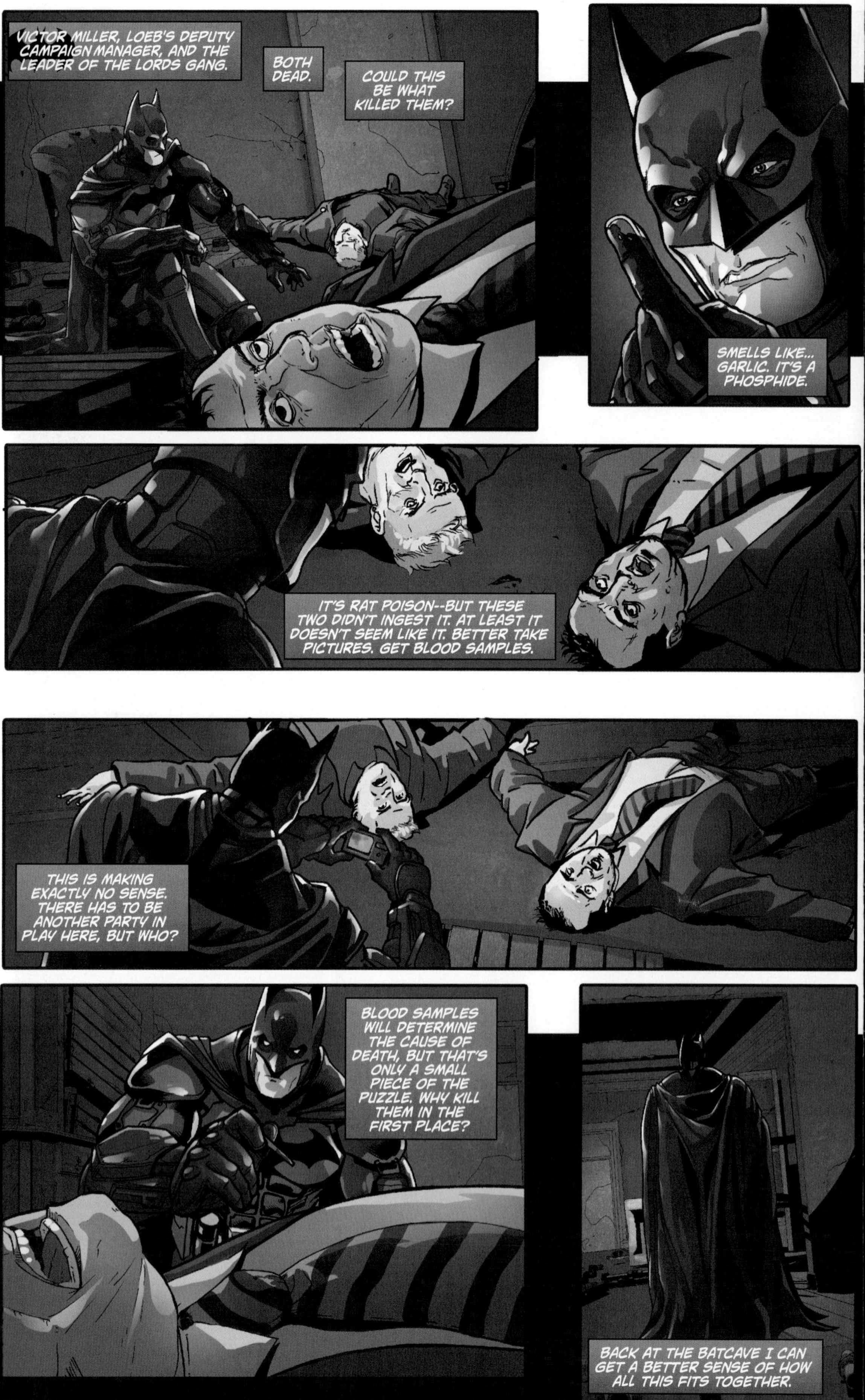
VICTOR MILLER, LOEB'S DEPUTY CAMPAIGN MANAGER, AND THE LEADER OF THE LORDS GANG.
BOTH DEAD.
COULD THIS BE WHAT KILLED THEM?
SMELLS LIKE... GARLIC. IT'S A PHOSPHIDE.
IT'S RAT POISON--BUT THESE TWO DIDN'T INGEST IT. AT LEAST IT DOESN'T SEEM LIKE IT. BETTER TAKE PICTURES. GET BLOOD SAMPLES.
THIS IS MAKING EXACTLY NO SENSE. THERE HAS TO BE ANOTHER PARTY IN PLAY HERE, BUT WHO?
BLOOD SAMPLES WILL DETERMINE THE CAUSE OF DEATH, BUT THAT'S ONLY A SMALL PIECE OF THE PUZZLE. WHY KILL THEM IN THE FIRST PLACE?
BACK AT THE BATCAVE I CAN GET A BETTER SENSE OF HOW ALL THIS FITS TOGETHER.

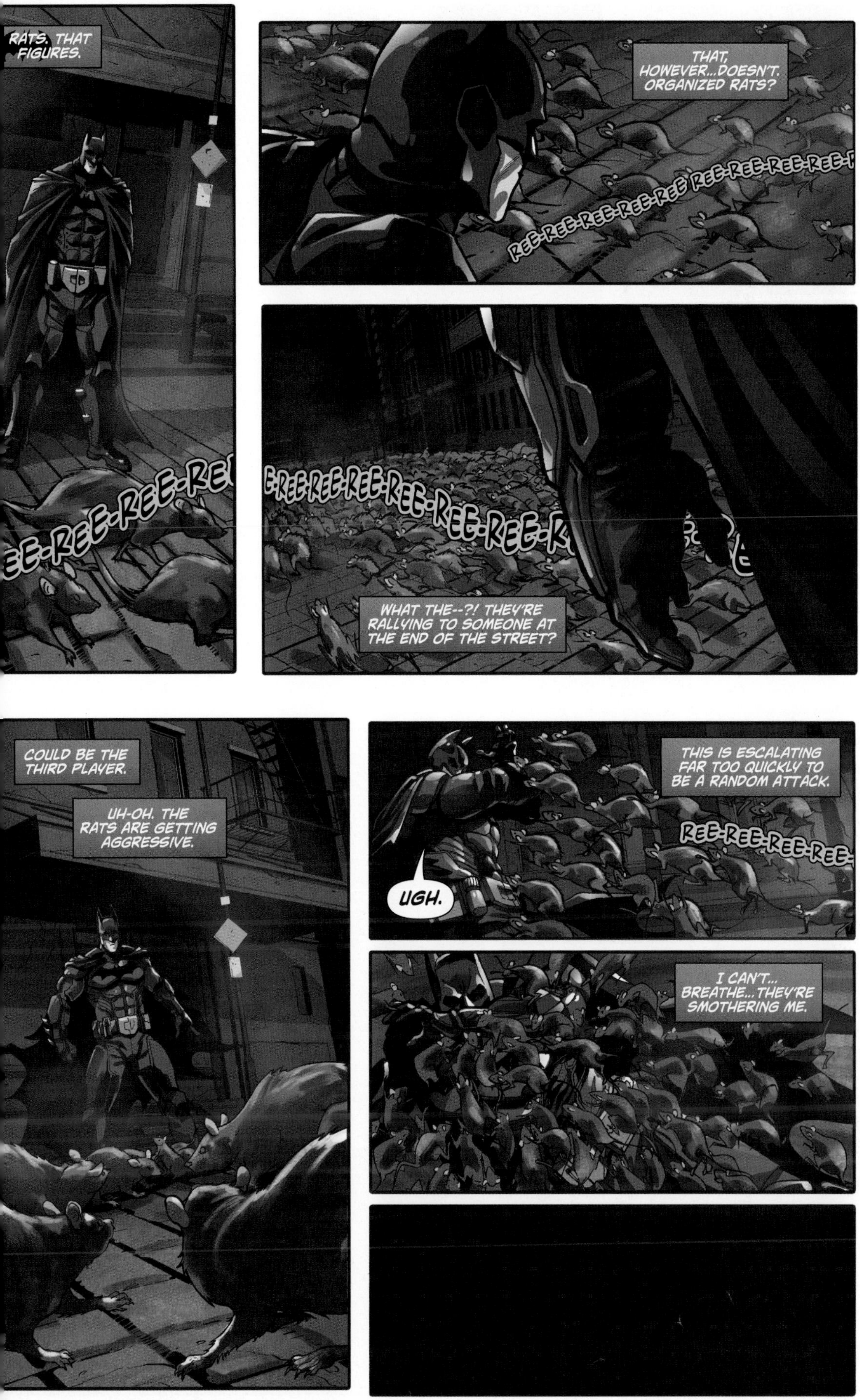
RATS. THAT FIGURES.
EE-REE-REE-REE
THAT, HOWEVER...DOESN'T. ORGANIZED RATS?
REE-REE-REE-REE-REE-REE-REE-REE-REE-REE-R
E-REE-REE-REE-REE-REE-REE-REE-R
WHAT THE--?! THEY'RE RALLYING TO SOMEONE AT THE END OF THE STREET?
COULD BE THE THIRD PLAYER.
UH-OH. THE RATS ARE GETTING AGGRESSIVE.
THIS IS ESCALATING FAR TOO QUICKLY TO BE A RANDOM ATTACK.
REE-REE-REE-REE-
UGH.
I CAN'T... BREATHE...THEY'RE SMOTHERING ME.

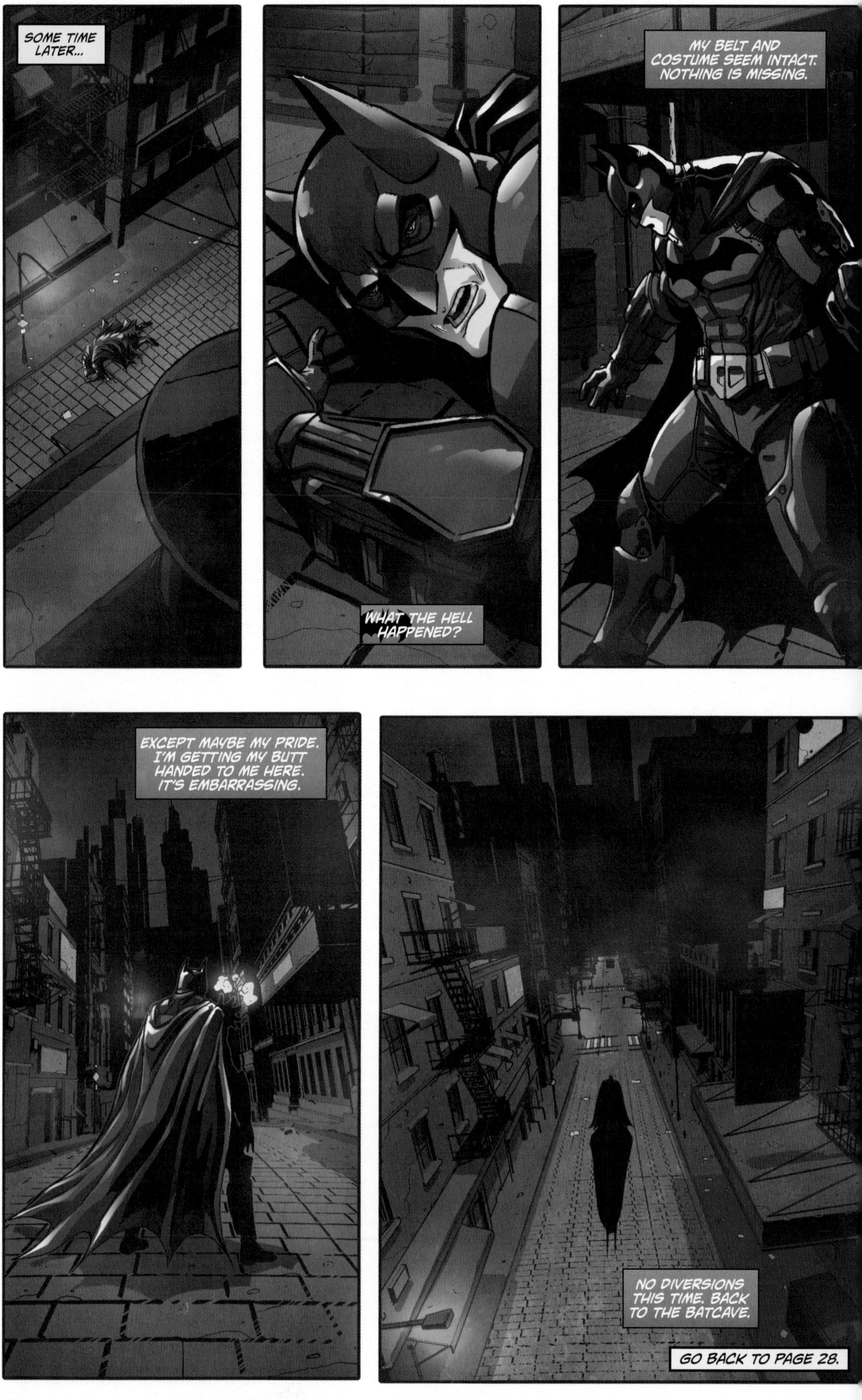
SOME TIME LATER...
WHAT THE HELL HAPPENED?
MY BELT AND COSTUME SEEM INTACT. NOTHING IS MISSING.
EXCEPT MAYBE MY PRIDE. I'M GETTING MY BUTT HANDED TO ME HERE. IT'S EMBARRASSING.
NO DIVERSIONS THIS TIME. BACK TO THE BATCAVE.
GO BACK TO PAGE 28.

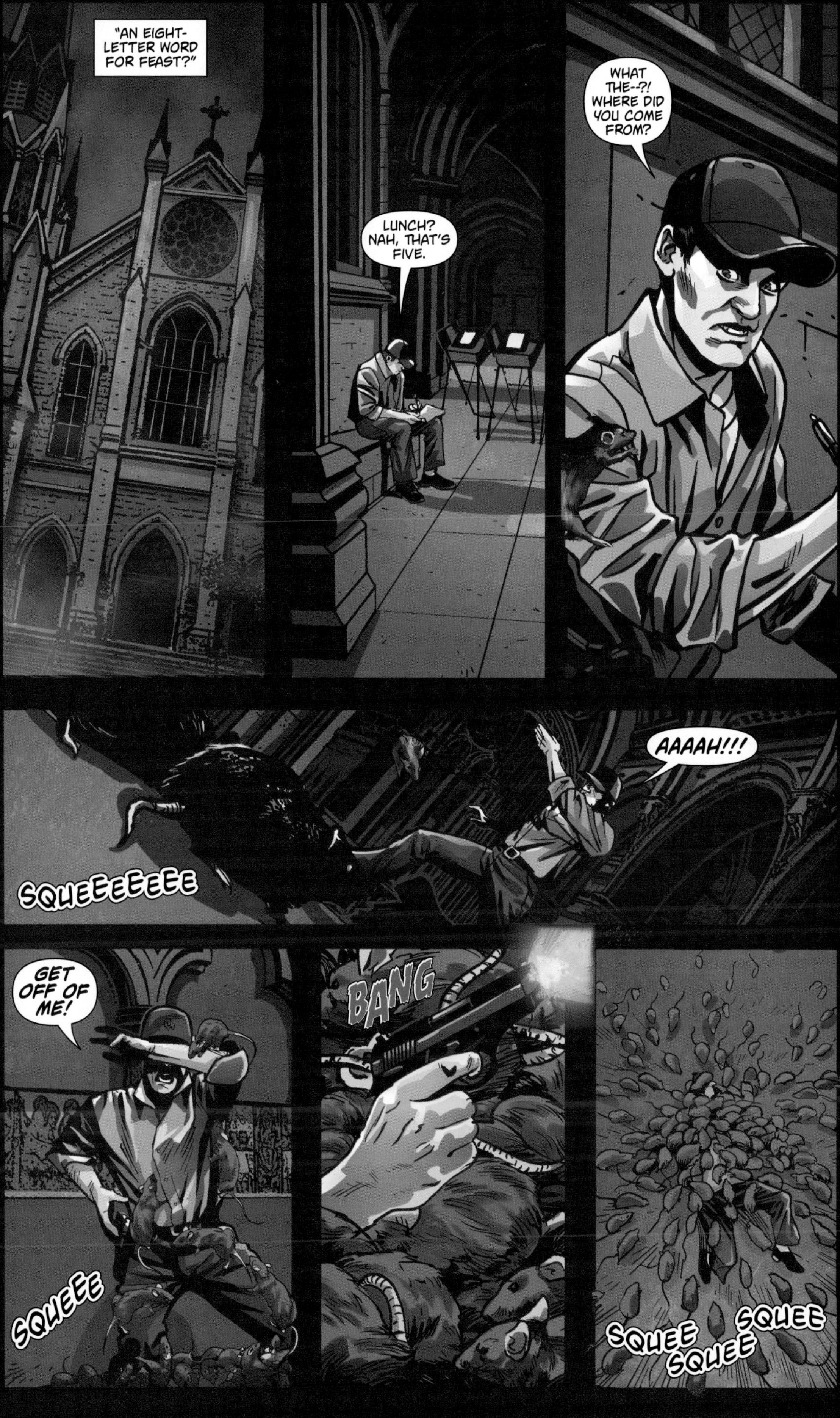
"AN EIGHT-LETTER WORD FOR FEAST?"
LUNCH? NAH, THAT'S FIVE.
WHAT THE--?! WHERE DID YOU COME FROM?
AAAAH!!!
SQUEEEEEEEE
GET OFF OF ME!
SQUEEE
BANG
SQUEE SQUEE SQUEE

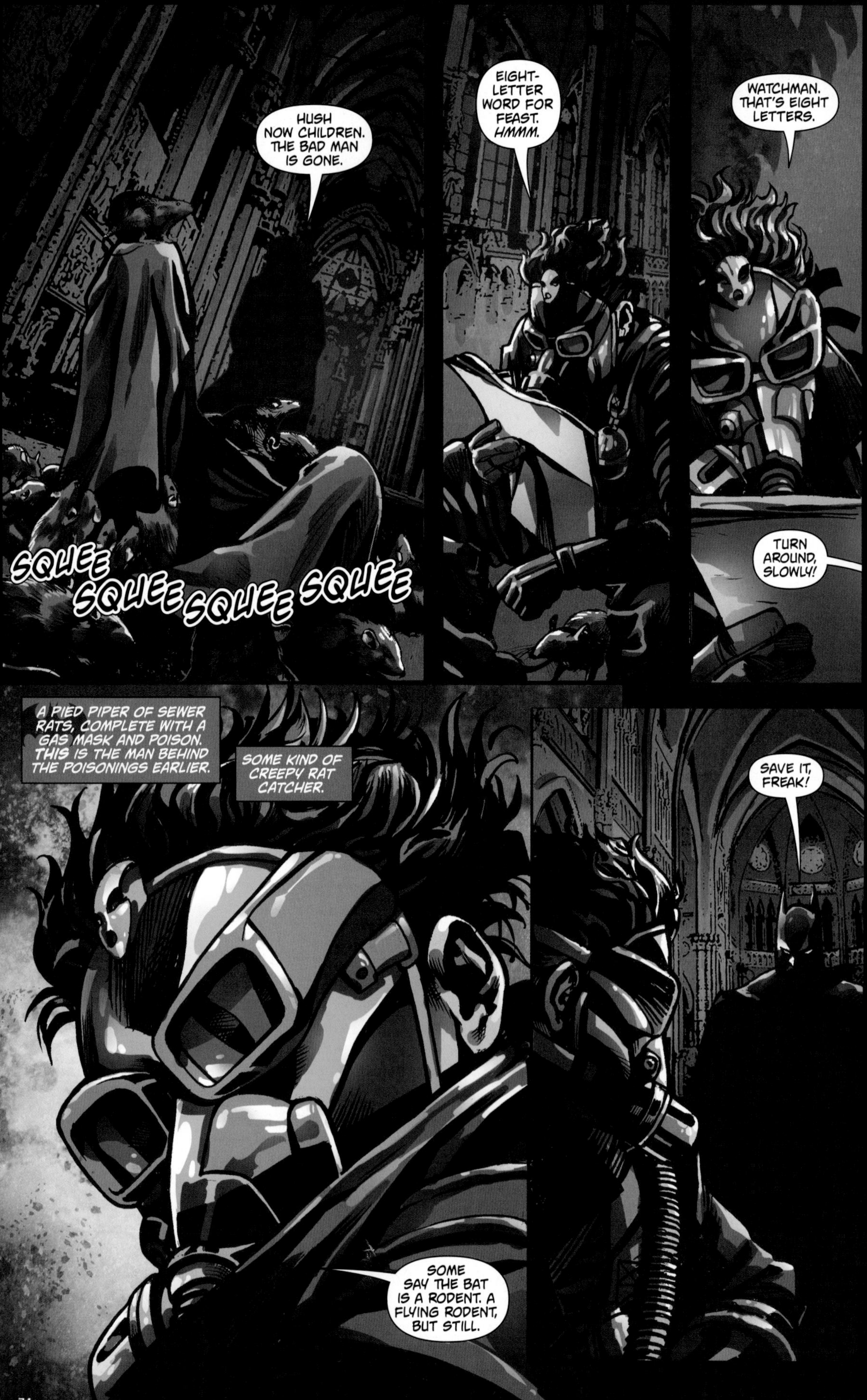
HUSH NOW CHILDREN. THE BAD MAN IS GONE.
SQUEE SQUEE SQUEE SQUEE
EIGHT-LETTER WORD FOR FEAST. *HMMM.*
WATCHMAN. THAT'S EIGHT LETTERS.
TURN AROUND, SLOWLY!
A PIED PIPER OF SEWER RATS, COMPLETE WITH A GAS MASK AND POISON. **THIS** IS THE MAN BEHIND THE POISONINGS EARLIER.
SOME KIND OF CREEPY RAT CATCHER.
SOME SAY THE BAT IS A RODENT. A FLYING RODENT, BUT STILL.
SAVE IT, FREAK!

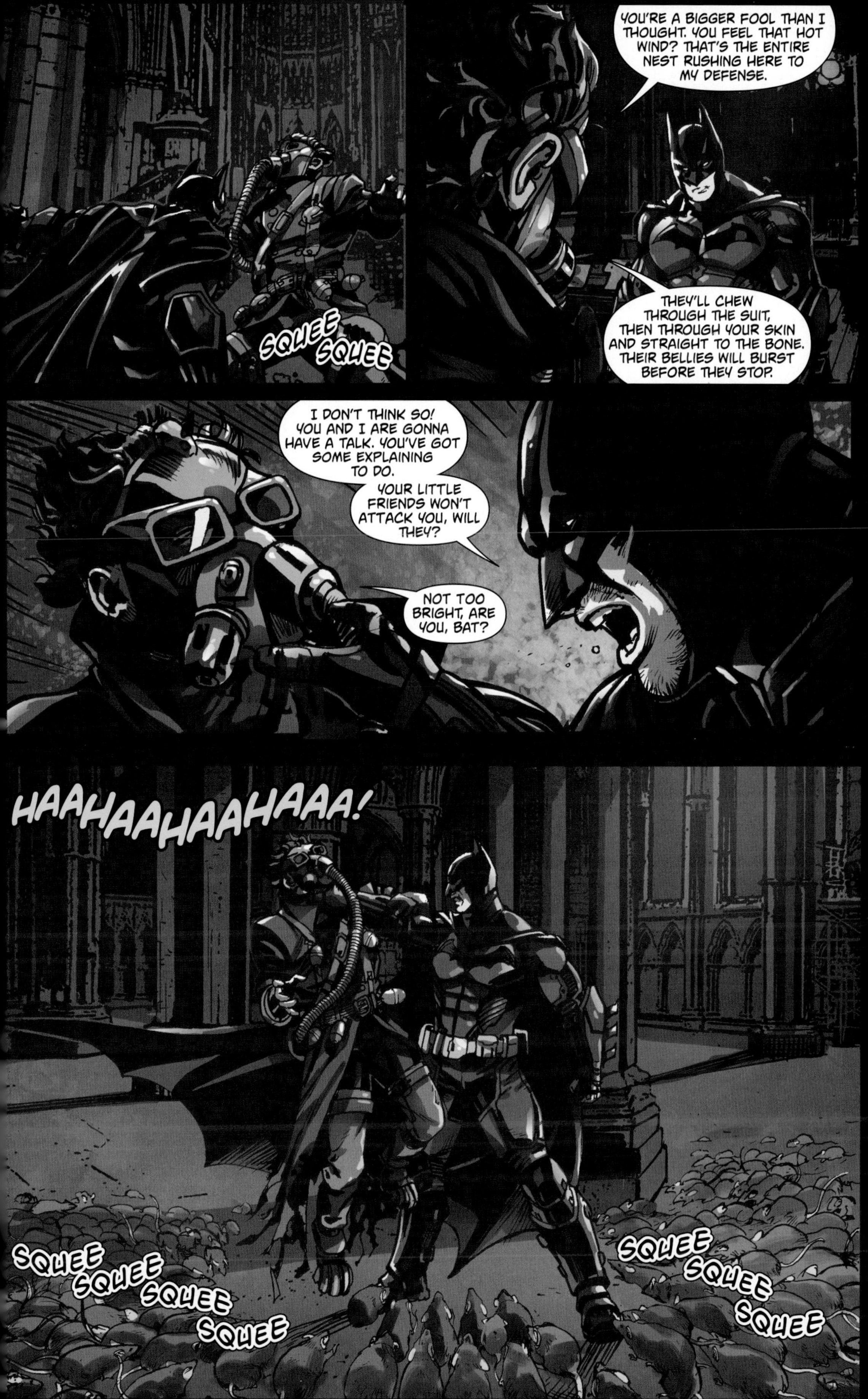
SQUEE SQUEE
YOU'RE A BIGGER FOOL THAN I THOUGHT. YOU FEEL THAT HOT WIND? THAT'S THE ENTIRE NEST RUSHING HERE TO MY DEFENSE.
THEY'LL CHEW THROUGH THE SUIT, THEN THROUGH YOUR SKIN AND STRAIGHT TO THE BONE. THEIR BELLIES WILL BURST BEFORE THEY STOP.
I DON'T THINK SO! YOU AND I ARE GONNA HAVE A TALK. YOU'VE GOT SOME EXPLAINING TO DO.
YOUR LITTLE FRIENDS WON'T ATTACK YOU, WILL THEY?
NOT TOO BRIGHT, ARE YOU, BAT?
HAAHAAHAAHAAA!
SQUEE SQUEE SQUEE SQUEE
SQUEE SQUEE SQUEE

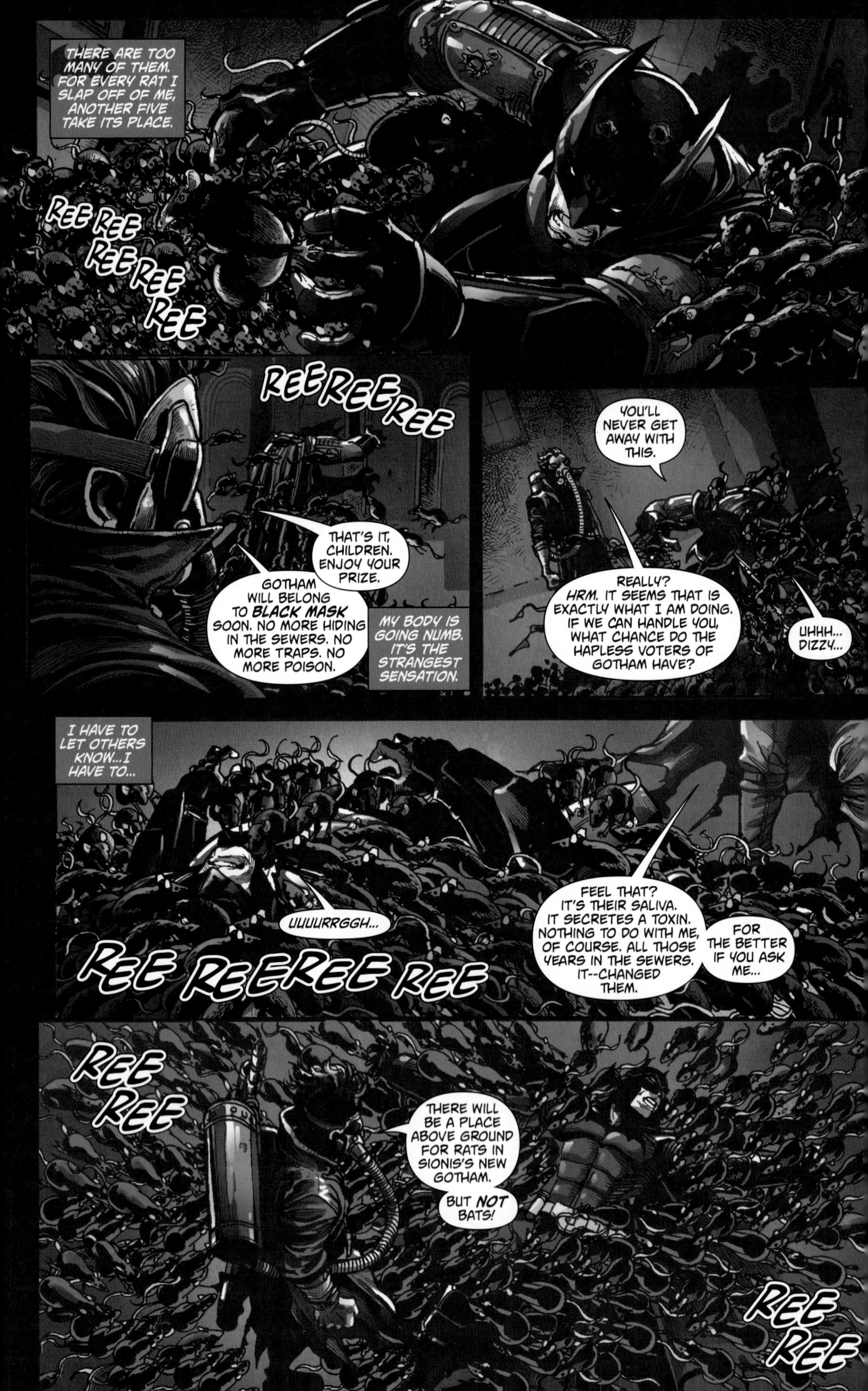
THERE ARE TOO MANY OF THEM. FOR EVERY RAT I SLAP OFF OF ME, ANOTHER FIVE TAKE ITS PLACE.
REE REE REE REE REE
REEREEREE
THAT'S IT, CHILDREN. ENJOY YOUR PRIZE.
GOTHAM WILL BELONG TO BLACK MASK SOON. NO MORE HIDING IN THE SEWERS. NO MORE TRAPS. NO MORE POISON.
MY BODY IS GOING NUMB. IT'S THE STRANGEST SENSATION.
YOU'LL NEVER GET AWAY WITH THIS.
REALLY? HRM. IT SEEMS THAT IS EXACTLY WHAT I AM DOING. IF WE CAN HANDLE YOU, WHAT CHANCE DO THE HAPLESS VOTERS OF GOTHAM HAVE?
UHHH... DIZZY...
I HAVE TO LET OTHERS KNOW...I HAVE TO...
UUUURRGGH...
REE REEREE REE
FEEL THAT? IT'S THEIR SALIVA. IT SECRETES A TOXIN. NOTHING TO DO WITH ME, OF COURSE. ALL THOSE YEARS IN THE SEWERS. IT--CHANGED THEM.
FOR THE BETTER IF YOU ASK ME...
REE REE
THERE WILL BE A PLACE ABOVE GROUND FOR RATS IN SIONIS'S NEW GOTHAM.
BUT NOT BATS!
REE REE

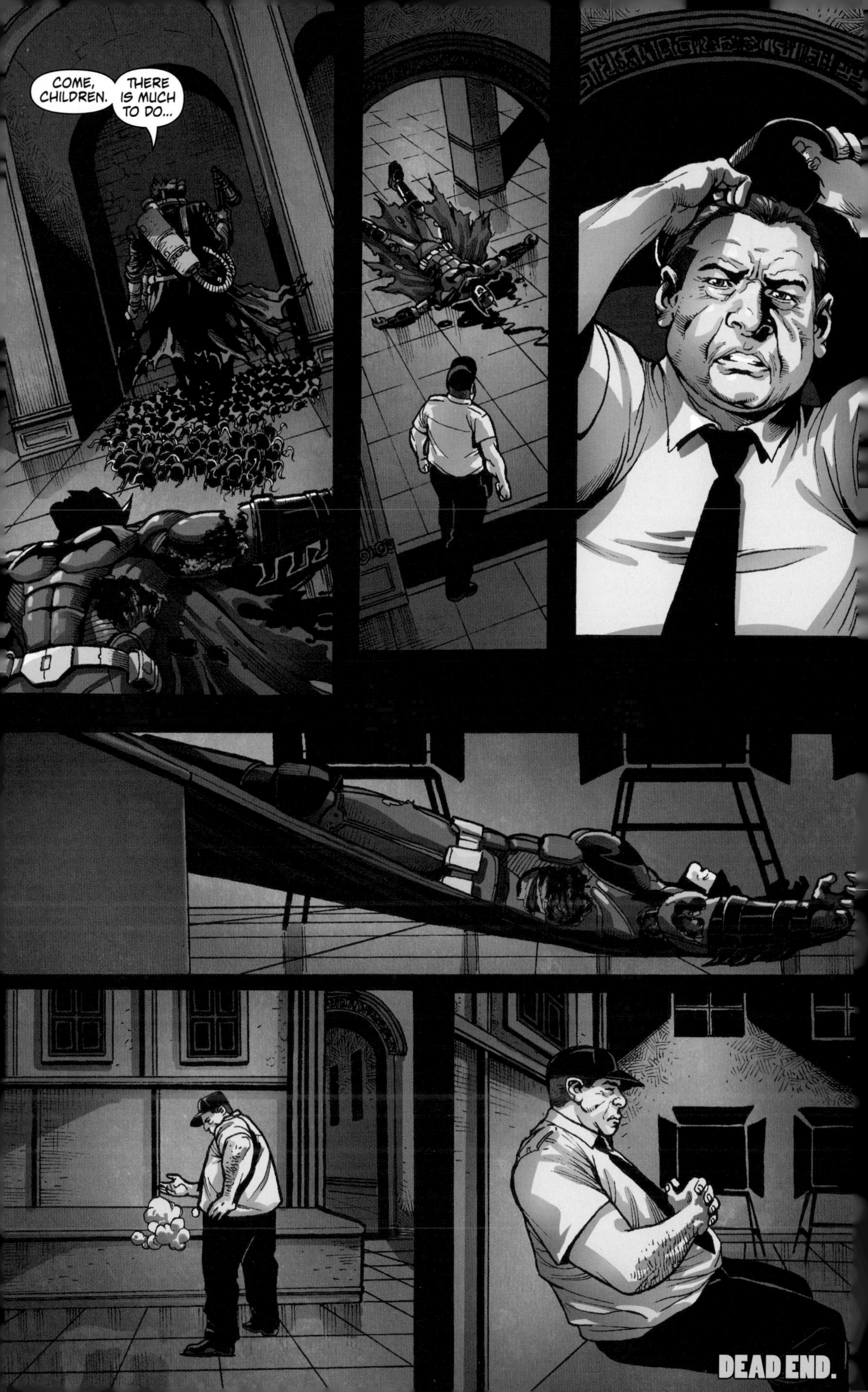
COME, CHILDREN.
THERE IS MUCH TO DO...
DEAD END.

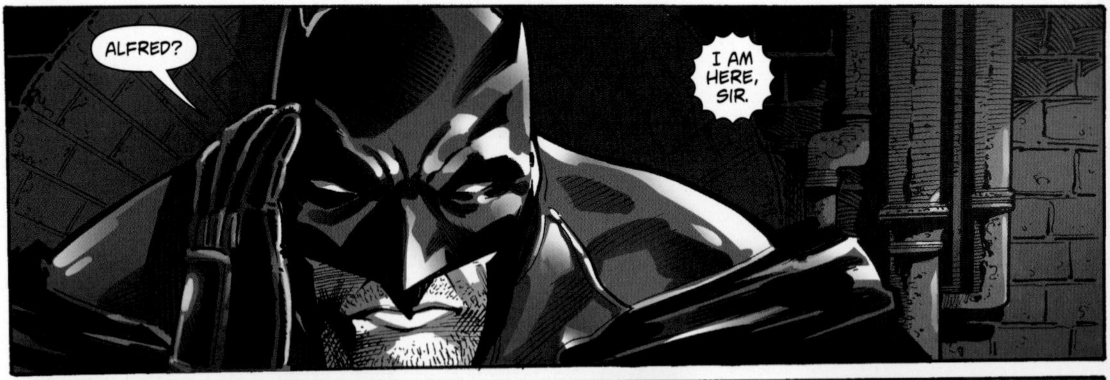
ALFRED?
I AM HERE, SIR.

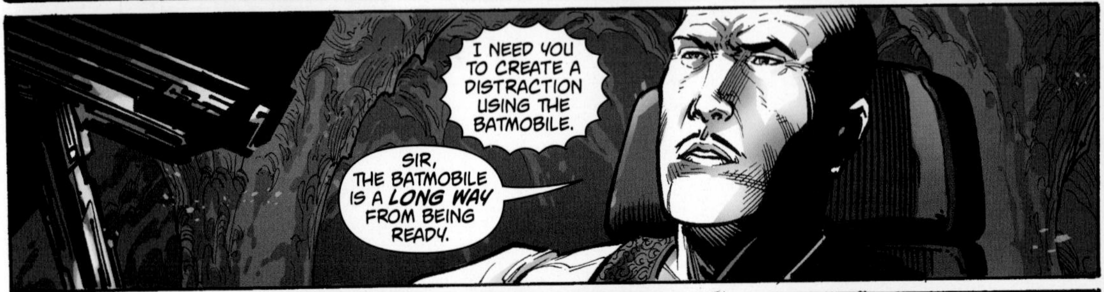
I NEED YOU TO CREATE A DISTRACTION USING THE BATMOBILE.
SIR, THE BATMOBILE IS A **LONG WAY** FROM BEING READY.

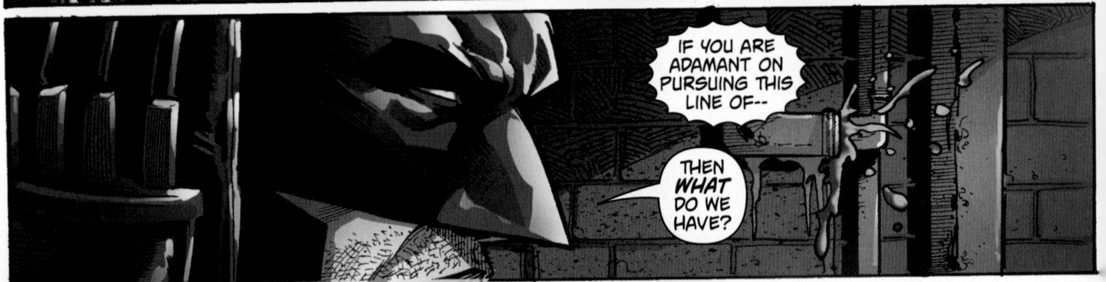
IF YOU ARE ADAMANT ON PURSUING THIS LINE OF--
THEN **WHAT** DO WE HAVE?

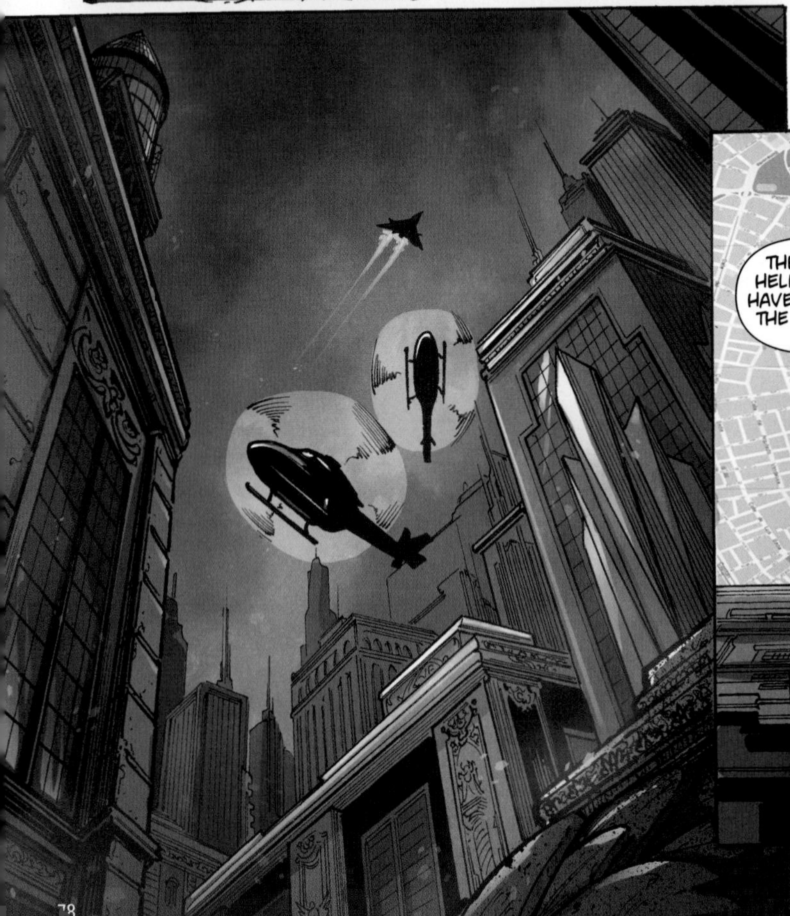

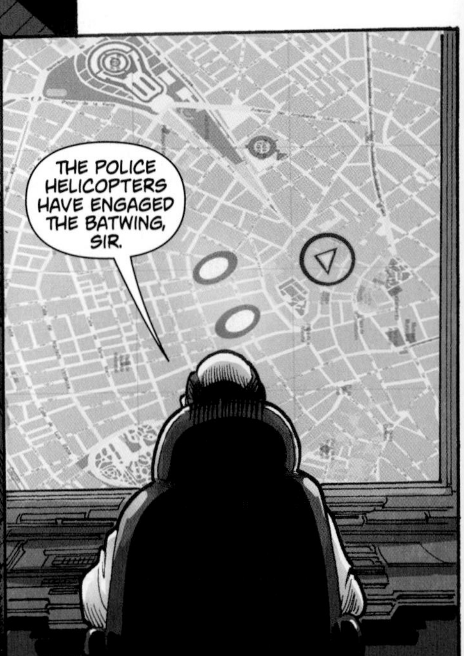
THE POLICE HELICOPTERS HAVE ENGAGED THE BATWING, SIR.

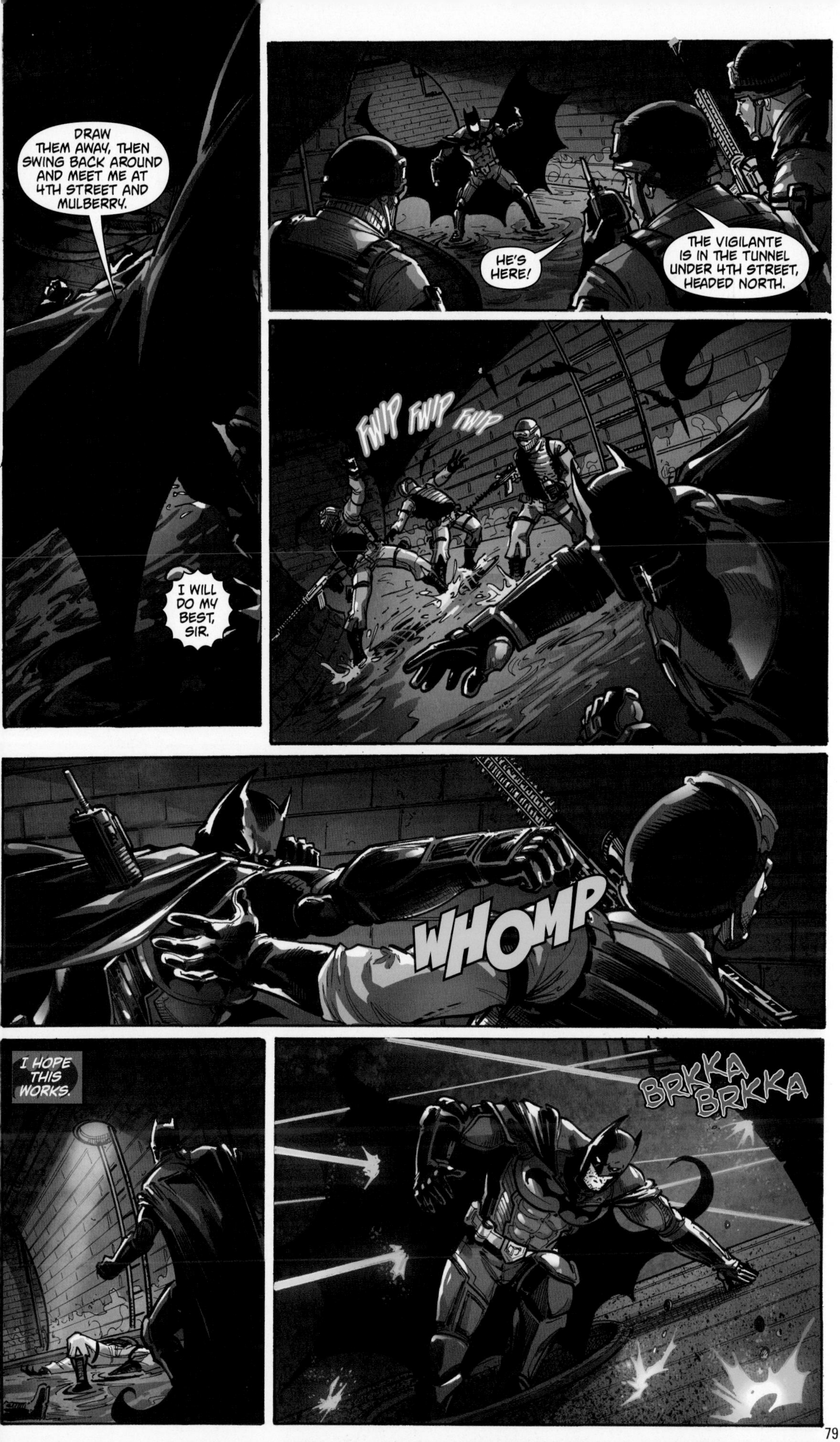
DRAW THEM AWAY, THEN SWING BACK AROUND AND MEET ME AT 4TH STREET AND MULBERRY.
I WILL DO MY BEST, SIR.
HE'S HERE!
THE VIGILANTE IS IN THE TUNNEL UNDER 4TH STREET, HEADED NORTH.
FWIP FWIP FWIP
WHOMP
I HOPE THIS WORKS.
BRKKA BRKKA

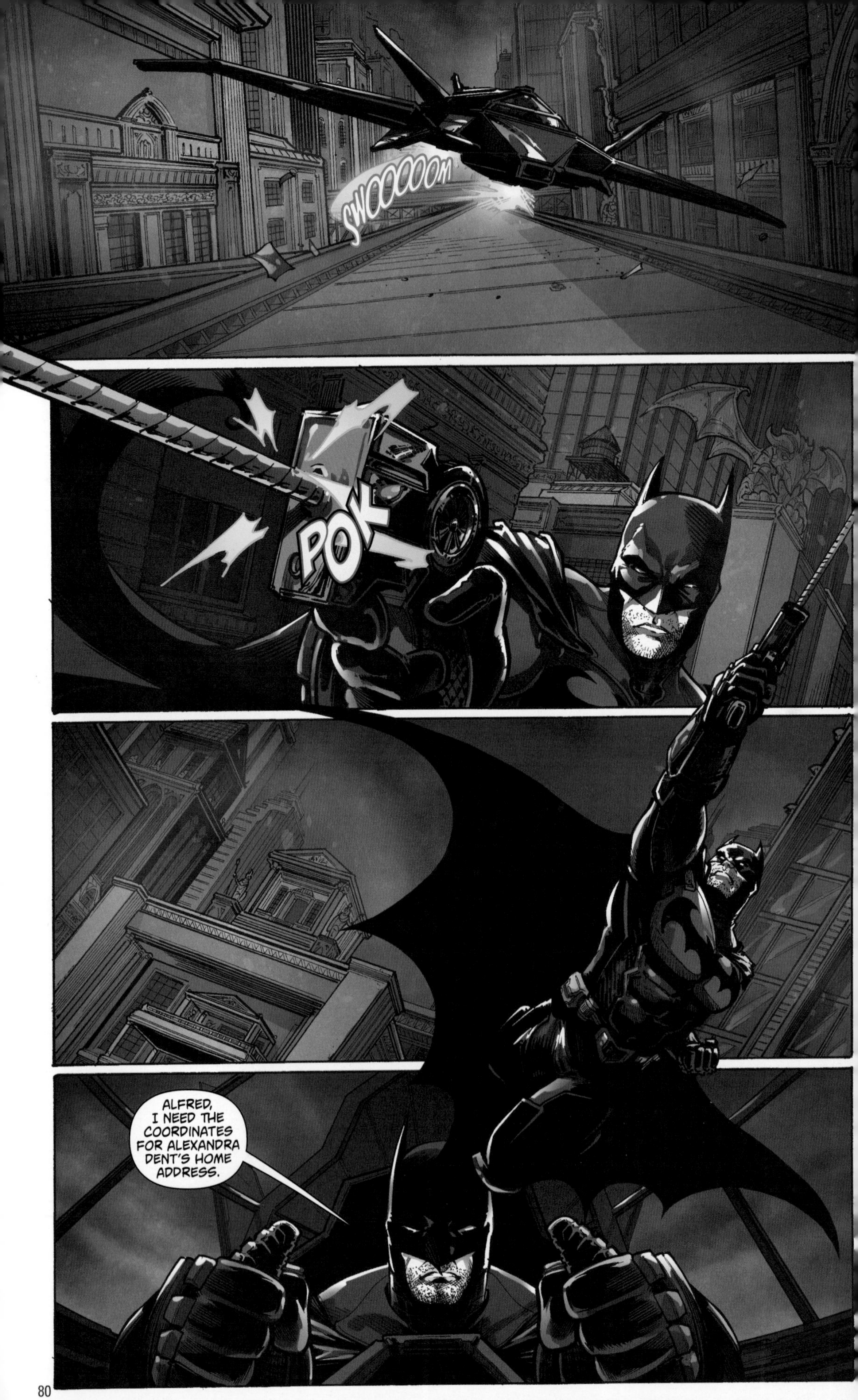
SWOOOOOM
POK
ALFRED, I NEED THE COORDINATES FOR ALEXANDRA DENT'S HOME ADDRESS.

SIR, MS. DENT LIVES IN A TOWNHOME AT--

ONE MOMENT, ALFRED.

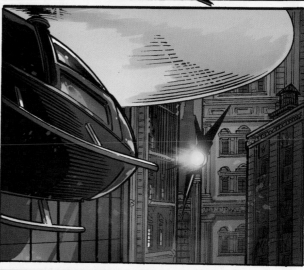

I DON'T HAVE TIME FOR THIS. MORE IMPORTANTLY, ALEXANDRA DENT DOESN'T HAVE TIME FOR THIS. I NEED TO FIND A WAY TO END THIS QUICKLY WITHOUT ANYONE GETTING HURT.

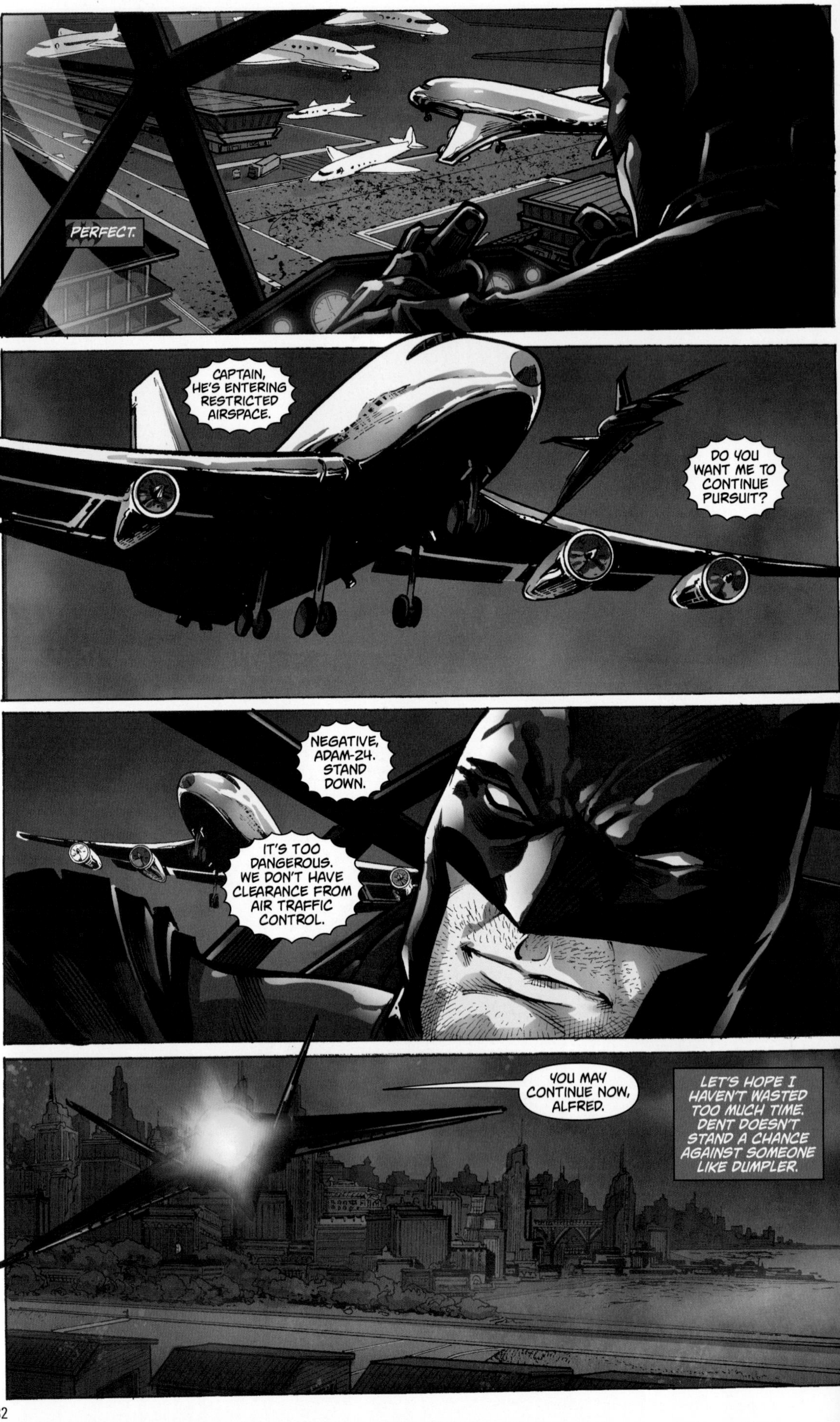
PERFECT.
CAPTAIN, HE'S ENTERING RESTRICTED AIRSPACE.
DO YOU WANT ME TO CONTINUE PURSUIT?
NEGATIVE, ADAM-24. STAND DOWN.
IT'S TOO DANGEROUS. WE DON'T HAVE CLEARANCE FROM AIR TRAFFIC CONTROL.
YOU MAY CONTINUE NOW, ALFRED.
LET'S HOPE I HAVEN'T WASTED TOO MUCH TIME. DENT DOESN'T STAND A CHANCE AGAINST SOMEONE LIKE DUMPLER.

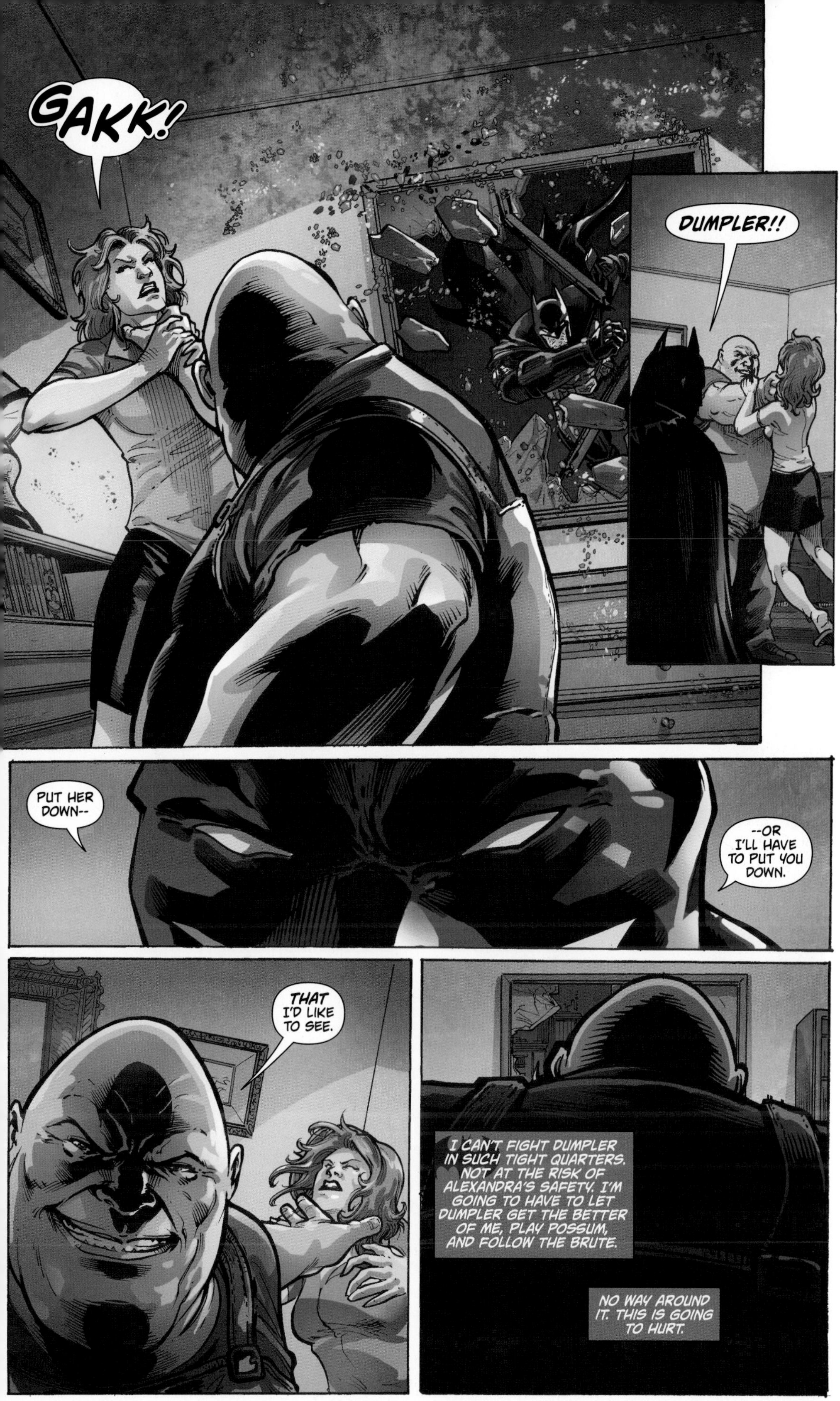

GAKK!
DUMPLER!!
PUT HER DOWN--
--OR I'LL HAVE TO PUT YOU DOWN.
THAT I'D LIKE TO SEE.
I CAN'T FIGHT DUMPLER IN SUCH TIGHT QUARTERS. NOT AT THE RISK OF ALEXANDRA'S SAFETY. I'M GOING TO HAVE TO LET DUMPLER GET THE BETTER OF ME, PLAY POSSUM, AND FOLLOW THE BRUTE.
NO WAY AROUND IT. THIS IS GOING TO HURT.

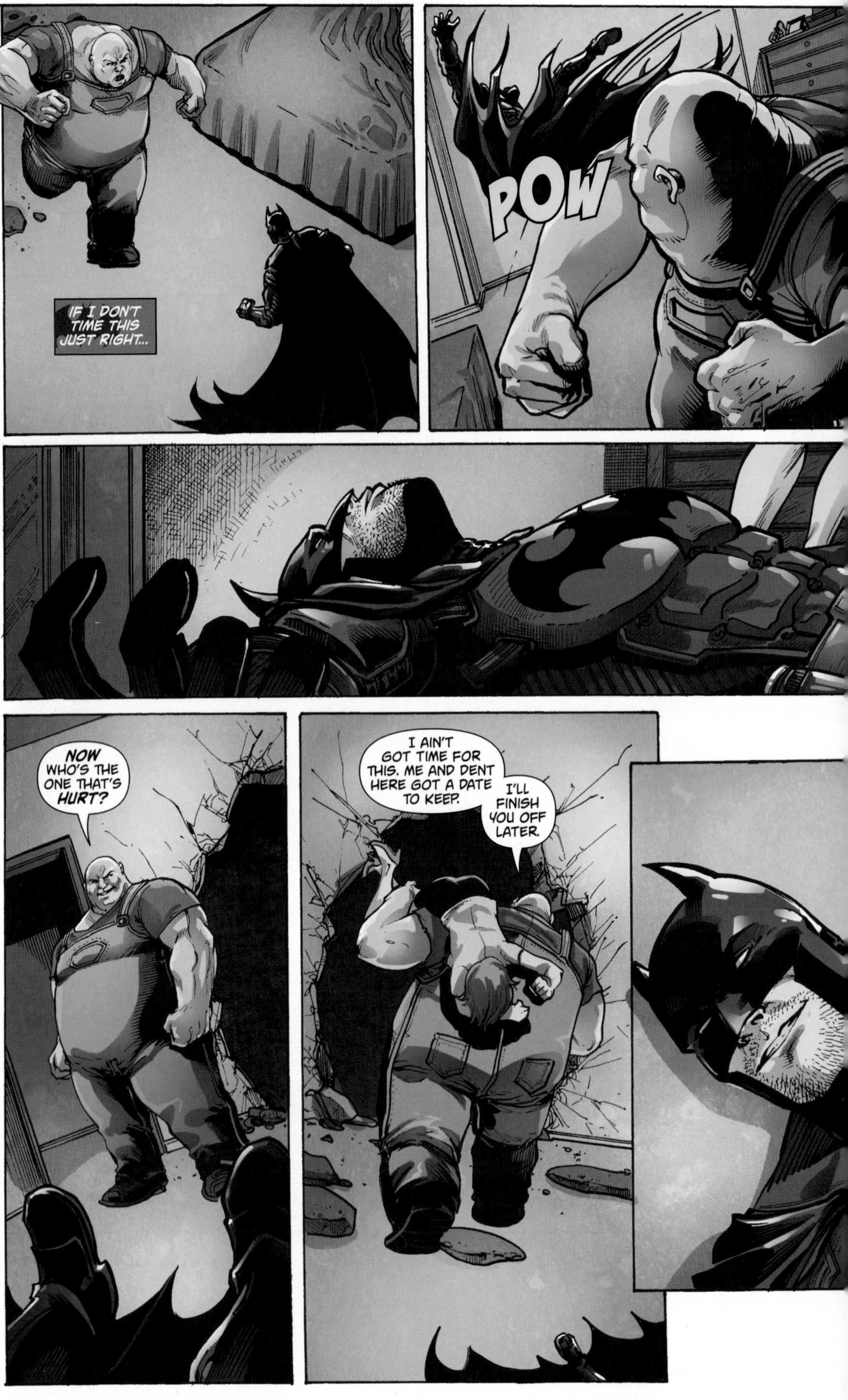
IF I DON'T TIME THIS JUST RIGHT...
POW
NOW WHO'S THE ONE THAT'S HURT?
I AIN'T GOT TIME FOR THIS. ME AND DENT HERE GOT A DATE TO KEEP.
I'LL FINISH YOU OFF LATER.

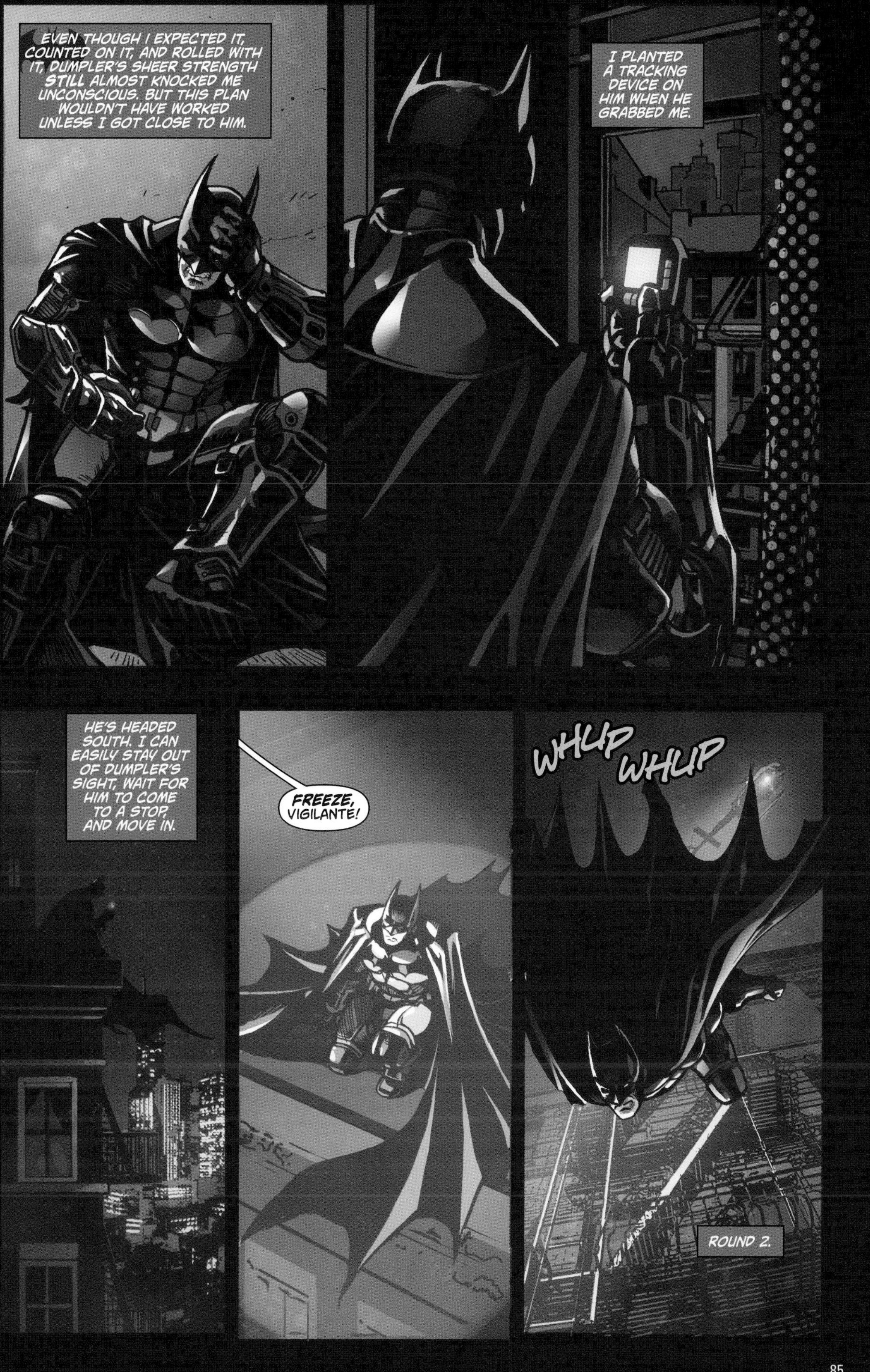
EVEN THOUGH I EXPECTED IT, COUNTED ON IT, AND ROLLED WITH IT, DUMPLER'S SHEER STRENGTH STILL ALMOST KNOCKED ME UNCONSCIOUS. BUT THIS PLAN WOULDN'T HAVE WORKED UNLESS I GOT CLOSE TO HIM.
I PLANTED A TRACKING DEVICE ON HIM WHEN HE GRABBED ME.
HE'S HEADED SOUTH. I CAN EASILY STAY OUT OF DUMPLER'S SIGHT, WAIT FOR HIM TO COME TO A STOP, AND MOVE IN.
FREEZE, VIGILANTE!
WHUP WHUP
ROUND 2.

WHUP WHUP
WHUP WHUP

KPOK

THE HELICOPTER IS MAKING THIS MORE COMPLICATED.

WHUP
WHUP
WHUP
WHUP
WHUP

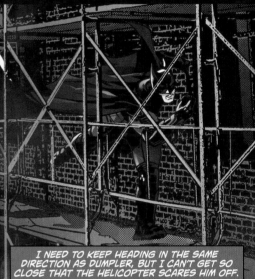

I NEED TO KEEP HEADING IN THE SAME DIRECTION AS DUMPLER, BUT I CAN'T GET SO CLOSE THAT THE HELICOPTER SCARES HIM OFF.

WHUP WHUP
WHUP

THERE. TRACKER SAYS DUMPLER'S STOPPED.

WHUP WHUP WHUP
WHUP

TIME TO LOSE GOTHAM'S FINEST.

WHUP WHUP WHUP WHUP
WHUP

OKAY, BOYS. STAY CLOSE.

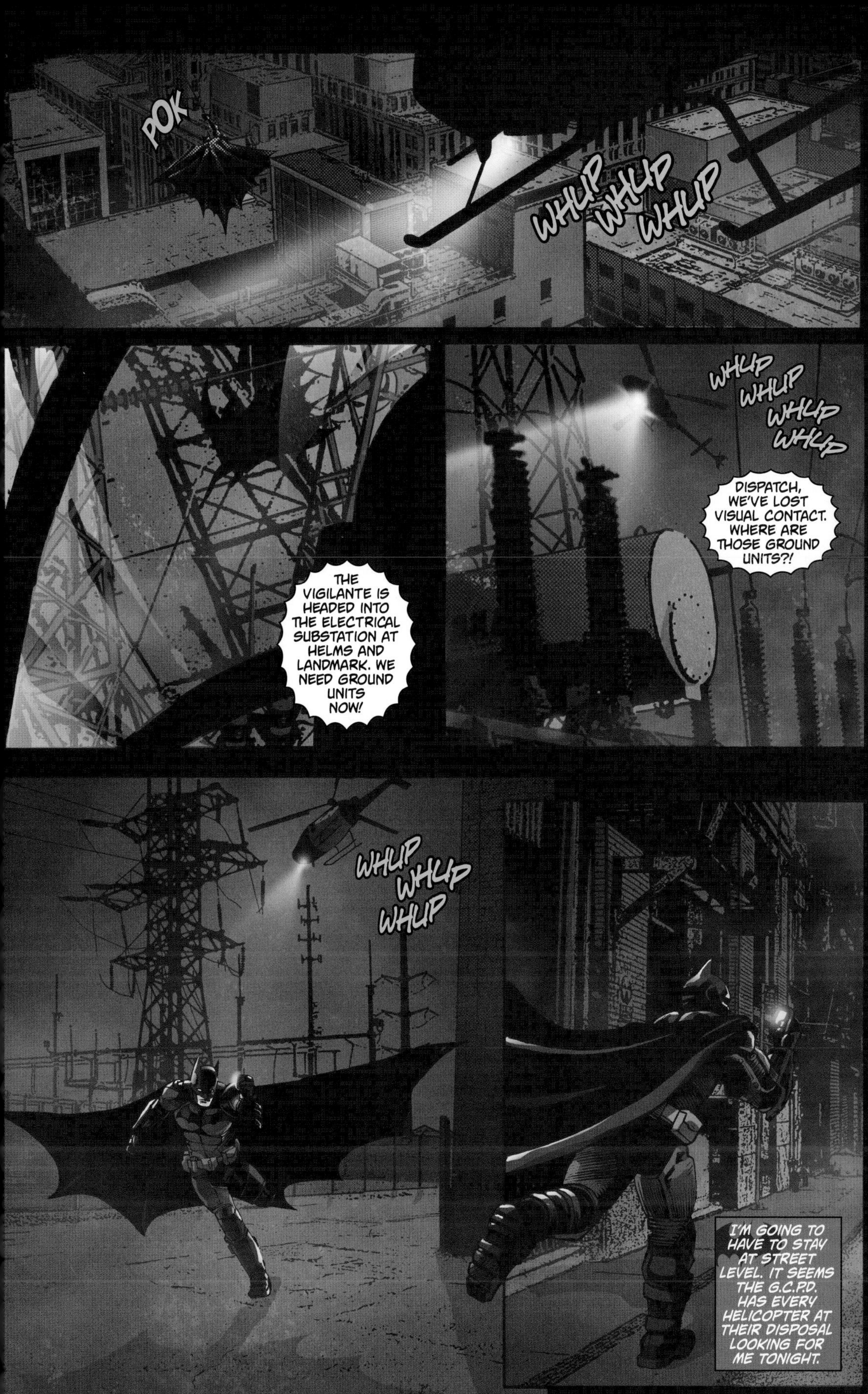
POK
WHUP WHUP WHUP
THE VIGILANTE IS HEADED INTO THE ELECTRICAL SUBSTATION AT HELMS AND LANDMARK. WE NEED GROUND UNITS NOW!
WHUP WHUP WHUP WHUP
DISPATCH, WE'VE LOST VISUAL CONTACT. WHERE ARE THOSE GROUND UNITS?!
WHUP WHUP WHUP
I'M GOING TO HAVE TO STAY AT STREET LEVEL. IT SEEMS THE G.C.P.D. HAS EVERY HELICOPTER AT THEIR DISPOSAL LOOKING FOR ME TONIGHT.

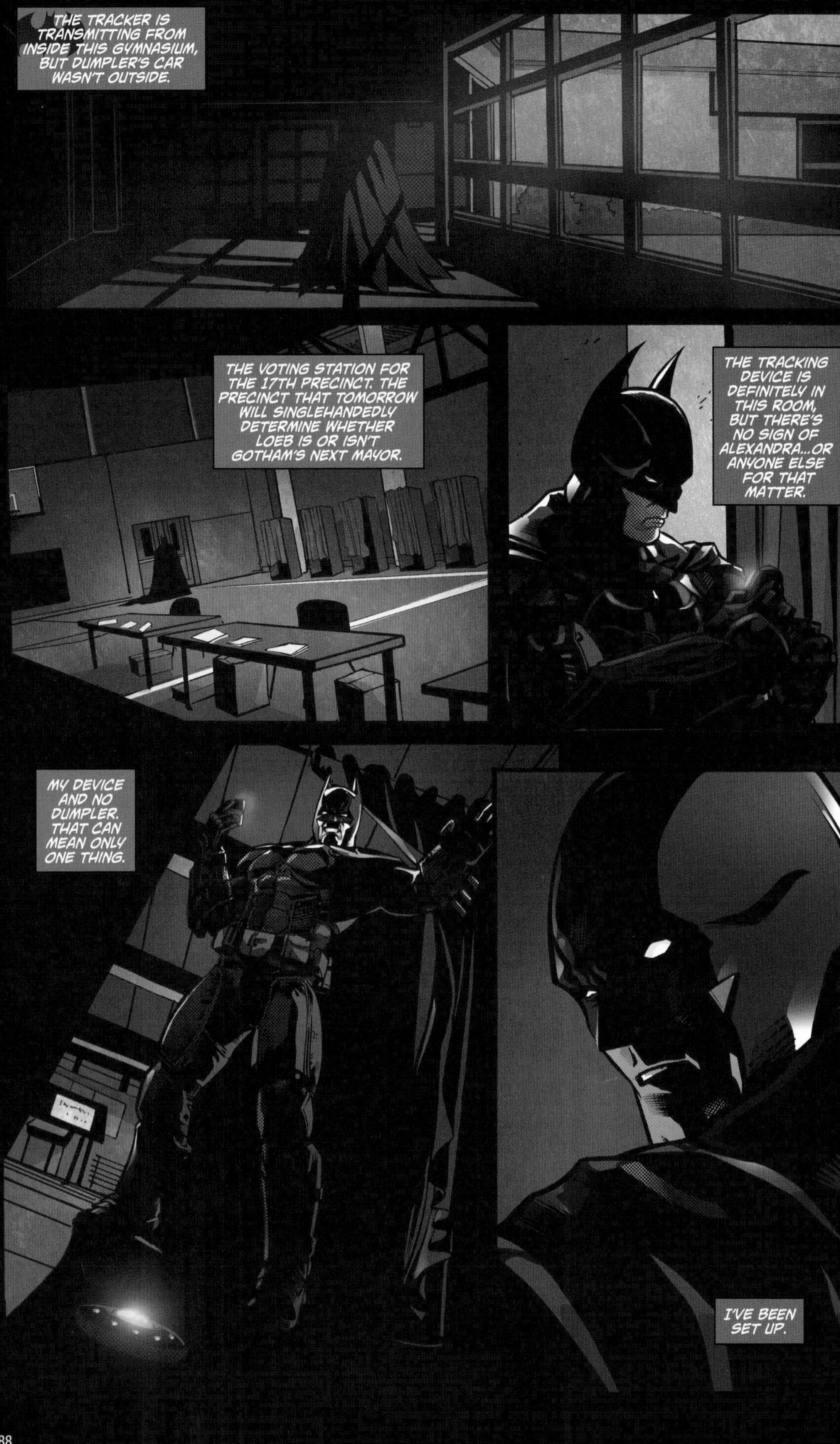
THE TRACKER IS TRANSMITTING FROM INSIDE THIS GYMNASIUM, BUT DUMPLER'S CAR WASN'T OUTSIDE.
THE VOTING STATION FOR THE 17TH PRECINCT. THE PRECINCT THAT TOMORROW WILL SINGLEHANDEDLY DETERMINE WHETHER LOEB IS OR ISN'T GOTHAM'S NEXT MAYOR.
THE TRACKING DEVICE IS DEFINITELY IN THIS ROOM, BUT THERE'S NO SIGN OF ALEXANDRA...OR ANYONE ELSE FOR THAT MATTER.
MY DEVICE AND NO DUMPLER. THAT CAN MEAN ONLY ONE THING.
I'VE BEEN SET UP.

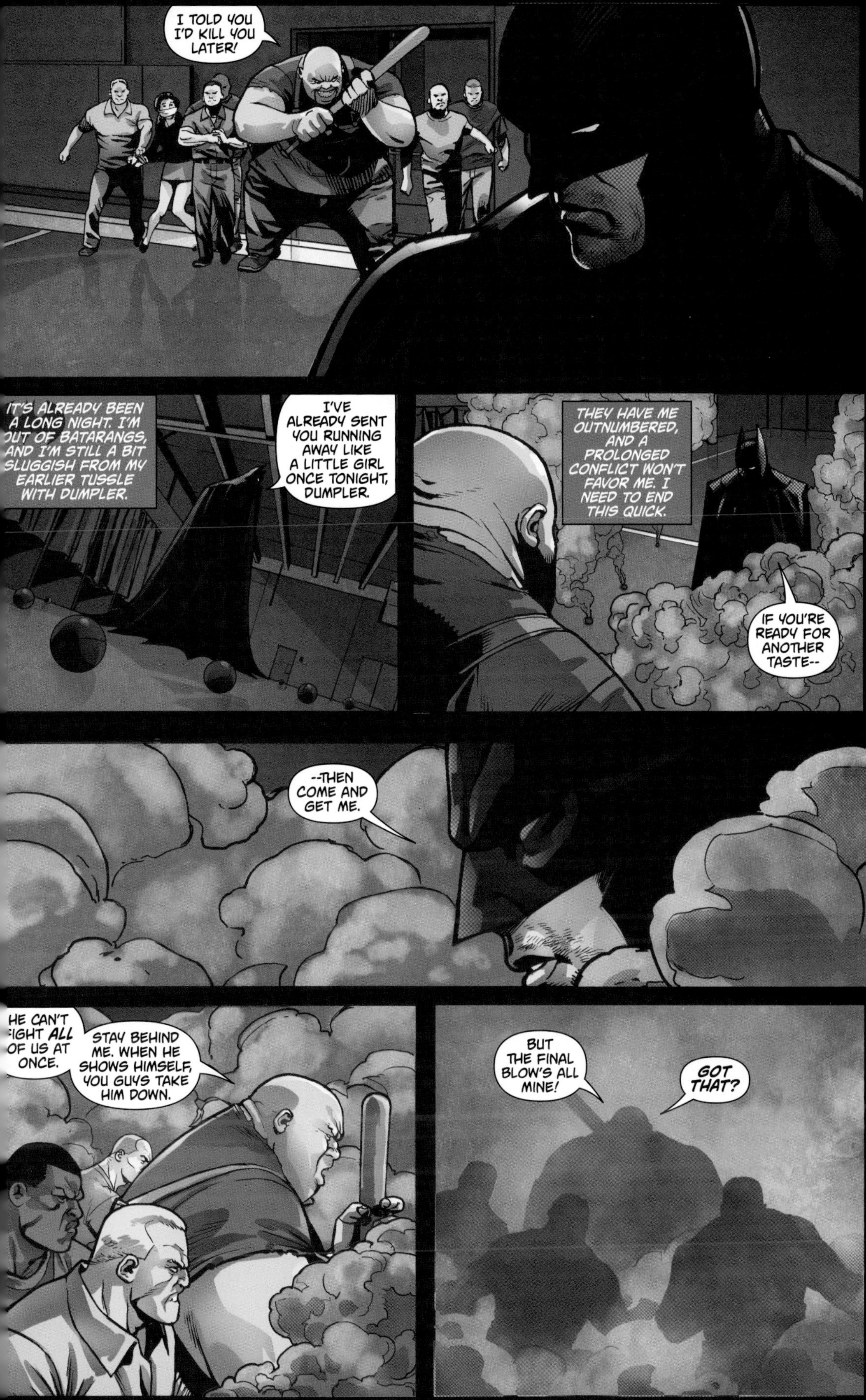
I TOLD YOU I'D KILL YOU LATER!
IT'S ALREADY BEEN A LONG NIGHT. I'M OUT OF BATARANGS, AND I'M STILL A BIT SLUGGISH FROM MY EARLIER TUSSLE WITH DUMPLER.
I'VE ALREADY SENT YOU RUNNING AWAY LIKE A LITTLE GIRL ONCE TONIGHT, DUMPLER.
THEY HAVE ME OUTNUMBERED, AND A PROLONGED CONFLICT WON'T FAVOR ME. I NEED TO END THIS QUICK.
IF YOU'RE READY FOR ANOTHER TASTE--
--THEN COME AND GET ME.
HE CAN'T FIGHT ALL OF US AT ONCE.
STAY BEHIND ME. WHEN HE SHOWS HIMSELF, YOU GUYS TAKE HIM DOWN.
BUT THE FINAL BLOW'S ALL MINE!
GOT THAT?

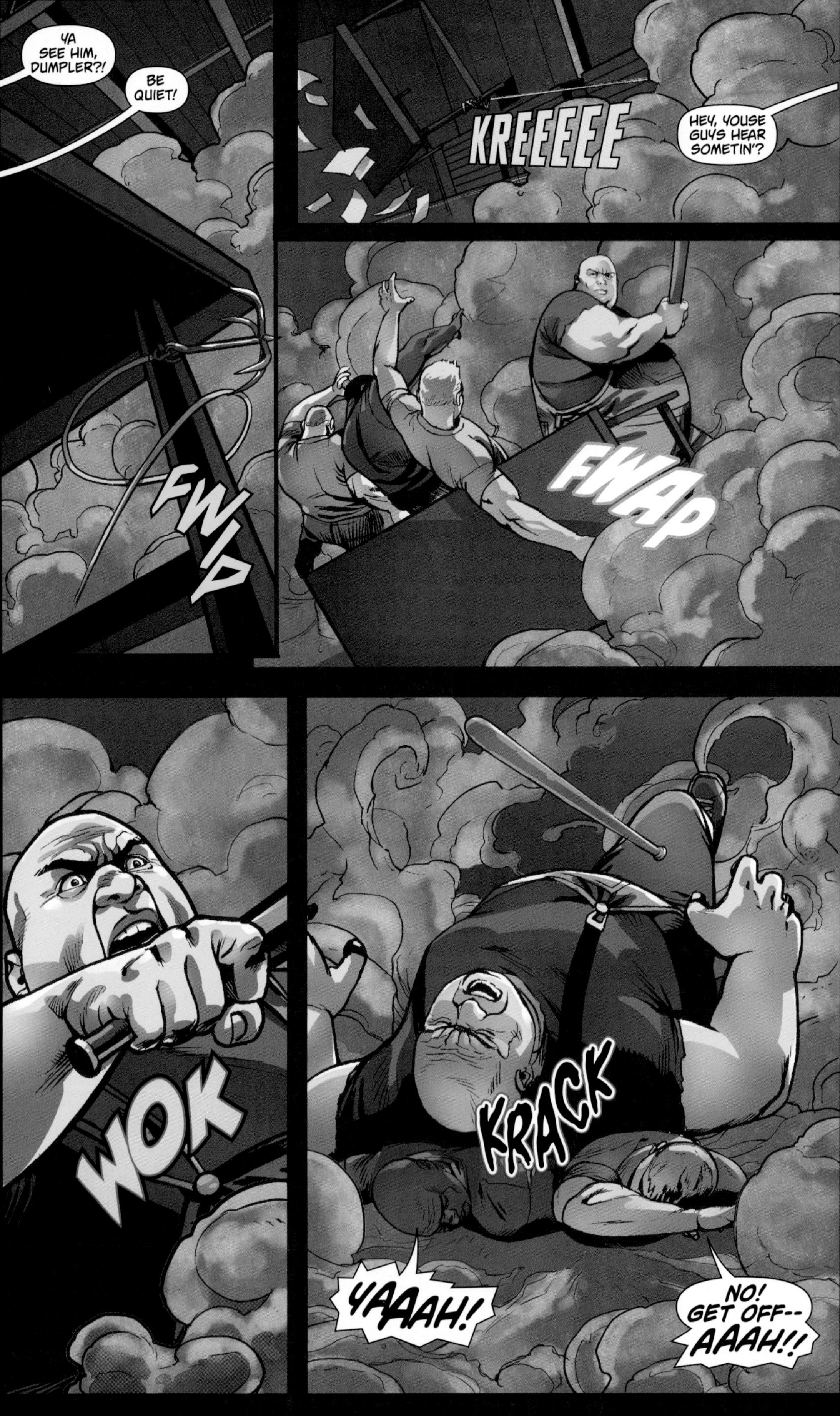

YA SEE HIM, DUMPLER?!
BE QUIET!
FWIP
KREEEEE
HEY, YOUSE GUYS HEAR SOMETIN'?
FWAP
WOK
KRACK
YAAAH!
NO! GET OFF-- AAAH!!

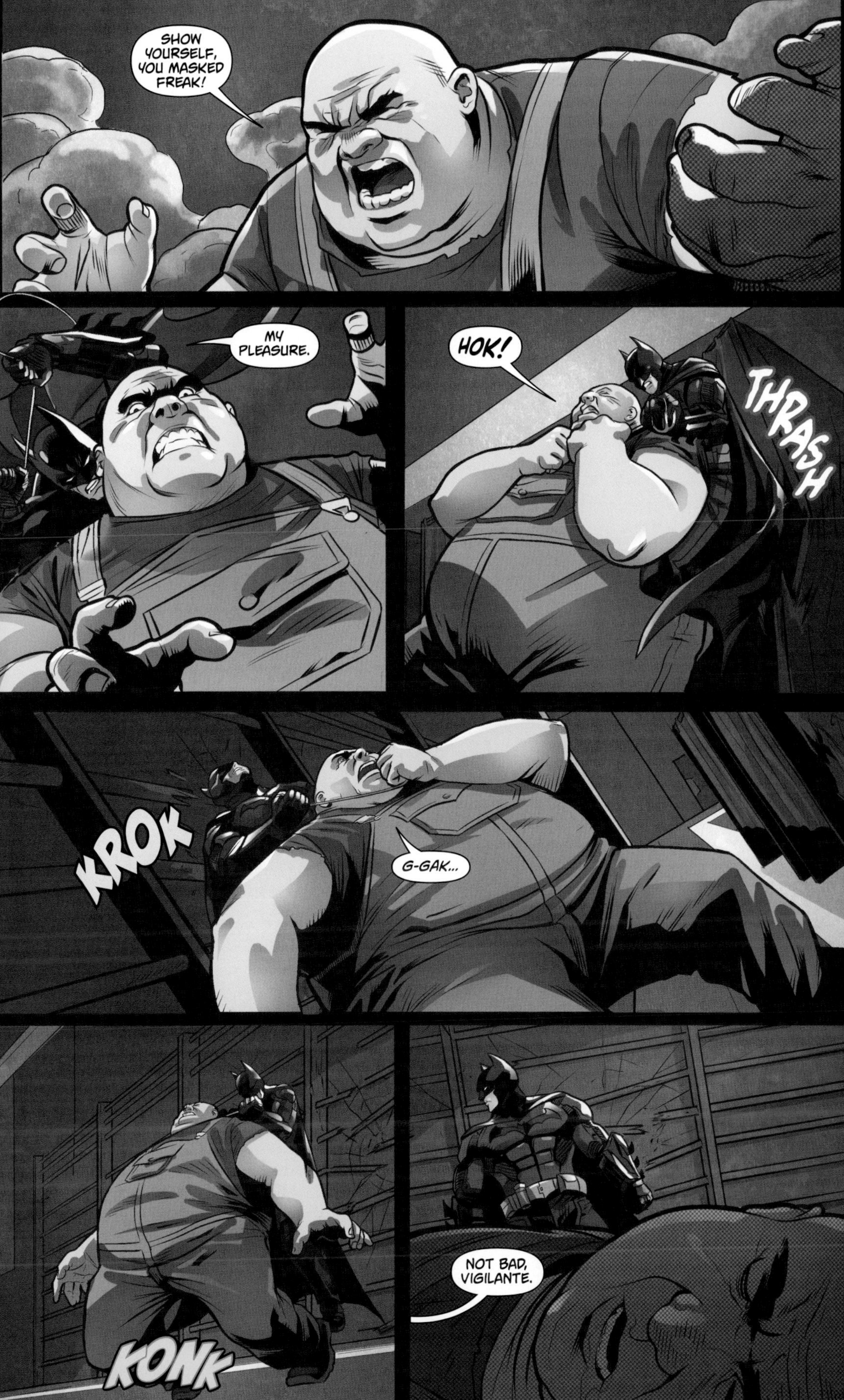
SHOW YOURSELF, YOU MASKED FREAK!
MY PLEASURE.
HOK!
THRASH
KROK
G-GAK...
KONK
NOT BAD, VIGILANTE.

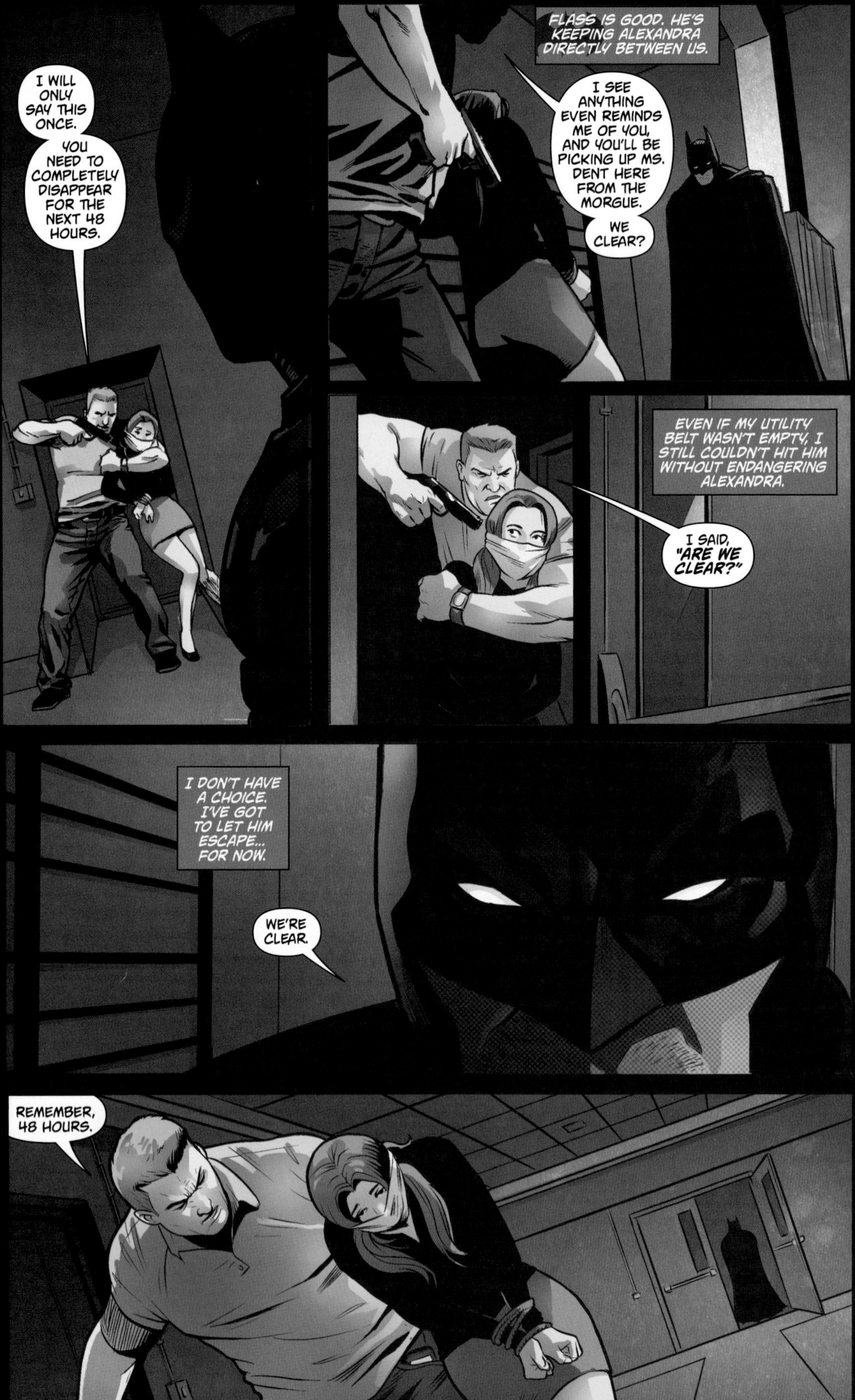
I WILL ONLY SAY THIS ONCE.
YOU NEED TO COMPLETELY DISAPPEAR FOR THE NEXT 48 HOURS.
FLASS IS GOOD. HE'S KEEPING ALEXANDRA DIRECTLY BETWEEN US.
I SEE ANYTHING EVEN REMINDS ME OF YOU, AND YOU'LL BE PICKING UP MS. DENT HERE FROM THE MORGUE.
WE CLEAR?
EVEN IF MY UTILITY BELT WASN'T EMPTY, I STILL COULDN'T HIT HIM WITHOUT ENDANGERING ALEXANDRA.
I SAID, "ARE WE CLEAR?"
I DON'T HAVE A CHOICE. I'VE GOT TO LET HIM ESCAPE... FOR NOW.
WE'RE CLEAR.
REMEMBER, 48 HOURS.

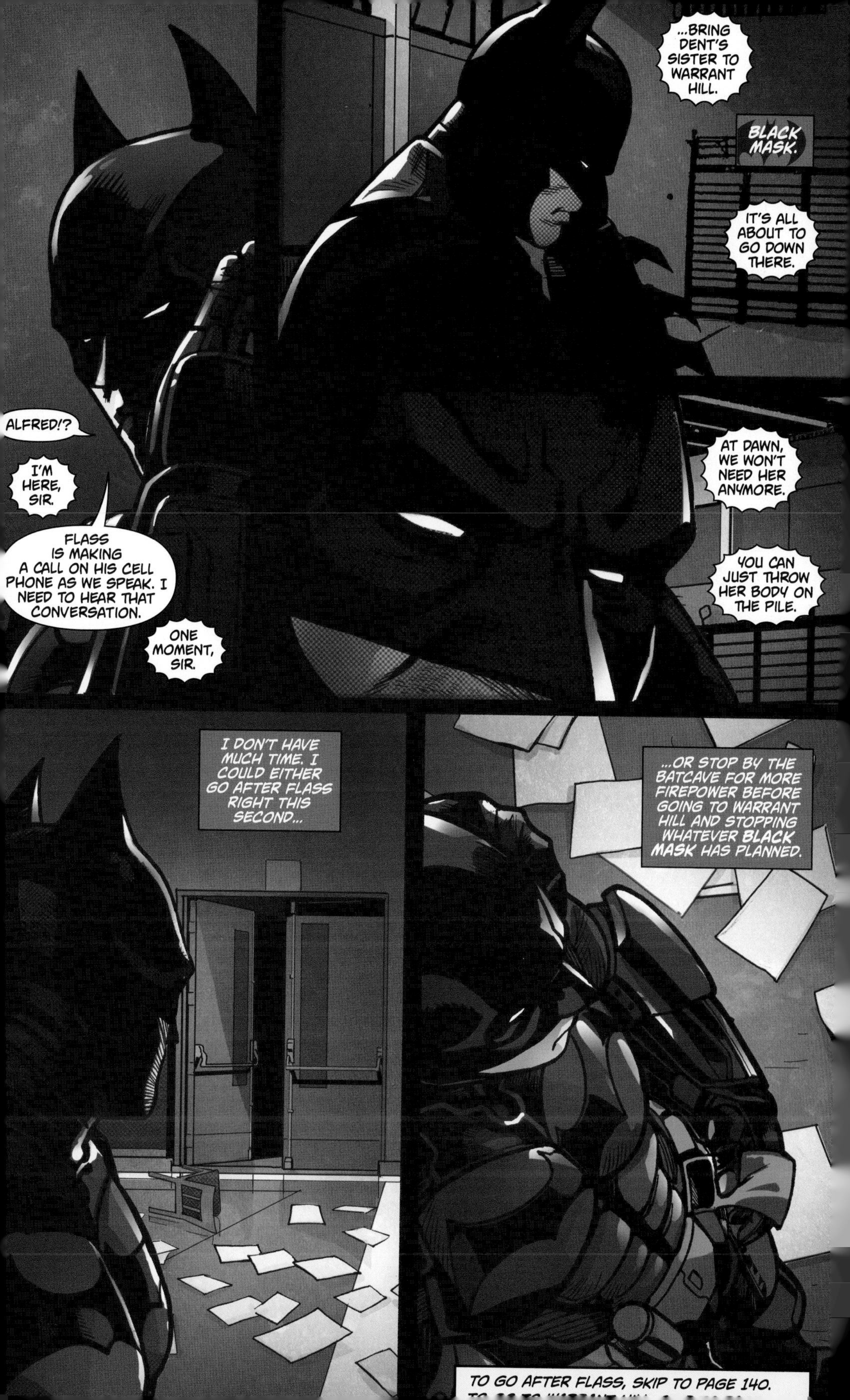
ALFRED!?
I'M HERE, SIR.
FLASS IS MAKING A CALL ON HIS CELL PHONE AS WE SPEAK. I NEED TO HEAR THAT CONVERSATION.
ONE MOMENT, SIR.
...BRING DENT'S SISTER TO WARRANT HILL.
BLACK MASK.
IT'S ALL ABOUT TO GO DOWN THERE.
AT DAWN, WE WON'T NEED HER ANYMORE.
YOU CAN JUST THROW HER BODY ON THE PILE.
I DON'T HAVE MUCH TIME. I COULD EITHER GO AFTER FLASS RIGHT THIS SECOND...
...OR STOP BY THE BATCAVE FOR MORE FIREPOWER BEFORE GOING TO WARRANT HILL AND STOPPING WHATEVER BLACK MASK HAS PLANNED.
TO GO AFTER FLASS, SKIP TO PAGE 140.

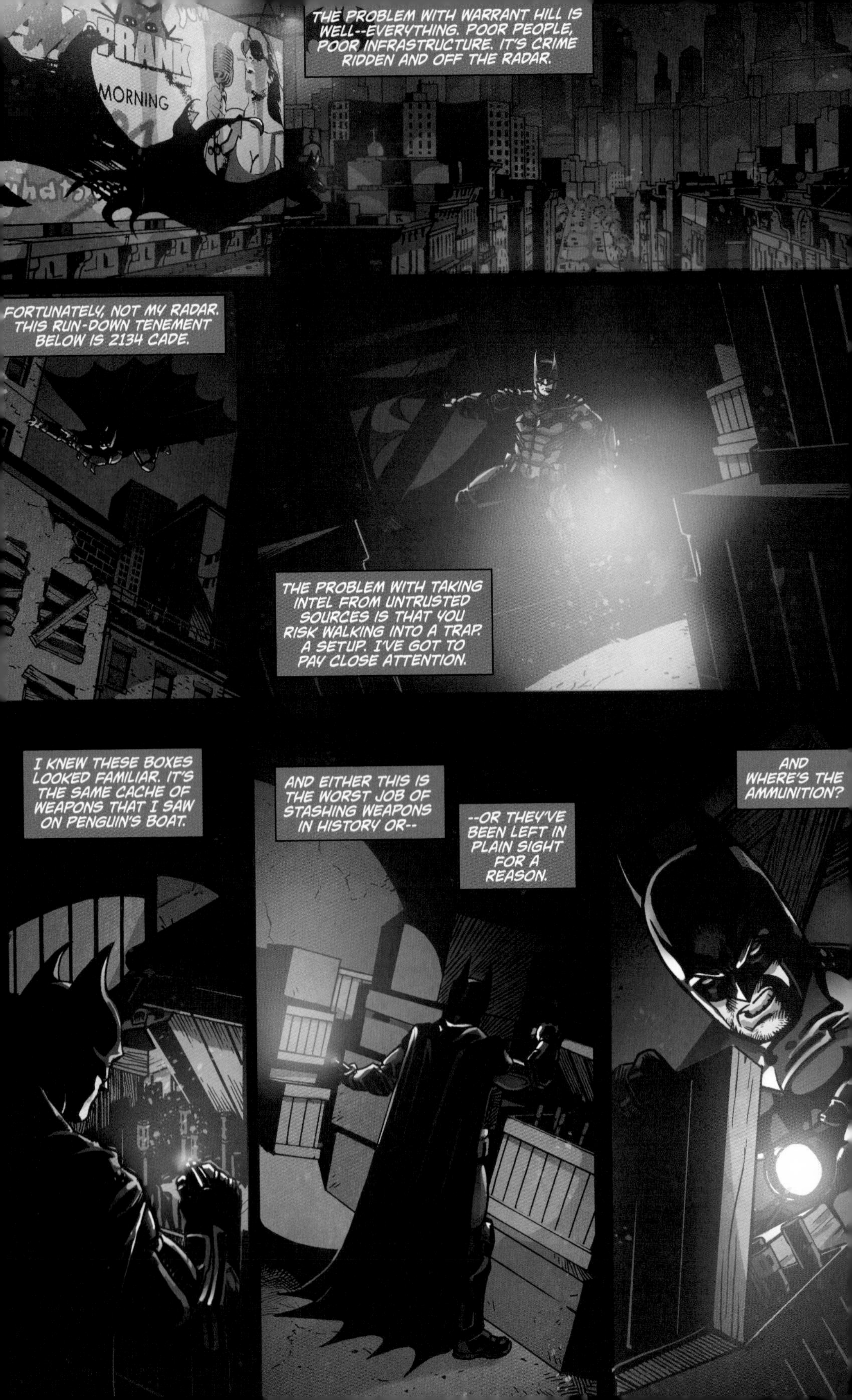
THE PROBLEM WITH WARRANT HILL IS WELL--EVERYTHING. POOR PEOPLE, POOR INFRASTRUCTURE. IT'S CRIME RIDDEN AND OFF THE RADAR.
MORNING
FORTUNATELY, NOT MY RADAR. THIS RUN-DOWN TENEMENT BELOW IS 2134 CADE.
THE PROBLEM WITH TAKING INTEL FROM UNTRUSTED SOURCES IS THAT YOU RISK WALKING INTO A TRAP. A SETUP. I'VE GOT TO PAY CLOSE ATTENTION.
I KNEW THESE BOXES LOOKED FAMILIAR. IT'S THE SAME CACHE OF WEAPONS THAT I SAW ON PENGUIN'S BOAT.
AND EITHER THIS IS THE WORST JOB OF STASHING WEAPONS IN HISTORY OR--
--OR THEY'VE BEEN LEFT IN PLAIN SIGHT FOR A REASON.
AND WHERE'S THE AMMUNITION?

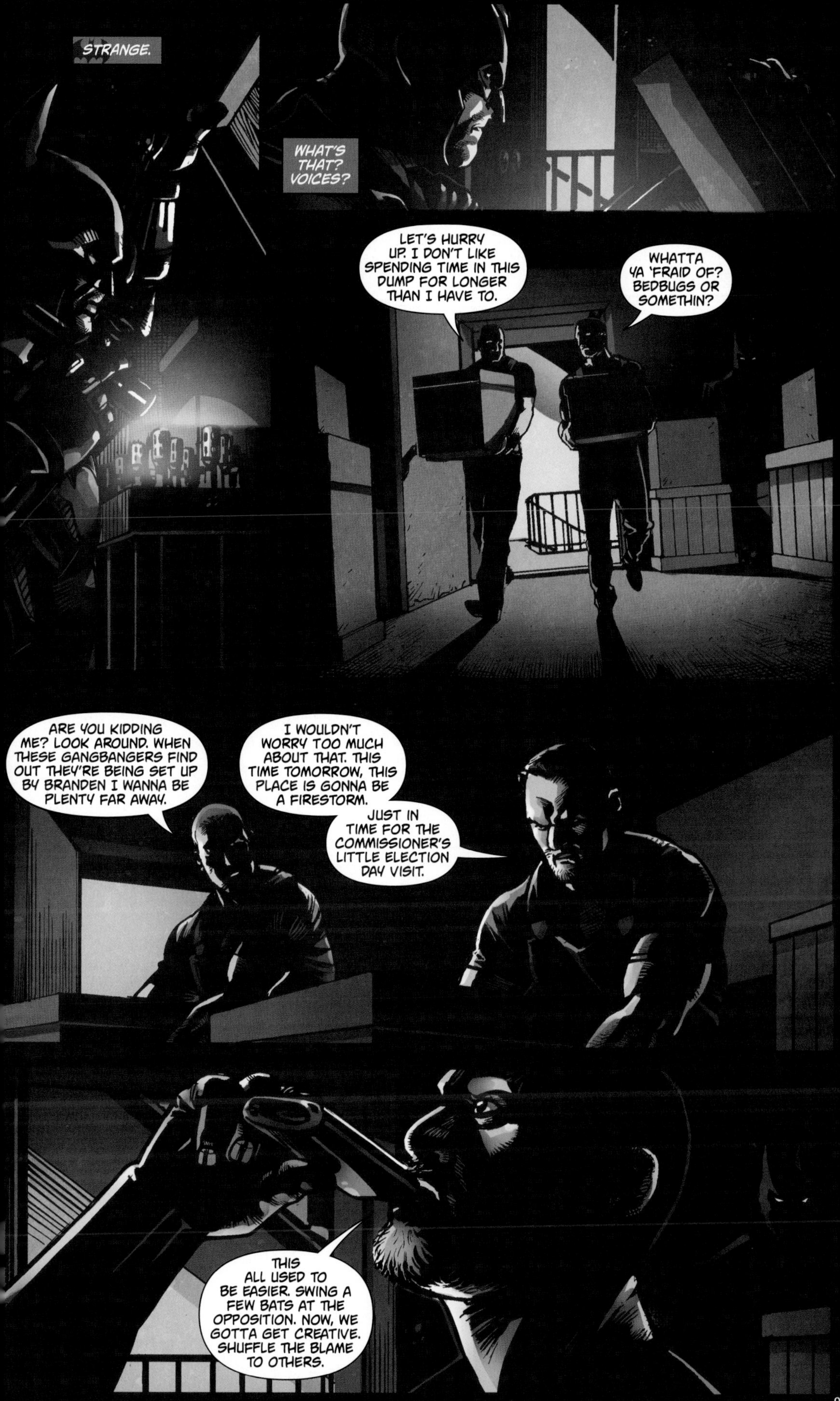
STRANGE.
WHAT'S THAT? VOICES?
LET'S HURRY UP. I DON'T LIKE SPENDING TIME IN THIS DUMP FOR LONGER THAN I HAVE TO.
WHATTA YA 'FRAID OF? BEDBUGS OR SOMETHIN?
ARE YOU KIDDING ME? LOOK AROUND. WHEN THESE GANGBANGERS FIND OUT THEY'RE BEING SET UP BY BRANDEN I WANNA BE PLENTY FAR AWAY.
I WOULDN'T WORRY TOO MUCH ABOUT THAT. THIS TIME TOMORROW, THIS PLACE IS GONNA BE A FIRESTORM.
JUST IN TIME FOR THE COMMISSIONER'S LITTLE ELECTION DAY VISIT.
THIS ALL USED TO BE EASIER. SWING A FEW BATS AT THE OPPOSITION. NOW, WE GOTTA GET CREATIVE. SHUFFLE THE BLAME TO OTHERS.

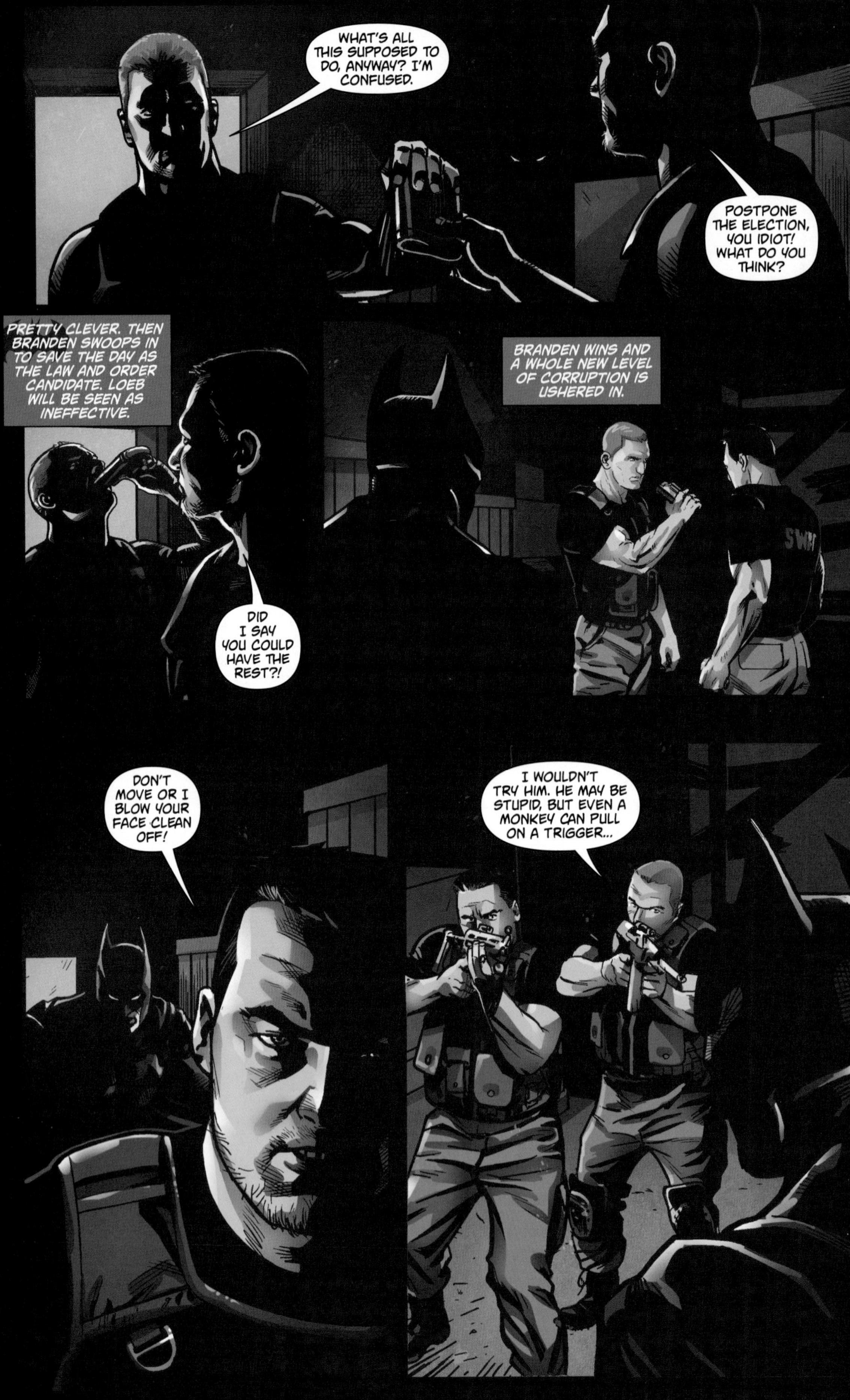
WHAT'S ALL THIS SUPPOSED TO DO, ANYWAY? I'M CONFUSED.
POSTPONE THE ELECTION, YOU IDIOT! WHAT DO YOU THINK?
PRETTY CLEVER. THEN BRANDEN SWOOPS IN TO SAVE THE DAY AS THE LAW AND ORDER CANDIDATE. LOEB WILL BE SEEN AS INEFFECTIVE.
DID I SAY YOU COULD HAVE THE REST?!
BRANDEN WINS AND A WHOLE NEW LEVEL OF CORRUPTION IS USHERED IN.
DON'T MOVE OR I BLOW YOUR FACE CLEAN OFF!
I WOULDN'T TRY HIM. HE MAY BE STUPID, BUT EVEN A MONKEY CAN PULL ON A TRIGGER...

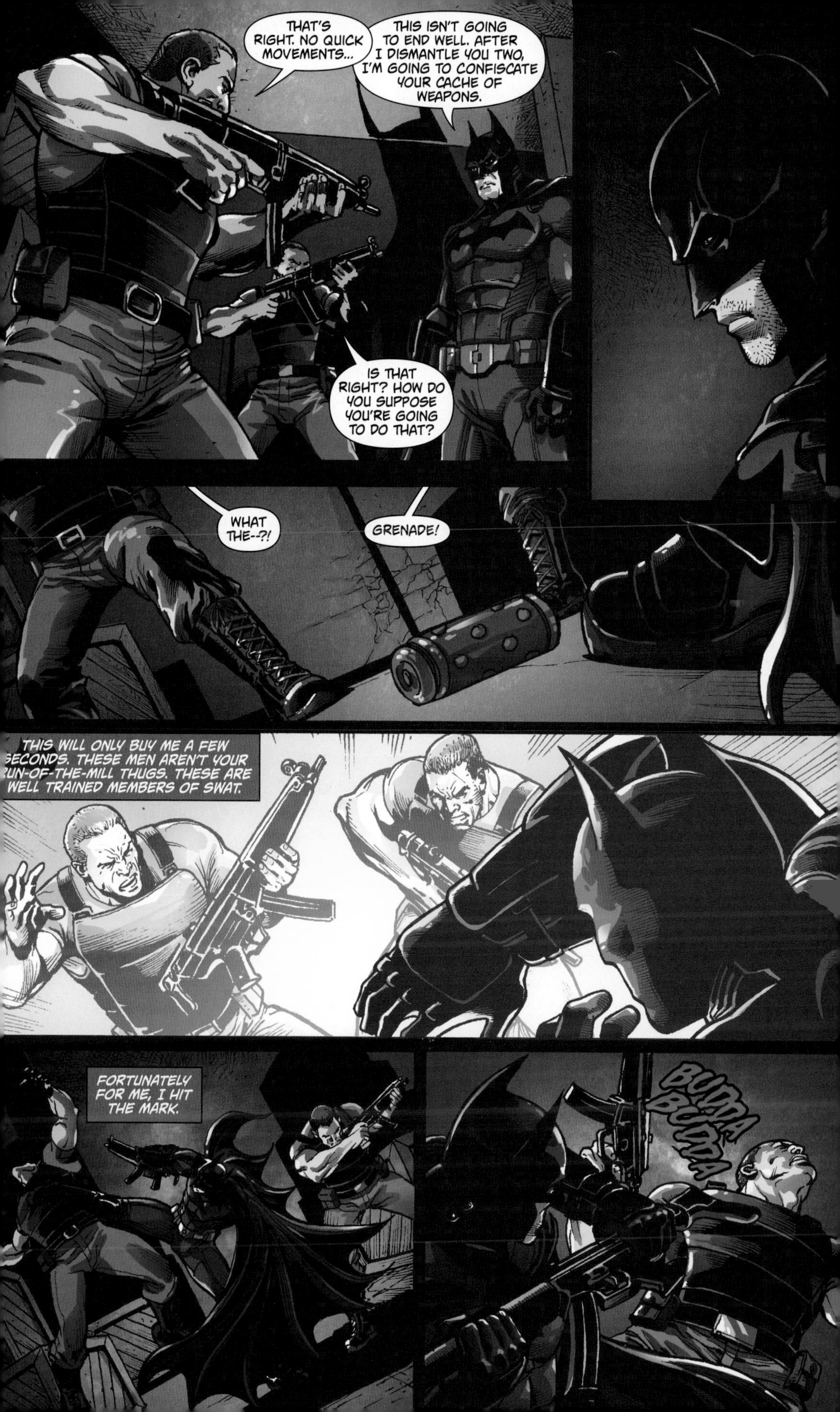
THAT'S RIGHT. NO QUICK MOVEMENTS...
THIS ISN'T GOING TO END WELL. AFTER I DISMANTLE YOU TWO, I'M GOING TO CONFISCATE YOUR CACHE OF WEAPONS.
IS THAT RIGHT? HOW DO YOU SUPPOSE YOU'RE GOING TO DO THAT?
WHAT THE--?!
GRENADE!
THIS WILL ONLY BUY ME A FEW SECONDS. THESE MEN AREN'T YOUR RUN-OF-THE-MILL THUGS. THESE ARE WELL TRAINED MEMBERS OF SWAT.
FORTUNATELY FOR ME, I HIT THE MARK.
BUDDA
BUDDA

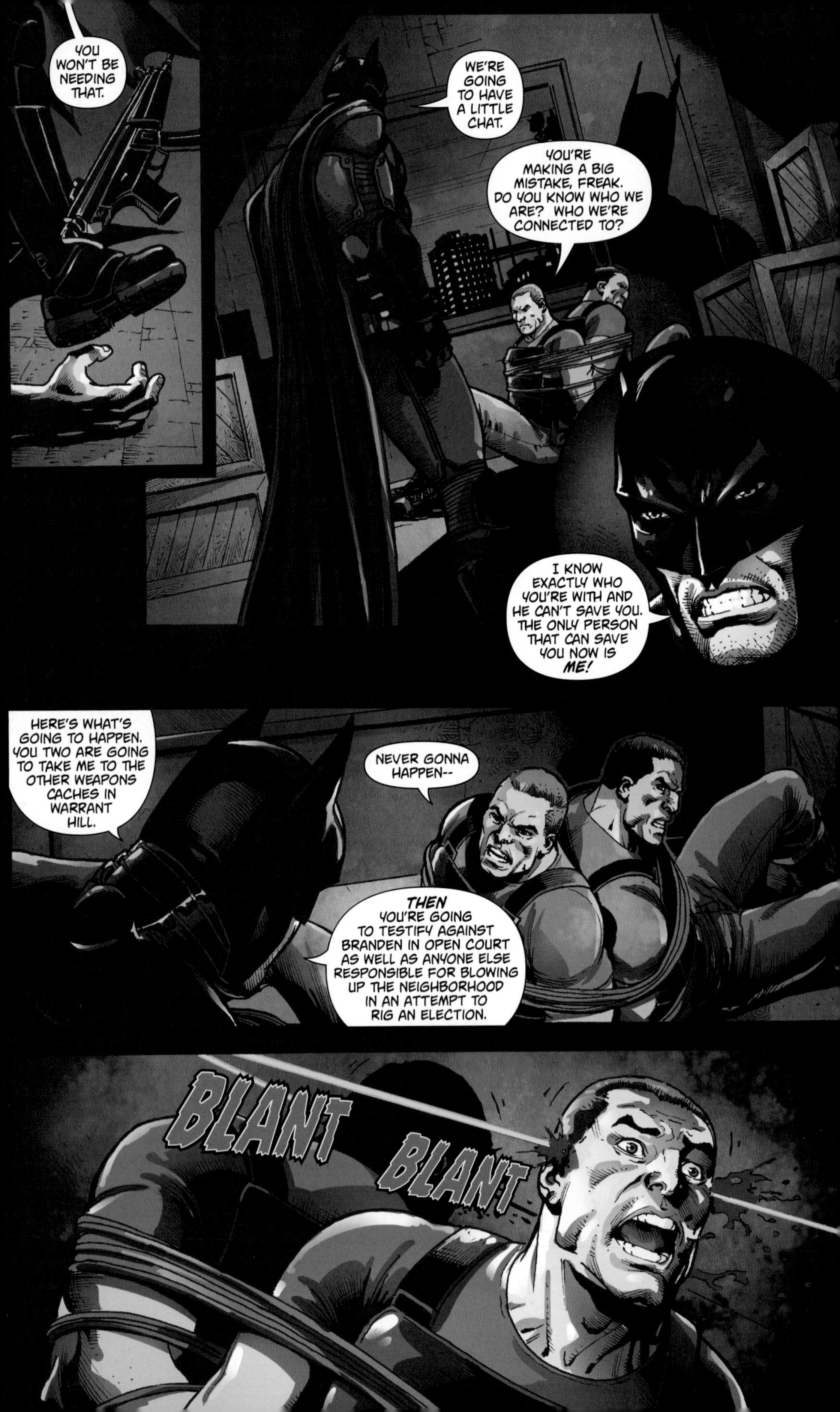
YOU WON'T BE NEEDING THAT.
WE'RE GOING TO HAVE A LITTLE CHAT.
YOU'RE MAKING A BIG MISTAKE, FREAK. DO YOU KNOW WHO WE ARE? WHO WE'RE CONNECTED TO?
I KNOW EXACTLY WHO YOU'RE WITH AND HE CAN'T SAVE YOU. THE ONLY PERSON THAT CAN SAVE YOU NOW IS ME!
HERE'S WHAT'S GOING TO HAPPEN. YOU TWO ARE GOING TO TAKE ME TO THE OTHER WEAPONS CACHES IN WARRANT HILL.
NEVER GONNA HAPPEN--
THEN YOU'RE GOING TO TESTIFY AGAINST BRANDEN IN OPEN COURT AS WELL AS ANYONE ELSE RESPONSIBLE FOR BLOWING UP THE NEIGHBORHOOD IN AN ATTEMPT TO RIG AN ELECTION.
BLANT
BLANT

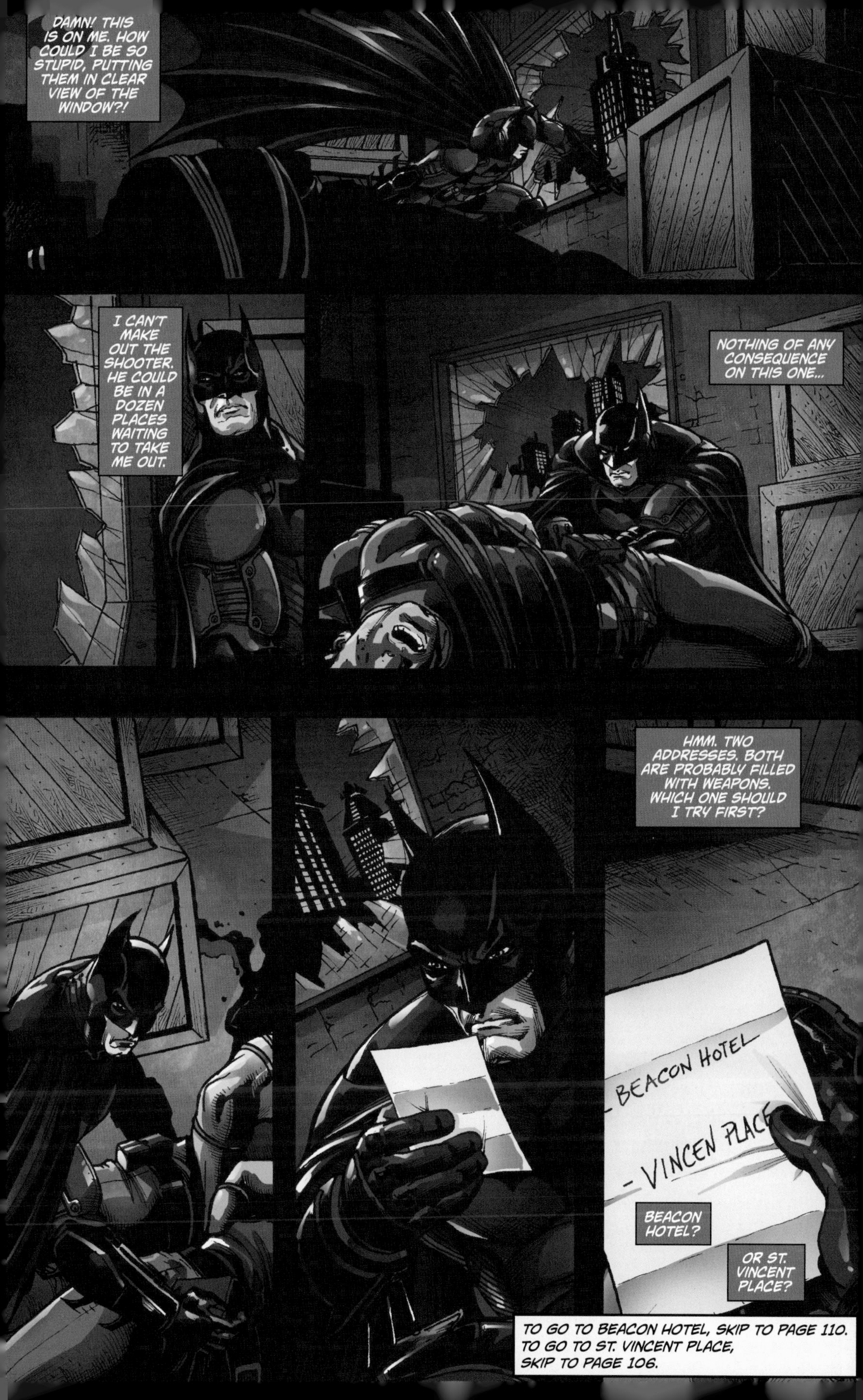
DAMN! THIS IS ON ME. HOW COULD I BE SO STUPID, PUTTING THEM IN CLEAR VIEW OF THE WINDOW?!
I CAN'T MAKE OUT THE SHOOTER. HE COULD BE IN A DOZEN PLACES WAITING TO TAKE ME OUT.
NOTHING OF ANY CONSEQUENCE ON THIS ONE...
HMM. TWO ADDRESSES. BOTH ARE PROBABLY FILLED WITH WEAPONS. WHICH ONE SHOULD I TRY FIRST?
BEACON HOTEL
VINCEN PLACE
BEACON HOTEL?
OR ST. VINCENT PLACE?

TO GO TO BEACON HOTEL, SKIP TO PAGE 110.
TO GO TO ST. VINCENT PLACE, SKIP TO PAGE 106.

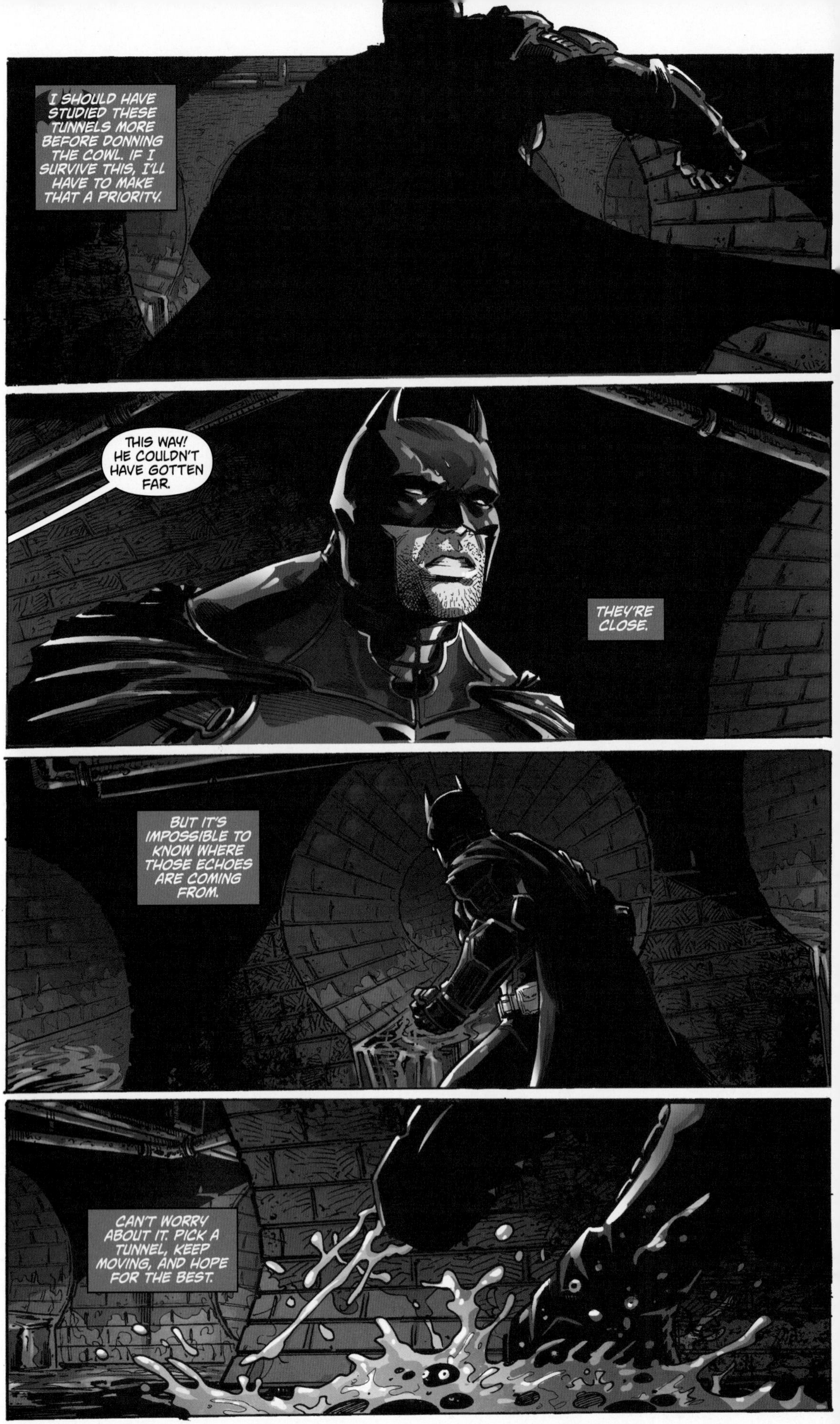
I SHOULD HAVE STUDIED THESE TUNNELS MORE BEFORE DONNING THE COWL. IF I SURVIVE THIS, I'LL HAVE TO MAKE THAT A PRIORITY.
THIS WAY! HE COULDN'T HAVE GOTTEN FAR.
THEY'RE CLOSE.
BUT IT'S IMPOSSIBLE TO KNOW WHERE THOSE ECHOES ARE COMING FROM.
CAN'T WORRY ABOUT IT. PICK A TUNNEL, KEEP MOVING, AND HOPE FOR THE BEST.

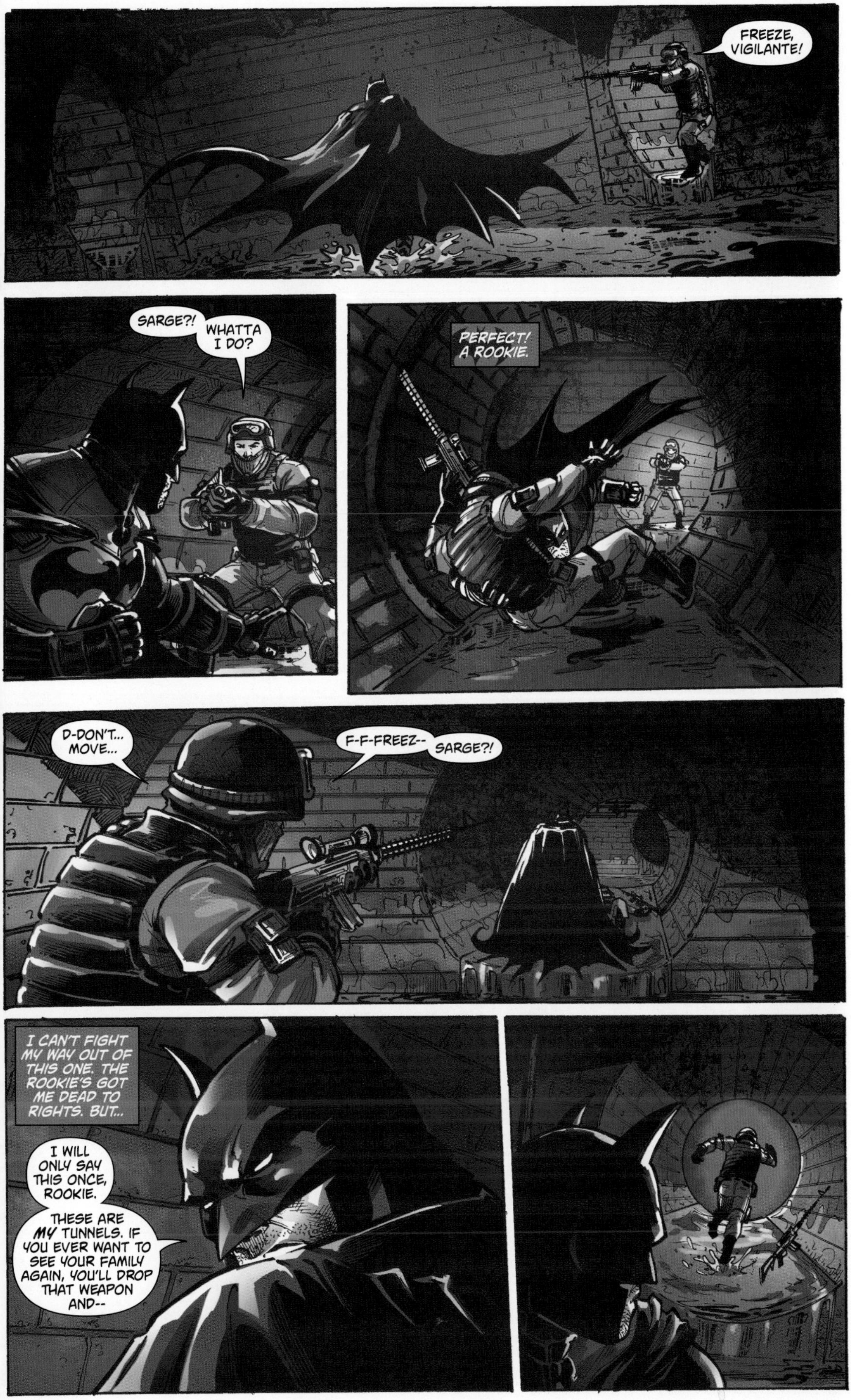
FREEZE, VIGILANTE!
SARGE?!
WHATTA I DO?
PERFECT! A ROOKIE.
D-DON'T... MOVE...
F-F-FREEZ--
SARGE?!
I CAN'T FIGHT MY WAY OUT OF THIS ONE. THE ROOKIE'S GOT ME DEAD TO RIGHTS. BUT...
I WILL ONLY SAY THIS ONCE, ROOKIE.
THESE ARE MY TUNNELS. IF YOU EVER WANT TO SEE YOUR FAMILY AGAIN, YOU'LL DROP THAT WEAPON AND--

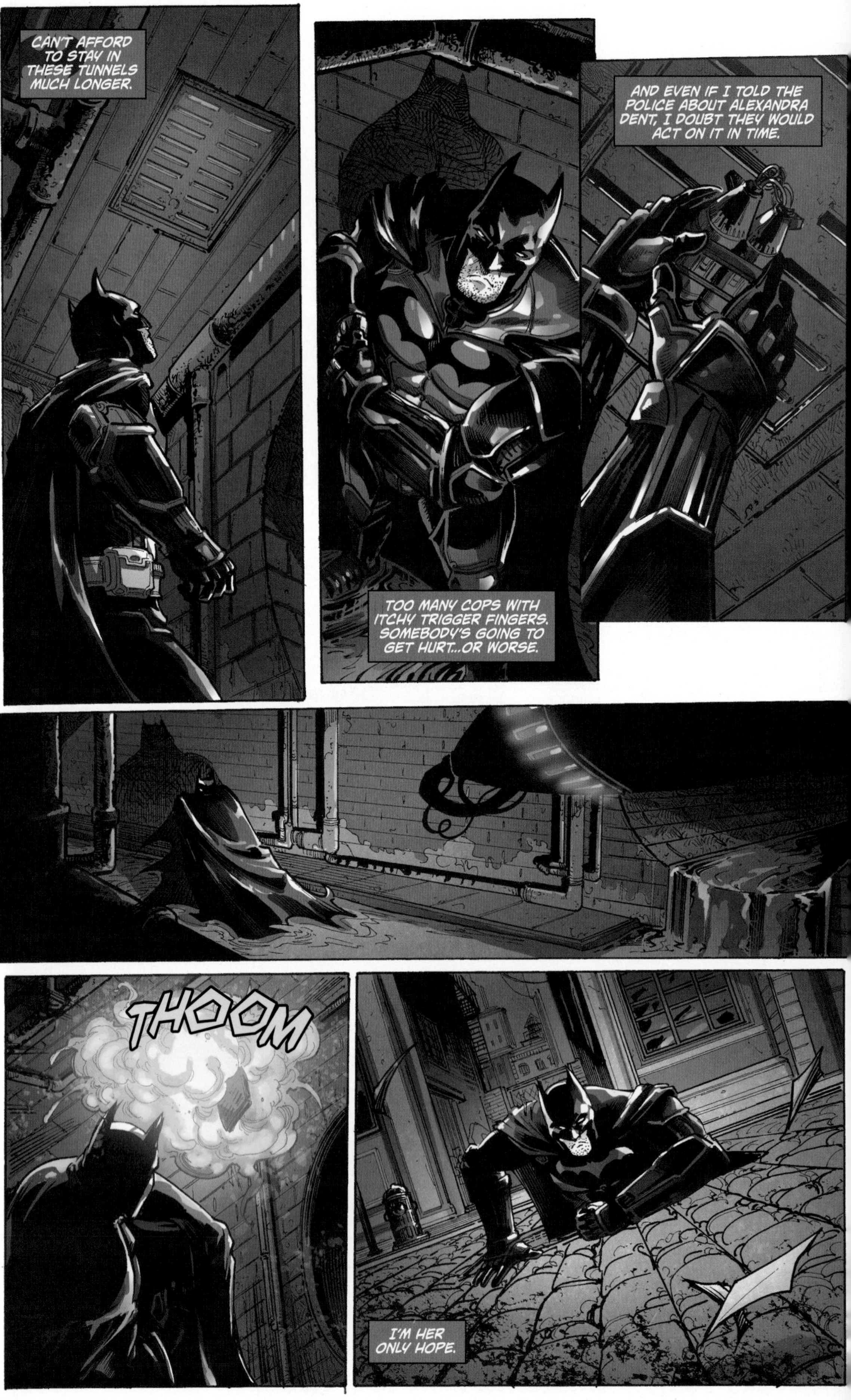
CAN'T AFFORD TO STAY IN THESE TUNNELS MUCH LONGER.
TOO MANY COPS WITH ITCHY TRIGGER FINGERS. SOMEBODY'S GOING TO GET HURT...OR WORSE.
AND EVEN IF I TOLD THE POLICE ABOUT ALEXANDRA DENT, I DOUBT THEY WOULD ACT ON IT IN TIME.
THOOM
I'M HER ONLY HOPE.

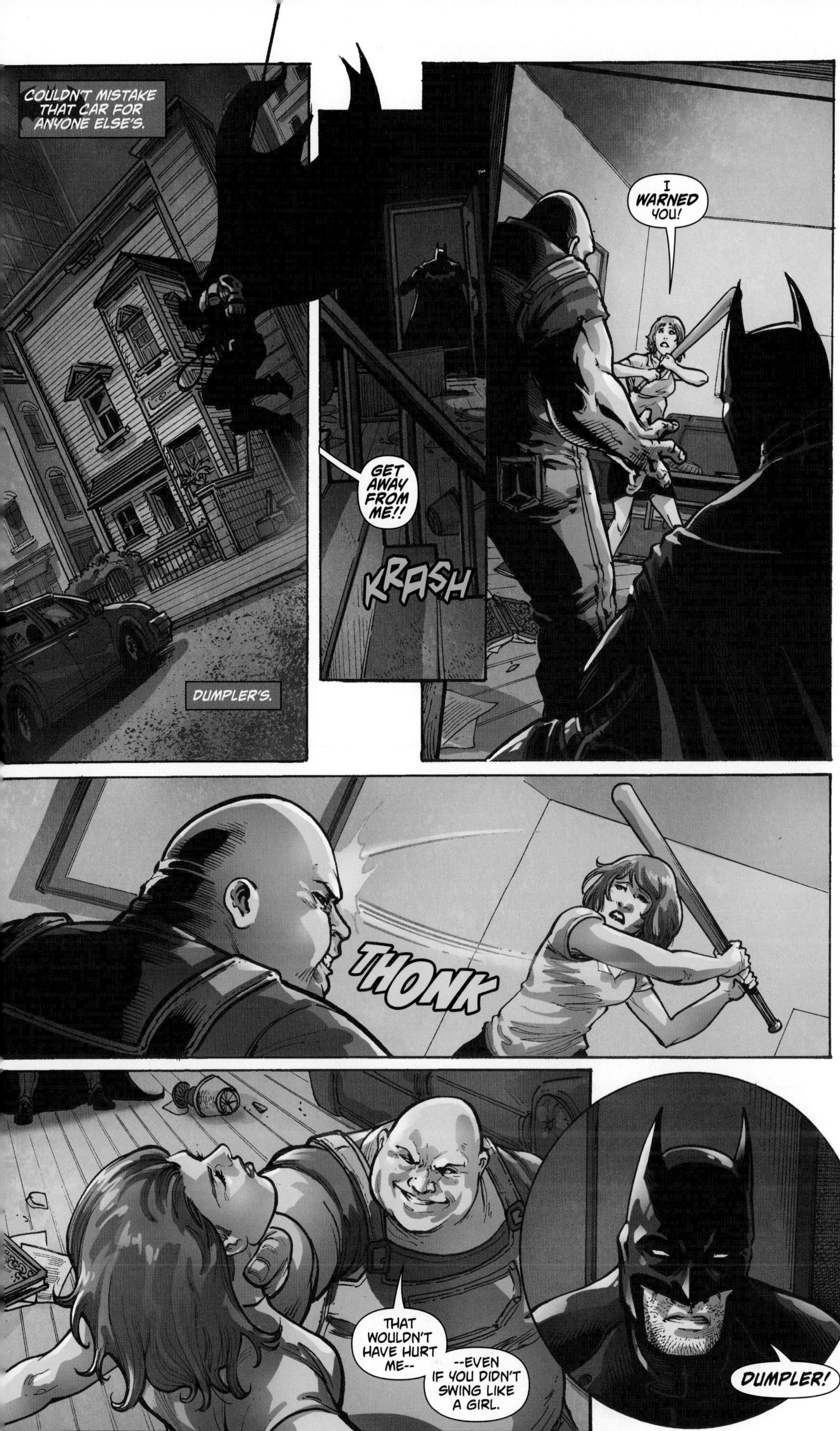
COULDN'T MISTAKE THAT CAR FOR ANYONE ELSE'S.
DUMPLER'S.
GET AWAY FROM ME!!
KRASH
I WARNED YOU!
THONK
THAT WOULDN'T HAVE HURT ME--
--EVEN IF YOU DIDN'T SWING LIKE A GIRL.
DUMPLER!

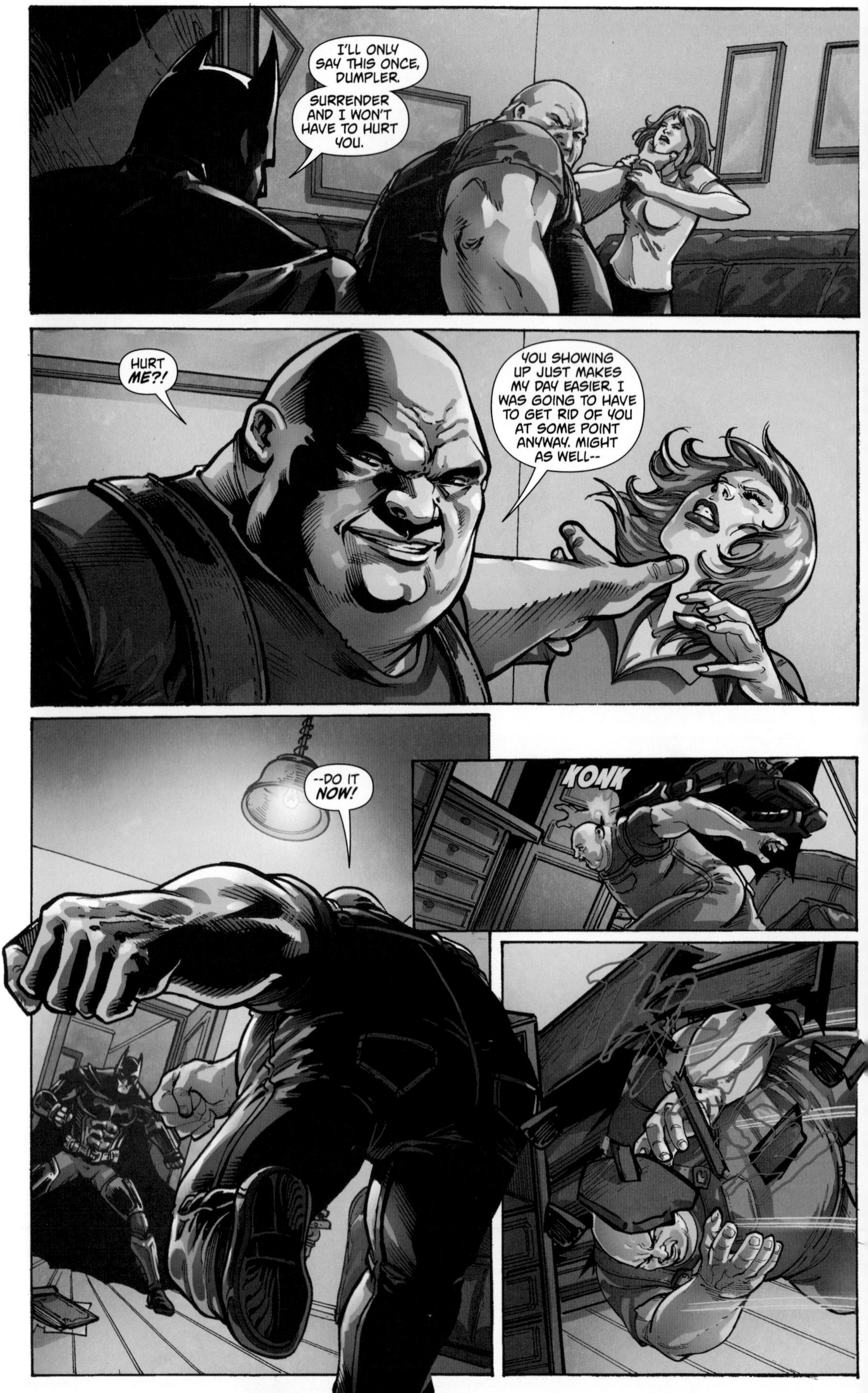
I'LL ONLY SAY THIS ONCE, DUMPLER.
SURRENDER AND I WON'T HAVE TO HURT YOU.
HURT *ME?!*
YOU SHOWING UP JUST MAKES MY DAY EASIER. I WAS GOING TO HAVE TO GET RID OF YOU AT SOME POINT ANYWAY. MIGHT AS WELL--
--DO IT *NOW!*
KONK

KAK

TONK

YWAK

YOU TWO JUST DON'T GET IT, DO YOU?

IT TAKES A LOT MORE THAN A BASEBALL BAT OR A SISSY KICK TO COME CLOSE TO SLOWING ME DOWN.

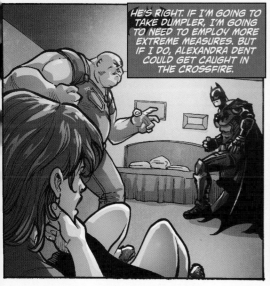

HE'S RIGHT. IF I'M GOING TO TAKE DUMPLER, I'M GOING TO NEED TO EMPLOY MORE EXTREME MEASURES. BUT IF I DO, ALEXANDRA DENT COULD GET CAUGHT IN THE CROSSFIRE.

I SEE TWO OPTIONS HERE. GET HIM IN CLOSE AND USE MY GRAPNEL AT POINT-BLANK RANGE...

...OR I THROW THE FIGHT AND LET DUMPLER KIDNAP ALEXANDRA. IF I FOLLOW HIM, HE MAY LEAD ME TO BIGGER FISH.

TO USE YOUR GRAPNEL, SKIP TO PAGE 114.
TO THROW THE FIGHT, GO BACK TO PAGE 84.

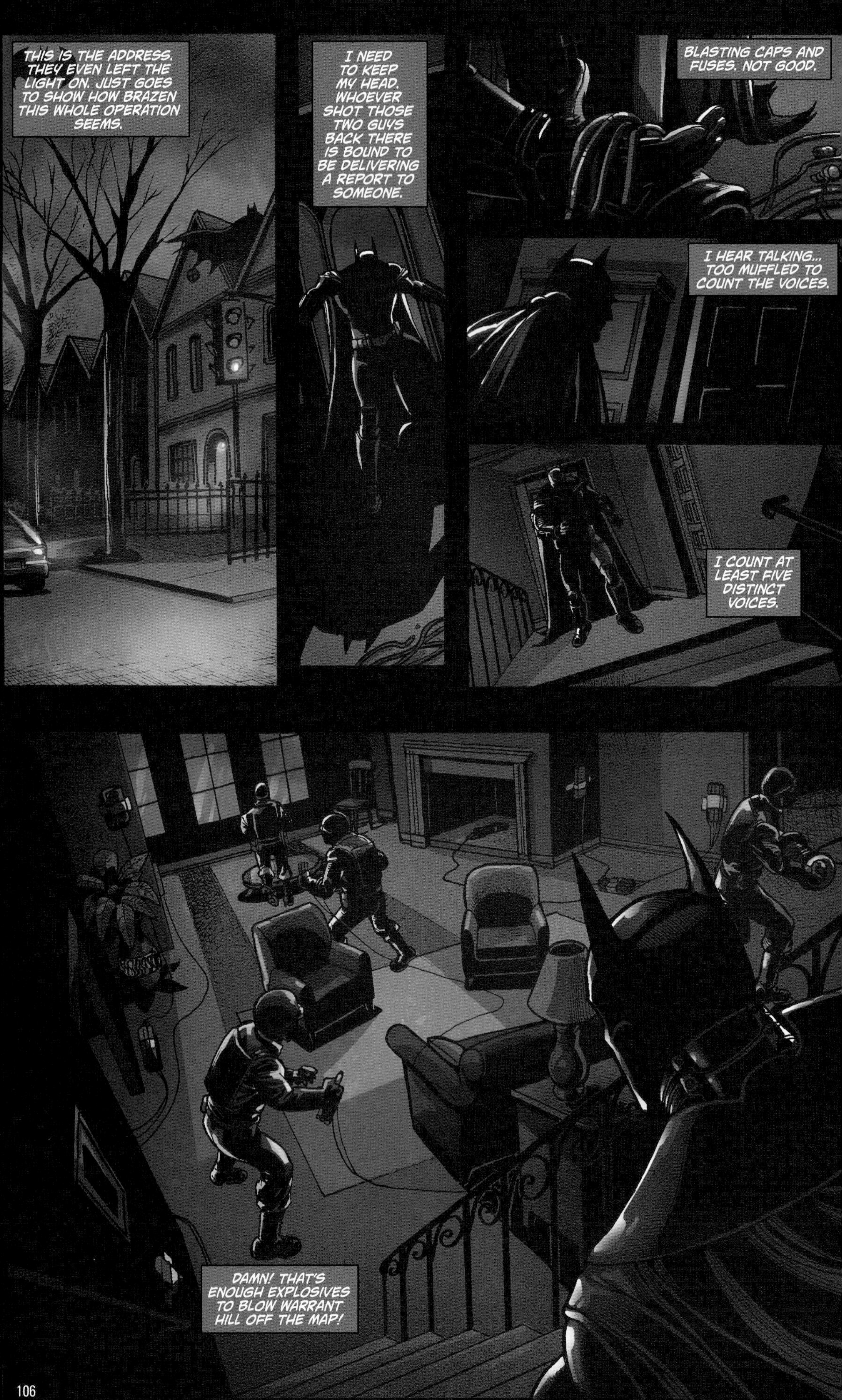
THIS IS THE ADDRESS. THEY EVEN LEFT THE LIGHT ON. JUST GOES TO SHOW HOW BRAZEN THIS WHOLE OPERATION SEEMS.
I NEED TO KEEP MY HEAD. WHOEVER SHOT THOSE TWO GUYS BACK THERE IS BOUND TO BE DELIVERING A REPORT TO SOMEONE.
BLASTING CAPS AND FUSES. NOT GOOD.
I HEAR TALKING... TOO MUFFLED TO COUNT THE VOICES.
I COUNT AT LEAST FIVE DISTINCT VOICES.
DAMN! THAT'S ENOUGH EXPLOSIVES TO BLOW WARRANT HILL OFF THE MAP!

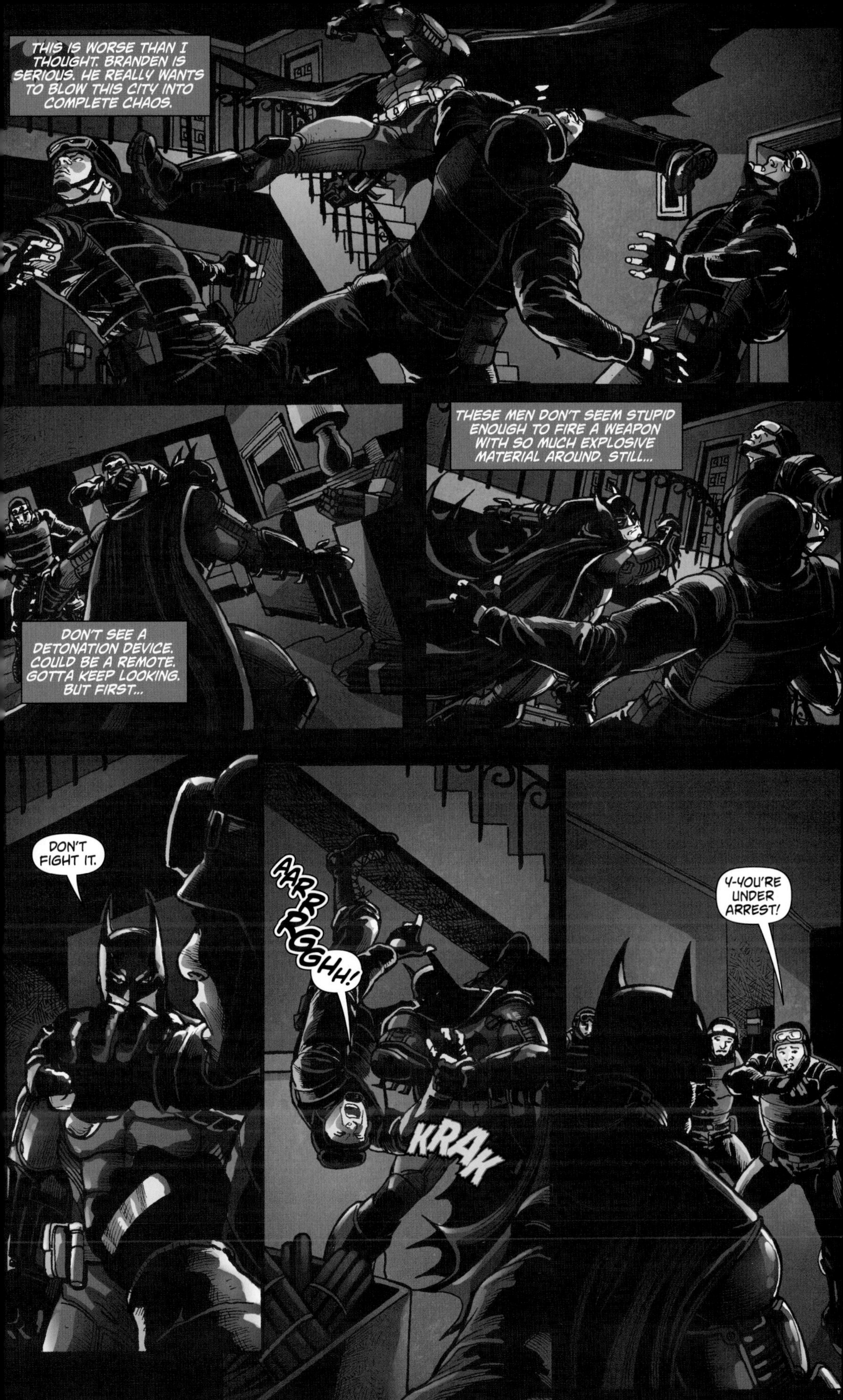
THIS IS WORSE THAN I THOUGHT. BRANDEN IS SERIOUS. HE REALLY WANTS TO BLOW THIS CITY INTO COMPLETE CHAOS.
DON'T SEE A DETONATION DEVICE. COULD BE A REMOTE. GOTTA KEEP LOOKING. BUT FIRST...
THESE MEN DON'T SEEM STUPID ENOUGH TO FIRE A WEAPON WITH SO MUCH EXPLOSIVE MATERIAL AROUND. STILL...
DON'T FIGHT IT.
AARRRGGHH!
KRAK
Y-YOU'RE UNDER ARREST!

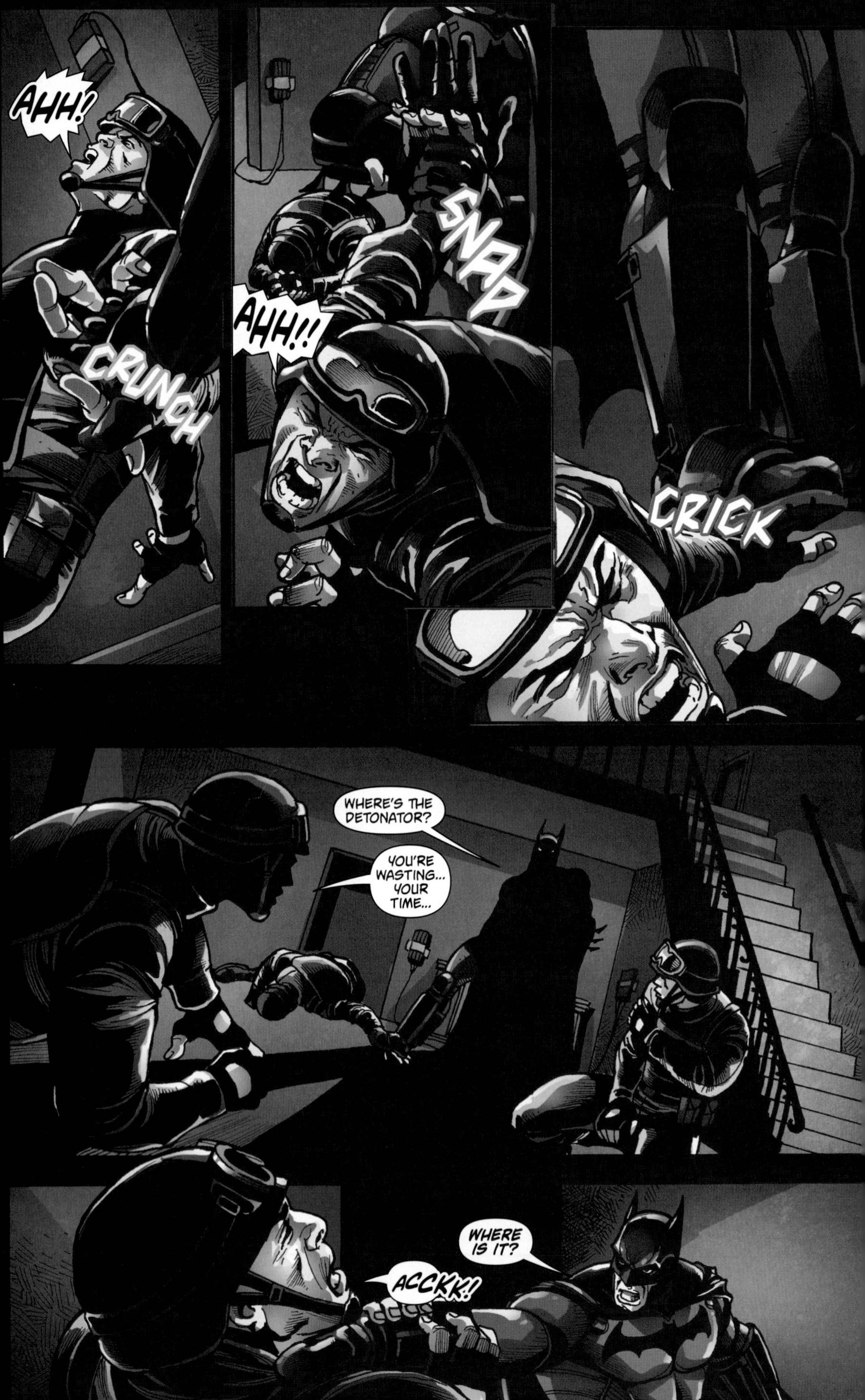

AHH!
CRUNCH
AHH!!
SNAP
CRICK
WHERE'S THE DETONATOR?
YOU'RE WASTING... YOUR TIME...
WHERE IS IT?
ACCKK!

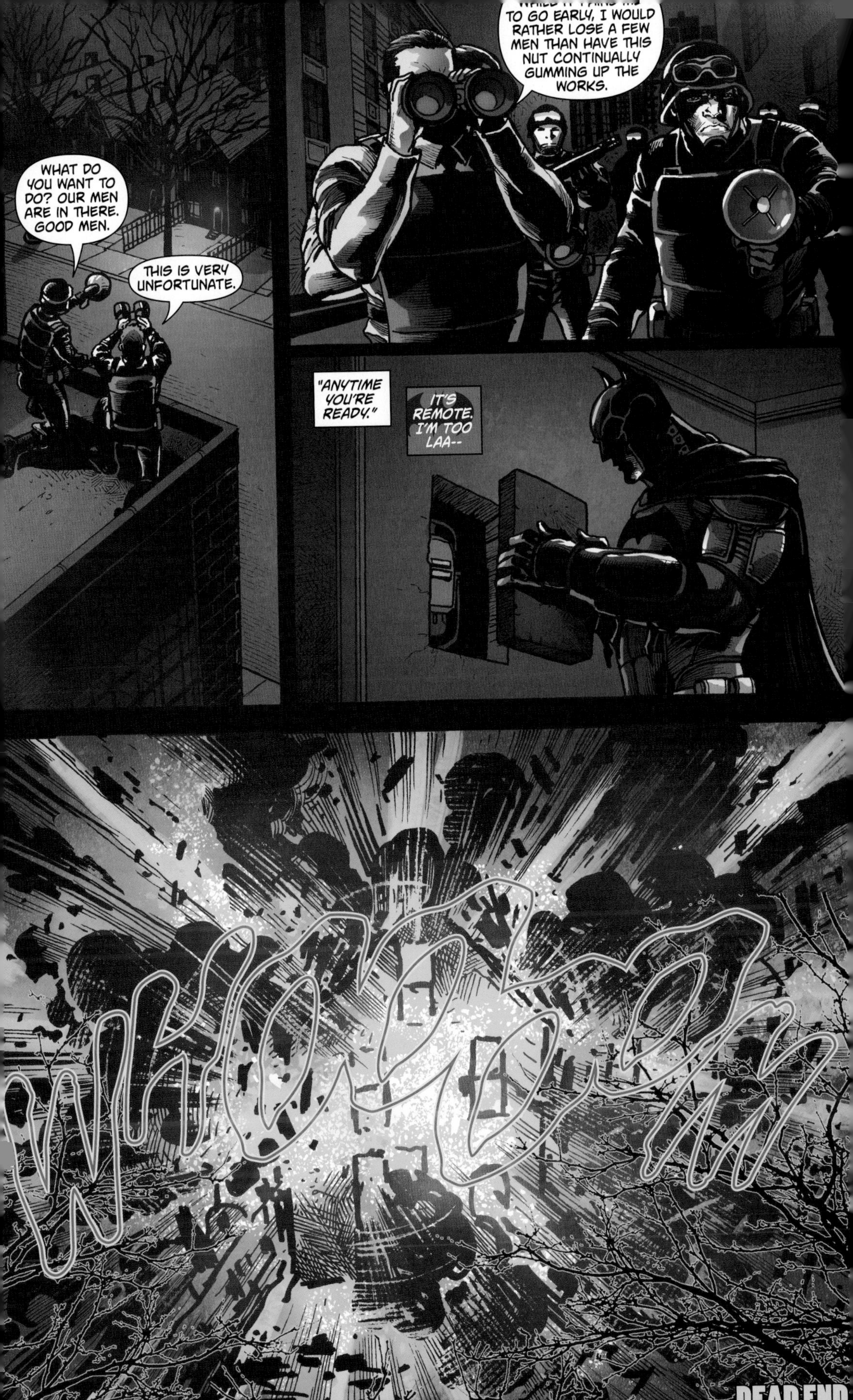
WHAT DO YOU WANT TO DO? OUR MEN ARE IN THERE. GOOD MEN.
THIS IS VERY UNFORTUNATE.
TO GO EARLY, I WOULD RATHER LOSE A FEW MEN THAN HAVE THIS NUT CONTINUALLY GUMMING UP THE WORKS.
"ANYTIME YOU'RE READY."
IT'S REMOTE. I'M TOO LAA--

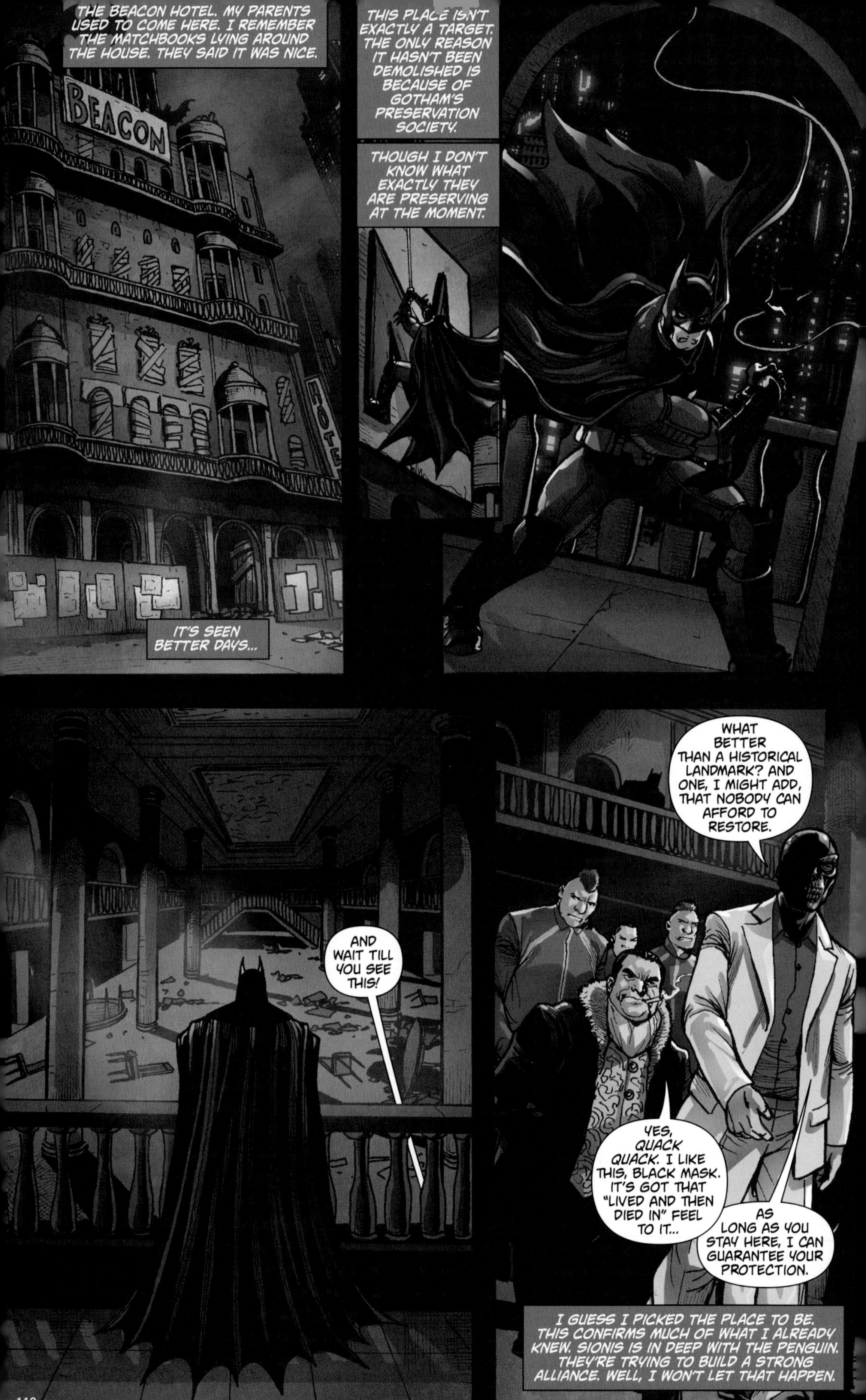
THE BEACON HOTEL. MY PARENTS USED TO COME HERE. I REMEMBER THE MATCHBOOKS LYING AROUND THE HOUSE. THEY SAID IT WAS NICE.
BEACON
HOTE
IT'S SEEN BETTER DAYS...
THIS PLACE ISN'T EXACTLY A TARGET. THE ONLY REASON IT HASN'T BEEN DEMOLISHED IS BECAUSE OF GOTHAM'S PRESERVATION SOCIETY.
THOUGH I DON'T KNOW WHAT EXACTLY THEY ARE PRESERVING AT THE MOMENT.
AND WAIT TILL YOU SEE THIS!
WHAT BETTER THAN A HISTORICAL LANDMARK? AND ONE, I MIGHT ADD, THAT NOBODY CAN AFFORD TO RESTORE.
YES, QUACK QUACK. I LIKE THIS, BLACK MASK. IT'S GOT THAT "LIVED AND THEN DIED IN" FEEL TO IT...
AS LONG AS YOU STAY HERE, I CAN GUARANTEE YOUR PROTECTION.
I GUESS I PICKED THE PLACE TO BE. THIS CONFIRMS MUCH OF WHAT I ALREADY KNEW. SIONIS IS IN DEEP WITH THE PENGUIN. THEY'RE TRYING TO BUILD A STRONG ALLIANCE. WELL, I WON'T LET THAT HAPPEN.

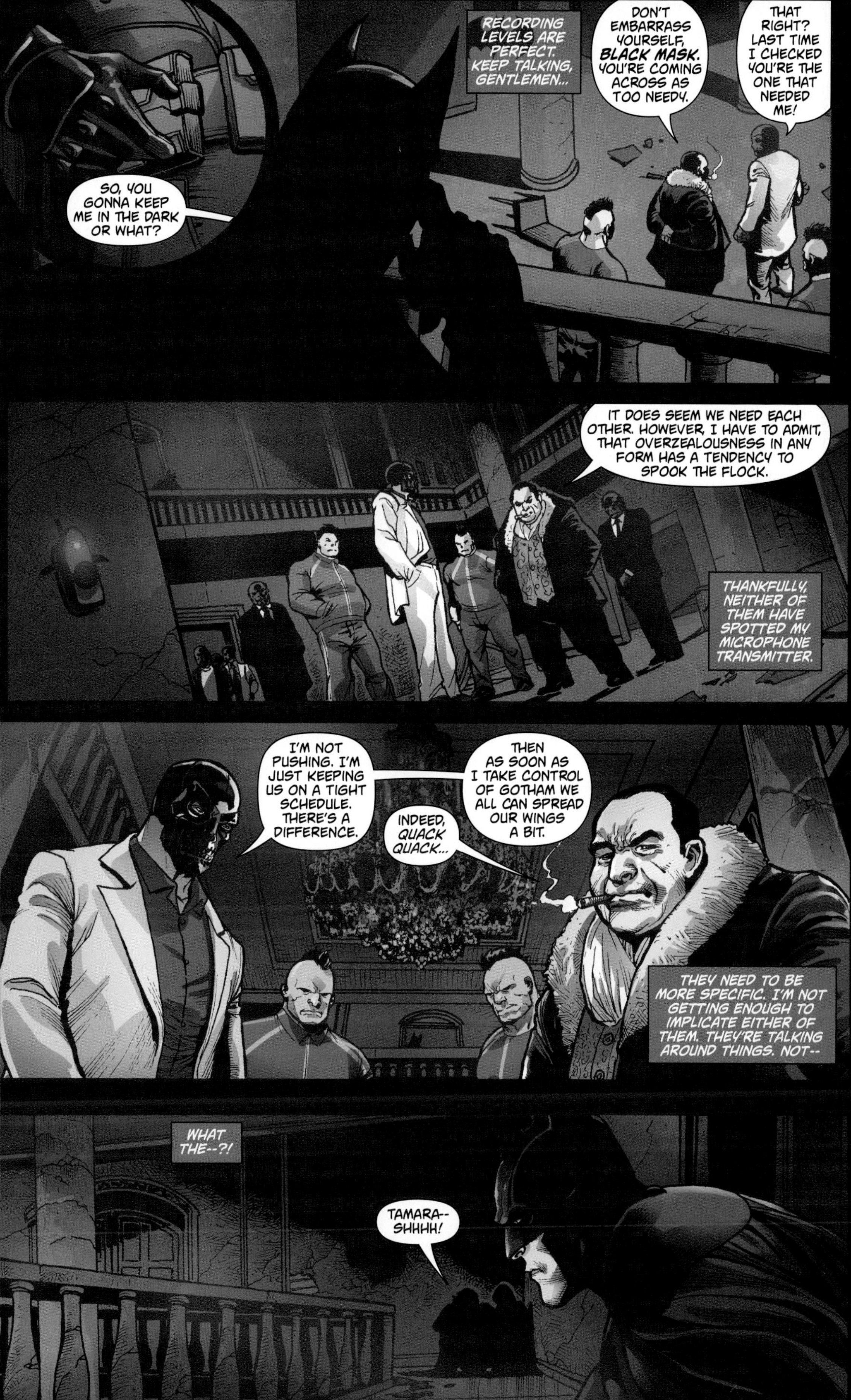
RECORDING LEVELS ARE PERFECT. KEEP TALKING, GENTLEMEN...
SO, YOU GONNA KEEP ME IN THE DARK OR WHAT?
DON'T EMBARRASS YOURSELF, BLACK MASK. YOU'RE COMING ACROSS AS TOO NEEDY.
THAT RIGHT? LAST TIME I CHECKED YOU'RE THE ONE THAT NEEDED ME!
IT DOES SEEM WE NEED EACH OTHER. HOWEVER, I HAVE TO ADMIT, THAT OVERZEALOUSNESS IN ANY FORM HAS A TENDENCY TO SPOOK THE FLOCK.
THANKFULLY, NEITHER OF THEM HAVE SPOTTED MY MICROPHONE TRANSMITTER.
I'M NOT PUSHING. I'M JUST KEEPING US ON A TIGHT SCHEDULE. THERE'S A DIFFERENCE.
INDEED, QUACK QUACK...
THEN AS SOON AS I TAKE CONTROL OF GOTHAM WE ALL CAN SPREAD OUR WINGS A BIT.
THEY NEED TO BE MORE SPECIFIC. I'M NOT GETTING ENOUGH TO IMPLICATE EITHER OF THEM. THEY'RE TALKING AROUND THINGS. NOT--
WHAT THE--?!
TAMARA-SHHHH!

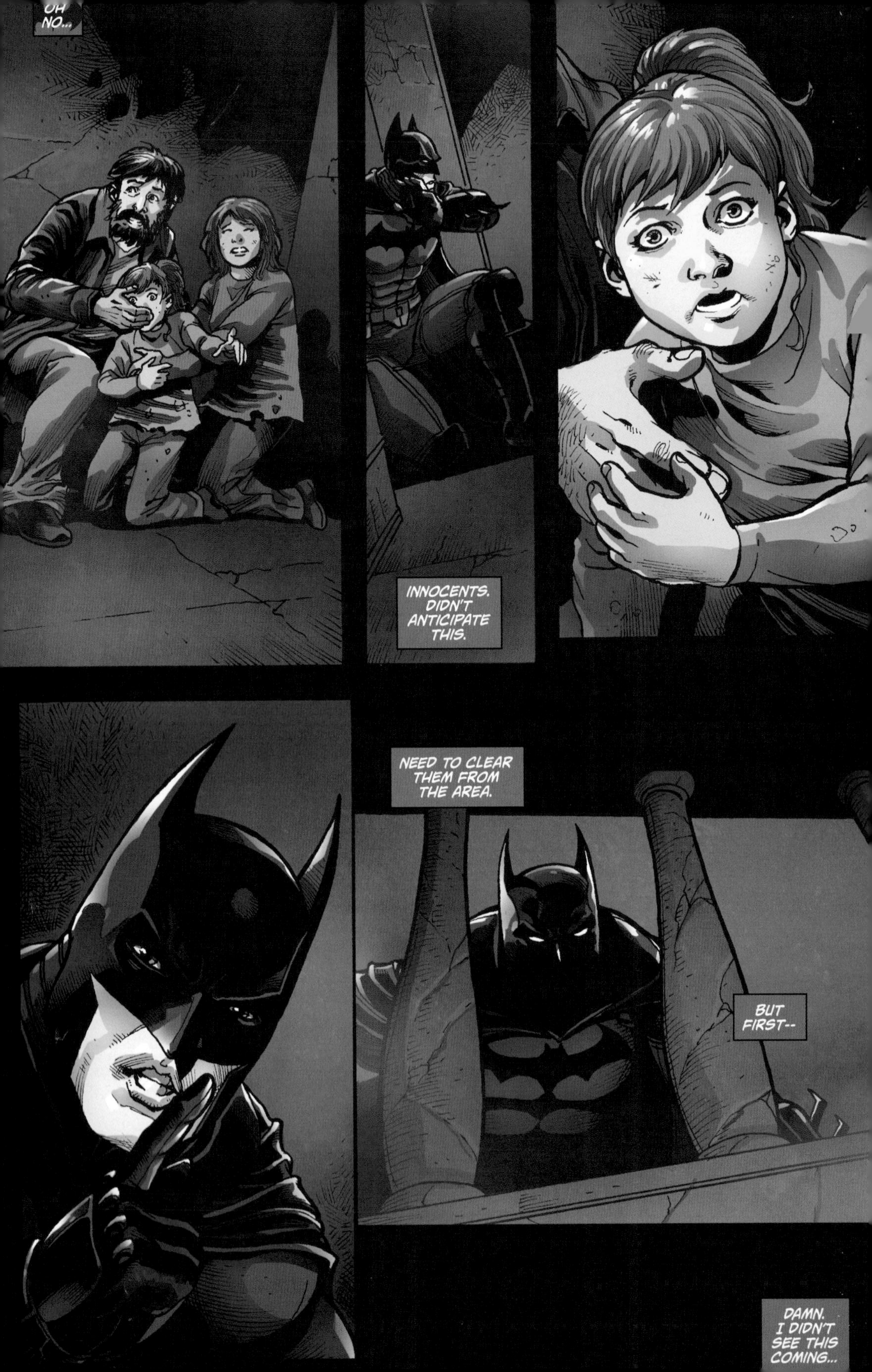
OH NO...
INNOCENTS. DIDN'T ANTICIPATE THIS.
NEED TO CLEAR THEM FROM THE AREA.
BUT FIRST--
DAMN. I DIDN'T SEE THIS COMING...

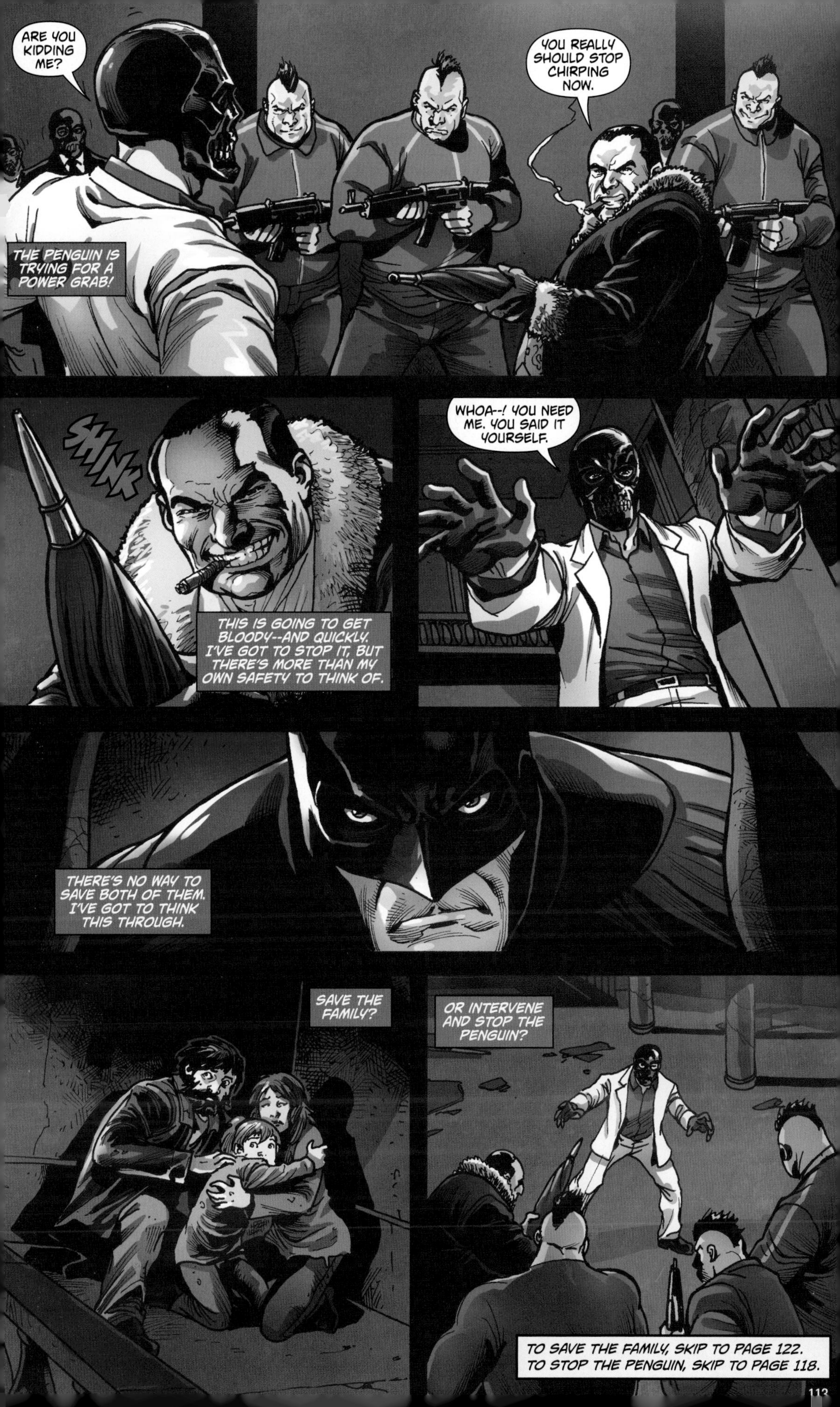
ARE YOU KIDDING ME?
THE PENGUIN IS TRYING FOR A POWER GRAB!
YOU REALLY SHOULD STOP CHIRPING NOW.
SHINK
THIS IS GOING TO GET BLOODY--AND QUICKLY. I'VE GOT TO STOP IT, BUT THERE'S MORE THAN MY OWN SAFETY TO THINK OF.
WHOA--! YOU NEED ME. YOU SAID IT YOURSELF.
THERE'S NO WAY TO SAVE BOTH OF THEM. I'VE GOT TO THINK THIS THROUGH.
SAVE THE FAMILY?
OR INTERVENE AND STOP THE PENGUIN?
TO SAVE THE FAMILY, SKIP TO PAGE 122.
TO STOP THE PENGUIN, SKIP TO PAGE 118.

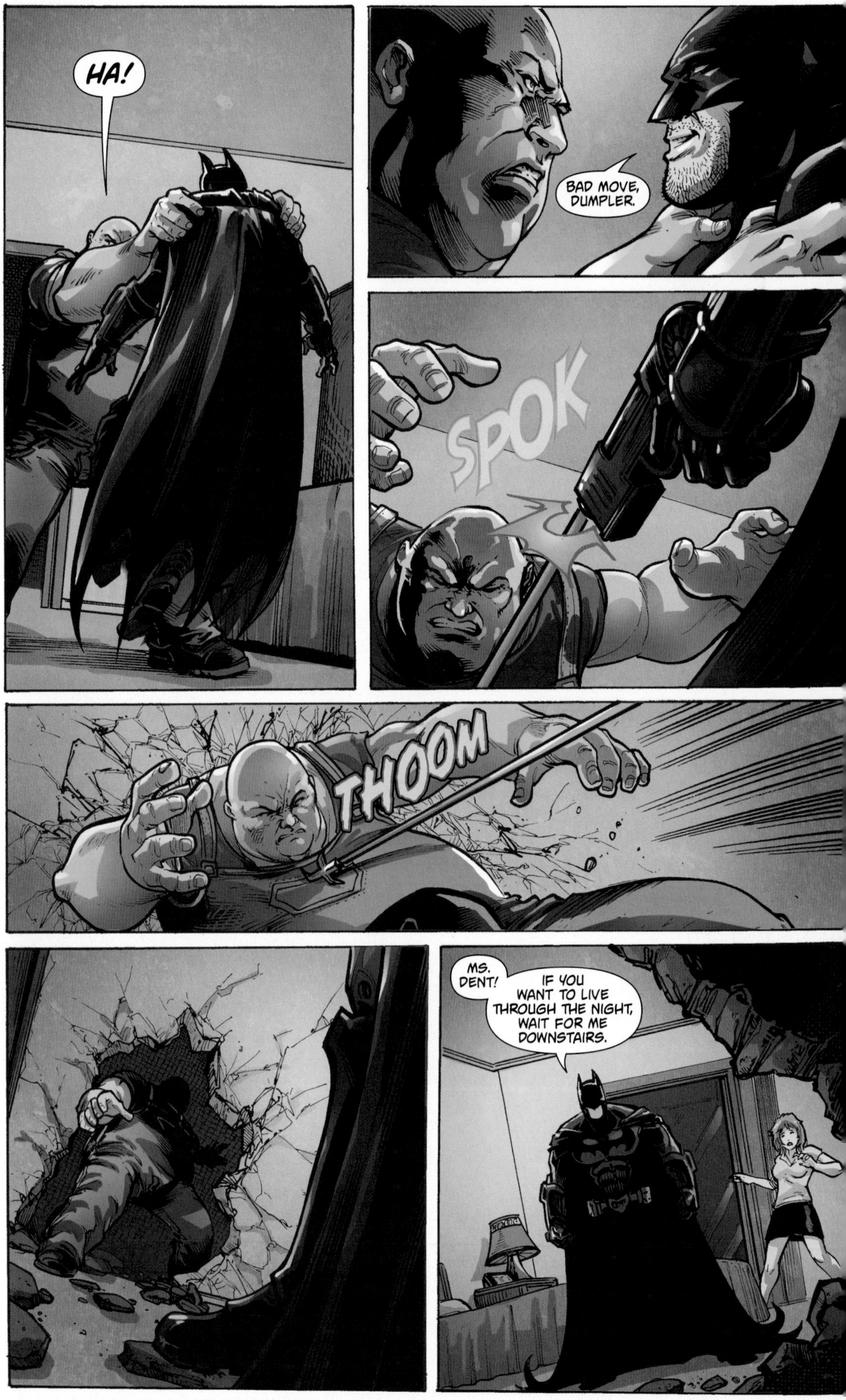
HA!
BAD MOVE, DUMPLER.
SPOK
THOOM
MS. DENT!
IF YOU WANT TO LIVE THROUGH THE NIGHT, WAIT FOR ME DOWNSTAIRS.

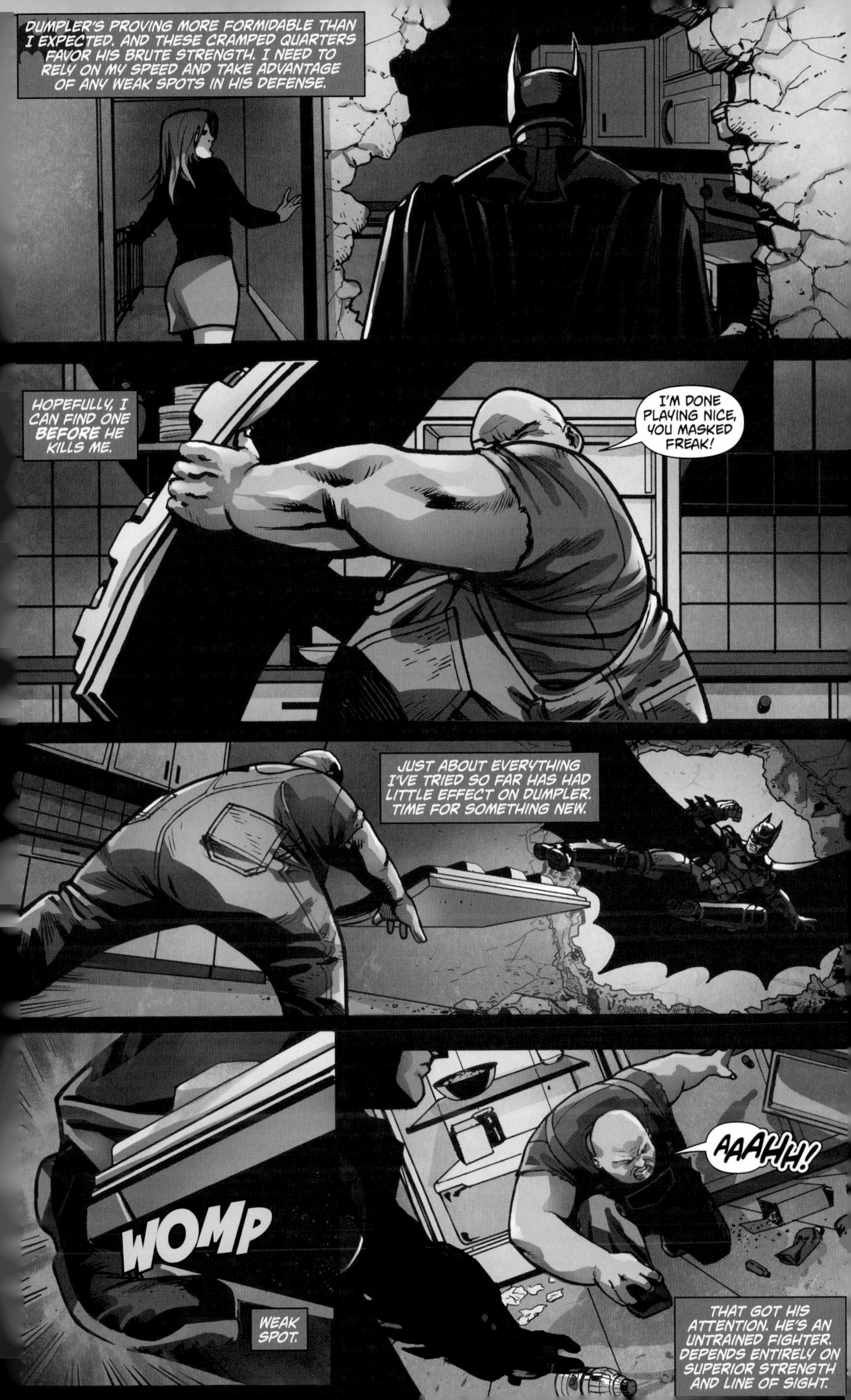
DUMPLER'S PROVING MORE FORMIDABLE THAN I EXPECTED. AND THESE CRAMPED QUARTERS FAVOR HIS BRUTE STRENGTH. I NEED TO RELY ON MY SPEED AND TAKE ADVANTAGE OF ANY WEAK SPOTS IN HIS DEFENSE.
HOPEFULLY, I CAN FIND ONE BEFORE HE KILLS ME.
I'M DONE PLAYING NICE, YOU MASKED FREAK!
JUST ABOUT EVERYTHING I'VE TRIED SO FAR HAS HAD LITTLE EFFECT ON DUMPLER. TIME FOR SOMETHING NEW.
WOMP
WEAK SPOT.
AAAHH!
THAT GOT HIS ATTENTION. HE'S AN UNTRAINED FIGHTER. DEPENDS ENTIRELY ON SUPERIOR STRENGTH AND LINE OF SIGHT.

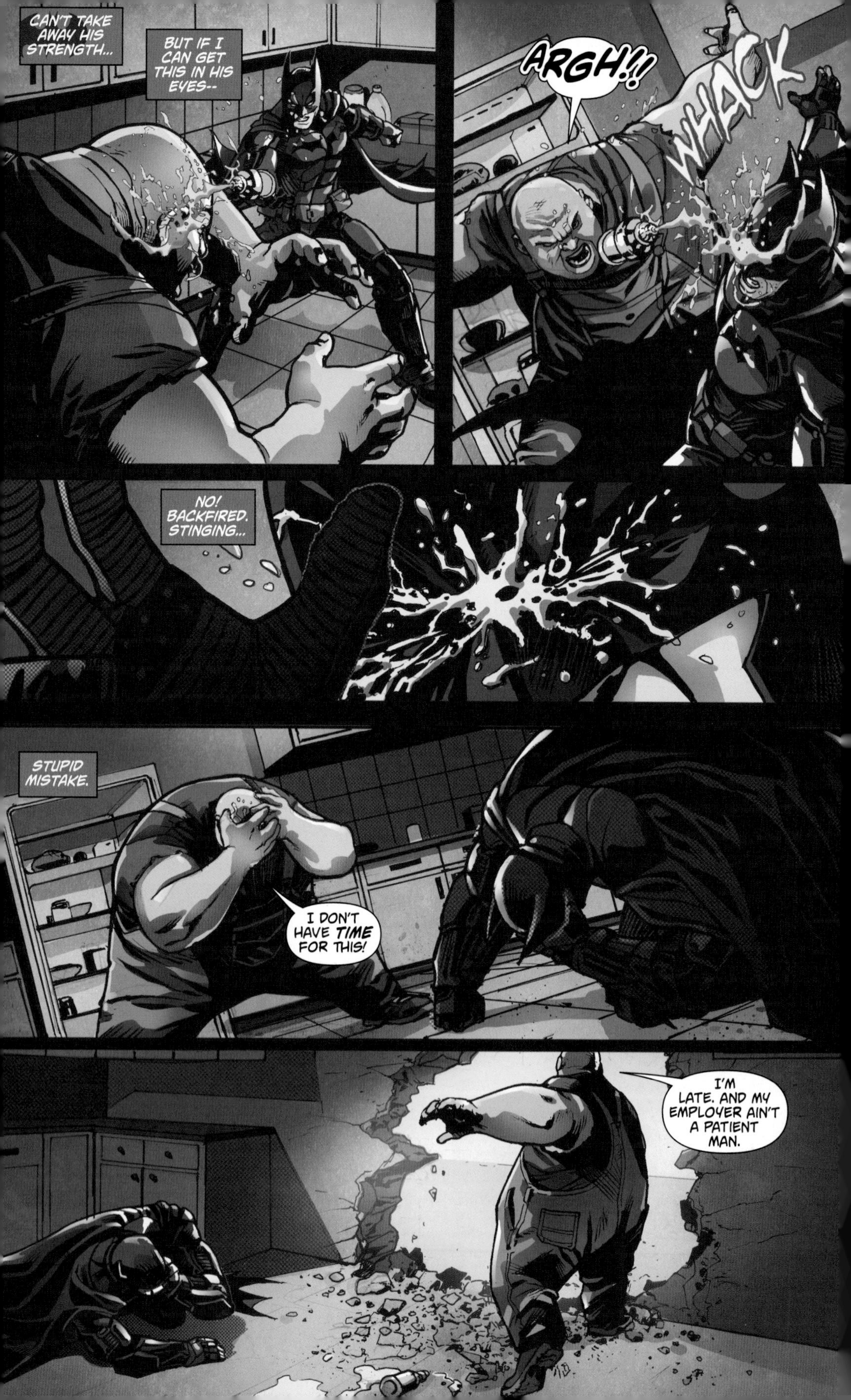
CAN'T TAKE AWAY HIS STRENGTH...
BUT IF I CAN GET THIS IN HIS EYES--
ARGH!!
WHACK
NO! BACKFIRED. STINGING...
STUPID MISTAKE.
I DON'T HAVE TIME FOR THIS!
I'M LATE. AND MY EMPLOYER AIN'T A PATIENT MAN.

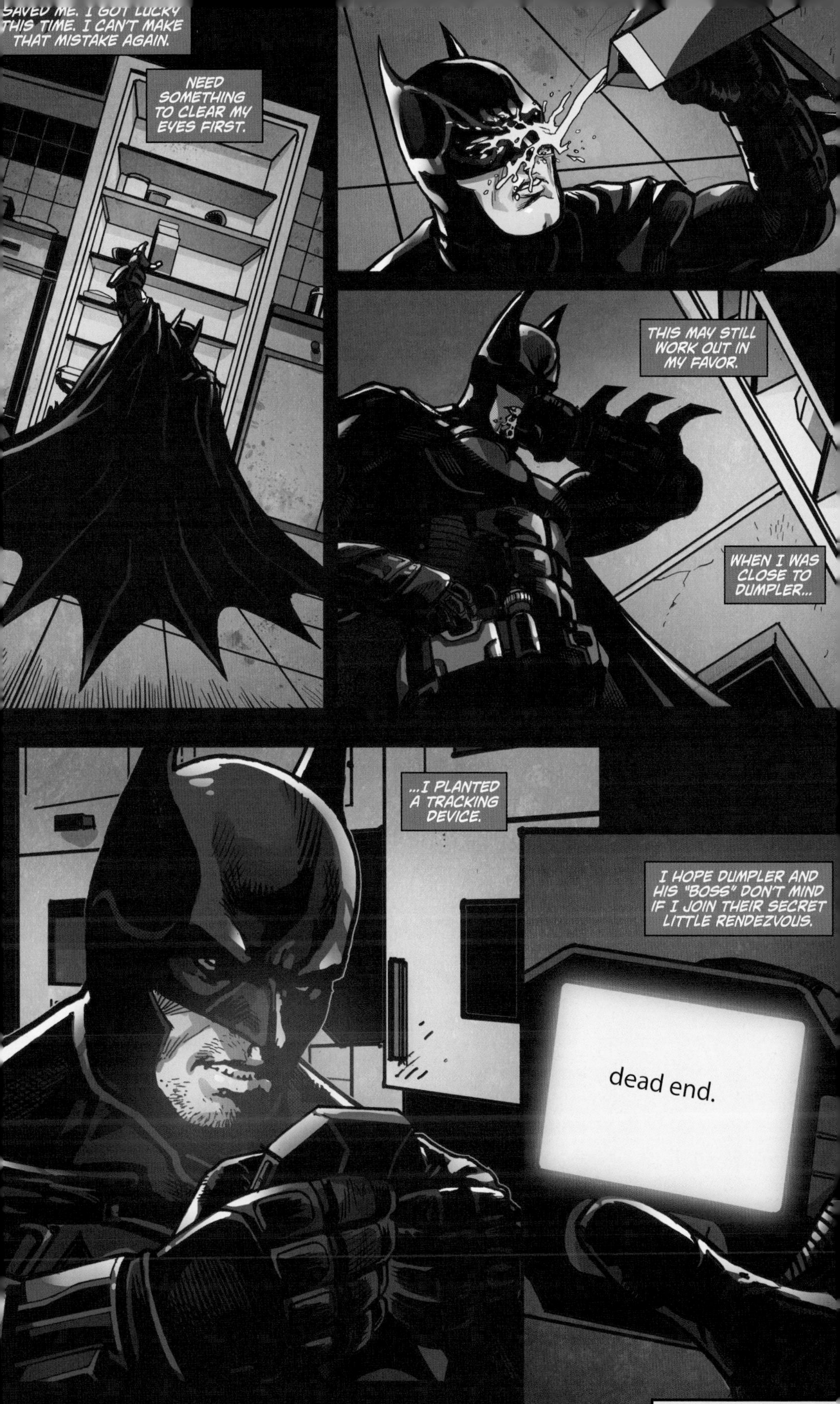
SAVED ME. I GOT LUCKY THIS TIME. I CAN'T MAKE THAT MISTAKE AGAIN.
NEED SOMETHING TO CLEAR MY EYES FIRST.
THIS MAY STILL WORK OUT IN MY FAVOR.
WHEN I WAS CLOSE TO DUMPLER...
...I PLANTED A TRACKING DEVICE.
I HOPE DUMPLER AND HIS "BOSS" DON'T MIND IF I JOIN THEIR SECRET LITTLE RENDEZVOUS.
dead end.

GO BACK TO PAGE 88.

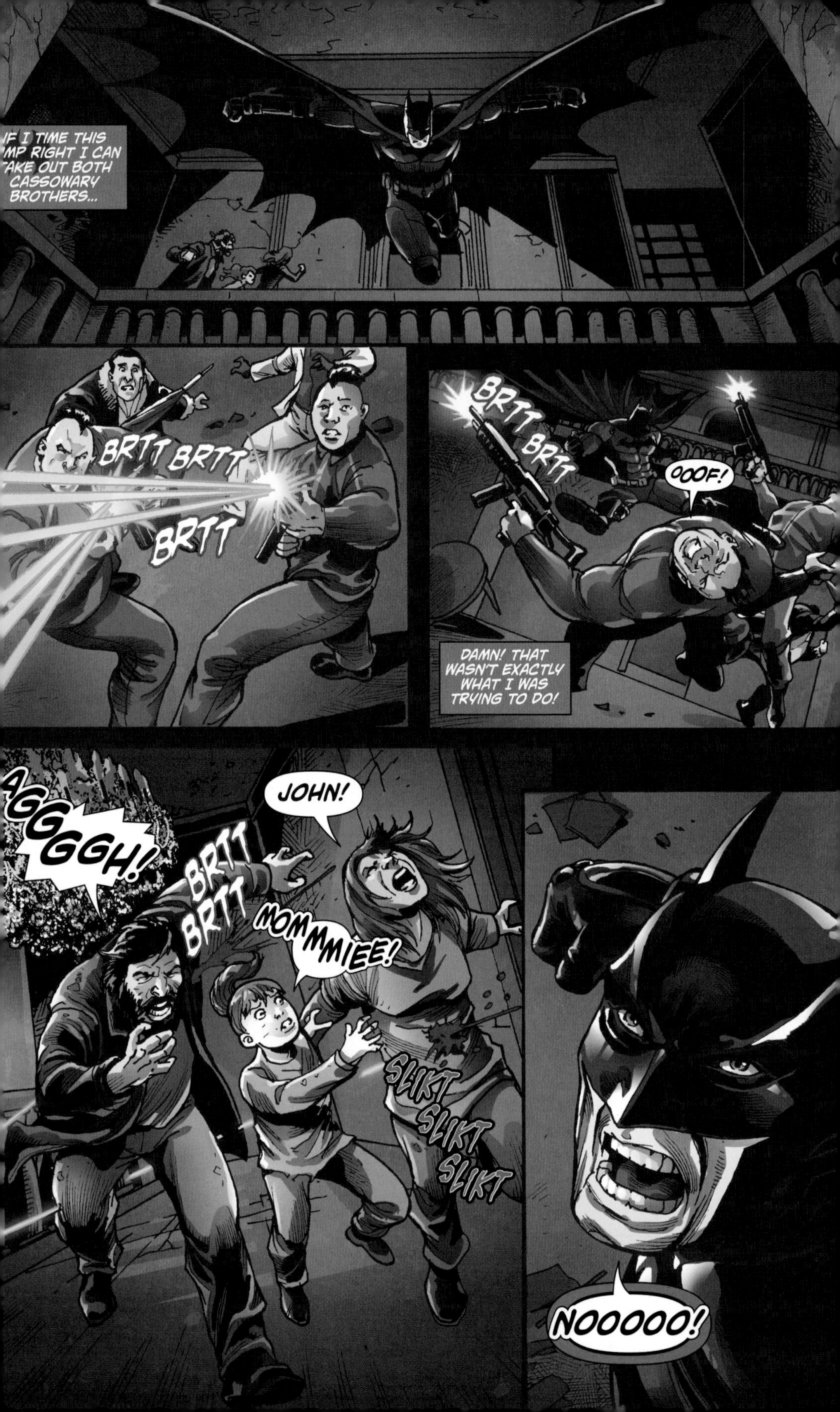
IF I TIME THIS
MP RIGHT I CAN
AKE OUT BOTH
CASSOWARY
BROTHERS...
BRTT BRTT
BRTT
BRTT
BRTT
OOOF!
DAMN! THAT WASN'T EXACTLY WHAT I WAS TRYING TO DO!
AGGGGH!
JOHN!
BRTT
BRTT
MOMMMIEE!
SLIKT
SLIKT
SLIKT
NOOOOO!

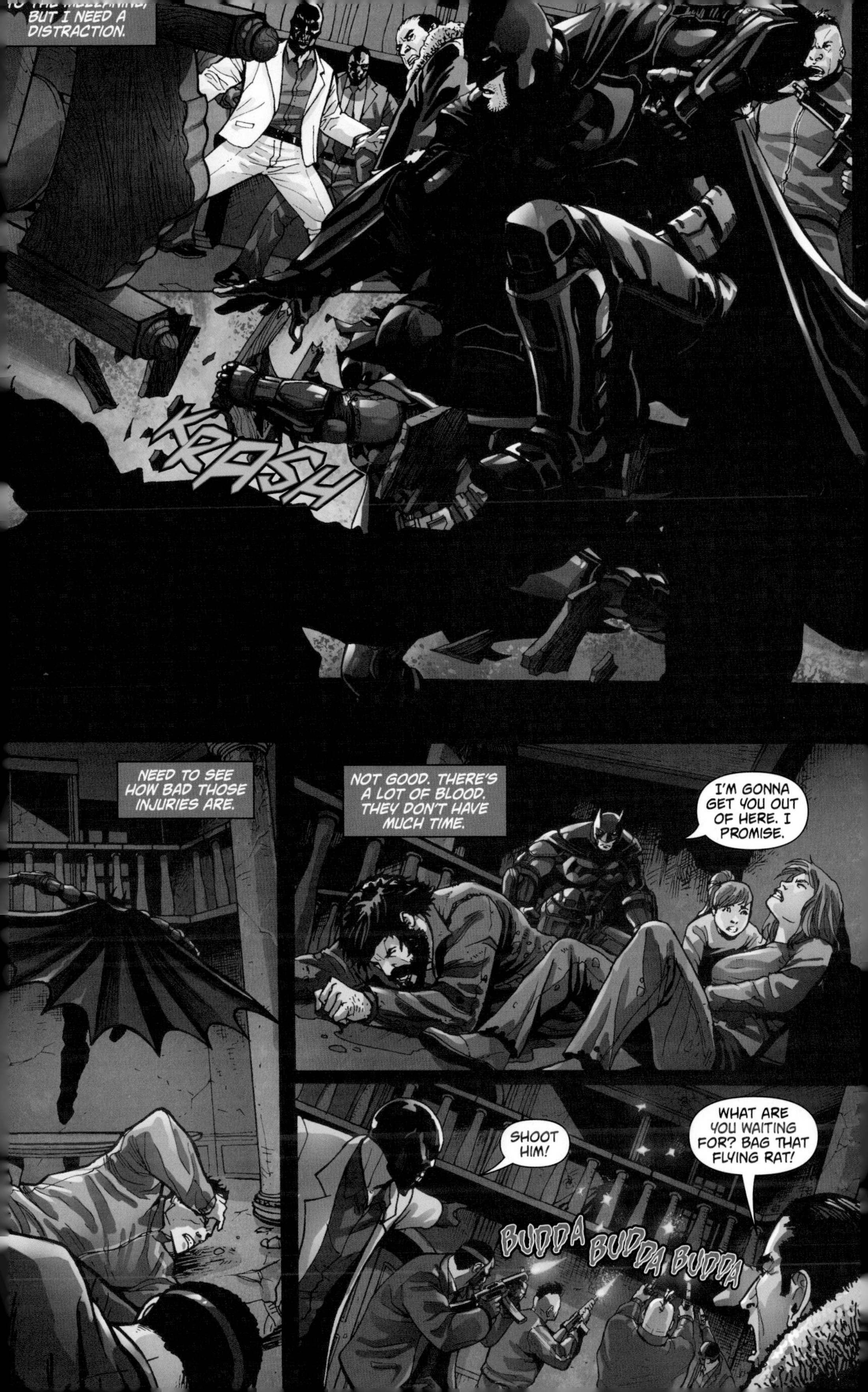
BUT I NEED A DISTRACTION.
KRASH
NEED TO SEE HOW BAD THOSE INJURIES ARE.
NOT GOOD. THERE'S A LOT OF BLOOD. THEY DON'T HAVE MUCH TIME.
I'M GONNA GET YOU OUT OF HERE. I PROMISE.
SHOOT HIM!
WHAT ARE YOU WAITING FOR? BAG THAT FLYING RAT!
BUDDA BUDDA BUDDA

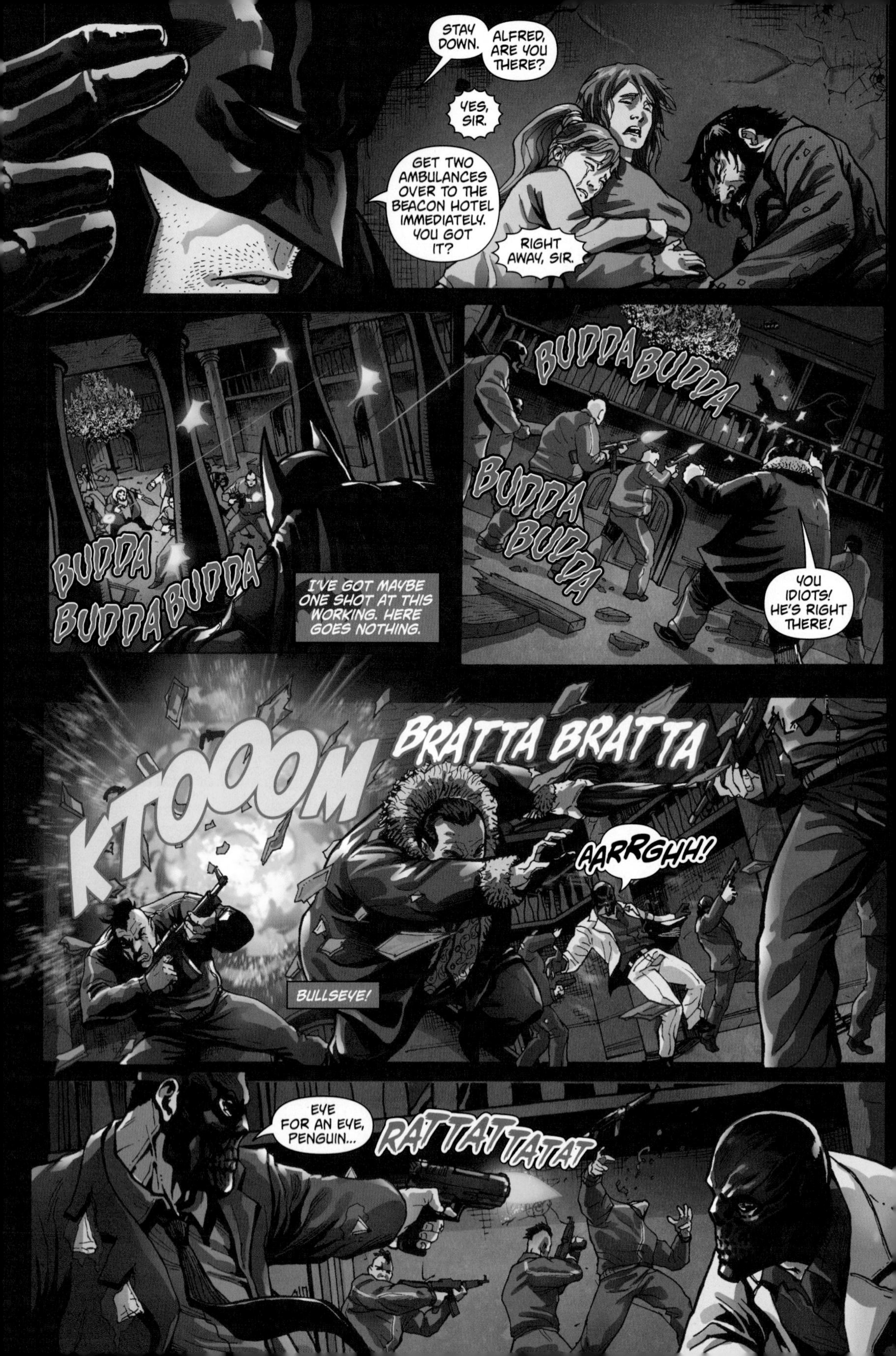
STAY DOWN.
ALFRED, ARE YOU THERE?
YES, SIR.
GET TWO AMBULANCES OVER TO THE BEACON HOTEL IMMEDIATELY. YOU GOT IT?
RIGHT AWAY, SIR.
BUDDA BUDDA BUDDA
I'VE GOT MAYBE ONE SHOT AT THIS WORKING. HERE GOES NOTHING.
BUDDA BUDDA
BUDDA BUDDA
YOU IDIOTS! HE'S RIGHT THERE!
KTOOOM
BRATTA BRATTA
AARRGHH!
BULLSEYE!
EYE FOR AN EYE, PENGUIN...
RATTAT TATAT

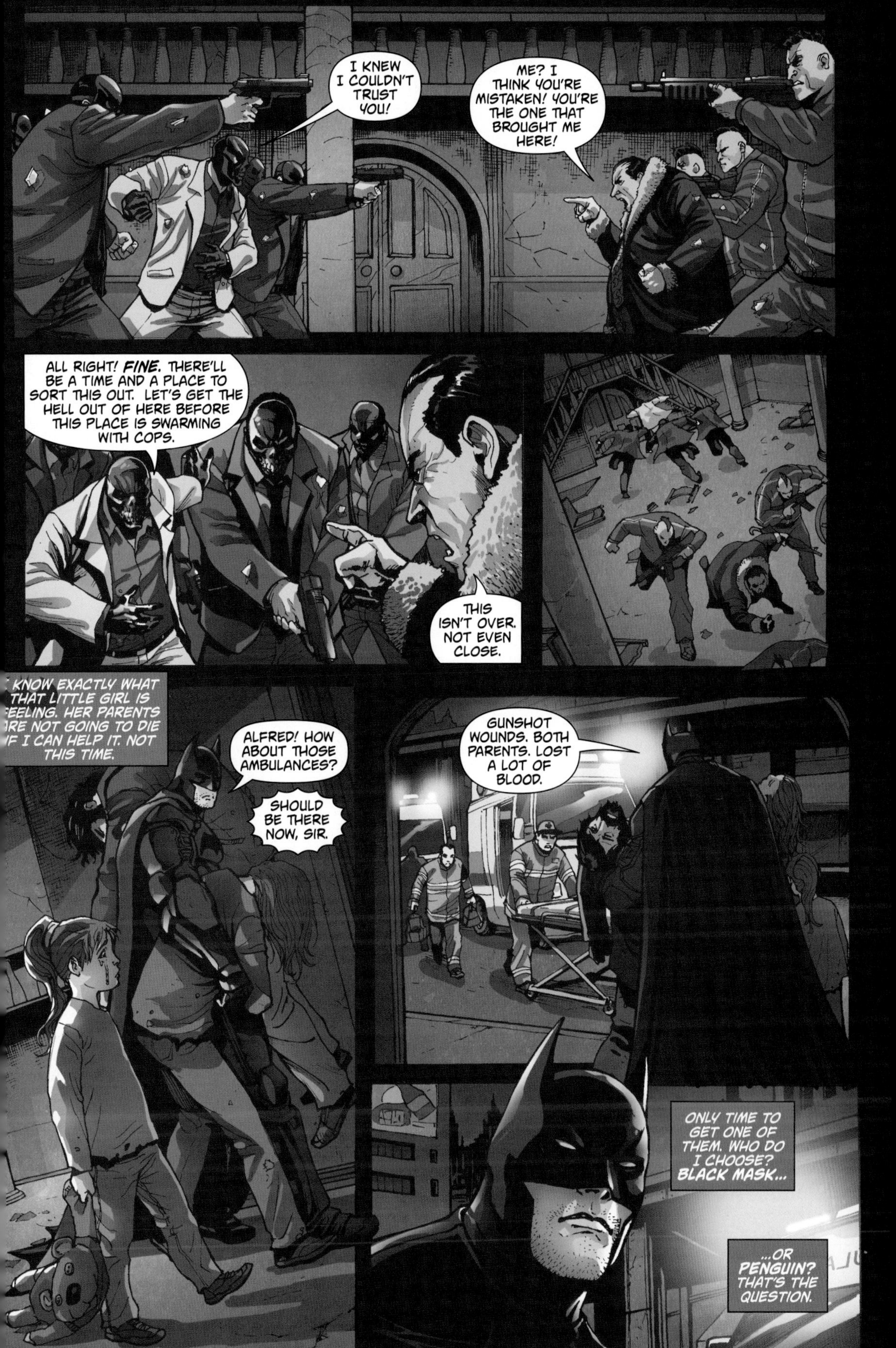
I KNEW I COULDN'T TRUST YOU!
ME? I THINK YOU'RE MISTAKEN! YOU'RE THE ONE THAT BROUGHT ME HERE!
ALL RIGHT! FINE. THERE'LL BE A TIME AND A PLACE TO SORT THIS OUT. LET'S GET THE HELL OUT OF HERE BEFORE THIS PLACE IS SWARMING WITH COPS.
THIS ISN'T OVER. NOT EVEN CLOSE.
KNOW EXACTLY WHAT THAT LITTLE GIRL IS EELING. HER PARENTS RE NOT GOING TO DIE F I CAN HELP IT. NOT THIS TIME.
ALFRED! HOW ABOUT THOSE AMBULANCES?
SHOULD BE THERE NOW, SIR.
GUNSHOT WOUNDS. BOTH PARENTS. LOST A LOT OF BLOOD.
ONLY TIME TO GET ONE OF THEM. WHO DO I CHOOSE? BLACK MASK...
...OR PENGUIN? THAT'S THE QUESTION.
TO GO AFTER BLACK MASK, SKIP TO PAGE 126.
TO STOP THE PENGUIN, SKIP TO PAGE 133.

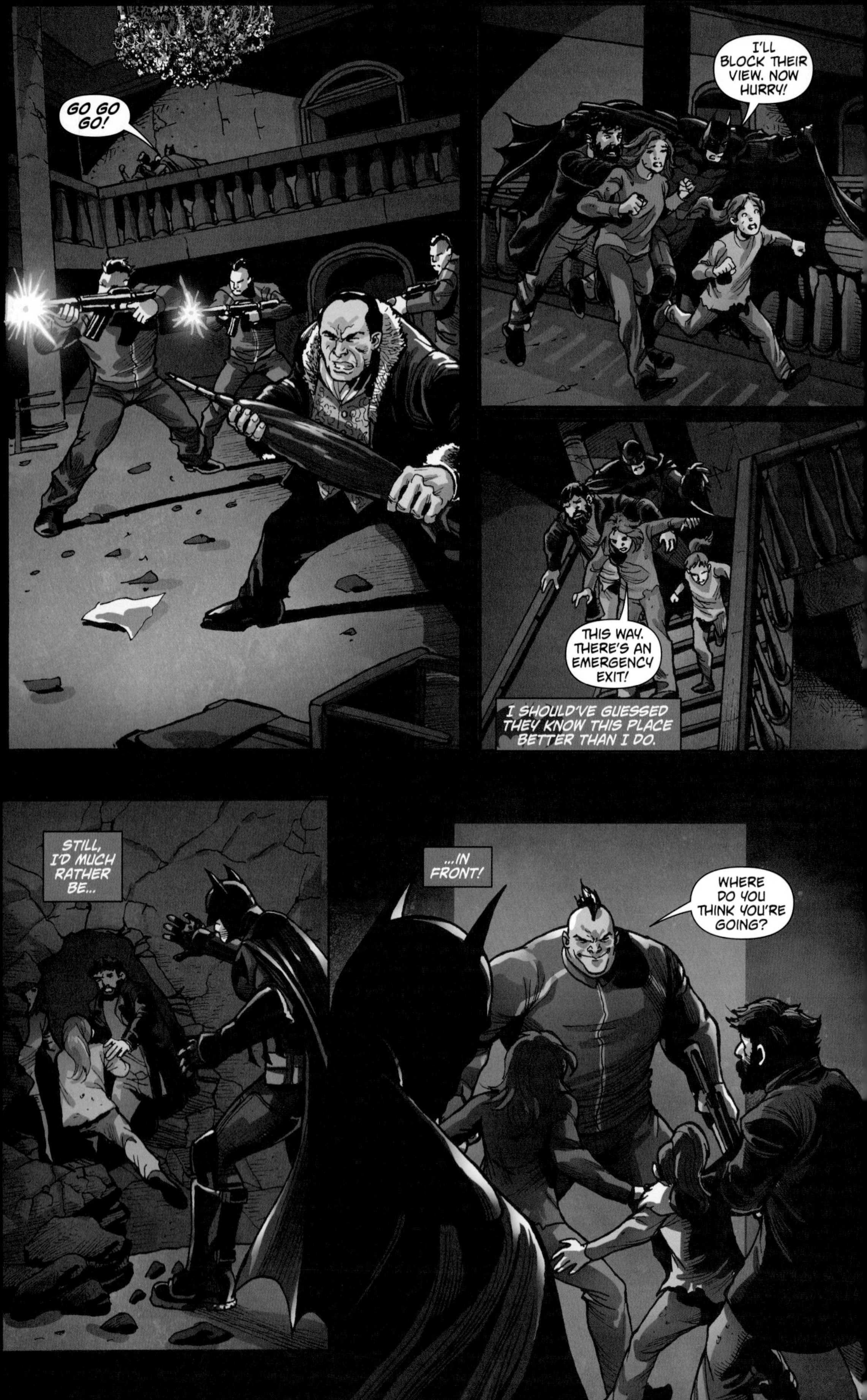
GO GO GO!
I'LL BLOCK THEIR VIEW. NOW HURRY!
THIS WAY. THERE'S AN EMERGENCY EXIT!
I SHOULD'VE GUESSED THEY KNOW THIS PLACE BETTER THAN I DO.
STILL, I'D MUCH RATHER BE...
...IN FRONT!
WHERE DO YOU THINK YOU'RE GOING?

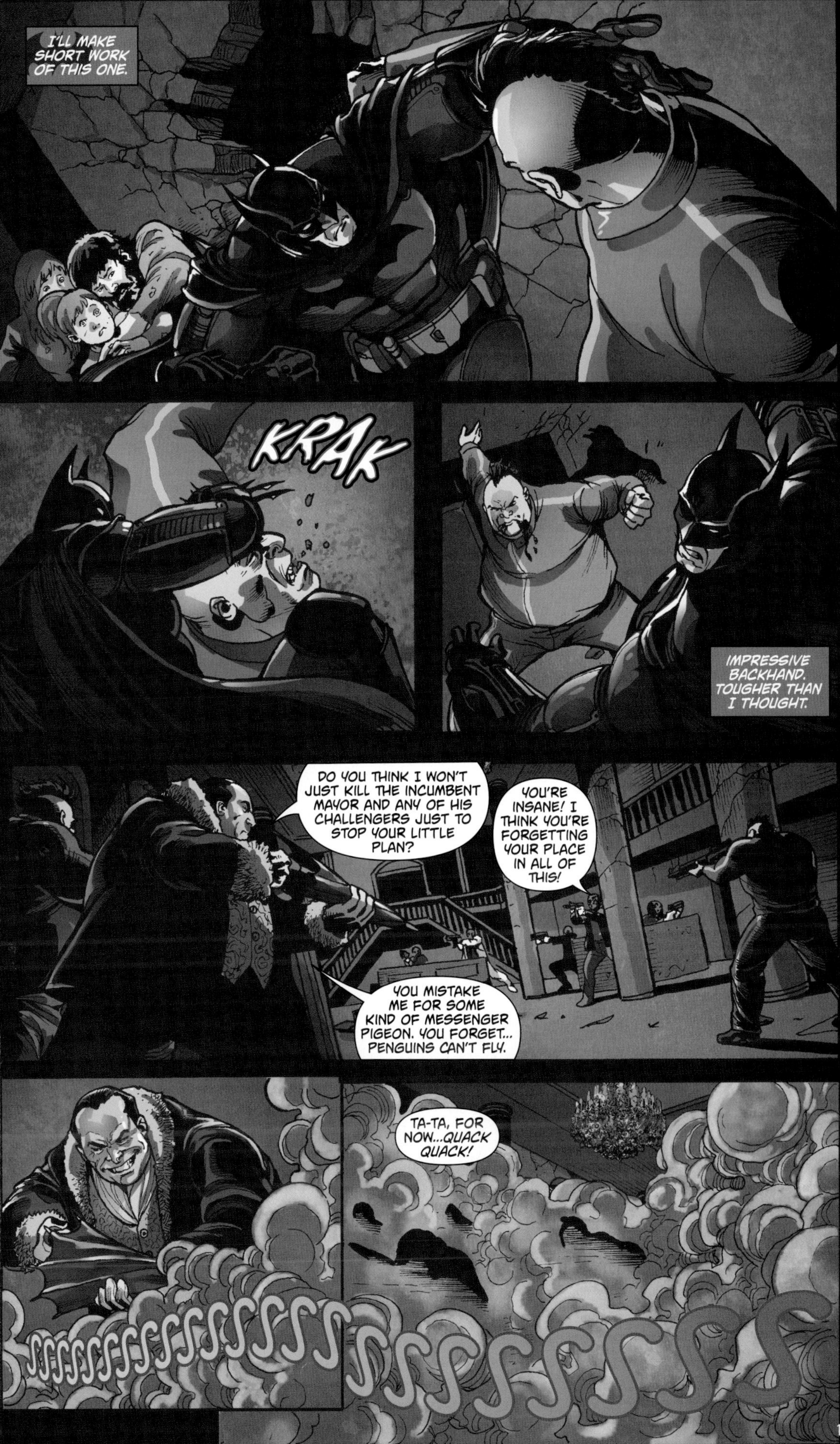

I'LL MAKE SHORT WORK OF THIS ONE.
KRAK
IMPRESSIVE BACKHAND. TOUGHER THAN I THOUGHT.
DO YOU THINK I WON'T JUST KILL THE INCUMBENT MAYOR AND ANY OF HIS CHALLENGERS JUST TO STOP YOUR LITTLE PLAN?
YOU'RE INSANE! I THINK YOU'RE FORGETTING YOUR PLACE IN ALL OF THIS!
YOU MISTAKE ME FOR SOME KIND OF MESSENGER PIGEON. YOU FORGET... PENGUINS CAN'T FLY.
TA-TA, FOR NOW...QUACK QUACK!
SSSSSSSSSSSSSSSSSSSSSSSSSSS

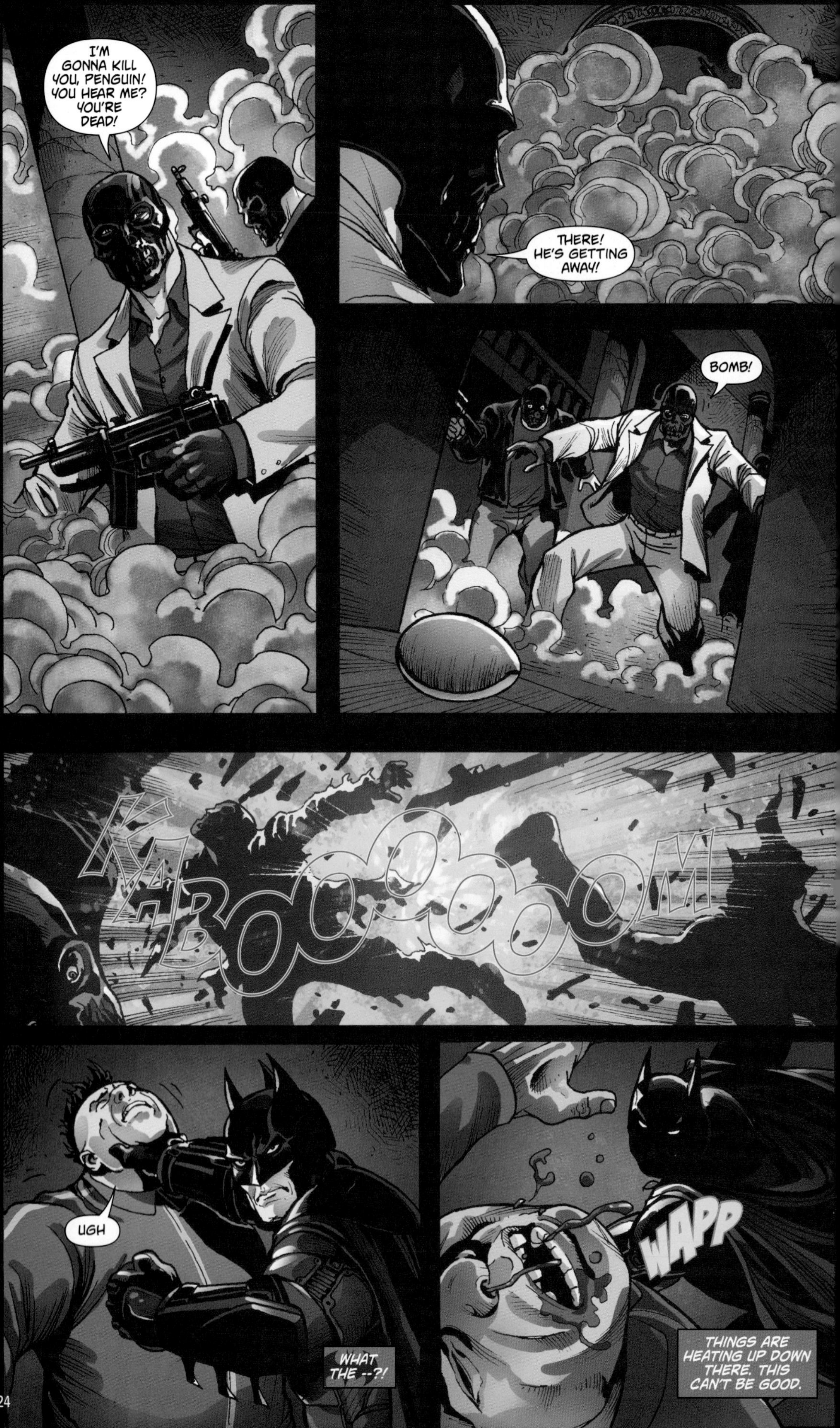
I'M GONNA KILL YOU, PENGUIN! YOU HEAR ME? YOU'RE DEAD!
THERE! HE'S GETTING AWAY!
BOMB!
KABOOOOOOOM
UGH
WHAT THE --?!
WAPP
THINGS ARE HEATING UP DOWN THERE. THIS CAN'T BE GOOD.

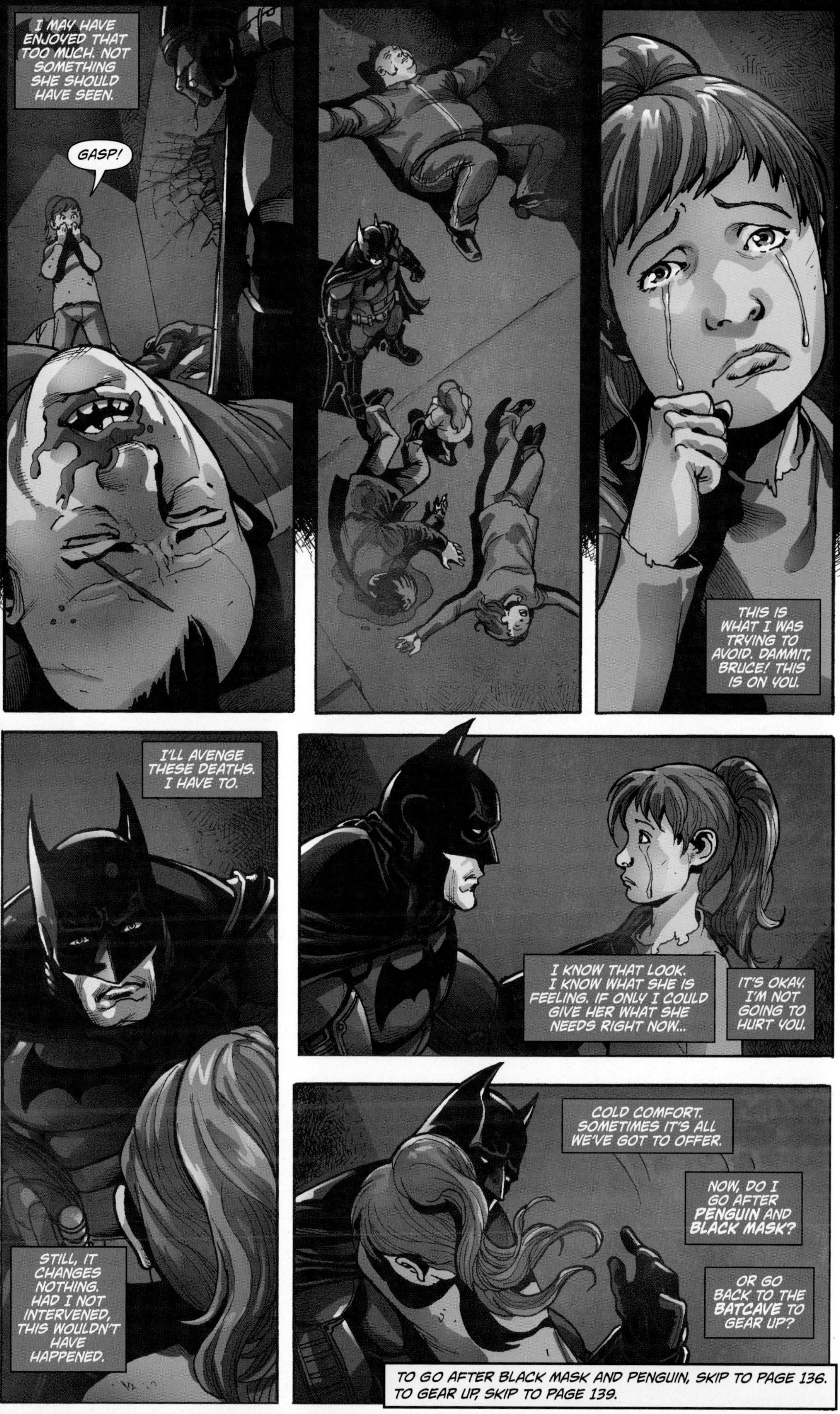
I MAY HAVE ENJOYED THAT TOO MUCH. NOT SOMETHING SHE SHOULD HAVE SEEN.
GASP!
THIS IS WHAT I WAS TRYING TO AVOID. DAMMIT, BRUCE! THIS IS ON YOU.
I'LL AVENGE THESE DEATHS. I HAVE TO.
STILL, IT CHANGES NOTHING. HAD I NOT INTERVENED, THIS WOULDN'T HAVE HAPPENED.
I KNOW THAT LOOK. I KNOW WHAT SHE IS FEELING. IF ONLY I COULD GIVE HER WHAT SHE NEEDS RIGHT NOW...
IT'S OKAY. I'M NOT GOING TO HURT YOU.
COLD COMFORT. SOMETIMES IT'S ALL WE'VE GOT TO OFFER.
NOW, DO I GO AFTER PENGUIN AND BLACK MASK?
OR GO BACK TO THE BATCAVE TO GEAR UP?

TO GO AFTER BLACK MASK AND PENGUIN, SKIP TO PAGE 136.
TO GEAR UP, SKIP TO PAGE 139.

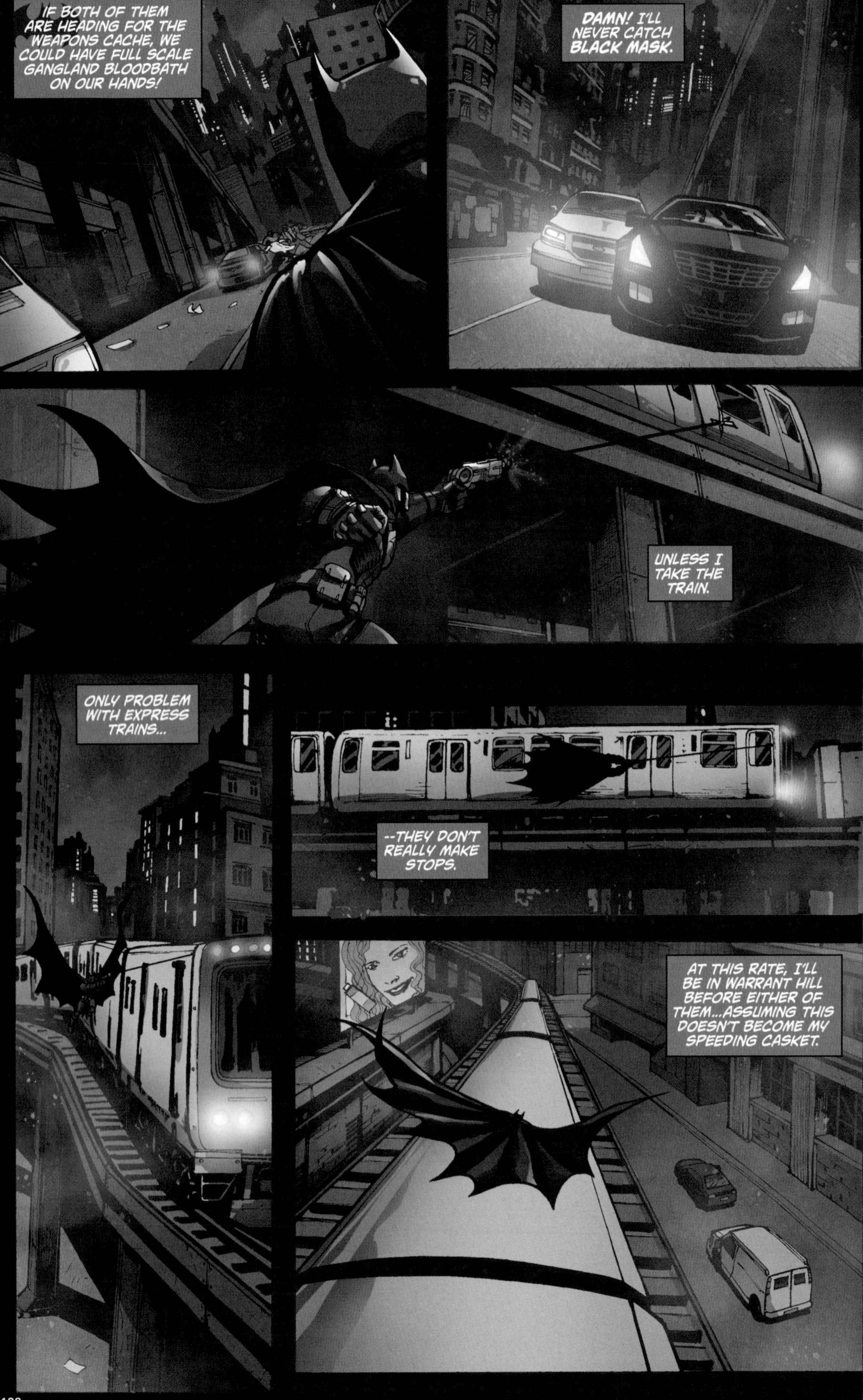
IF BOTH OF THEM ARE HEADING FOR THE WEAPONS CACHE, WE COULD HAVE FULL SCALE GANGLAND BLOODBATH ON OUR HANDS!
DAMN! I'LL NEVER CATCH BLACK MASK.
UNLESS I TAKE THE TRAIN.
ONLY PROBLEM WITH EXPRESS TRAINS...
--THEY DON'T REALLY MAKE STOPS.
AT THIS RATE, I'LL BE IN WARRANT HILL BEFORE EITHER OF THEM...ASSUMING THIS DOESN'T BECOME MY SPEEDING CASKET.

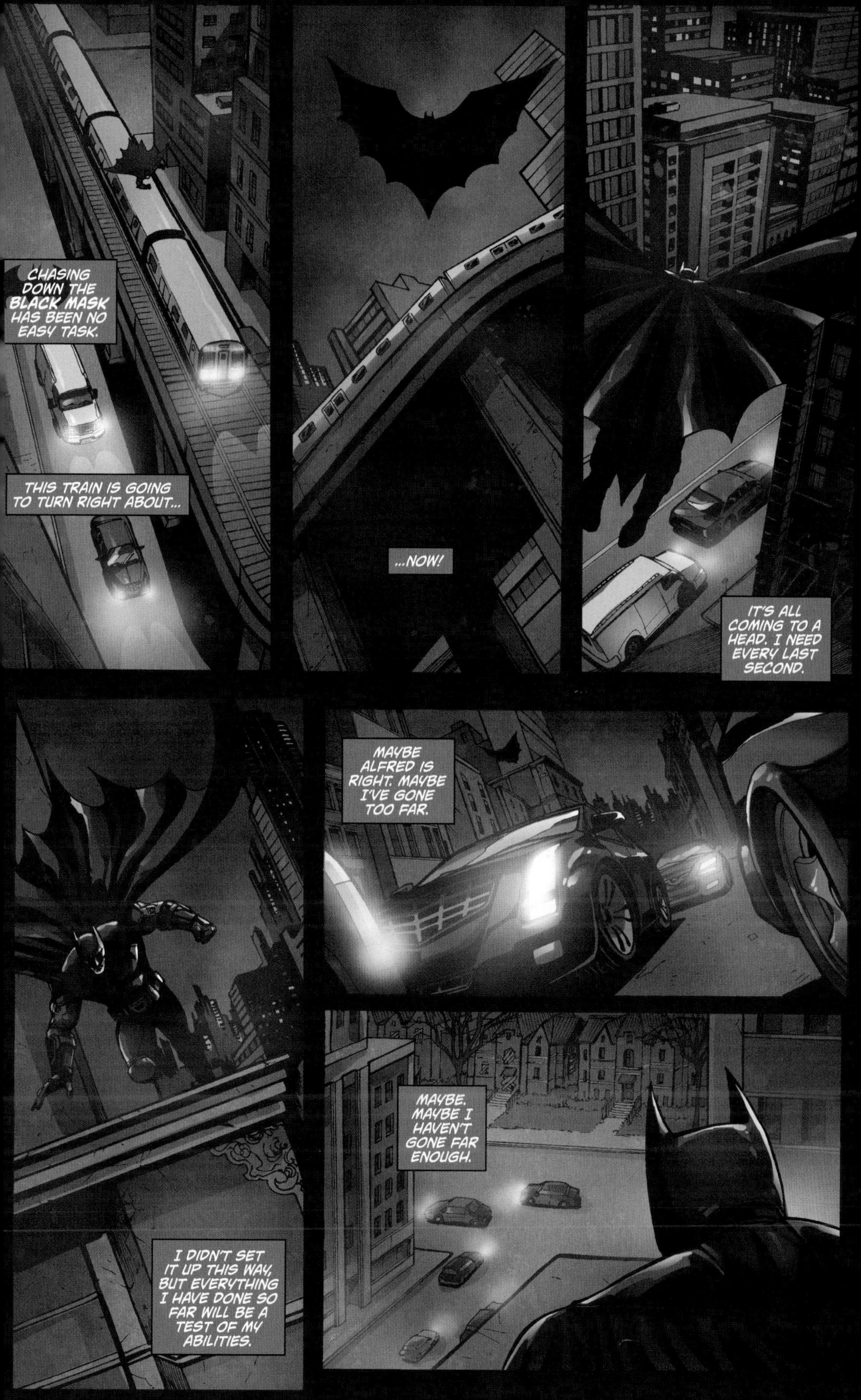
CHASING DOWN THE BLACK MASK HAS BEEN NO EASY TASK.
THIS TRAIN IS GOING TO TURN RIGHT ABOUT...
...NOW!
IT'S ALL COMING TO A HEAD. I NEED EVERY LAST SECOND.
I DIDN'T SET IT UP THIS WAY, BUT EVERYTHING I HAVE DONE SO FAR WILL BE A TEST OF MY ABILITIES.
MAYBE ALFRED IS RIGHT. MAYBE I'VE GONE TOO FAR.
MAYBE. MAYBE I HAVEN'T GONE FAR ENOUGH.

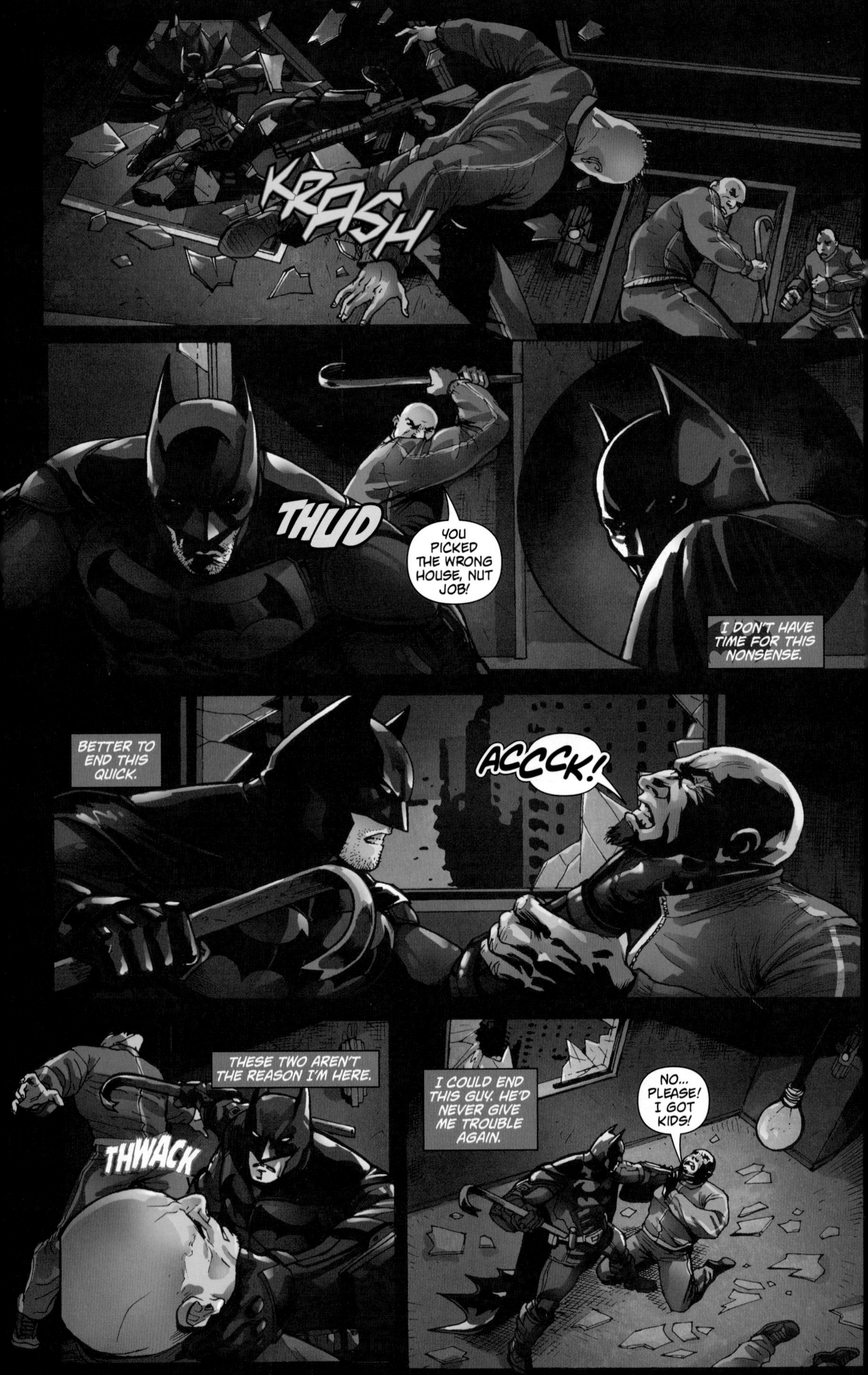
KRASH
THUD
YOU PICKED THE WRONG HOUSE, NUT JOB!
I DON'T HAVE TIME FOR THIS NONSENSE.
BETTER TO END THIS QUICK.
ACCCK!
THESE TWO AREN'T THE REASON I'M HERE.
THWACK
I COULD END THIS GUY. HE'D NEVER GIVE ME TROUBLE AGAIN.
NO... PLEASE! I GOT KIDS!

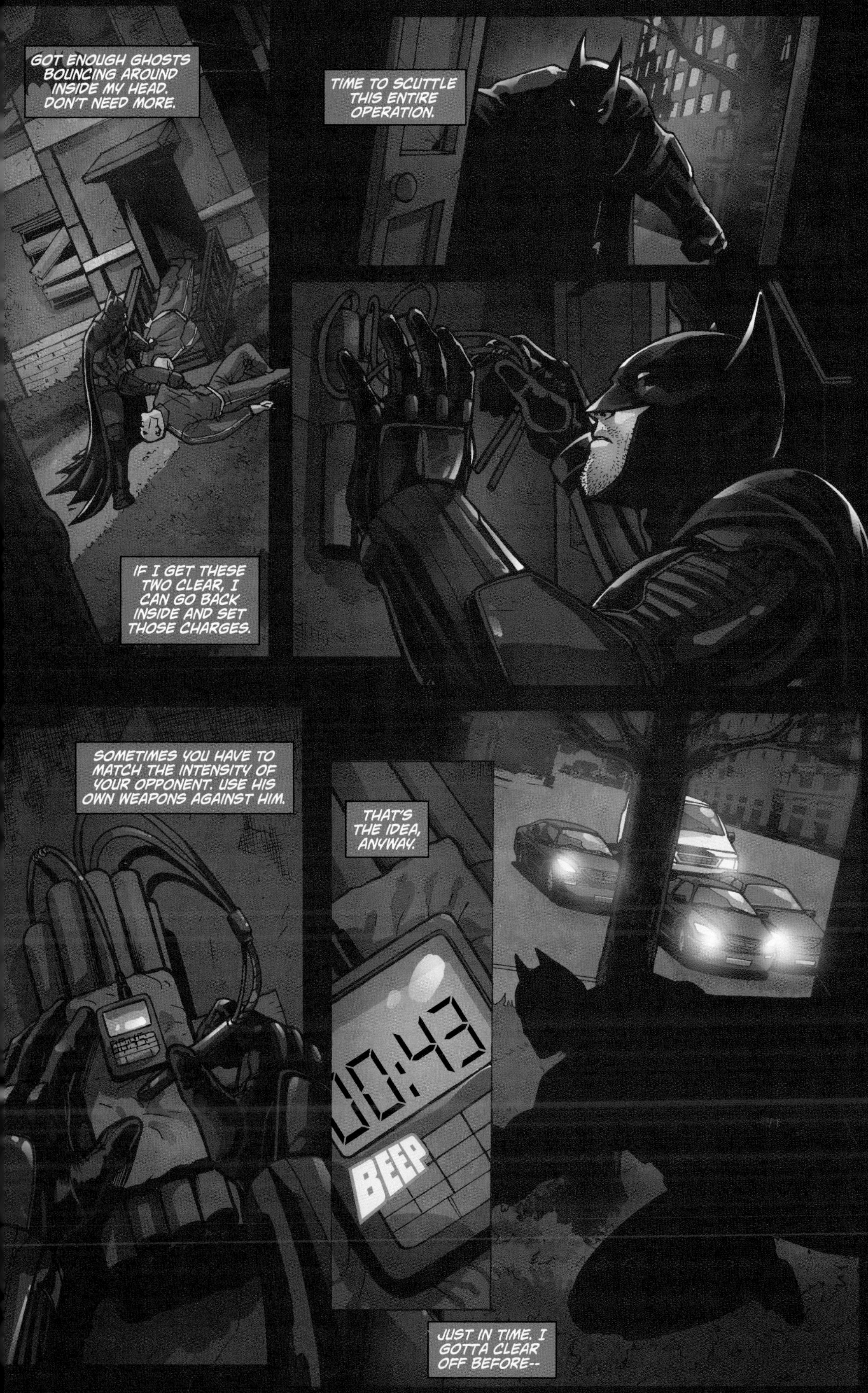
GOT ENOUGH GHOSTS BOUNCING AROUND INSIDE MY HEAD. DON'T NEED MORE.
IF I GET THESE TWO CLEAR, I CAN GO BACK INSIDE AND SET THOSE CHARGES.
TIME TO SCUTTLE THIS ENTIRE OPERATION.
SOMETIMES YOU HAVE TO MATCH THE INTENSITY OF YOUR OPPONENT. USE HIS OWN WEAPONS AGAINST HIM.
THAT'S THE IDEA, ANYWAY.
00:43
BEEP
JUST IN TIME. I GOTTA CLEAR OFF BEFORE--

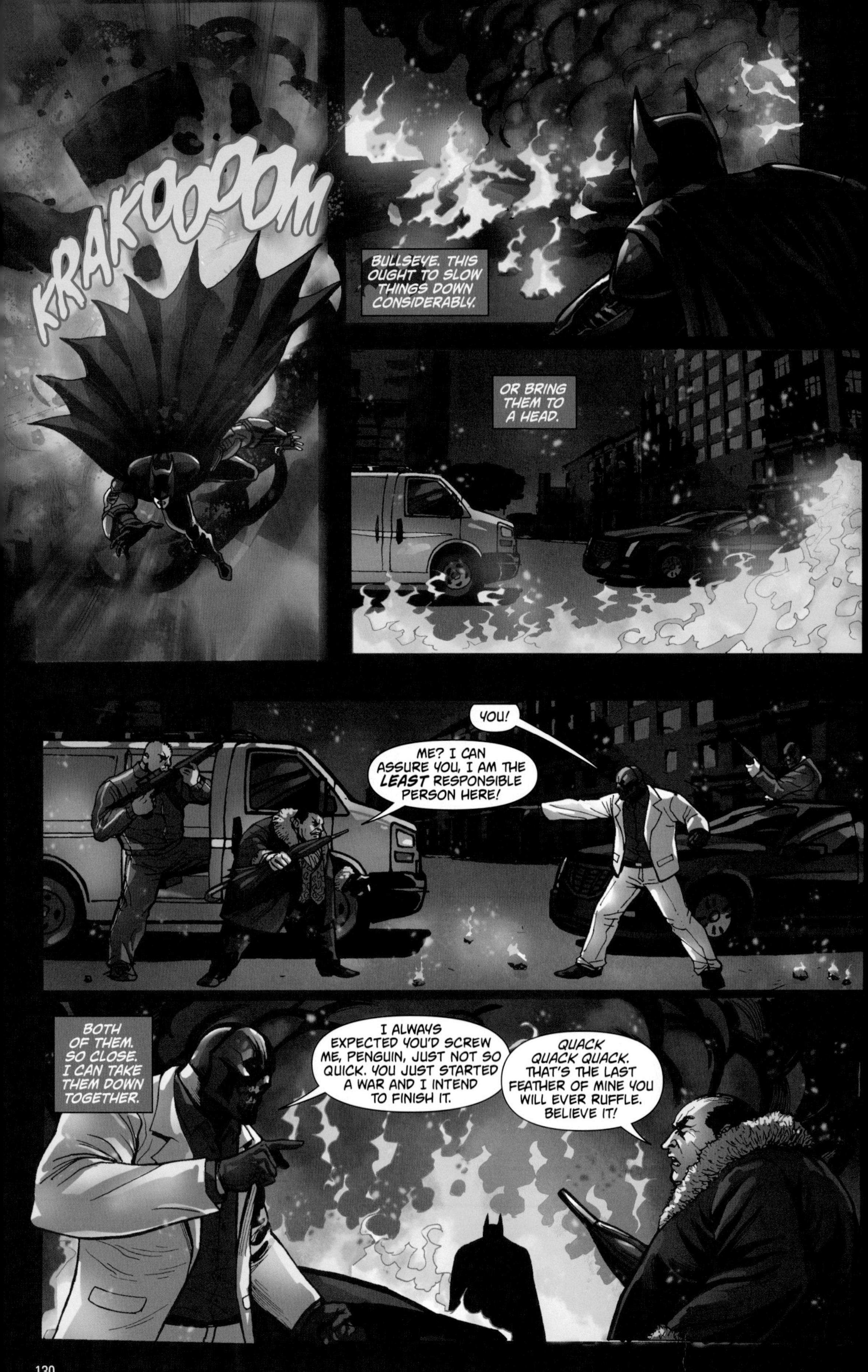
KRAKOOOOM
BULLSEYE. THIS OUGHT TO SLOW THINGS DOWN CONSIDERABLY.
OR BRING THEM TO A HEAD.
YOU!
ME? I CAN ASSURE YOU, I AM THE **LEAST** RESPONSIBLE PERSON HERE!
BOTH OF THEM. SO CLOSE. I CAN TAKE THEM DOWN TOGETHER.
I ALWAYS EXPECTED YOU'D SCREW ME, PENGUIN, JUST NOT SO QUICK. YOU JUST STARTED A WAR AND I INTEND TO FINISH IT.
QUACK QUACK QUACK. THAT'S THE LAST FEATHER OF MINE YOU WILL EVER RUFFLE. BELIEVE IT!

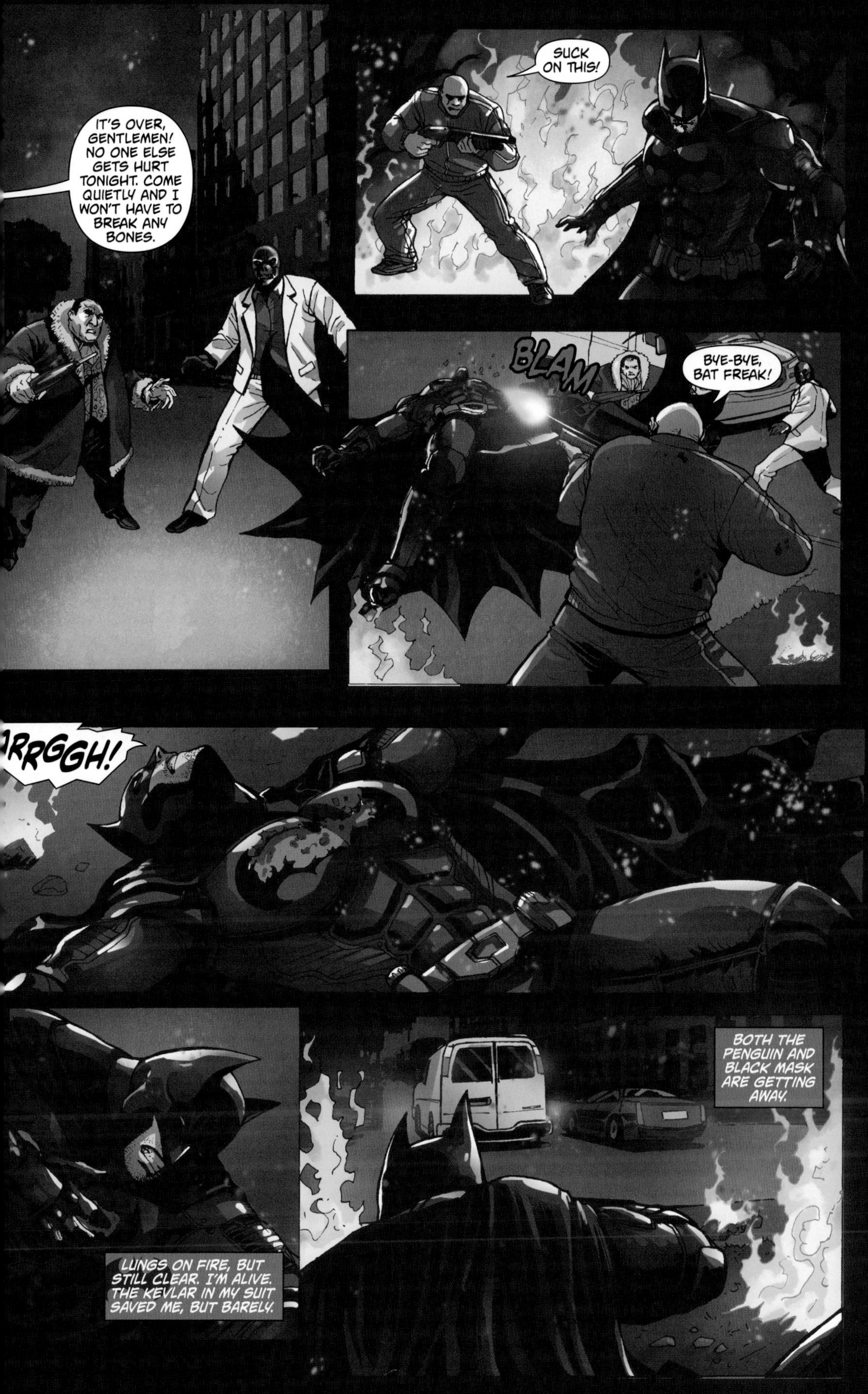
IT'S OVER, GENTLEMEN! NO ONE ELSE GETS HURT TONIGHT. COME QUIETLY AND I WON'T HAVE TO BREAK ANY BONES.
SUCK ON THIS!
BLAM
BYE-BYE, BAT FREAK!
ARRGGH!
LUNGS ON FIRE, BUT STILL CLEAR. I'M ALIVE. THE KEVLAR IN MY SUIT SAVED ME, BUT BARELY.
BOTH THE PENGUIN AND BLACK MASK ARE GETTING AWAY.

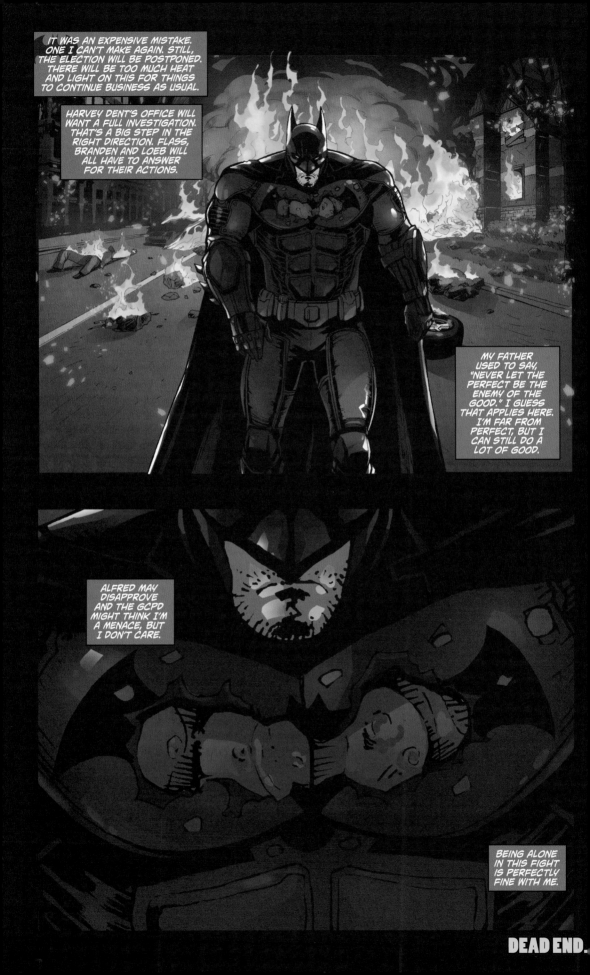

IT WAS AN EXPENSIVE MISTAKE. ONE I CAN'T MAKE AGAIN. STILL, THE ELECTION WILL BE POSTPONED. THERE WILL BE TOO MUCH HEAT AND LIGHT ON THIS FOR THINGS TO CONTINUE BUSINESS AS USUAL.

HARVEY DENT'S OFFICE WILL WANT A FULL INVESTIGATION. THAT'S A BIG STEP IN THE RIGHT DIRECTION. FLASS, BRANDEN AND LOEB WILL ALL HAVE TO ANSWER FOR THEIR ACTIONS.

MY FATHER USED TO SAY, "NEVER LET THE PERFECT BE THE ENEMY OF THE GOOD." I GUESS THAT APPLIES HERE. I'M FAR FROM PERFECT, BUT I CAN STILL DO A LOT OF GOOD.

ALFRED MAY DISAPPROVE AND THE GCPD MIGHT THINK I'M A MENACE, BUT I DON'T CARE.

BEING ALONE IN THIS FIGHT IS PERFECTLY FINE WITH ME.

DEAD END.

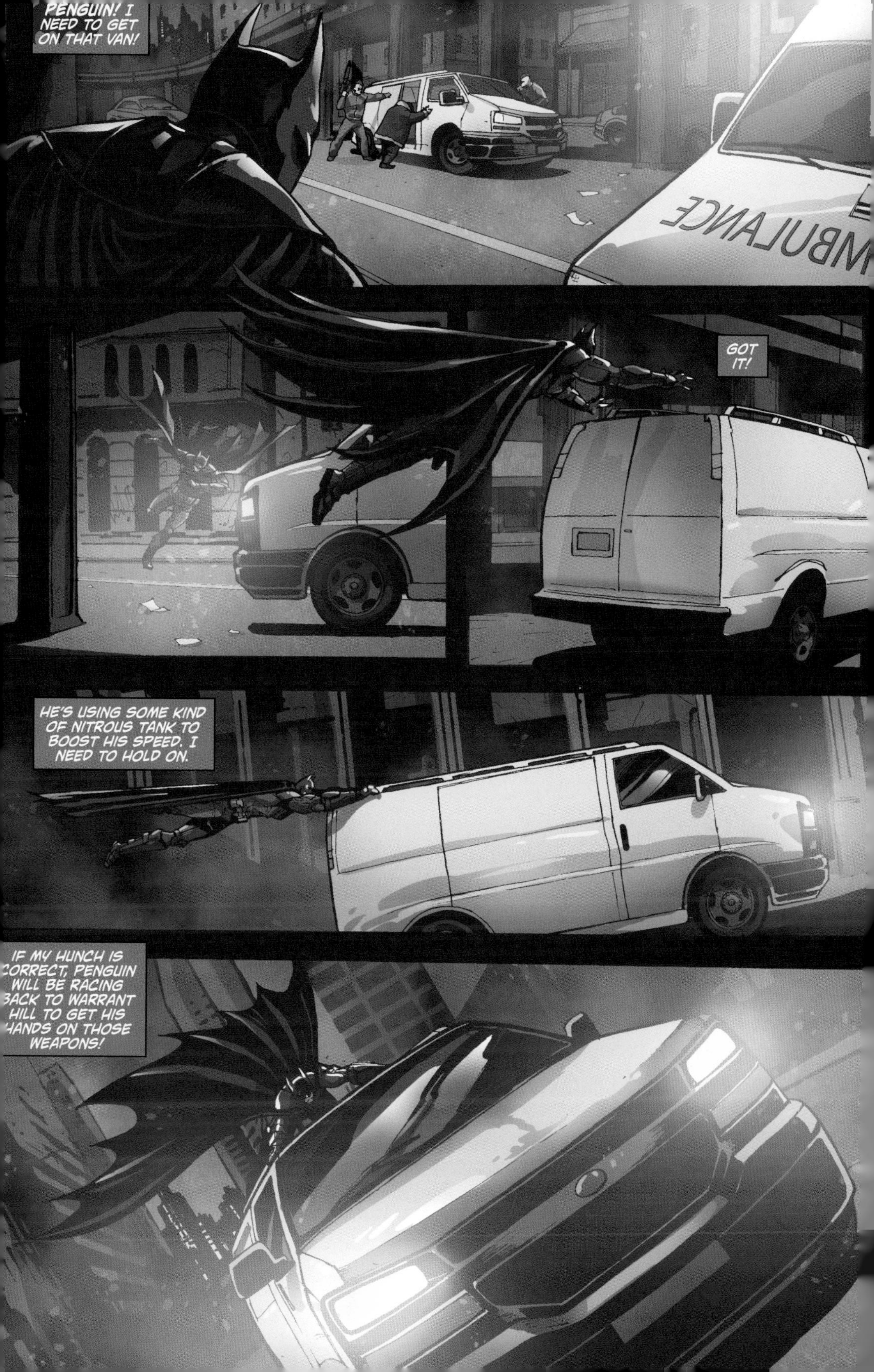
PENGUIN! I NEED TO GET ON THAT VAN!
AMBULANCE
GOT IT!
HE'S USING SOME KIND OF NITROUS TANK TO BOOST HIS SPEED. I NEED TO HOLD ON.
IF MY HUNCH IS CORRECT, PENGUIN WILL BE RACING BACK TO WARRANT HILL TO GET HIS HANDS ON THOSE WEAPONS!

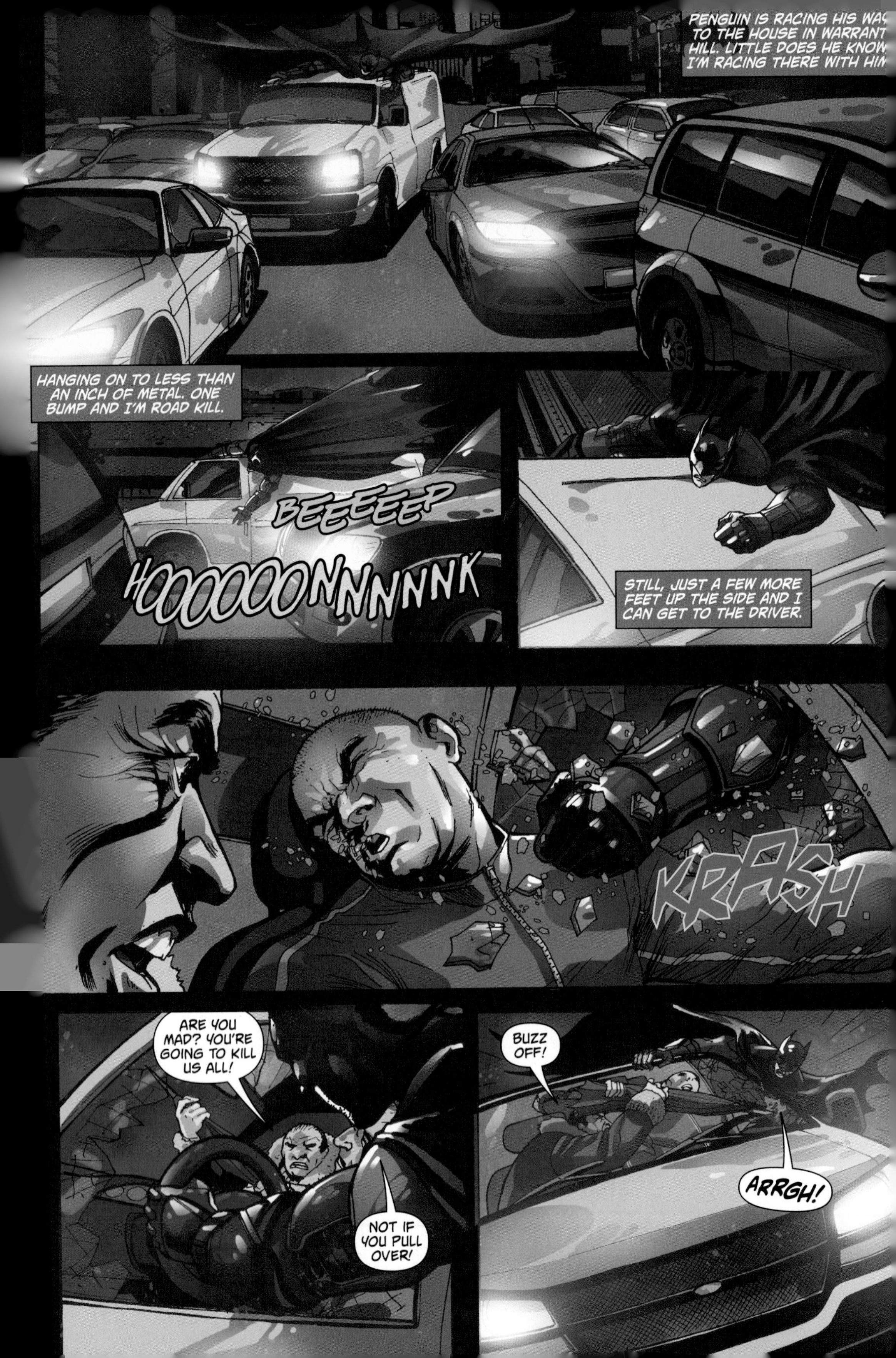
PENGUIN IS RACING HIS WAY TO THE HOUSE IN WARRANT HILL. LITTLE DOES HE KNOW I'M RACING THERE WITH HIM
HANGING ON TO LESS THAN AN INCH OF METAL. ONE BUMP AND I'M ROAD KILL.
BEEEEEEP
HOOOOOOONNNNNK
STILL, JUST A FEW MORE FEET UP THE SIDE AND I CAN GET TO THE DRIVER.
KRASH
ARE YOU MAD? YOU'RE GOING TO KILL US ALL!
NOT IF YOU PULL OVER!
BUZZ OFF!
ARRGH!

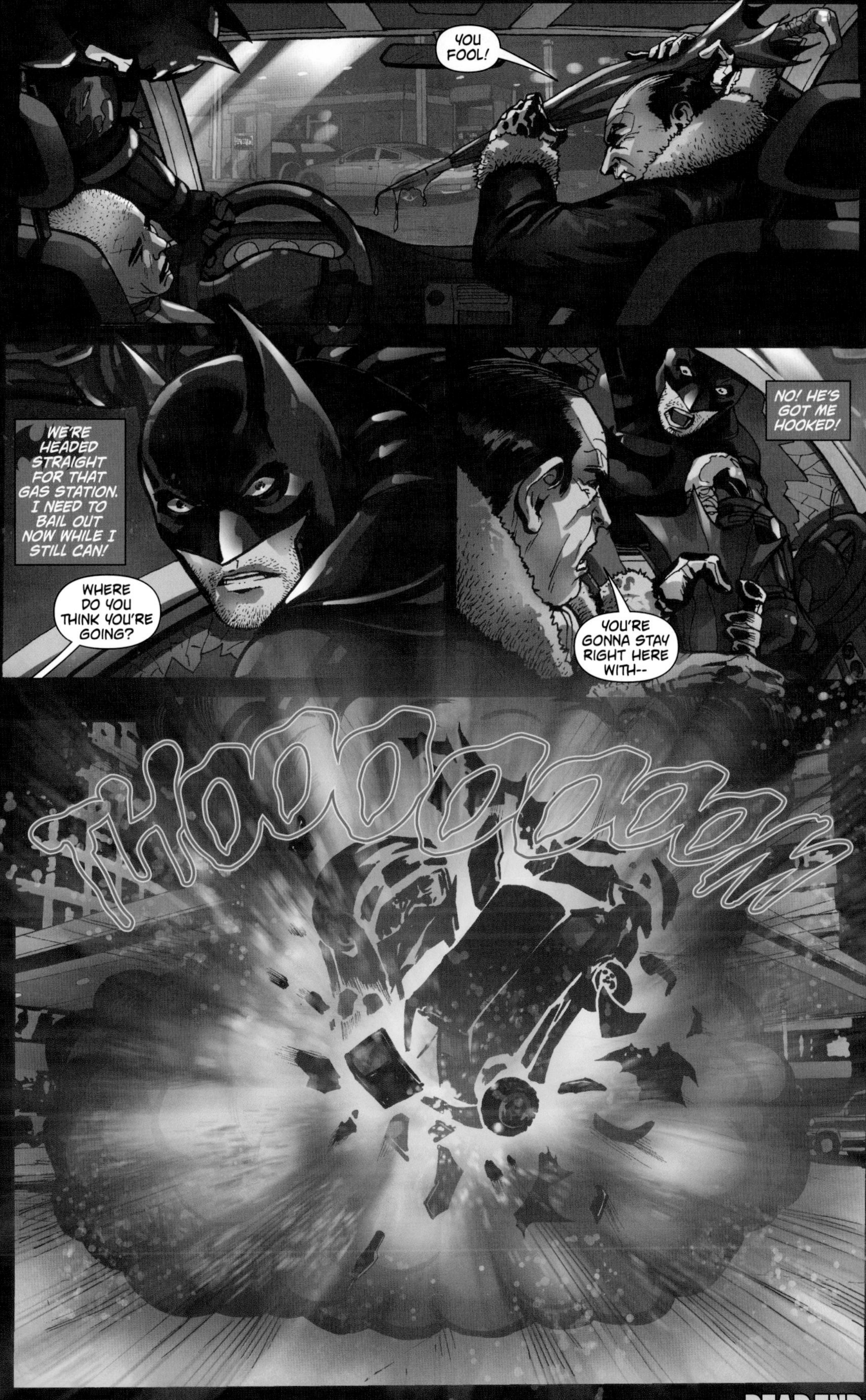
YOU FOOL!
WE'RE HEADED STRAIGHT FOR THAT GAS STATION. I NEED TO BAIL OUT NOW WHILE I STILL CAN!
WHERE DO YOU THINK YOU'RE GOING?
NO! HE'S GOT ME HOOKED!
YOU'RE GONNA STAY RIGHT HERE WITH--
THOOOOOOOOM

DEAD END.

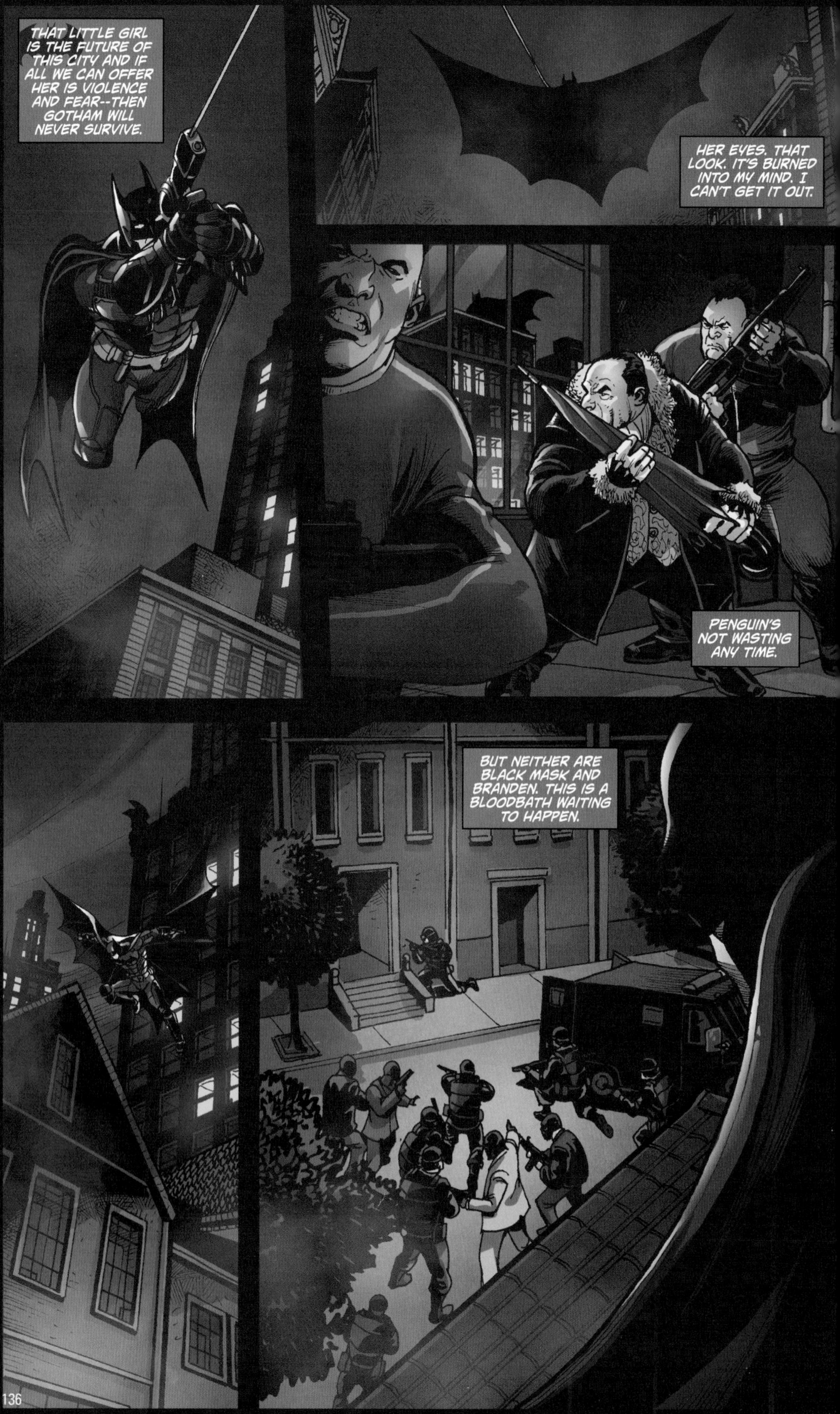
THAT LITTLE GIRL IS THE FUTURE OF THIS CITY AND IF ALL WE CAN OFFER HER IS VIOLENCE AND FEAR--THEN GOTHAM WILL NEVER SURVIVE.
HER EYES. THAT LOOK. IT'S BURNED INTO MY MIND. I CAN'T GET IT OUT.
PENGUIN'S NOT WASTING ANY TIME.
BUT NEITHER ARE BLACK MASK AND BRANDEN. THIS IS A BLOODBATH WAITING TO HAPPEN.

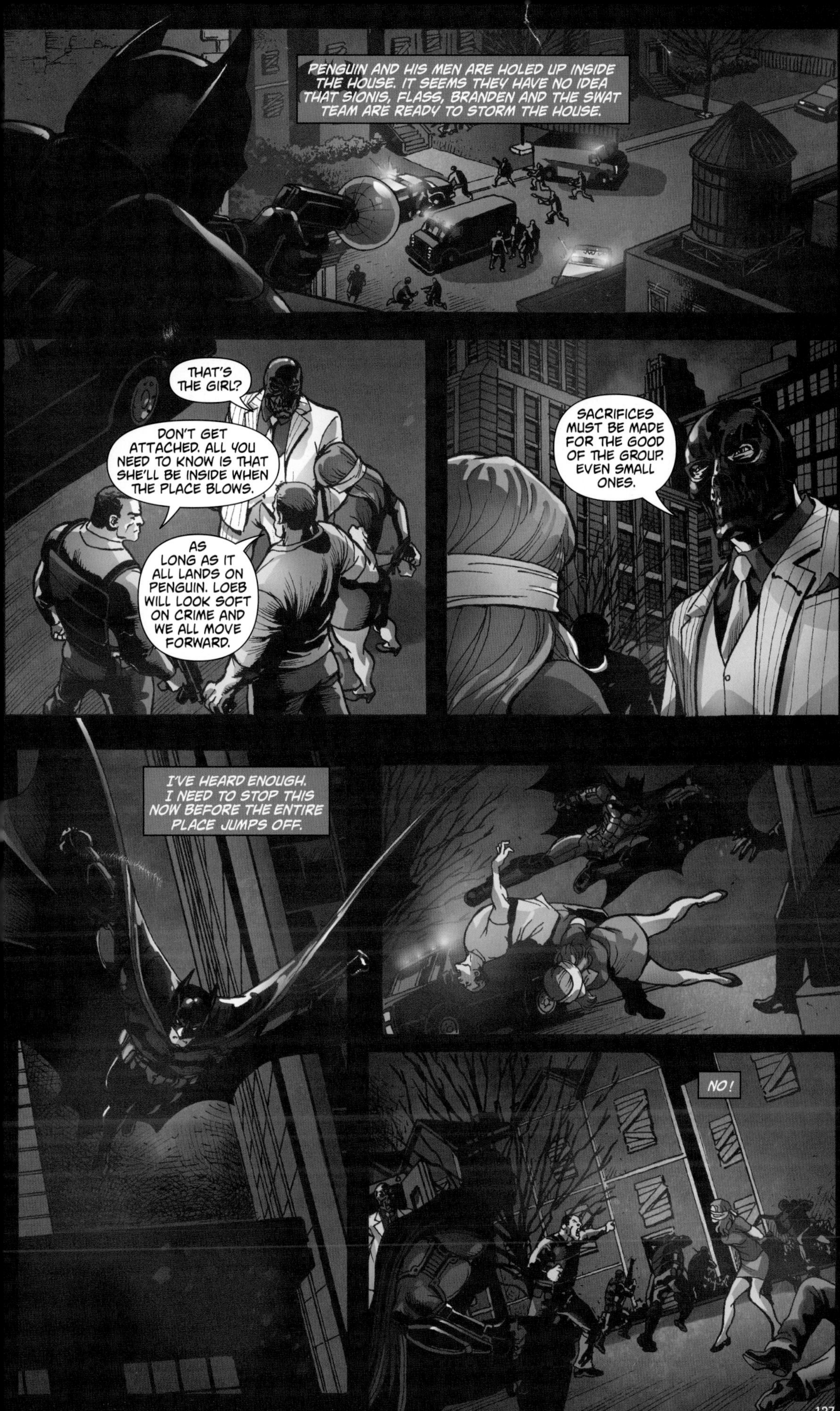
PENGUIN AND HIS MEN ARE HOLED UP INSIDE THE HOUSE. IT SEEMS THEY HAVE NO IDEA THAT SIONIS, FLASS, BRANDEN AND THE SWAT TEAM ARE READY TO STORM THE HOUSE.
THAT'S THE GIRL?
DON'T GET ATTACHED. ALL YOU NEED TO KNOW IS THAT SHE'LL BE INSIDE WHEN THE PLACE BLOWS.
AS LONG AS IT ALL LANDS ON PENGUIN. LOEB WILL LOOK SOFT ON CRIME AND WE ALL MOVE FORWARD.
SACRIFICES MUST BE MADE FOR THE GOOD OF THE GROUP. EVEN SMALL ONES.
I'VE HEARD ENOUGH. I NEED TO STOP THIS NOW BEFORE THE ENTIRE PLACE JUMPS OFF.
NO!

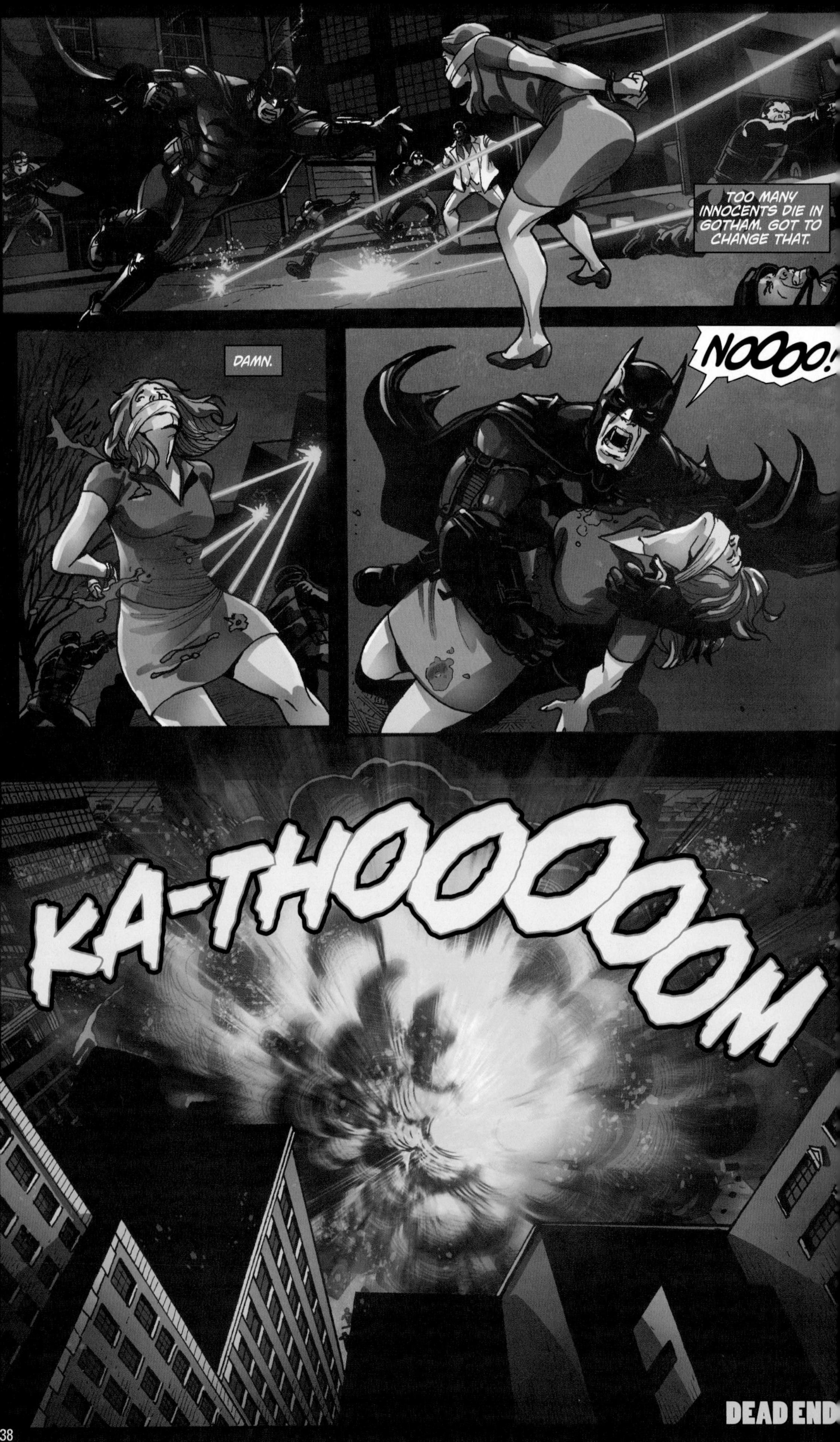
TOO MANY INNOCENTS DIE IN GOTHAM. GOT TO CHANGE THAT.
DAMN.
NOOOO!
KA-THOOOOOOM
DEAD END

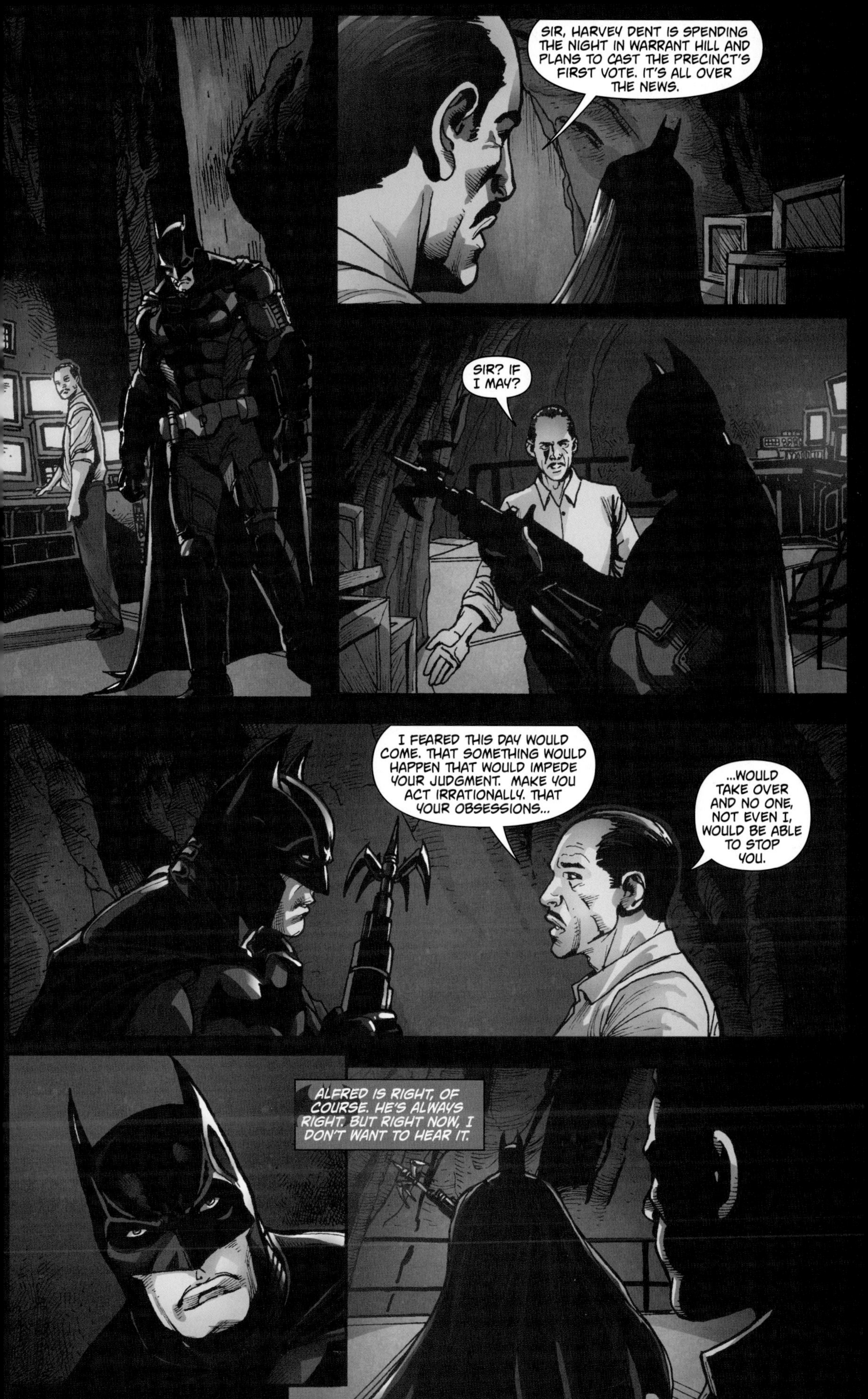
SIR, HARVEY DENT IS SPENDING THE NIGHT IN WARRANT HILL AND PLANS TO CAST THE PRECINCT'S FIRST VOTE. IT'S ALL OVER THE NEWS.
SIR? IF I MAY?
I FEARED THIS DAY WOULD COME. THAT SOMETHING WOULD HAPPEN THAT WOULD IMPEDE YOUR JUDGMENT. MAKE YOU ACT IRRATIONALLY. THAT YOUR OBSESSIONS...
...WOULD TAKE OVER AND NO ONE, NOT EVEN I, WOULD BE ABLE TO STOP YOU.
ALFRED IS RIGHT, OF COURSE. HE'S ALWAYS RIGHT. BUT RIGHT NOW, I DON'T WANT TO HEAR IT.

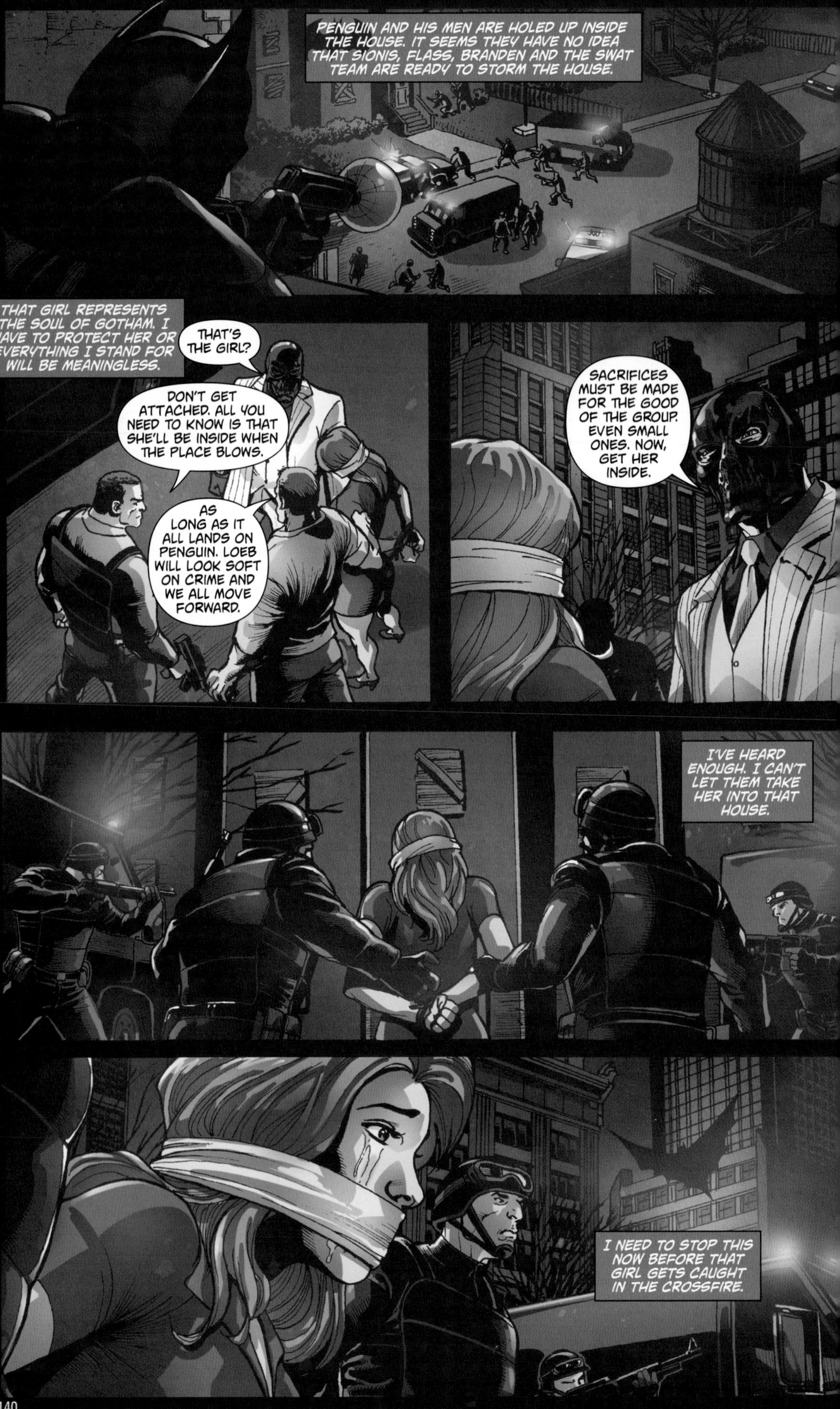
PENGUIN AND HIS MEN ARE HOLED UP INSIDE THE HOUSE. IT SEEMS THEY HAVE NO IDEA THAT SIONIS, FLASS, BRANDEN AND THE SWAT TEAM ARE READY TO STORM THE HOUSE.
THAT GIRL REPRESENTS THE SOUL OF GOTHAM. I HAVE TO PROTECT HER OR EVERYTHING I STAND FOR WILL BE MEANINGLESS.
THAT'S THE GIRL?
DON'T GET ATTACHED. ALL YOU NEED TO KNOW IS THAT SHE'LL BE INSIDE WHEN THE PLACE BLOWS.
AS LONG AS IT ALL LANDS ON PENGUIN. LOEB WILL LOOK SOFT ON CRIME AND WE ALL MOVE FORWARD.
SACRIFICES MUST BE MADE FOR THE GOOD OF THE GROUP. EVEN SMALL ONES. NOW, GET HER INSIDE.
I'VE HEARD ENOUGH. I CAN'T LET THEM TAKE HER INTO THAT HOUSE.
I NEED TO STOP THIS NOW BEFORE THAT GIRL GETS CAUGHT IN THE CROSSFIRE.

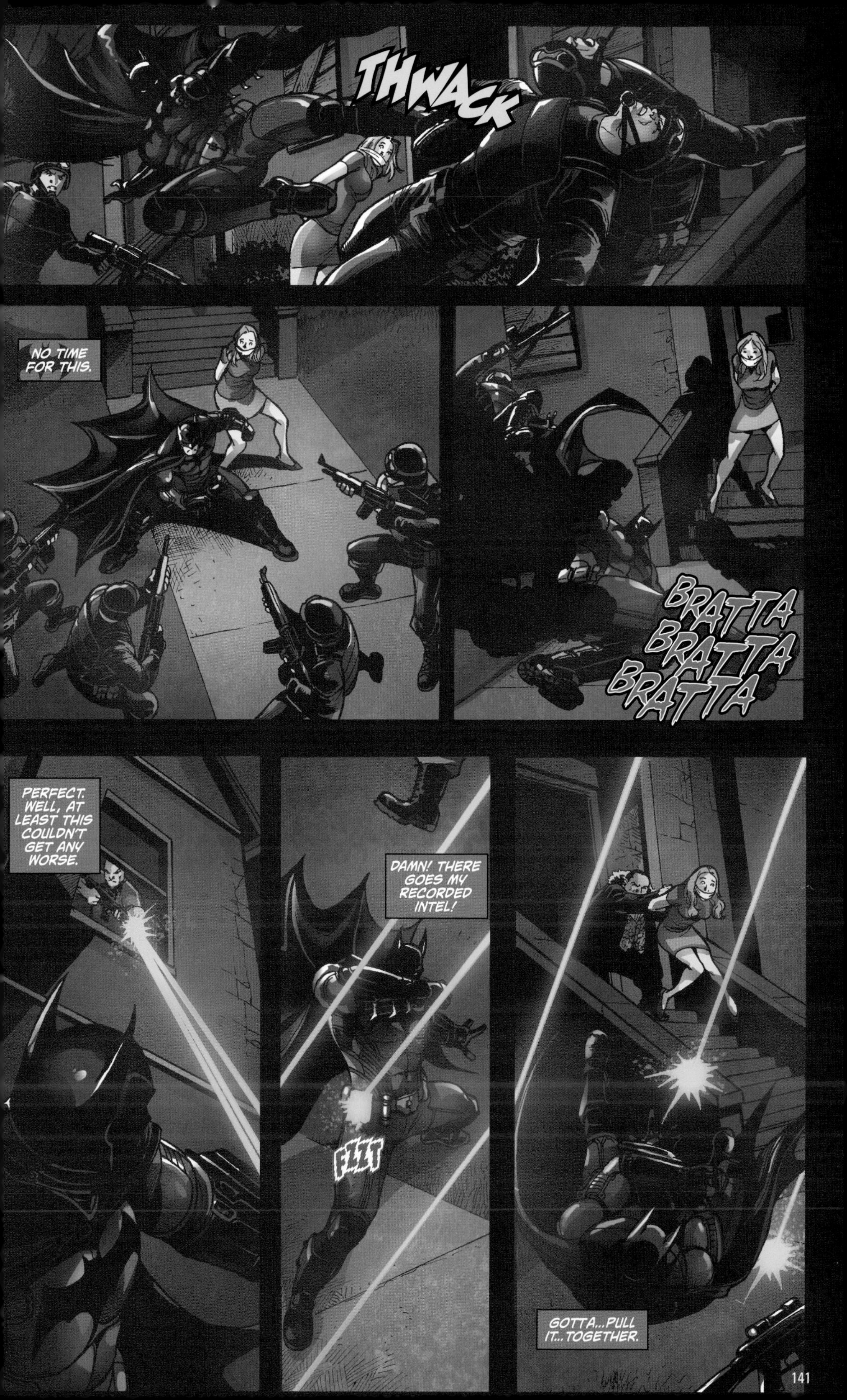
THWACK
NO TIME FOR THIS.
BRATTA BRATTA BRATTA
PERFECT. WELL, AT LEAST THIS COULDN'T GET ANY WORSE.
DAMN! THERE GOES MY RECORDED INTEL!
FZZT
GOTTA...PULL IT...TOGETHER.

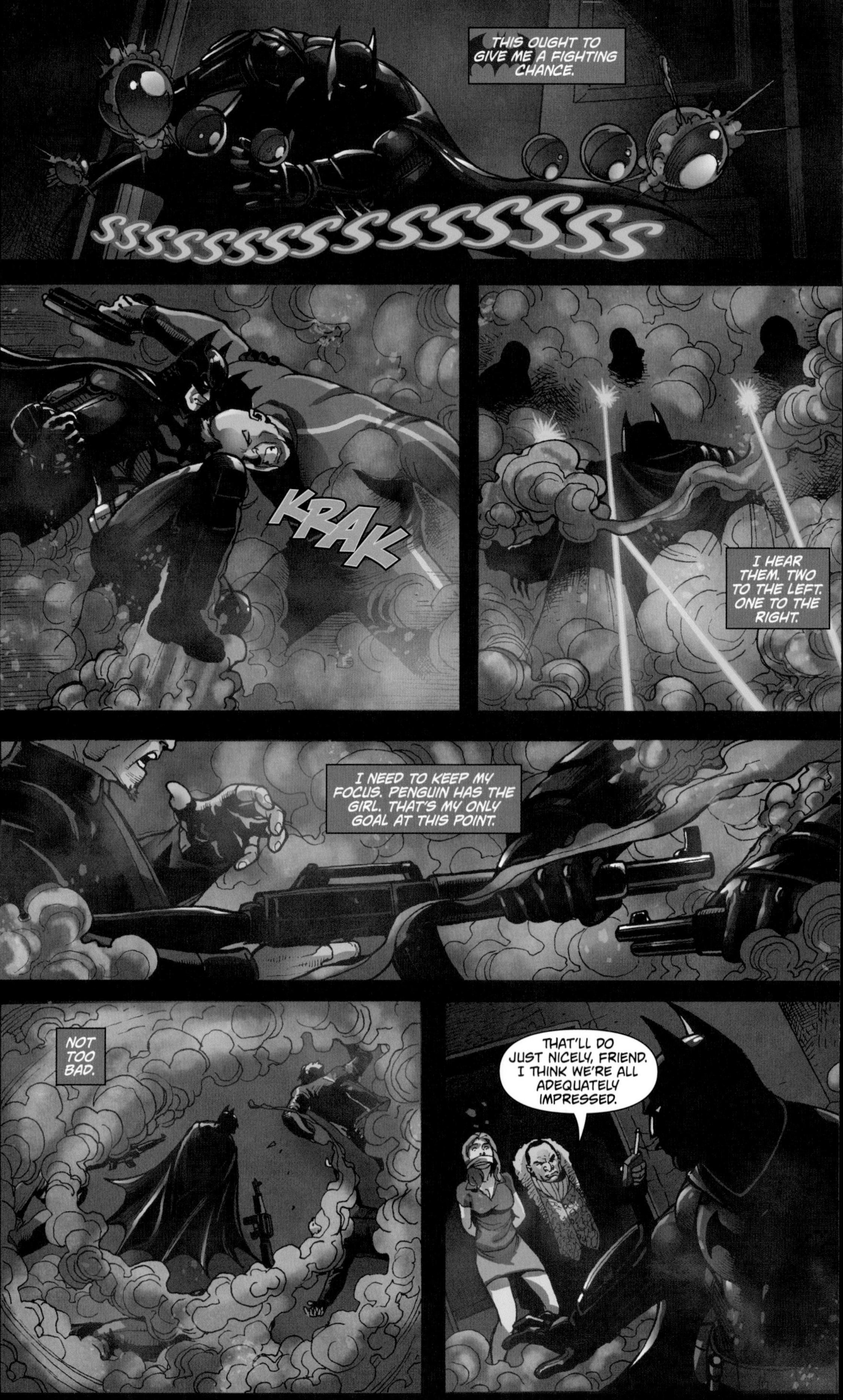
THIS OUGHT TO GIVE ME A FIGHTING CHANCE.
SSSSSSSSSSSSSSS
KRAK
I HEAR THEM. TWO TO THE LEFT. ONE TO THE RIGHT.
I NEED TO KEEP MY FOCUS. PENGUIN HAS THE GIRL. THAT'S MY ONLY GOAL AT THIS POINT.
NOT TOO BAD.
THAT'LL DO JUST NICELY, FRIEND. I THINK WE'RE ALL ADEQUATELY IMPRESSED.

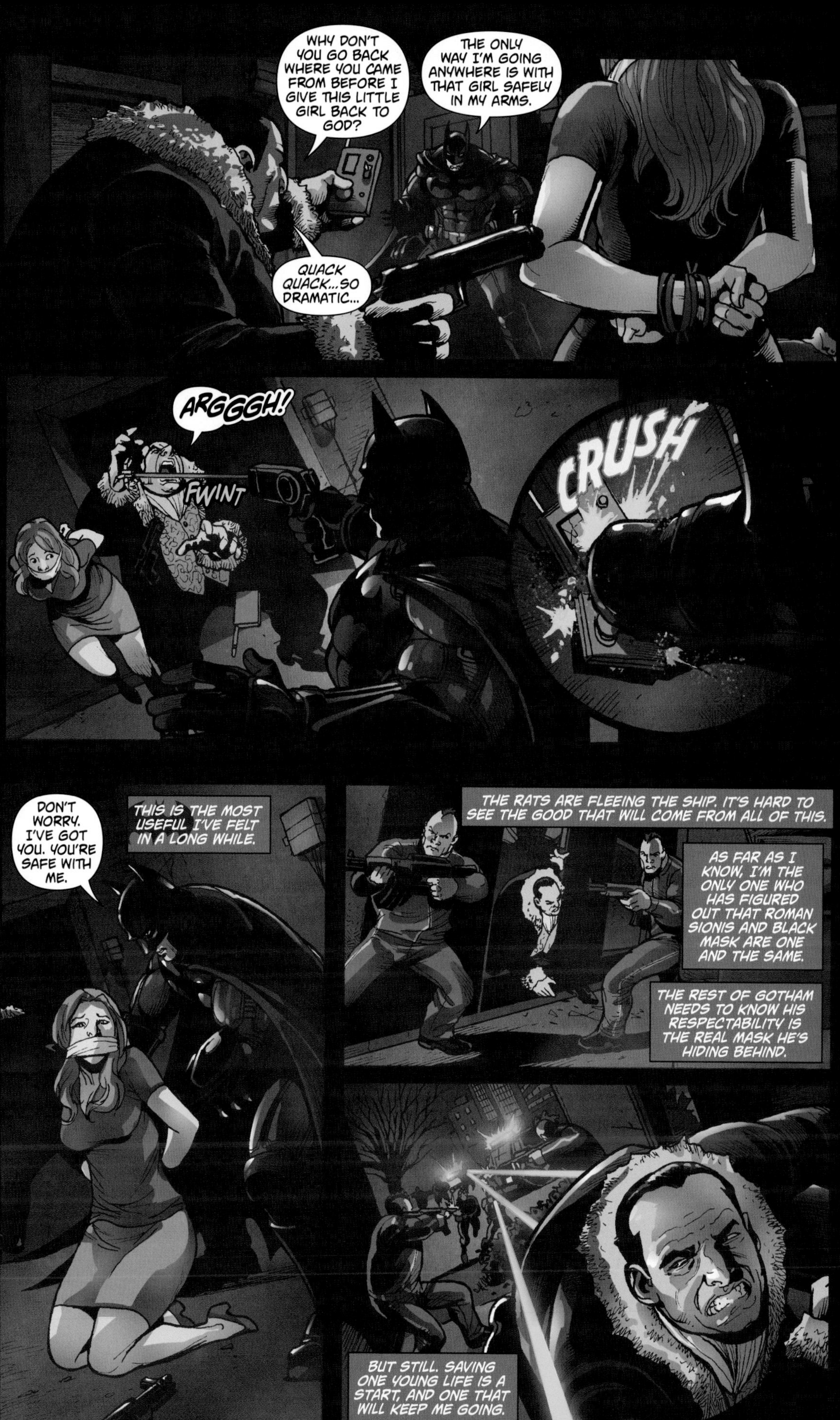
WHY DON'T YOU GO BACK WHERE YOU CAME FROM BEFORE I GIVE THIS LITTLE GIRL BACK TO GOD?
THE ONLY WAY I'M GOING ANYWHERE IS WITH THAT GIRL SAFELY IN MY ARMS.
QUACK QUACK...SO DRAMATIC...
ARGGGH!
FWINT
CRUSH
DON'T WORRY. I'VE GOT YOU. YOU'RE SAFE WITH ME.
THIS IS THE MOST USEFUL I'VE FELT IN A LONG WHILE.
THE RATS ARE FLEEING THE SHIP. IT'S HARD TO SEE THE GOOD THAT WILL COME FROM ALL OF THIS.
AS FAR AS I KNOW, I'M THE ONLY ONE WHO HAS FIGURED OUT THAT ROMAN SIONIS AND BLACK MASK ARE ONE AND THE SAME.
THE REST OF GOTHAM NEEDS TO KNOW HIS RESPECTABILITY IS THE REAL MASK HE'S HIDING BEHIND.
BUT STILL. SAVING ONE YOUNG LIFE IS A START, AND ONE THAT WILL KEEP ME GOING.

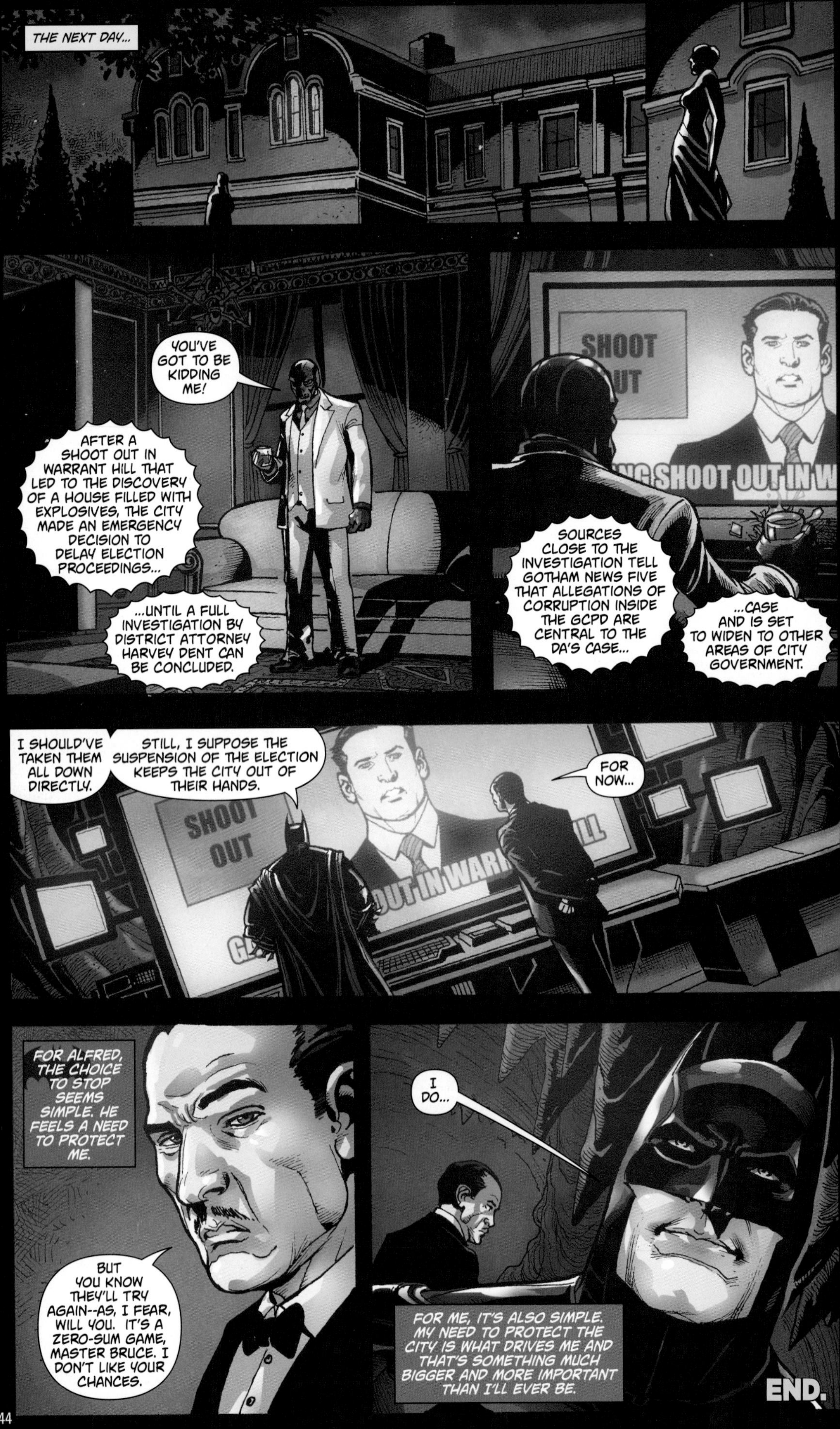
THE NEXT DAY...
YOU'VE GOT TO BE KIDDING ME!
AFTER A SHOOT OUT IN WARRANT HILL THAT LED TO THE DISCOVERY OF A HOUSE FILLED WITH EXPLOSIVES, THE CITY MADE AN EMERGENCY DECISION TO DELAY ELECTION PROCEEDINGS...
...UNTIL A FULL INVESTIGATION BY DISTRICT ATTORNEY HARVEY DENT CAN BE CONCLUDED.
SHOOT OUT
SOURCES CLOSE TO THE INVESTIGATION TELL GOTHAM NEWS FIVE THAT ALLEGATIONS OF CORRUPTION INSIDE THE GCPD ARE CENTRAL TO THE DA'S CASE...
...CASE AND IS SET TO WIDEN TO OTHER AREAS OF CITY GOVERNMENT.
I SHOULD'VE TAKEN THEM ALL DOWN DIRECTLY.
STILL, I SUPPOSE THE SUSPENSION OF THE ELECTION KEEPS THE CITY OUT OF THEIR HANDS.
FOR NOW...
SHOOT OUT
FOR ALFRED, THE CHOICE TO STOP SEEMS SIMPLE. HE FEELS A NEED TO PROTECT ME.
BUT YOU KNOW THEY'LL TRY AGAIN--AS, I FEAR, WILL YOU. IT'S A ZERO-SUM GAME, MASTER BRUCE. I DON'T LIKE YOUR CHANCES.
I DO...
FOR ME, IT'S ALSO SIMPLE. MY NEED TO PROTECT THE CITY IS WHAT DRIVES ME AND THAT'S SOMETHING MUCH BIGGER AND MORE IMPORTANT THAN I'LL EVER BE.
END.

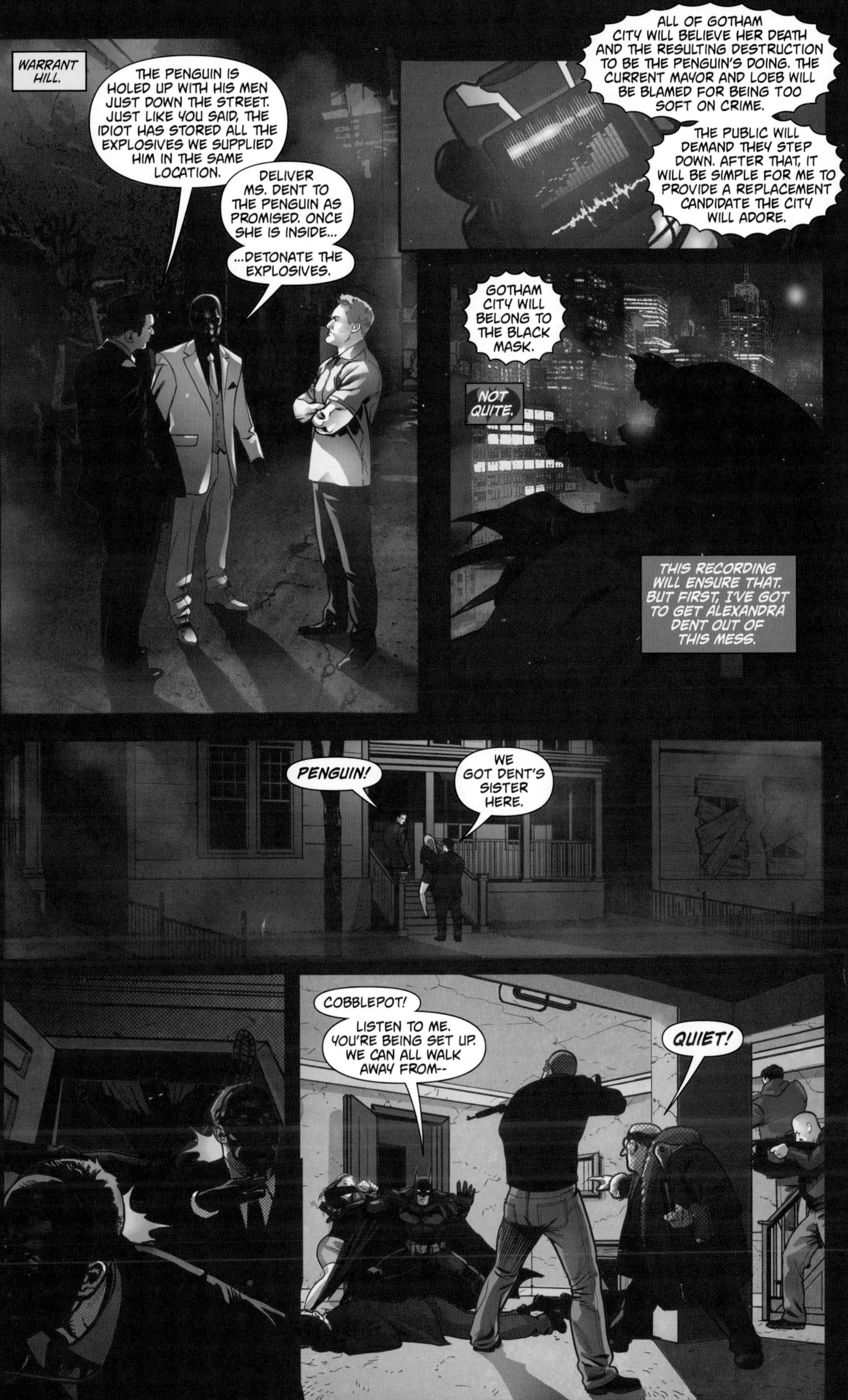
WARRANT HILL.
THE PENGUIN IS HOLED UP WITH HIS MEN JUST DOWN THE STREET. JUST LIKE YOU SAID, THE IDIOT HAS STORED ALL THE EXPLOSIVES WE SUPPLIED HIM IN THE SAME LOCATION.
DELIVER MS. DENT TO THE PENGUIN AS PROMISED. ONCE SHE IS INSIDE...
...DETONATE THE EXPLOSIVES.
ALL OF GOTHAM CITY WILL BELIEVE HER DEATH AND THE RESULTING DESTRUCTION TO BE THE PENGUIN'S DOING. THE CURRENT MAYOR AND LOEB WILL BE BLAMED FOR BEING TOO SOFT ON CRIME.
THE PUBLIC WILL DEMAND THEY STEP DOWN. AFTER THAT, IT WILL BE SIMPLE FOR ME TO PROVIDE A REPLACEMENT CANDIDATE THE CITY WILL ADORE.
GOTHAM CITY WILL BELONG TO THE BLACK MASK.
NOT QUITE.
THIS RECORDING WILL ENSURE THAT. BUT FIRST, I'VE GOT TO GET ALEXANDRA DENT OUT OF THIS MESS.
PENGUIN!
WE GOT DENT'S SISTER HERE.
COBBLEPOT!
LISTEN TO ME. YOU'RE BEING SET UP. WE CAN ALL WALK AWAY FROM--
QUIET!

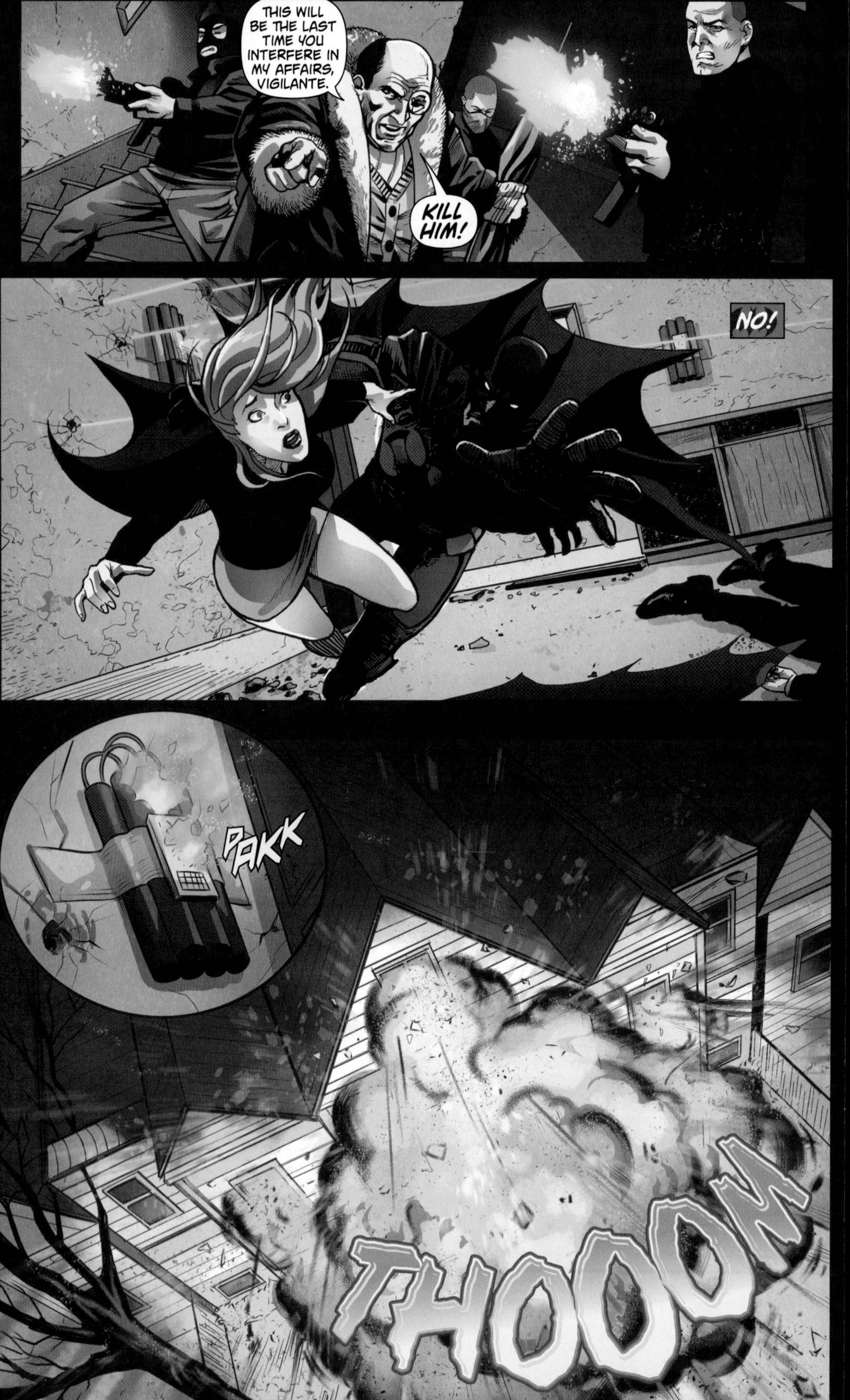

THIS WILL BE THE LAST TIME YOU INTERFERE IN MY AFFAIRS, VIGILANTE.
KILL HIM!
NO!
DAKK
THOOOM

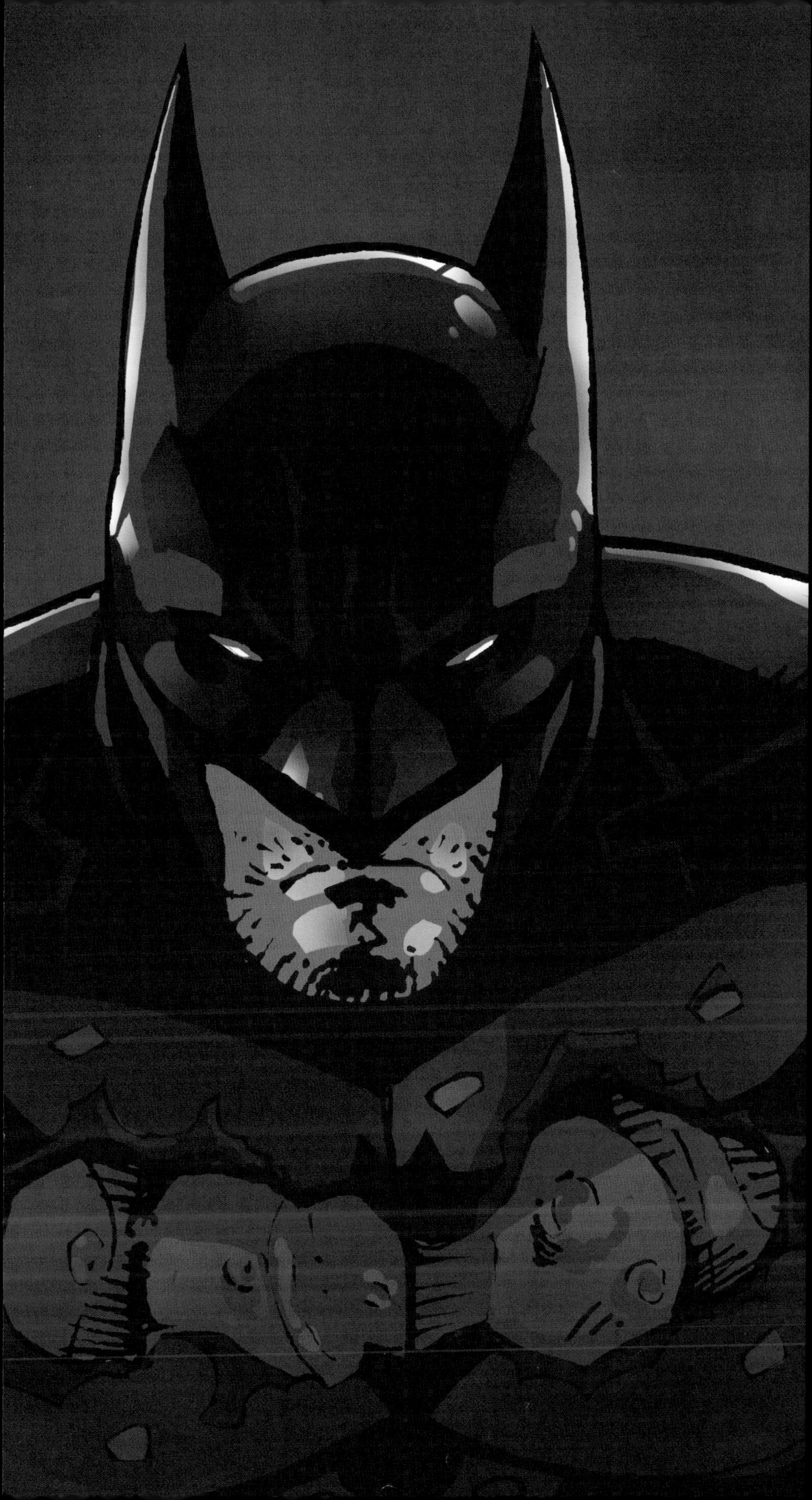

Origins of Arkham

Behind the scenes of the BATMAN: ARKHAM ORIGINS development

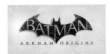

DC² MULTIVERSE

ARKHAM ORIGINS ROADMAP

x = Dead End

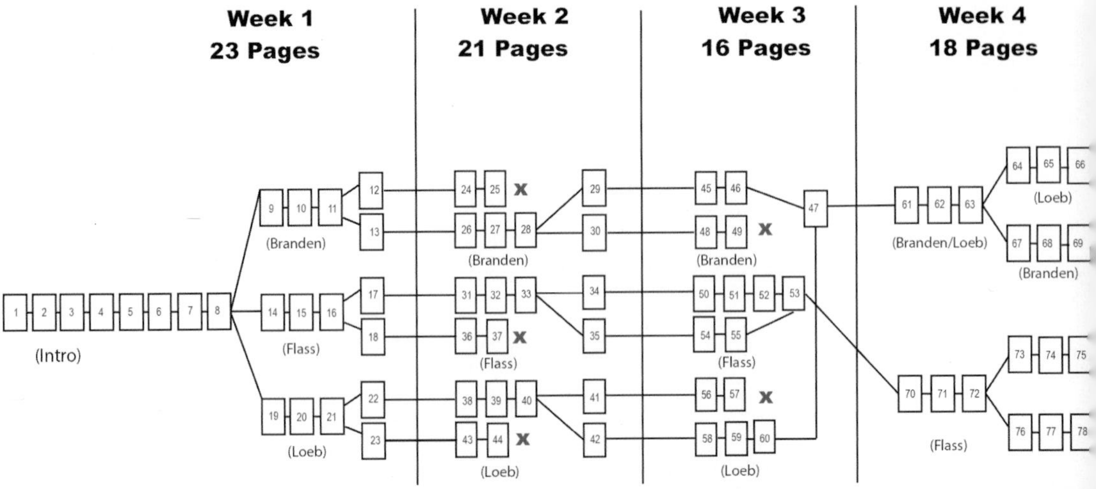
Week 1
23 Pages
Week 2
21 Pages
Week 3
16 Pages
Week 4
18 Pages
(Intro)
(Branden)
(Flass)
(Loeb)
(Branden)
(Flass)
(Loeb)
(Branden)
(Flass)
(Loeb)
(Branden/Loeb)
(Loeb)
(Branden)
(Flass)

Here is the roadmap created by the editors to help outline the progress and development of the story.

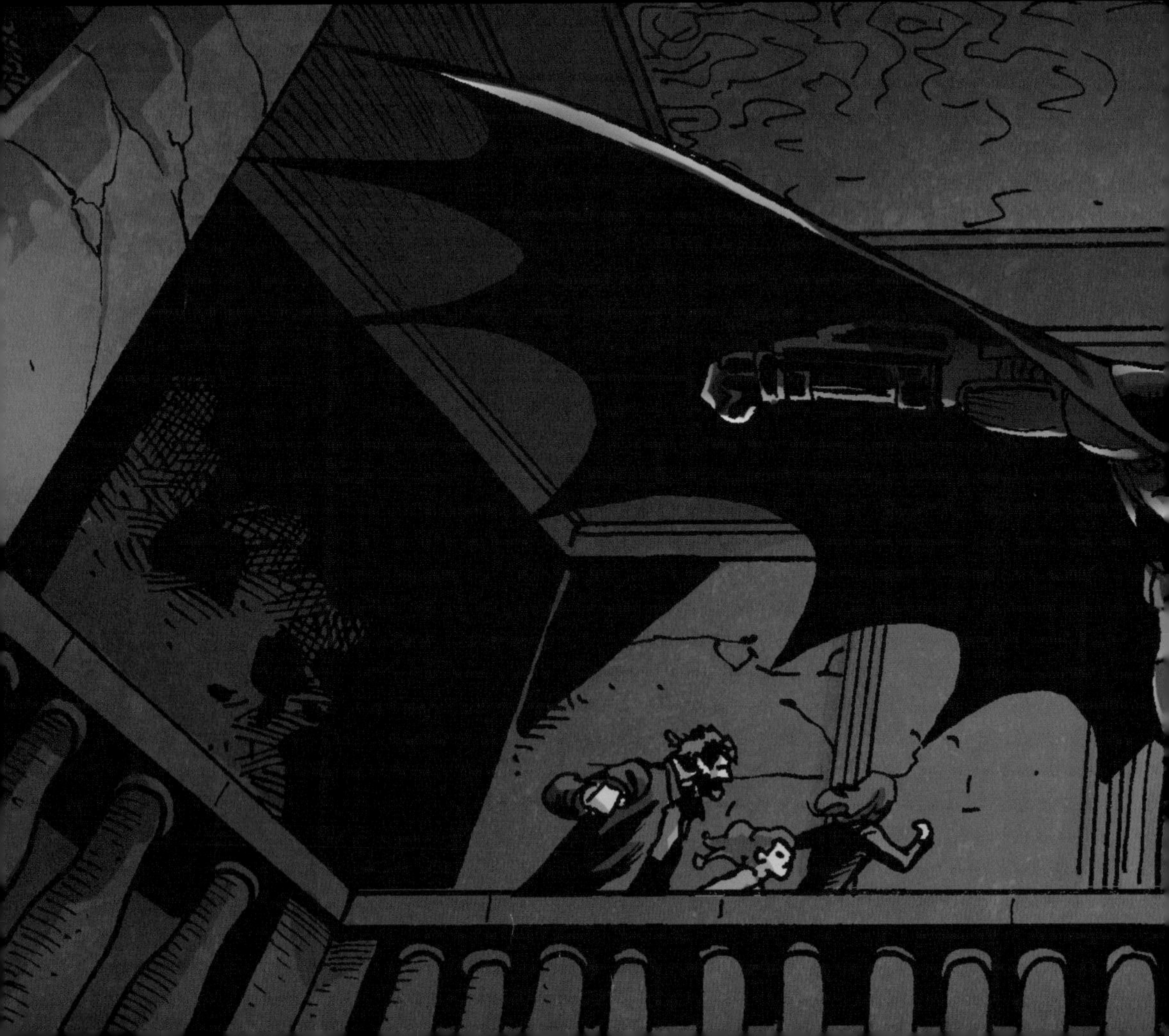

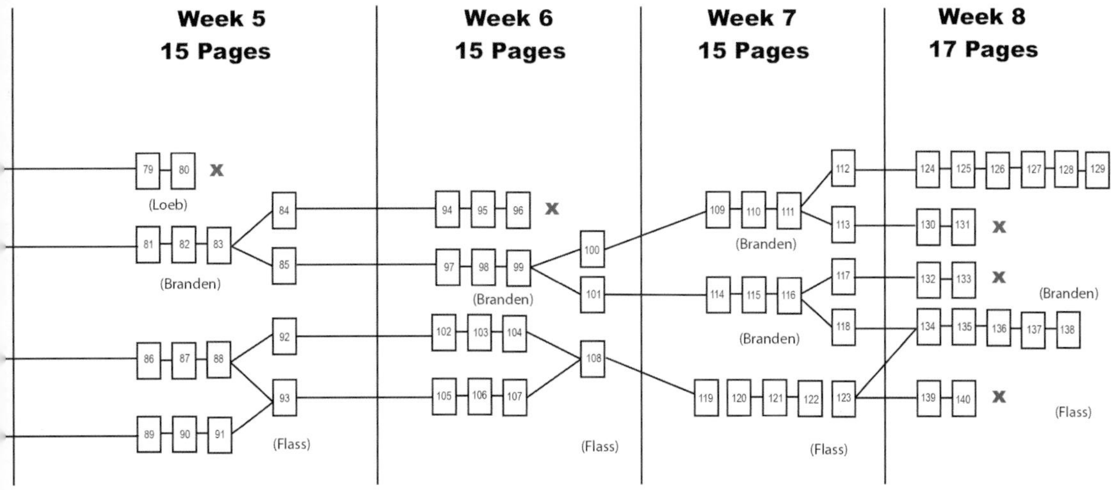
Week 5
15 Pages
Week 6
15 Pages
Week 7
15 Pages
Week 8
17 Pages
79
80
X
(Loeb)
81
82
83
84
85
(Branden)
86
87
88
89
90
91
92
93
(Flass)
94
95
96
X
97
98
99
(Branden)
100
101
102
103
104
105
106
107
108
(Flass)
109
110
111
112
113
(Branden)
114
115
116
117
118
(Branden)
119
120
121
122
123
(Flass)
124
125
126
127
128
129
130
131
X
132
133
X
(Branden)
134
135
136
137
138
139
140
X
(Flass)

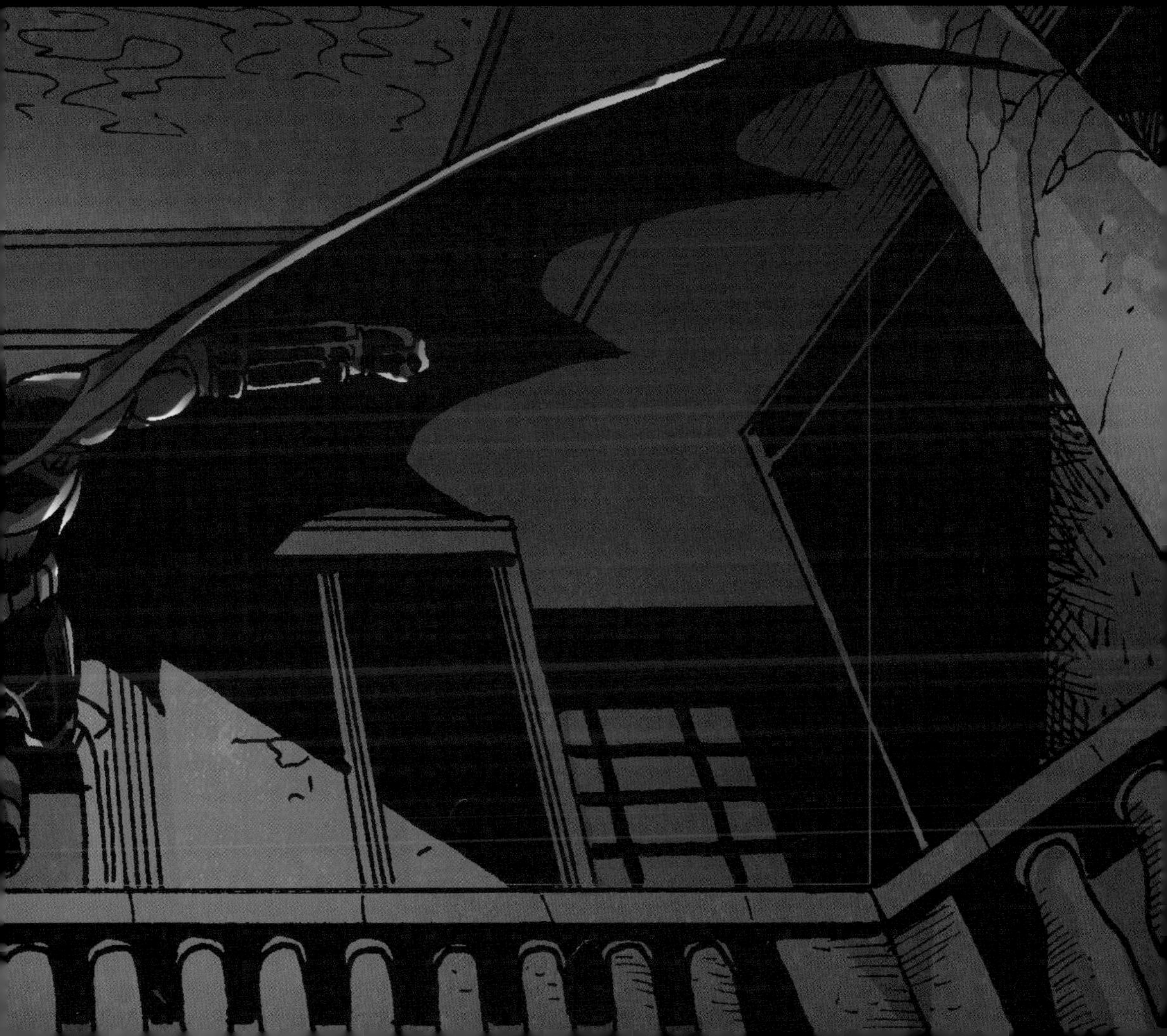

For the digital release of the story, there were many panels that had multiple versions drawn in order to properly animate the story. The following are examples of those panels. Page 23

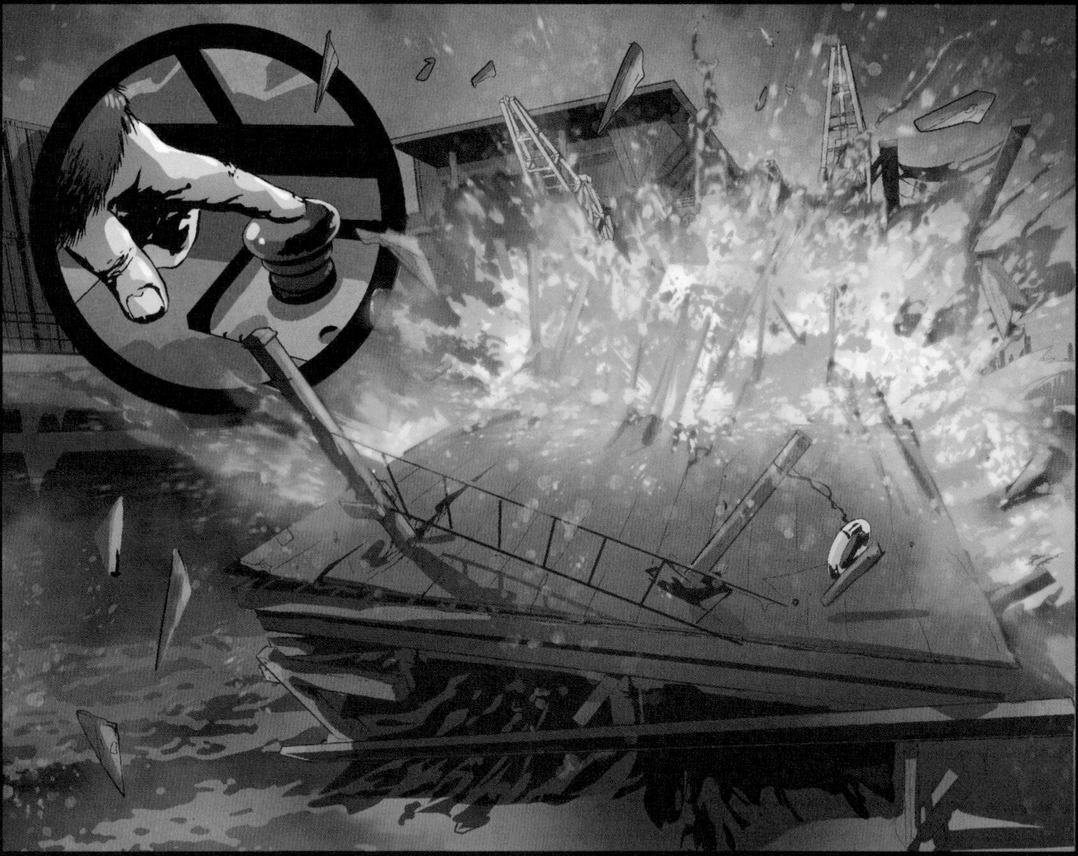

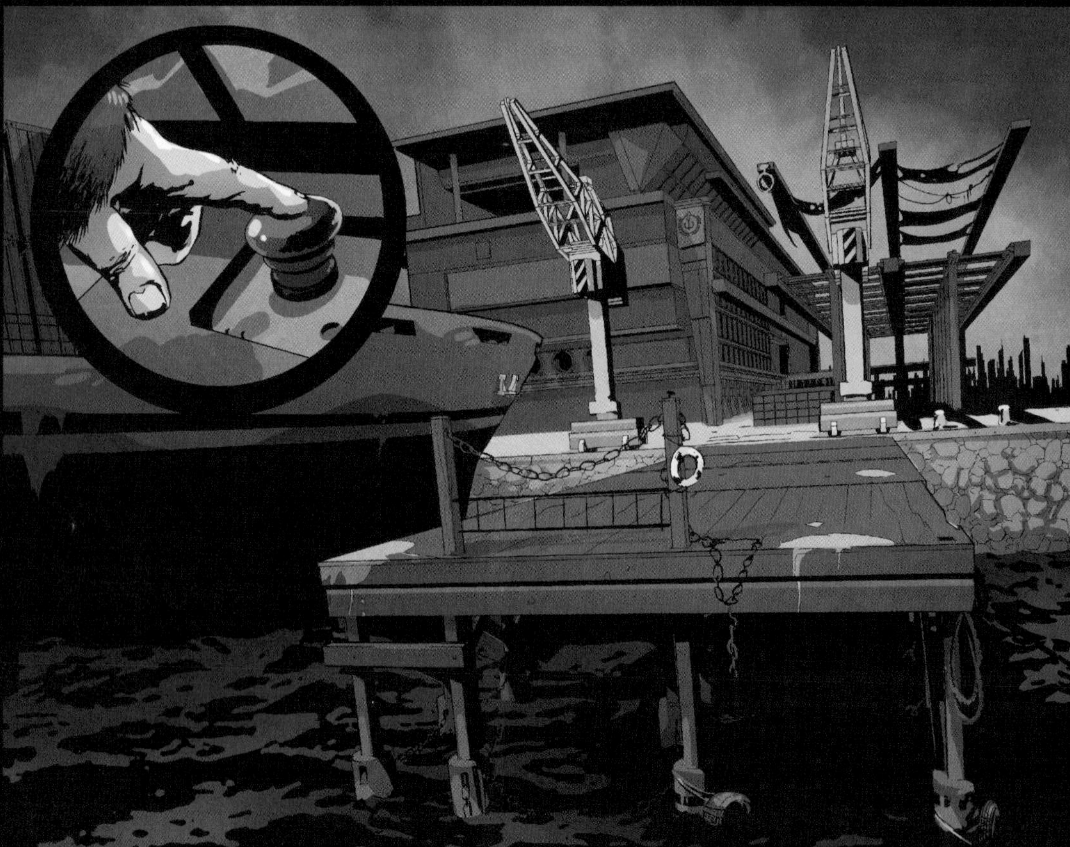

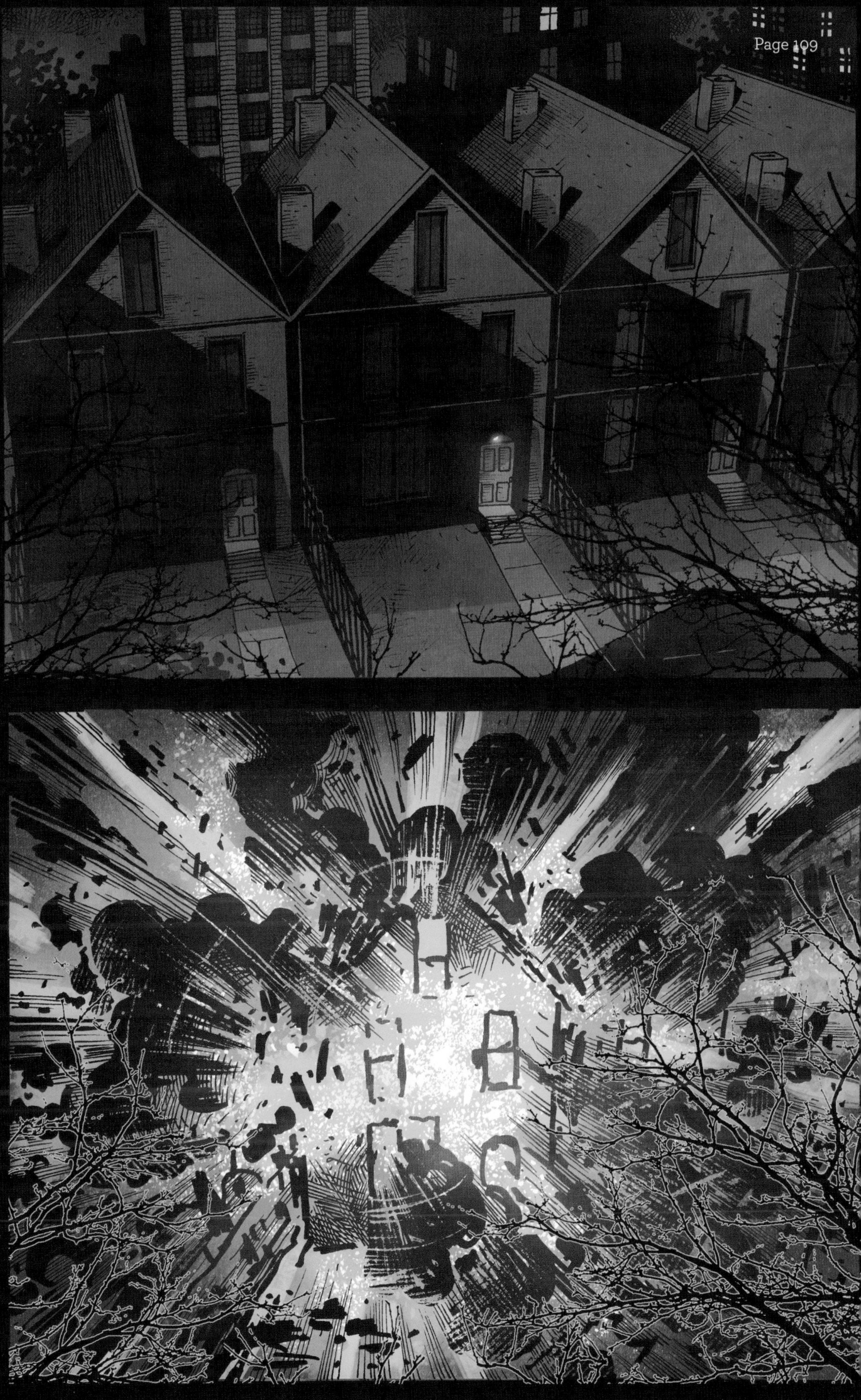

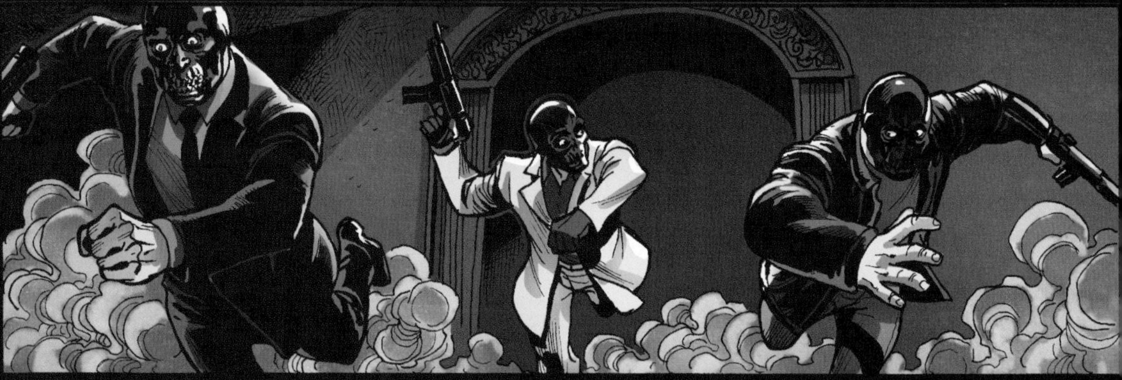

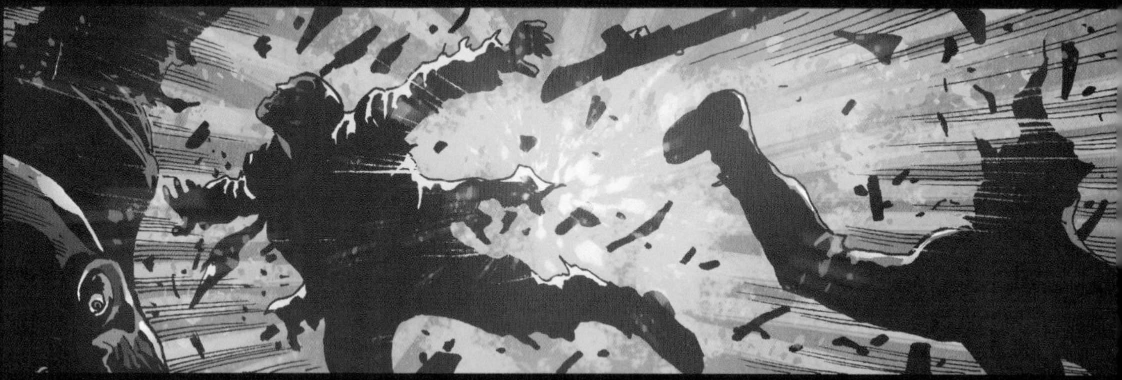

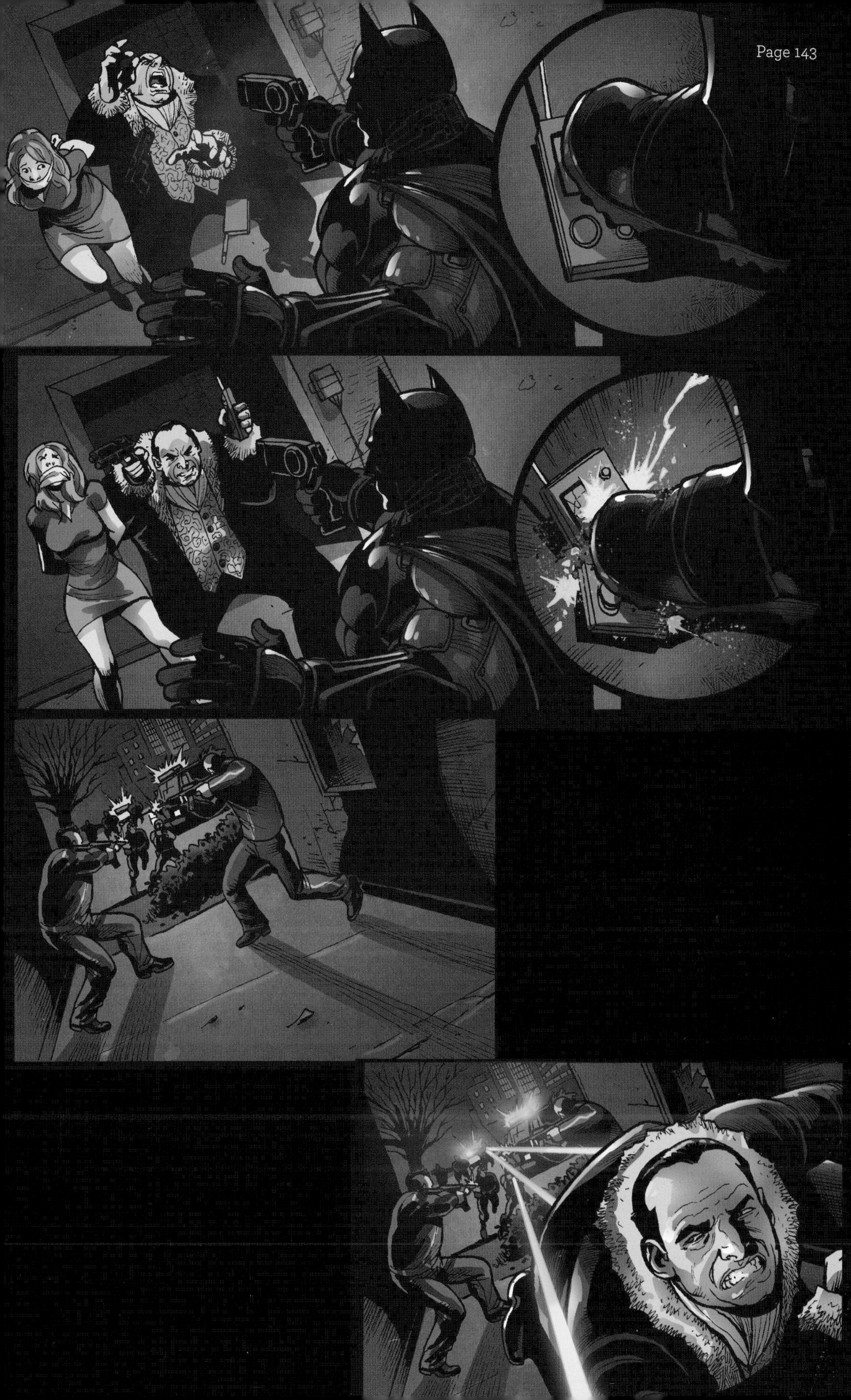

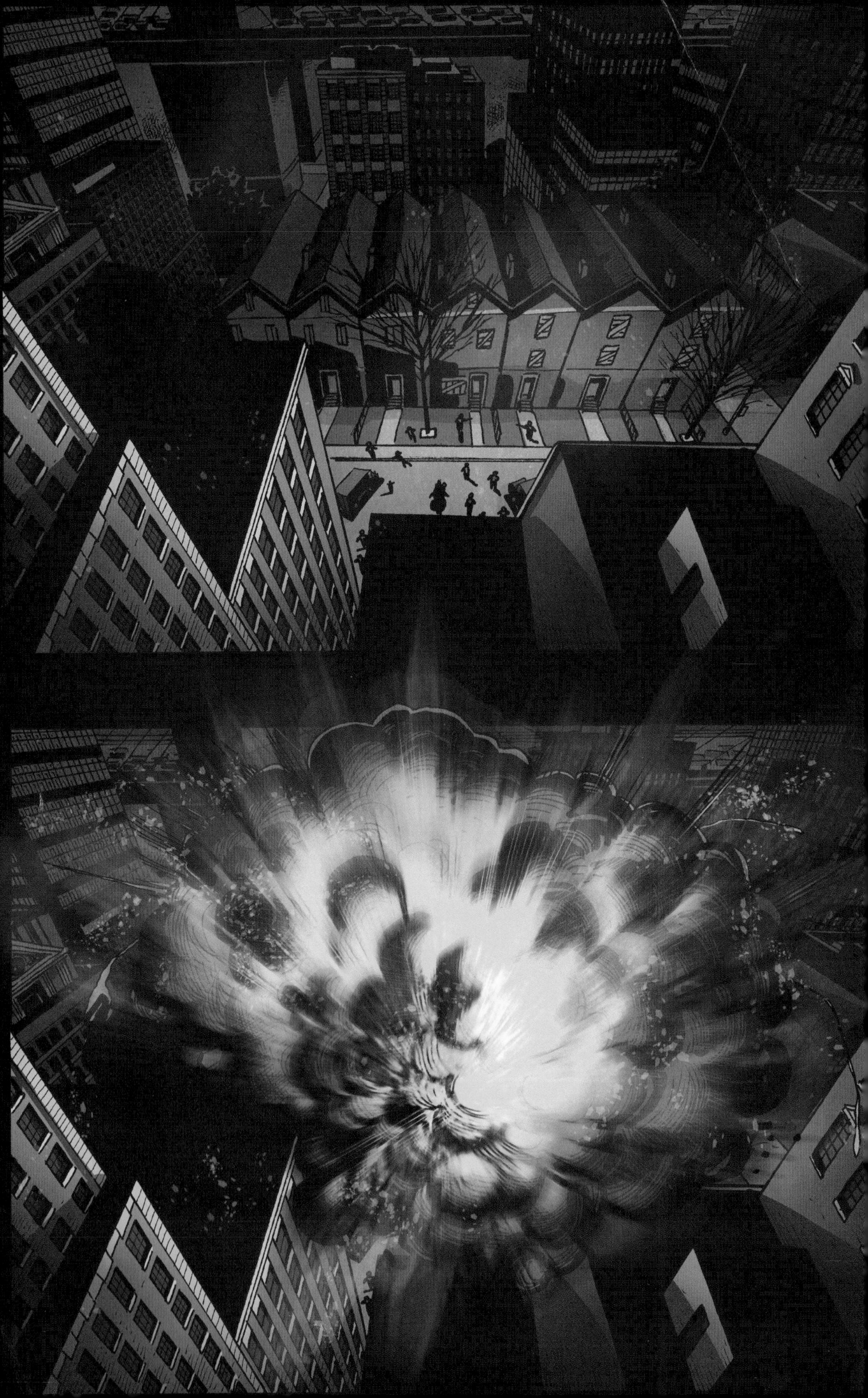